CLASS AND OTHER IDENTITIES

International Studies in Social History
General Editor: Marcel van der Linden,
International Institute of Social History, Amsterdam

Trade Unions, Immigration, and Immigrants in Europe, 1960–1993
Edited by Rinus Penninx and Judith Roosblad

Class and Other Identities
Edited by Lex Heerma van Voss and Marcel van der Linden

Rebellious Families
Edited by Jan Kok

CLASS AND OTHER IDENTITIES

Gender, Religion and Ethnicity in the
Writing of European Labour History

EDITED BY
LEX HEERMA VAN VOSS
AND
MARCEL VAN DER LINDEN

Berghahn Books
New York • Oxford

First published in 2002 by

Berghahn Books
www.BerghahnBooks.com

Library of Congress Cataloging-in-Publication Data
Class and other identities : gender, religion and ethnicity in the
writing of European labour history / edited by Lex Heerma van
Voss and Marcel van der Linden.
    p. cm. -- (International studies in social history ; v. 2)
    Includes bibliographical references and index.
    ISBN 1-57181-787-5 (cl : alk. paper) --
ISBN 1-57181-301-2 (pbk. : alk. paper)
    1. Labor--Historiography.   2. Labor movement--
Historiography.   I. Heerma van Voss, Lex.   II. Linden, Marcel
van der, 1952– III. Series

HD8374 .C58 2002
331.8'07'22'--dc21   2002020767

British Library Cataloguing in Publication Data
A catalogue record for this book is available
from the British Library.

ISBN 1–57181–787–5 (hardback)
ISBN 1–57181–301–2 (paperback)

CONTENTS

References

LIST OF ABBREVIATIONS

BDIC	Bibliothèque de Documentation Internationale Contemporaine
HISMA	Historical International Social Mobility Analysis
IALHI	International Association of Labour History Institutions
IISH	International Institute of Social History
ITH	Internationale Tagung der Historiker der Arbeiterbewegung
PCI	Partito Comunista Italiano
PSA	Parti socialiste autonome (1958)
PSU	Parti socialiste unifié
SED	Sozialistische Einheitspartei Deutschlands (East Germany)
SFIO	Section française de l'Internationale ouvrière
SPD	Sozialdemokratische Partei Deutschlands
SSLH	Society for the Study of Labour History
TUC	Trades Union Congress

CHAPTER 1

INTRODUCTION[1]

Marcel van der Linden and Lex Heerma van Voss

West European labour historiography is now approximately one-and-a-half centuries old. Over the course of time, in a tempo that has varied in different countries, periods and subjects, a considerable body of literature has accumulated in many languages. Communication among researchers has been somewhat intermittent through the years. Labour historians are often not well informed about each others' work, although almost all of them are familiar with the writings of a few (primarily British) 'great' men and women. This relative lack of knowledge of each others' debates and research results is all the more remarkable in light of the fact that national developments in labour historiography have often paralleled each other to a striking degree.

Five Periods of West European Labour History

The term 'labour history' has a dual meaning. Strictly speaking, the concept refers to the history of the labour movement: trade unions, cooperatives, strikes, etc. More broadly interpreted, the concept also refers to the history of the working classes: the development of labour relations, family life, mentalities, etc. This ambiguity seems characteristic of the term in English. In most other European languages labour movement history and working-class history cannot be summed up in a single term.[2]

'Broad' labour history is older than 'narrow' labour history.[3] Broad labour history could be written as soon as capitalist development had advanced to a certain point in Western Europe and the need arose to situate historically the corresponding social changes in general and the 'social question' in particular.[4] Projects along these lines were undertaken as early as the aftermath of the 1848 revolutions. One true pioneer was Emile Levasseur (1828–1911), who in the late 1850s and 1860s published a four-volume study of the French 'working classes' since Julius Caesar. Levasseur had a very broad conception of the 'working classes' ('All those who earned their living in and from industry, from simple apprentices to great merchants') and paid little attention and gave scant appreciation to the labour movement. Levasseur considered that the 'social question' was above all a matter of will-power. If workers would shed their childish lack of foresight, then they could dramatically improve their living conditions through thrift and industriousness.[5] Levasseur's example was soon followed by others, albeit often authors of lesser calibre. Fernando Garrido's extensive *Historia de las clases trabajadores*, for example, a book in which the history of the Spanish 'wealth-producing' classes was laid out ideologically rather than empirically, was published in 1870.[6]

'Narrow' labour history began to develop only in the 1870s. Political as well as theoretical factors contributed to its rise. Politically, it was significant that labour movements began to be visible on a national scale from the late 1860s on. The British TUC (Trades Union Congress) was established in 1868, and in the following decades national trade union federations were founded in virtually all of Western Europe, with a major chronological clustering in the years 1888–99. In this same period the rise of working-class parties began. German Social Democracy was the first in this field in 1875; all the other Western European countries followed suit in the subsequent thirty years, with the exception of Britain (1918) and Ireland (1922).

At the same time that these developments made clear to everyone that labour movements had come to stay, a theoretical obstacle was also removed. During most of the nineteenth century the doctrine of the 'wage fund' had had broad support among economists and other social scientists. According to this theory there exists a 'natural wage', which collective economic action is incapable of influencing. This standpoint was perhaps best known in the form of the 'iron law of wages' as propagated in the 1860s by the German workers' leader Ferdinand Lassalle, who used it as an argument for political action instead of trade union action.[7] The fact that not only most intellectuals but also substantial groups of workers saw the 'natural wage' theory as plausible was doubtless related to the many defeats with which nineteenth-century strikes often ended, and to the fragility and brief life span of existing labour organisations.[8] In about 1870 the wage-fund theory began to lose its credibility. The most significant turning-point was an essay by John Stuart Mill in which he broke with the concept.[9] There had of course been earlier critics, but until then the impact of their criticisms had been limited. Clearly the time was ripe for this turn-around, because within a few years many intellectuals in Europe and North America supported this paradigm shift.[10] Various causes have been given for this willingness to change standpoint, but evidently the consolidation of the British union movement played a role in it.[11]

This combination of political and theoretical shifts was sufficient reason for a number of scholars to concern themselves with labour movement history. These labour historians generally belonged to the political left; most of them were socialists or socially conscious liberals. The work of the German economist Lujo von Brentano (1844–1931), who published *On the History and Development of Gilds, and the Origin of Trade-Unions* in 1870, was epoch-making. His works still make a surprisingly fresh impression today, in part because he joined extensive historical knowledge with clear theoretical insights.[12]

From the 1880s on economic historians, who were interested in the evolution of wages and prices, came to the aid of 'narrow' and 'broad' labour history. An early but still much valued work in this field was James E. Thorold Rogers (1823–90) book on the evolution of wages in England since the thirteenth century.[13]

In the late 1880s the foundations were laid for labour history in all its basic forms (broad, narrow and quantitative). If we examine its further development up to the present, then both institutional aspects (archives, libraries, university chairs, associations and journals) and substantive aspects (objects of study, methods and theories employed) are important. Starting from this basis, we can distinguish five different periods.

First of all, the period *from the 1890s to the First World War.* In this period the first institutional foundations were laid for all later developments. In several countries archives were assembled, which naturally were often small and relatively insignificant to begin with. Important initiatives were taken in 'narrow' labour history in social democratic milieux. After the German SPD (Sozialdemokratische Partei Deutschlands) had set up a party archive in exile in Switzerland as early as 1882,[14] its example was followed in the early twentieth century in Sweden (1902), Norway (1908), Denmark and Finland (1909).[15] Socially conscious liberals and Christians set to work on 'broad' documentation and study of the working class and its living and working conditions. The most important example is the foundation of the Musée Social in Paris (1894) by the Comte de Chambrun.[16] His example had an inspirational effect throughout Europe. The Swiss minister Paul Pflüger, for example, spurred on by a visit to the French capital in 1900, began to collect the materials on the 'social question' that formed the basis in 1906 for the still existing Schweizerische Sozialarchiv.[17]

The first scholarly journals in the field also originated in this period. 'Broad' labour history (together with many other subjects) was occasionally on offer in the *Vierteljahrschrift für Sozial- und Wirtschaftsgeschichte*, founded in 1903 and still being published today. Some of the periodical's founders were progressive in orientation; its central figure, Ludo M. Hartmann, was a social democrat.[18] 'Narrow' labour history received a major stimulus in 1911 when one of Hartmann's collaborators, the legal expert and Austro-Marxist Carl Grünberg (1861–1940), founded the *Archiv für die Geschichte des Sozialismus und der Arbeiterbewegung*, which became generally known as *Grünbergs Archiv*. Grünberg (who would also become the first director of the Frankfurt Institute for Social Research in 1924)[19] sought to fill a gap with his journal. 'In all the vast field of political economy', he wrote in October 1909 to his kindred spirit Karl Kautsky, 'there scarcely exists any area in which so little systematic and intensive work is done as in labour movement history, despite its great importance. And that also holds true – though not to as great an extent as for bourgeois 'national economics' – for the exponents of scientific socialism.'[20]

Meanwhile the number of major studies in labour history, in the narrow and broad sense, was growing steadily. Narrow labour history was the subject of Sidney and Beatrice Webb's pioneering *History of Trade Unionism* (1894)[21] among other works, but also of other thorough studies, such as those by the well-known German 'revisionist' social democrat Eduard Bernstein on the labour movement in Berlin, Nettlau's major biography of Bakunin and Guillaume's history of the First International.[22] The growing interest in 'broad' labour history was expressed, among other ways, in Georges d'Avenel and Henri Hauser's ambitious works,[23] and above all, of course, in John and Barbara Hammond's magnificent trilogy covering the period 1760–1832: *The Village Labourer* (1912), *The Town Labourer* (1917) and *The Skilled Labourer* (1920).[24]

Robert René Kuczynski made a major quantitative contribution with his monumental study of wages and working hours, as did Carl von Tyszka's work following in Kuczynski's footsteps.[25]

The second period can be defined as *the interwar years*. It was a turbulent time, with revolutionary situations in 1917–20, hyperinflation and economic depression, and the rise of dictatorships in Southern and Central Europe. From an institutional point of view a defensive attitude predominated. The labour historiography that was carried on by labour movement activists themselves degenerated in this period to some extent into a 'scholarship of legitimation'. Tendencies in this direction had existed already before 1914; but the polarisation between social democrats and Communists and the process of Stalinisation transformed much historical writing in the 1920s into an instrument of self-justification.

> From that point on, historical discussion was shaped by the view that the working-class parties had of themselves and the image they wished to project. Control over sources and a voluntarist attitude toward history facilitated the task and conditioned research. Facts which corresponded to official versions of the past were extricated and declared essential. Those which were contradictory or were not of service in the immediate situation were considered marginal or inopportune. Such a flexible system of classification was organized around one single invariable consideration – the requirements of a utilitarian, projective history whose ultimate result was the manipulation of the past.[26]

One bright spot in this context was the foundation of the politically independent International Institute of Social History in Amsterdam in 1935 – a step meant to save archives threatened by the rise of Fascism and Stalinism.[27] The IISH began in 1936 to publish a yearbook (the *International Review for Social History*) and a *Bulletin*. In this way it filled, to some extent, the gap that had been opened six years earlier when *Grünbergs Archiv* ceased publication.[28]

While the scholarly output in the interwar years was comparatively rather meagre, there were nonetheless several important contributions made. Innovations took place in the field of 'narrow' labour history in the strict sense. The scholarly biography came of age, as was apparent from Franz Mehring's study of Karl Marx and Gustav Mayer's of Friedrich Engels, two works that would also be published in other languages.[29] The German social democrat Max Quarck wrote a fine study of workers' organisations during the revolution of 1848–9; Ludwig Brügel completed a vast history of Austrian social democracy; the Dutch trade union leader Jan Oudegeest published a thorough but very partisan history of 'his' labour movement; and the British Guild Socialist, G.D.H. Cole, began his fruitful career with – among other things – an extensive 'short' history of the British labour movement, in which he paid serious attention to 'ordinary' people's historical experiences and activities.[30] In Sweden in the 1930s social democratic academics and politicians set up a large-scale project, 'The History of the Swedish Working Class', which was completed only in 1957 and comprised a total of twelve volumes.[31] In France Georges Bourgin (1879–1958) and Edouard Dolléans (1877–1954) edited a book series, in which institutional labour history was not overlooked. While Bourgin made his greatest contribution as a historian of the Paris Commune of 1871, Dolléans was looking, at an early date, beyond France's borders. His intellectual range was shown by two publications: on the one hand his great, pre-First World War study of British Chartism, with a preface by Sidney Webb, and on the other hand the trilogy on institutional labour history that he began in the 1930s, with a preface by Lucien Febvre, one of the founders of the Annales school.[32] In the Netherlands A.J.C. Rüter, later director of the IISH, published an extensive doctoral thesis on the great transport strikes of 1903.[33]

Pioneering contributions also appeared in the field of 'broad' labour history. In 1930 Ivy Pinchbeck published an innovative study in which the social history of the Industrial Revolution in Britain, as charted by the Hammonds, was corrected by focusing on female workers.[34] In the Netherlands Izaäk Brugmans (1896–1992) earned his doctorate with a study of the nineteenth-century working class.[35] In Britain A.L. Morton (1903–87) published a 'people's history' of England that would inspire a whole generation of postwar British Marxist historians.[36] Here and there attempts were made to link 'narrow' and 'broad' labour history with each other, for example in a pioneering study by Juan Diaz del Moral (1870–1948) on agricultural labourers in Andalusia.[37] The work of the Norwegian Edvard Bull (1881–1932), an undogmatic Marxist who would serve briefly as his country's Minister of Foreign Affairs just before he died, also achieved a certain renown by bridging the gap between 'broad' and 'narrow' labour history.[38] Struck by the fact that his country's Labour Party joined the Communist International as a bloc for a few years (1919–23), while the Danish and Swedish labour parties took up much more moderate positions, Bull tried to give a social explanation of the three Scandinavian labour movements' different degrees of radicalism. His hypothesis, which emphasised the divergent tempo of industrialisation processes, inspired discussion well into the 1970s.[39]

It is probably no accident that the crisis years of the 1930s witnessed an unprecedented blossoming of historical writings on wages and prices. Beginning in 1936, the Rockefeller Foundation subsidised a large-scale international research programme on the evolution of wages and prices from the Middle Ages to the nineteenth century. W.H. Beveridge directed the project, first from London and later from Oxford. His collaborators included Moritz Elsas, E.F. Gay, Earl Hamilton, Henri Hauser, Nicolaas Posthumus and Alfred Pribam.[40]

The third period coincides more or less with *the postwar boom of the late 1940s to the mid-1960s*. In these years, under the impact of the Second World War, the European labour movement was in the process of rethinking its own past. In 1951 the well-known publisher Giangiacomo Feltrinelli (1926–72) founded a library in Milan, named after himself, that commanded considerable financial resources and grew to become Italy's largest labour history collection.

Since 1958 the Feltrinelli Institute has published an authoritative annual review (*Annali*). Other Italian initiatives quickly followed. In 1950 the Istituto Gramsci, linked to the PCI (Partito Comunista Italiano), was founded in Rome, and in 1959 it began publishing its journal *Studi Storici*. In 1952 Domenico Demarco founded the Istituto di storia economica e sociale at the University of Naples.

The Institut français d'histoire sociale, which has played an important role through its journal *Actualité de l'histoire* (later *Le Mouvement Social*), was founded in France in 1949. The driving force behind it was Jean Maitron (1910–87), who not only was a historian of note himself but also gained considerable influence through his organisational work. Maitron will continue to be known above all as the initiator of a vast biographical dictionary, whose first volume appeared in 1964.[41]

A Social History Study Circle was founded in 1953 in milieux close to the International Institute of Social History in Amsterdam, with a bulletin that would later grow to become a leading journal in the Netherlands, the *Tijdschrift voor Sociale Geschiedenis*. A Social History Working Group (Arbeitskreis Sozialgeschichte), in which Werner Conze (1910–86) and Theodor Schieder (1908–84) played key roles, began in West Germany in 1957 with government support. The Arbeitskreis was responsible for a prestigious book series under the title 'Industrial World', in which twenty-five volumes appeared between 1962 and 1995. The social democratic Friedrich Ebert Foundation made its presence felt as well. In 1961 it launched a long series of voluminous yearbooks under the title *Archiv für Sozialgeschichte*. In 1959 the Verein für Geschichte der Arbeiterbewegung (Association for Labour Movement History) was founded in Austria. Britain followed in 1960 with the Society for the Study of Labour History.

'Narrow' labour history was stimulated in this period in many ways. There was a formidable upsurge in Italy – historians were making up for lost time after twenty years of dictatorship – manifested in a great number of institutional studies.[42] But 'broad' labour history became a livelier field as well. One important pioneer in Italy was Giuliano Procacci (*1926), who published several important essays in the 1950s and early 1960s on the living and working conditions of the industrial and agrarian working class.[43] Others quickly followed his example.

A beginning was made in this period on a renewal of labour history's foundations. Methodologically Ernest Labrousse (1895–1988) played a great role.[44] As professor at the Sorbonne, Labrousse influenced a whole generation of French social and labour historians in the years after 1945. 'It was his programme for a statistical evaluation of serial sources that was seized on by Braudel and his collaborators and made into a trademark of the *Annales* school of historiography.[45] In the English-speaking world the work of John Saville (*1916), Eric Hobsbawm (*1917), Asa Briggs (*1921) and E.P. Thompson (1924–93) was of great importance. Thompson's *The Making of the English Working Class* (1963), in particular, had a truly overwhelming impact.[46]

The fourth period runs *from the late 1960s to the mid-1980s*. Around 1970 the field began to spread its wings far and wide under the influence of the student movement. Many new journals were founded and the number of scholarly studies expanded to unheard-of proportions. The explosion of publications has been so great that we cannot do justice to it here.[47] Hobsbawm pointed out that this revival was 'largely political':

> the radicalization of generations of students and (in due course) junior professors in the 1960s. In Britain, in the USA, in West Germany (where there has been a remarkable revival in such studies), in Italy among the new left, and doubtless elsewhere, radicalization has produced a substantial crop of new labour historians, whose interest in the subject is basically that of political commitment though their competence as researchers may be greater and their scope somewhat wider.[48]

This period also saw a new interest in comparative labour history. For the first time, daily life was studied systematically as well. Attempts to bridge the gap between academic history and interested workers led to movements such as the History Workshops in Britain and later in several other countries as well.[49] New centres that were established include the Ludwig Boltzmann Institut für Gesellschafts- und Kulturgeschichte in Linz (1968), the brainchild of Karl R. Stadler (1913–87), a left-wing socialist historian who had lived in the UK as a political refugee from 1938 on and returned to Austria only in 1968.[50] In May 1968 the Working Group on the History of the Workers' Movement in Switzerland was formed in Lausanne, which, though it ceased to exist after only a few years, produced a number of interesting publications in the meantime.[51] A year later the Archiv der sozialen Demokratie was established in Bonn-Bad Godesberg. A library was built up in Bochum in the period 1972–80, leading in 1980 to the establishment of the Institut zur Erforschung der europäischen Arbeiterbewegung (since 1999 called the Institut für soziale Bewegungen). In 1973 the foundation of the Irish Labour History Society took place.

The first major studies in 'broad' labour history appeared at this time. Erich Gruner (*1915) published his 1,100–page study on the nineteenth-century Swiss working class.[52] The prolific Spanish historian Manuel Tuñón de Lara produced substantial contributions to 'broad' as well as 'narrow' labour history.[53] The pioneering works of

Rolande Trempé on the Carmaux miners, Yves Lequin on the working class of Lyons and the surrounding area, and Michelle Perrot on striking workers in the late nineteenth century all appeared in France.[54] All these French studies were, in Lequin's words, 'inspired by Labroussian thought'. 'All three of them are among those who gave priority to analysing productive forces and their development, whereby they methodically adopted a mode of investigation that moves from the constantly changing economic structure to collective relationships and cultural phenomena.'[55] In Italy too, partly under the impact of student protests and the 'hot autumn' of 1969, there was an enormous blossoming of labour history. Among the most influential authors were the left-wing socialist Stefano Merli (1925–94), who in 1969 founded the journal *Classe*, which tried to combine current political analyses with historical studies. Merli also published a huge monograph on the rise of the factory proletariat, which would be considered a classic for many years.[56] In the wake of the Portuguese 'revolution of the carnations', labour history changed from a political taboo to a 'fashionable topic, with all the ephemeral earmarks of fashion'.[57] There was a veritable explosion of publications, culminating in Carlos da Fonseca's four-volume *História do movimento operário e das ideias socialistas em Portugal*.[58] In Sweden labour history became 'one of the main fields of historical research at the universities', as manifested, for example, in a great number of dissertations.[59] In the Netherlands it was, above all, the historians Ger Harmsen and Theo van Tijn, with their competing 'schools', who made major contributions.[60] Considerable attention was now devoted for the first time to the Christian labour movement, alongside the socialist, communist and anarchist movements.[61]

In this fourth period, interest in Western European labour history also grew in the United States. There had of course been interest before among individual US researchers (such as Walter Galenson, Val Lorwin and Maurice Neufeld),[62] but now there was a fully-fledged breakthrough. This development was also manifested in the founding in 1972 of the US-based *Newsletter: European Labor and Working Class History*, a journal that was renamed three years later *International Labor and Working-Class History*. The driving force behind this project was Robert F. Wheeler (1940–77), a labour historian who died young after specialising in the Weimar Republic.[63]

The fifth period (*since the mid-1980s*), finally, is a period of paradoxes. On the one hand, major synthetic works are now coming out that are the fruit of twenty or thirty years of intellectual labour. Erich Gruner and his students have completed their three-volume study, over 3,200 pages long, covering the growth of the Swiss working class from 1880 to the First World War.[64] A team of Norwegian authors has published six solid volumes covering 'broad' and 'narrow' labour history from the mid-nineteenth century to the 1980s.[65] In Austria five volumes on 'narrow' labour history were published under Wolfgang Maderthaner's supervision.[66] In Sweden six volumes were published on the trade union movement after the Second World War.[67] The most ambitious project has been (and is) undoubtedly the series of monumental studies launched by Gerhard A. Ritter (*1929) in the 1970s, *Geschichte der Arbeiter und der Arbeiterbewegung in Deutschland seit dem Ende des 18. Jahrhunderts* (History of the Workers and Workers' Movement in Germany since the End of the Eighteenth Century).[68] But on the other hand, the maturing of the discipline has been accompanied by a certain decline in interest, though this has varied from one country to the next.[69] A cluster of factors has probably played a role in this process. In some cases the discipline's high level of development has itself made it less interesting for young researchers.[70] But the conservative ideological climate may also have played a role, along with cutbacks in university budgets.[71] Attention has been shifting to other aspects of social and economic history (culture, for example, and entrepreneurs).[72] We have seen visible signs of these shifts in the journals. Periodicals that published preponderantly or largely articles on labour history for a long time are now devoting proportionately more attention to other subjects. This shift is clearly visible, for example in the *Archiv für Sozialgeschichte* and the *Tijdschrift voor Sociale Geschiedenis*. It is telling that the Italian journal *Movimento operaio e socialista* (Labour and Socialist Movement) was transformed in 1991 into *Ventesimo Secolo* (Twentieth Century) – a name change that accompanied a clearly reduced interest in its earlier field of work.

Long-Term Shifts

It goes without saying that this overview has had to be rough and impressionistic. No integrated study of the development of Western European labour history exists, and we cannot fill the gap with this brief introduction. The periodisation that we have suggested should not serve to conceal the fact that developments in different countries have diverged considerably. In countries where civil war or dictatorship had a great impact on the political culture (like Portugal, Spain and Finland), labour history has tended to concern itself more with political aspects than in countries with consolidated parliamentary democracies (like Sweden and Britain). Emphases vary between countries with big Communist parties and countries where social democracy has predominated. Christian trade union movements that merged into unified labour federations after 1945 have received less attention from historians than those that maintained their independent existence.[73] And while 'broad' labour history made its breakthrough in some countries early in the twentieth century, in other countries this occurred much later. Despite this unevenness, however, we can point to certain red threads and patterns in the discipline's development.

First, *the relationship between labour history, labour movements and academic historical writing* seems to have changed in important ways over the course of time. Originally the practitioners of broad and narrow labour history were not professional historians. Historical writing at universities was being professionalised everywhere towards the end of the nineteenth century, and focused in the first instance on 'great' subjects such as wars, diplomacy, statesmen and so on. The powerless, poor and 'red' did not fall within its field of vision.[74] As a result, non-academics and academics who were not trained in history had the field to themselves. Important contributions were made mostly by the labour movements' own leaders and sympathisers, as well as by economists, legal scholars and, in some cases, physicians. Thanks in part to this situation, early writings in labour history were rather old-fashioned from a technical and methodological standpoint. 'It produced a great deal of traditional narrative and institutional history; only its subject matter was unusual.'[75]

The 'official' world of professional historians kept labour historians at arm's length for some time. It did sometimes happen that a professional historian played a role in the (political) labour movement, but that by no means implied that he or she had specialised in labour history.[76] For many years it remained difficult for labour historians to win academic recognition. Take Denmark in the 1930s:

> Two historians, Henry Bruun and Georg Nørregaard, made strictly empirical contributions built on large quantities of primary sources. This basic research did not, though, have any positive effect on working class history as an academic subject. Bruun tried to get his work accepted as a doctoral thesis at the University of Copenhagen, but it was rejected. Thus Nørregaard didn't even try to get his accepted. [...It] is quite impossible to understand why Bruun's thesis was rejected. But anyway, the result was that the topic couldn't attract scholars or research since it was perceived as a field from which no merits or scientific reputation could be derived.[77]

Such things also occurred in other countries.

This began to change after the Second World War, far more quickly in some countries than in others. France seems to have had a head start in this reversal.[78] Labour history was integrated to an increasing extent into professional historiography, it seems, while sometimes retaining close ties to the labour movement. Even when the conflicts seemed to have been thoroughly overcome, major studies still arose outside academia. What was probably the most influential book of the past half-century, Edward P. Thompson's *The Making of the English Working Class* in 1963, was a product of adult education courses.[79]

The increasingly academic face of labour history went together with a few other shifts. After 1945 there began an uneven but steady, systematic *convergence between 'narrow' and 'broad' labour history*. An important figure in this respect was the Belgian historian Jan Dhondt (1915–72), who endeavoured from the late 1940s on to go beyond the institutional approach to writing the history of workers' organisations through detailed analyses of rank-and-file militants.[80] Discontent with a purely 'narrowly' defined labour history spread visibly in the course of the 1950s. During the founding meeting of the British Society for the Study of Labour History in 1960, newly installed president, Asa Briggs, emphasised,

> there are new lines of approach which suggest themselves – for example, a study of the working class 'situation' taken in terms of health, leisure, etc. Social history in the fullest sense, including politics, but not tied exclusively to politics; studies which focus attention on class relations, the impact of other classes and class organisations on the workers; and a strictly economic history of labour.[81]

The best-known programmatic expression of this approach was Eric Hobsbawm's, in the introduction to his book *Labouring Men* in 1964. The point would be to focus on 'the working classes as such [… and] the economic and technical conditions that allowed labour movements to be effective, or which prevented them from being effective.'[82] An important example of a study in which this trend would be apparent was Claude Willard's *Les guesdistes* in 1965.[83]

This shift in approach began from very different starting points in different countries. In Britain, for instance, Marxists like Eric Hobsbawm, John Saville and E.P. Thompson took the lead. In the years 1946–56 they belonged to the Historians' Group of the Communist Party, and developed an approach there, in dialogue with kindred spirits like Christopher Hill, Rodney Hilton and Victor Kiernan, that saw workers' protest and organisations as expressions of structural and cultural processes of class formation.[84] In Germany, by contrast, the pioneers of the 'modern' approach to the history of the labour movement were Werner Conze and Theodor Schieder – former National Socialists who had been inspired in the 1930s by the then fashionable *Volksgeschichte* (folk history), and sought to pursue this approach in denazified form after the war.[85] At the same time we must realise that the social history that emerged in West Germany in the late 1950s 'cannot be fully understood in terms of this continuity. Even the students of Conze and Schieder, who have participated in the *Arbeitskreis*, went in directions that if not entirely different were nevertheless sufficiently complex to make them qualitatively different.'[86]

In France, where writers of 'event-centred' (*événementiel*) labour movement history had long been opposed by followers of the *Annales* school, whose structural and serial historiography had largely 'left people out', some rapprochement was apparent, especially after 1968. It was such a slow process, however, that Michelle Perrot felt impelled to remark in 1979: '[In French historiography] the study of the workers' movement has polarised historians for a long time and eclipsed other problems, such as the development of the working class and its culture. However, this is changing rapidly.'[87] Whatever the ways in which the rapprochement between 'broad' and 'narrow' labour history took place, it was a generalised phenomenon.

The first generations of labour historians generally examined labour movements and working classes in national isolation: each case was treated as a sort of 'monad'. Even when historians in one country described developments in another, they emphasised the distinctiveness of the different cases. One good example is the German scholar Werner Sombart (1863–1941), who published impressive essays on both the Italian and US working classes, but nonetheless began from a monadist premise.[88] Studies that dealt with the 'internationals' also did not usually break this pattern. This tendency was reinforced for a long time by the limited contacts that labour historians in different countries had with each other.

The first signs of change became visible in the 1960s. In 1964 a symposium was held in Vienna on 'Austria-Hungary and the [First] International'. Historians from not only Austria but also Czechoslovakia, Hungary, Italy, Yugoslavia and West and East Germany took part in the conference. On the spot the idea arose of organising an international gathering of labour historians the following year. In this way Linz, Austria, became and has since 1965 remained the meeting place each year of the International Conference of Historians of the Labour Movement (German acronym: ITH).[89] Since these gatherings were meant primarily as meeting places for scholars from the East and West and accordingly no qualitative criteria were used to restrict attendance, the average standard of the papers presented at them was usually not impressive.[90] The transformations in Eastern Europe landed the ITH in a crisis, which the organisers have been trying to resolve for a number of years through higher standards of quality.[91]

After the ITH other indications came quickly of a growing tendency towards supranational cooperation. In 1970 the International Association of Labour History Institutions (IALHI) was founded, an international meeting point for labour history archives and libraries. In 1974 there was an attempt to found a Nordic Society for Labour Movement History, as a forum for Danish, Norwegian, Swedish and Finnish historians. This attempt failed, however; cross-country contacts were nonetheless intensified in the framework of this project and several 'Nordic' labour history congresses took place. In 1997 'Lab-Net' was founded; this European collaborative network for labour historians maintains an electronic discussion list, and forms the labour network of the European Social Science History Conference.

More substantively as well, a significant shift became apparent from the 1970s on. A tendency towards transnationalisation was at work, which took two different forms. On the one hand, there were international comparative studies, which had been tried very sporadically before (for example in Sombart's work) but now grew explosively in number.[92] On the other hand, cross-border interactions were now taken much more seriously at every level of analysis. Transnational projects, in which researchers from several different countries try jointly to formulate hypotheses by comparing national case studies, have also become much more plentiful over the years. The number of studies of labour migration and remigration has mushroomed.[93] Much less attention has been paid so far to relations between European working classes and labour movements on the one hand and colonial societies on the other. True, there have been a reasonable number of studies on working-class parties' attitudes, but we still know very little by comparison about the attitudes of the rank and file.

The internationalisation of the discipline has been further advanced since the 1970s by the considerably increased interest on the part of US researchers. We have already mentioned the founding of the journal *International Labor and Working-Class History* in 1975. An important role has been played in this internationalisation by the Romanian-French historian Georges Haupt (1928–78), who raised the study of connections among national labour movements (above all in the period from roughly 1860 to 1930) to a higher level. Haupt not only stimulated countless other researchers and initiated many projects but also made very important contributions himself.[94] More generally, the growing interest in Western European labour history has been expressed in a swelling river of books and articles by US colleagues. Even their 'house organs' such as the *American Historical Review*, publish occasional contributions on the topic. One remarkable aspect of this interest is the overwhelming focus on the larger countries (Britain, France, Germany and Italy). Rarely do more than a handful of American historians concern themselves with smaller countries, except when a small country has exceptional characteristics that evoke curiosity (like the Swedish welfare state).

Labour history's academic prestige rose for many years, only to decline again in the last ten or fifteen, though it still seems reasonably high. Growing appreciation for it in academic circles reached an unprecedentedly high level in the late 1960s and 1970s. This can be seen in two ways. First, the influence of social history in general and labour history in particular on other historical subfields increased considerably. Political history, business history, cultural history: in all of them connections were attempted with labour history. General journals like *History, Historische Zeitschrift, Annales* and *Historisk Tidskrift* began publishing regular articles on labour history. Second, labour history's influence on the social sciences also increased greatly. Sociologists, political scientists, anthropologists and geographers integrated notions from labour history and in so doing enriched labour history. Leading social science journals published pieces on trade union history, workers' parties and strike waves. Simultaneously with this new popularity of labour history came a remarkable political turnaround. The 'old' labour history had been infused with an optimistic perspective, celebrating the emergence of mass organisation and stressing the dynamics of unity and organisation. From the 1960s on, however, the teleology of earlier phases was frequently turned upside down. The new generation tended to ask what had gone wrong with the movement. From a methodological point of view an 'epistemology of absence' (in Margaret Somers' words) became predominant:

> Rather than seeking to explain the presence of radically varying dispositions and practices, [labour historians] have concentrated disproportionately on explaining the absence of an expected outcome, namely the emergence of a revolutionary class consciousness among the Western working class.[95]

All this began to change again in the 1980s. Labour history became less popular among both historians and social scientists, and the teleological perspective was now put seriously in question. The organising categories of the 1960s and 1970s were increasingly subject to doubt, partly because they displayed certain continuities with those of the earlier phase.

A crucial factor in this second turnaround was not only the turning of the tide of '1968' and the dissipation of its characteristic illusions, but also the rise of new approaches to writing history. The women's movement, which came on the scene everywhere in Western Europe from 1969 on, began to win influence rapidly among labour historians as well. The number of studies of women's waged and non-waged labour, their involvement in social struggles and similar themes grew very quickly for a while. But it soon became clear that paying attention to women was not sufficient, because

> it is no less problematic to separate the history of women from history in general than to separate the history of men – and even more so, truly general history – from the history of women. Women's history concerns not merely half of humankind, but all of it.[96]

In this way the concept of gender made its appearance in the world of labour history and made necessary a fundamental rethinking of the discipline. A parallel development took place with 'ethnic minorities'. It became clear in this case as well that *other* identities besides those of the worker/wage-earner are essential to the reconstruction of historical processes. Both 'revisions' of the old labour history were very much hastened, incidentally, by the already mentioned increase in US intellectual influence. Many Western European discussions were spurred on by contributions from such US colleagues as Louise Tilly, Joan W. Scott, Claudia Koonz, Temma Kaplan, Donna Gabaccia, Leslie Moch and others.

One last tendency, still somewhat weak but nonetheless perceptible, is the opening up of labour history to the early modern period. For a long time – under the Webbs' influence – the axiom held sway that the rise of 'modern' capitalism and the 'modern' labour movement at the end of the eighteenth century constituted a fundamental historical break, a discontinuity relative to early modern labour relations and modes of social protest. This consensus was contested from the beginning; and in the last thirty years more and more historians have been not only paying attention to long-term continuities but also developing an intrinsic interest in the structures and processes that preceded the 'modern' period.[97]

As an overall summary we could say the following: in the third phase (1945–65) the institutional foundations of the field were consolidated, as is shown, for example, by the growth in the number of main periodicals (see Figure 1.1). In the fourth phase (1965–85), relying on the political conjuncture, it was possible to build higher on those foundations, so that this period became the disciplines golden decades. The high level of institutional presence reached in the fourth phase was maintained after 1985, but this period has unavoidably been one of reorientation and rethinking.

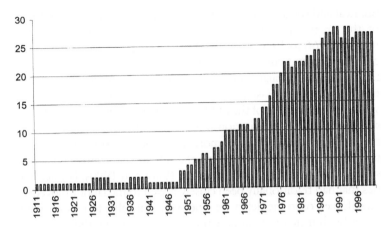

Figure 1.1 *Number of Main European Labour History Periodicals, 1911–2000 (as listed in References, this volume, 162–165)*

Challenges

The fifth period, from the mid-1980s on, was thus a period of mixed results for labour history. The number of professional historians working in labour history was great, given that many of them had begun to work in the field as students during the fourth period. As we have already mentioned, a few major projects were carried out in this period, but many social historians who had been trained in the previous period turned their attention to other subjects. Labour historians frequently combined their interest in the working class with these new focuses in social history. There were, for example, studies of the culture of the labour movement and working class, education, poverty, nationalism, migration and daily life.

A central supposition of much labour history came under fire, beginning in the 1980s: namely the idea that workers in principle would act in accordance with their long-term class interests. Every labour historian understood, of course, that there were all sorts of concrete historical situations in which workers had *not* acted in solidarity with their own class; but class solidarity was nonetheless usually treated by historians as one of their self-evident, basic assumptions. When workers did act in solidarity with their social class, researchers often judged this to be 'logical' and reported it without any further explanation. When, by contrast, workers let interests other than class interests prevail, that was something that called for an explanation.

This assumption of self-evident working-class solidarity was increasingly put in question from the 1980s on. There were clear political and social reasons for this development. The gradual decline of the great international wave of protest that had lasted from roughly 1966 to 1976, as well as the working class's changing social composition and culture, led to an erosion of the image of the militant, male, blue-collar, industrial worker.[98] At the decade's end the transformations in Eastern Europe and the Soviet Union seemed to symbolise the demise of the old-fashioned left, while at the same time real or perceived globalisation was moving ahead: these changes put the labour movement under more and more pressure. The political pendulum, which had swung to the left in the 1960s and 1970s, swung sharply back to the right in the 1980s and 1990s. Political parties that had traditionally been closely linked to the labour movement were forced onto the defensive, and were only able to reassert themselves by shifting rightward themselves and loosening their ties to the labour movement. From this time on the ideas 'that the growth of public spending should be curbed; that the welfare state can be defended but not extended; that privatization may be unavoidable and, when it eradicates monopolies, desirable; that equality, though still appealing as a goal, may be tempered by the need to preserve incentives and competition', among others, became basic assumptions of the major Western European left-wing parties.[99]

In addition to contemporary social and political developments, the already-mentioned enlargement of the field of history itself also provoked questions as to whether working-class solidarity was in fact so self-evidently logical a phenomenon. Women's and ethnic history made clear that workers were not only wage earners with specific occupational and class interests, but also had other identities, including ethnic, gendered and religious identities. Reality could no longer be reduced to the class struggle. In other words, labour historians were faced with a major challenge: they had to develop new organising categories and ask different questions about the past.

One road that was travelled in response was micro-history. Historians, including the *Les Révoltes Logiques* collective and the group around Robert Berdahl, had first explored this approach as early as the 1970s.[100] In the 1980s mainstream labour historians also began to appreciate these efforts. Various methods were tried out. First, there were studies of the life courses of concrete historical people. Workers' autobiographies constituted an outstanding source for this purpose.[101] Unfortunately not many workers left autobiographies behind; the workers who did were usually highly educated; and in addition most autobiographies were written towards the end of workers' lives and with didactic intent. Second, historians resorted to oral history, although of course this method could only be satisfactorily applied to the late nineteenth and twentieth centuries.[102] A third, more structural method consisted of reconstructing workers' life courses with the help of standard sources, such as censuses, population registries, voters' rolls, surveys, military service records, address books or household budgets.[103] Individuals' life courses and the life choices they made can be reconstructed by finding the same individuals repeatedly in a series of these sources. This makes it possible to determine, for example, which children stayed at home and which ones migrated in order to contribute to the family's income, and whether by migrating they rose out of the working class.[104] By re-analysing a survey by computer it is possible to determine, for example, whether the sons of the London working class in fact had the same occupations as their fathers, as the neighbourhood's inhabitants in their recollections would have us believe.[105] In short, tracking occupational and geographical mobility helps us to analyse class formation or the absence of it.

A second option was analysing the class and other major identities that workers had acted on in various situations.[106] The two approaches are not contradictory: as we have seen, the results of research into individual data on the micro-level can contribute to analysing various different possible identities.

Social class's most important competitor as an identity in historical research in this period was undoubtedly gender. The rise of gender as an analytical category must be linked to the new international feminist upsurge that began in the late 1960s, and its penetration into the scholarly world by way of Women's Studies.[107] The lecture that Joan Scott gave to the American Historical Association in 1985 on 'Gender: A Useful Category of Historical Analysis' had a great deal of influence in Western Europe.[108] Within labour history, interest in gender led in the first place to studies that looked at women's work as well as male work. Although the women studied in these cases were engaged in traditional wage labour, they had often been ignored or referred to only as strikebreakers. Sometimes they were engaged in typically female occupations, in other cases in occupations where men and women competed for access to the occupation and disputed the preconditions for admission.[109] There were also studies of women's work that had not been recognised as such in the past because it was considered immoral or was done at home.[110] Studies of these different forms of women's work pointed towards gender as an issue in the past. Historical actors such as employers, politicians, social reformers, the labour movement and women's movement had used images of femininity and masculinity in order to influence reality in the desired direction.[111] The gendered image of their work had sometimes been a reason for women to choose or reject a particular job, and had constituted a major object of struggle. These insights often only slowly gained ground among labour historians, just as it took time for the labour movement itself to get used to them.[112] Once femininity had gained visibility as an issue, masculinity began to as well. Male workers had earned respect for behaviour that was considered masculine, as expressed in heavy physical labour, toughness, drinking (but in some circumstances also not drinking), technical skill, homo-sociality (but not homosexuality), courage or fighting spirit, earning a wage sufficient to support a family, and refusal to break strikes (as workers – male soldiers might be considered masculine when they *did* break strikes). These and other aspects of the construction of masculinity also became objects of study.[113]

Interest in gender was greater initially in the United States than in Europe, where the proportion of women among social and labour historians also remained lower than in the USA. Roughly the same was true for the factors of race and ethnicity. Ethnic distinctions were more clearly visible in the USA than in Europe, and there was more of a tradition of seeing American society as an aggregate of different ethnic groups than was the case with European society.[114] Employers and workers themselves had used ethnicity in order to play different groups of workers off against each other, albeit not always successfully.[115] When nonwhite workers had been treated worse than white workers, it was logical that they had not organised on the basis of class solidarity with those who excluded them, but demanded first to be admitted to the trade on equal terms. Sometimes the disadvantaged ethnic group subsequently maintained its separate organisations, because isolation was seen as a source of strength.[116]

Parallel to the interest in the construction of gender identities, attention was also given to the construction of ethnic identity. In this way the 'whiteness' of Irish and Italian workers in the USA also became visible as a social construction. Poor Irish and Italian immigrants' social position had often been comparable to that of poor free African-Americans. It had been in these immigrants' interest to conquer segments of the labour market, drawing a sharp line in the process between themselves and the blacks, the group that could most easily be discriminated against. It was in employers' interest, that their employees should be divided, and they had encouraged the existence of these dividing lines.[117] Comparable developments were subsequently noted as well in countries other than the USA.[118]

Europe, too, had and has immigrants of colour and immigrants defined as nonwhite, whose disadvantaged position in the labour market has been comparable to the position of American women or ethnic groups.[119] Compared with the US situation, however, ethnic differences have been more important than racial ones, even if groups such as Jews or the Irish have often been referred to in Europe in racial terms as well. 'Foreigners', recognisable by their distinctive language, clothing, customs and religion, have had a special position, whether they had a different nationality or not: Bretons in Paris, Frisians in Amsterdam or Poles in the Ruhr Valley.[120] Feelings of solidarity with their ethnic group were potentially in competition with their feelings of class solidarity. The study of Irish workers in England included in this book fits with the European emphasis on ethnicity.

We have already mentioned religion in connection with ethnicity as a potential alternative source of solidarity to class. Industrialisation and proletarianisation were seen in the past as a threat to established religion, which they also influenced and changed.[121] The struggle over the societal order was therefore linked to the struggle over faith, and faith was sometimes also in competition with class as a point of crystallisation for solidarity. Workers were so strongly attached to their faith in some places, circumstances and periods that it outweighed their identification with their class.[122]

Gender, ethnicity and religion still do not exhaust all the identities in competition with class. Age or generation and nation are other alternatives that could be mentioned.[123] Gender, ethnicity and religion can, however, be considered the most important examples.

The third road that was travelled, finally, led to a reconsideration of the concept of the working class as such. We can make a distinction here between a weak version and a strong version of this approach. The weak version still uses the concept of class, but maintains that there are more facets to the concept than was once thought. Some advocates of this perspective no longer define class identity in terms of relations of production alone, for example, but also in terms of consumption.[124] This angle of approach brings women more to the forefront: one characteristic of the construction of femininity in the period when the 'male breadwinner' ideology reigned was that women were relegated more to the sphere of consumption than to the sphere of production. It is clear in any case that consumption has often been gender-specific.[125] Other historians have used sociological theorisations of social movements (such as so-called 'resource mobilisation theory') in order to acquire new insights into the logic of workers' collective action.[126]

The strong version of this approach puts the very concept of class itself into question. Reacting against monocausal explanations based exclusively on workers' class position, some historians have made a 'linguistic turn' and shifted their focus to discourse analysis.[127] They have de-linked the literary history of social movements from these movements' real history and thus attempted 'to elevate language above class in the history of modern labor and its movements'.[128] Some advocates of the linguistic turn have defended the idea that the concept of social class must be seen so much as an intellectual construction as to make it useless for analysing the past. It was only one step further to proclaim the death of social history.[129] In practice, however, historians were not able to avoid referring to differences among social classes, which have been very tangible differences for real historical actors, in describing their subjects.[130] Historical study of social classes has furnished abundant evidence of how tangible these differences have been.

Conclusion

The wealth of approaches that have been developed in the past two decades have made labour history an exciting enterprise, but also a very complex one. Much that seemed solid has melted into air. This has resulted in important new insights, but it also conceals a danger: the fragmentation of our historical images threatens to push connections among different historical processes outside our field of vision. There are postmodern historians who embrace this danger. They consider that the urge towards overarching interpretations and theories is not only futile but also misleading. They can even go so far as to propose 'the nostalgic experience of the past' as 'the matrix for a satisfactory analysis of historical experience.'[131] We have a different opinion. Current debates in labour history cannot conceal the fact that a considerable body of knowledge has demonstrably been accumulated in the last century and a half, and that our conceptual tools have become much more refined. In short, there is no question of successive interpretations that have been disconnected from each other and are equally valid scientifically. There has been *progress*.

Nor do we believe that the effort to give overarching interpretations should be abandoned. What we need now is a new theory that can situate different aspects (class, gender, ethnicity, etc.) of different forms of power (in wage labour, households, politics, etc.) within concrete causal processes, and that indicates which (individual or collective) subjects exercise this power and why.[132] A theory of this kind will never again have the same character as the classical syntheses we are familiar with from earlier phases of labour historiography (such as Oxford institutionalism, classical Marxism, etc.). The new developments have in particular focused our attention sharply on fundamental methodological difficulties that went unacknowledged or were inadequately recognised in the classical syntheses. We could refer to these difficulties as indeterminacy problems, analogous to some extent with the indeterminacy problems in physics, according to which some characteristics of elementary particles become harder to measure as other characteristics are measured more accurately.

At least two such indeterminacies exist in labour historiography. The first concerns the relationship between structure and agency. The more historians focus on concrete people, the more broader societal processes and structures fade into the background. Inversely, the more they examine structures and macro-processes, the more individual agents and their personal life stories fade out of the picture. There does not seem to be any solution to this dilemma: every approach has its price.

The second indeterminacy problem concerns the relationship between class, gender, ethnicity, religion and other aspects of historical analysis. The Australian feminist historian Ann Curthoys has pointed out how difficult it is to work *simultaneously* with concepts like sex (or gender), ethnicity (or race) and class:

> Trying to keep just two of these concepts in play has proved extremely difficult. ... But if keeping two such concepts in play is hard enough, look what happens when the third concept, be it ethnicity or class or sex, is brought seriously into play. The system, the analysis, becomes too complex to handle.[133]

Both indeterminacy problems mean that the perspective chosen unavoidably distorts any picture. But they do not mean that no knowable reality exists outside our scholarly discourses. Grand Narratives are still possible and desirable, but no single Grand Narrative can ever tell the whole story. Like floodlights, they produce a great deal of light, but they also cast things in shadow and can blind the observer.

We would like this volume to make a very modest contribution to the preparation of such partial Grand Narratives. The halting communication among labour historians from different countries that we mentioned at the beginning of this introduction is becoming more and more of an obstacle to this process. A good understanding of national developments demands historical study of transnational processes and international comparisons. We are convinced that better contacts and more cooperation across national frontiers would be to everyone's advantage. Labour historians from different countries have much to learn from each other in many areas (development of theory, research questions, methods and techniques). Exchanging knowledge will facilitate the interpretation of supranational connections *and* of local peculiarities. The fact that this book is limited to Western Europe does not imply any Eurocentrism, but results from purely practical considerations. We are very much aware that any serious Grand Narrative must ultimately embrace the whole world.[134]

This book originated at a congress that the International Institute of Social History organised in 1997 for the founding of LabNet, the European network of labour historians.[135] A substantial part of the meeting was devoted to a discussion of the most important categories in current labour history: class, gender, ethnicity and religion. Prominent specialists delved into these identities' meaning for European labour history. Their revised contributions are documented here. Each of the studies is organised in its own way: a systematic discussion of class by Mike Savage, an essay on ethnicity by John Belchem focusing on Irish workers' position in England, an overview of recent studies on religion by Patrick Pasture, and an essay on gender by Eileen Yeo that once more focuses particularly on the British case. Taken as a whole, they show how much livelier the new perspectives have made European labour history. The four essays are preceded by a historiographical overview by Jürgen Kocka, and followed by two comments from other continents by Janaki Nair and Alice Kessler-Harris.

This book's second part provides what we hope are useful tools for the study of *all* of Western European labour history. Along with an overview of professional journals, overviews of bibliographies, survey articles, biographical dictionaries, general surveys and websites are also included, together with an annotated list of important books.

Translated by Peter Drucker

Notes

1. We would like to express our appreciation to Gerd Callesen, Elina Katainen, Jaap Kloosterman, Wolfgang Maderthaner, Siegfried Mattl, Emmet O'Connor, Lars Olsson, Manuel Pérez Ledesma, François Valloton and Bart de Wilde for their comments on earlier versions of this introduction.

2. In German, for example, there exist both *Arbeitergeschichte* and *Arbeiterbewegungsgeschichte*, and in French *histoire du mouvement ouvrier* and *histoire ouvrière*.

3. Prior to the development of either form of labour history, contemporaneous studies were published by reformers or conservatives who were concerned about the condition of the subaltern classes or about social protest. Early examples are the physician Louis-René Villermé (1782–1863), whose *Tableau de l'état physique et moral des ouvriers employés dans les manufactures de coton, de laine et de soie*, 2 vols, Paris, 1840, gave a detailed description of French textile workers' working conditions, housing, clothing, etc.; and the philosopher Lorenz von Stein (1815–90), who explained in his book *Der Socialismus und Communismus des heutigen Frankreichs: Ein Beitrag zur Zeitgeschichte*, Leipzig, 1842, that the rise of French and British 'communism' should be studied in order to prevent a similar development in Germany. Other authors include the Belgians J. Mareska and J. Heyman, *Enquête sur le travail et la Condition physique et morale des ouvriers employés dans les manufactures de cotton à Gand*, Ghent, 1845. Later authors such as Frédéric LePlay, Henry Mayhew and others worked naturally along the same lines.

4. On this subject see e.g. Gerhard Oestreich, 'Die Fachhistorie und die Anfänge der sozialgeschichtlichen Forschung in Deutschland', *Historische Zeitschrift*, 208 (1969): 320–63.

5. Emile Levasseur, *Histoire des classes ouvrières en France depuis la conquête de Jules César jusqu'à la Révolution*, 2 vols, Paris, 1859, and *Histoire des classes ouvrières en France depuis 1789 jusqu'à nos jours*, 2 vols, Paris, 1867. The citation is on p. iii of the very first part.

6. Fernando Garrido, *Historia de las clases trabajadores*, 4 vols (1870; reprint: Algorta, 1970–1). We have accepted the characterisation by Manuel Pérez Ledesma, 'Manuel Tuñon de Lara y la historiografía española del movimiento obrero', in José Luis de la Granja and Alberto Reig Tapia (eds), *Manuel Tuñon de Lara: El compromiso con la historia: Su vida y su obra*, Bilbao, 1993, 197–215, here 201.

7. Lassalle formulated the 'iron law of wages' in, among other writings, the Open Letter that he addressed in 1863 to the Central Convocatory Committee for a General German Workers' Congress (see Lassalle's *Gesammelte Reden und Schriften*, vol. III, Berlin, 1919). The theory appeared in other variants as well. John Weston, for example, defended a version of it in the General Council of the International Working Men's Association (First International).

8. Rainer Zoll, *Der Doppelcharakter der Gewerkschaften: Zur Aktualität der Marxschen Gewerkschaftstheorie*, Frankfurt am Main, 1976, 55–7. Zoll adds: 'And nevertheless the "iron law of wages" was linked to a clear recognition of class distinctions; it implied an abandonment of all illusions about any possible individual advancement – which Lassalle also warned against.' (57)

9. John Stuart Mill, 'Thornton on Labour and Its Claims' [a review of W.T. Thornton, *On Labour, Its Wrongful Claims and Rightful Dues, Its Actual Present and Possible Future*, London, 1869], *Fortnightly Review*, May 1869, reprinted in Mill, *Collected Works*, vol. 5, Toronto, 1965, 631–68.

10. Although a second round of discussion took place between the mid-1880s and the mid-1890s. Scott Gordon, 'The Wage-Fund Controversy: The Second Round', *History of Political Economy*, 5 (1973): 14–35.

11. For another explanation see: T.W. Hutchison, 'The "Marginal Revolution" and the Decline and Fall of English Classical Political Economy', in R.D. Collison Black, A.W. Coats and D.W. Goodwin (eds), *The Marginal Revolution in Economics: Interpretation and Evaluation*, Durham, NC, 1973, 176–202, 194–202.

12. See e.g. Lujo Brentano, 'Die gewerbliche Arbeiterfrage', in Gustav Schönberg (ed.), *Handbuch der politischen Oekonomie*, Tübingen, 1882, vol. 1, 905–94. In this essay Brentano, anticipating Karl Polányi among others, contends that labour power is an entirely different sort of commodity from others. See also James J. Sheehan, *The Career of Lujo Brentano: A Study of Liberalism and Reform in Imperial Germany*, Chicago [etc.], 1966; E.P. Hennock, 'Lessons from England: Lujo Brentano on British Trade Unionism', *German History*, 11 (1993): 141–60.

    As far as we know there does not exist any comparative history of the earliest liberal labour historiography. One Dutch case study is: Ger Harmsen, 'De vroegste geschiedschrijving van de Nederlandse arbeidersbeweging, 1875–1905', in Mies Campfens, Margreet Schrevel and Fritjof Tichelman (eds), *Op een beteren weg: Schetsen uit de geschiedenis van de arbeidersbeweging aangeboden aan mevrouw dr. J.M. Welcker*, Amsterdam, 1985, 14–38.

13. James E. Thorold Rogers, *Six Centuries of Work and Wages*, London, 1884.

14. Paul Mayer, 'Die Geschichte des Sozialdemokratischen Parteiarchivs und das Schicksal des Marx-Engels-Nachlasses', *Archiv für Sozialgeschichte*, 6–7 (1966–67): 5–198.

15. Namely with the Arbetarebibliotek (Stockholm) – now the Arbetarrörelsens Arkiv och bibliotek – the Arbeiderbevegelsens Arkiv og Bibliotek (Oslo), the Työväen Arkisto (Helsinki) and the Arbejderbevaegelsens Bibliotek og Arkiv (Copenhagen). The Scandinavian archives diverged from the German model by, for example, working for the parties as well as the union movements.

16. On the origins of the Musée Social and its founder, see Janet Horne, 'Le Musée social: les métamorphoses d'une idée', *Le mouvement social*, no. 171 (April–June 1995): 47–69; Françoise Blum, 'Le Comte de Chambrun: catholique, mécène des protestants?', in Collette Chambelland (ed.), *Le Musée Social en son temps*, Preface Pierre Rosanvallon, Paris, 1998, 27–41. The Musée Social merged in 1963 with the Office Central des Oeuvres de Bienfaisance and has been known since then as the CEDIAS-Musée social. The foundation of the Musée Social was followed, even before the First World War, by the foundation of a second important French institution, namely the Bibliothèque de Documentation Internationale Contemporaine (BDIC) in 1914.

17. Theodor Pinkus, 'Das Schweizerische Sozialarchiv', *Internationale wissenschaftliche Korrespondenz zur Geschichte der deutschen Arbeiterbewegung*, no. 3 (December 1966): 21–2.

18. The context of these (primarily Austrian) experiments is described in Herbert Hassinger, 'Die Wirtschaftsgeschichte an Österreichs Hochschulen bis zum Ende des ersten Weltkrieges', in Wilhelm Abel et al. (eds), *Wirtschaft, Geschichte und Wirtschaftsgeschichte: Festschrift zum 65. Geburtstag von Friedrich Lütge*, Stuttgart, 1966, 407–29.

19. Grünberg had early made a proposal (in 1919) to found in Vienna an Austrian counterpart of the Musée Social, with Karl Kautsky as director. A few years later the Frankfurt Institute could be founded, thanks to financial support from Felix Weil, who had inherited a considerable fortune. Weil originally wanted another labour historian, Gustav Mayer, as director, but Mayer declined the honour when he found out that Weil himself wanted to have too much influence on the institute's day-to-day work (Gustav Mayer, *Erinnerungen: Vom Journalisten zum Historiker der deutschen Arbeiterbewegung*, Zürich, 1949, 340–1.) Grünberg accepted Weil's offer, and saw the new institute first and foremost as an 'institute for research on the history of socialism and the workers' movement'. When Max Horkheimer succeeded him in 1931 (Grünberg had had a stroke in 1928), he pointed out in his inaugural speech that Grünberg had built up a library of 50,000 titles on labour history in the institute's first four years. See Rolf Wiggershaus, *The Frankfurt School: Its History, Theories and Political Significance,* Cambridge, 1994, 21–4; Günther Nenning, 'Biographie', in *Indexband zu Archiv für die Geschichte des Sozialismus und der Arbeiterbewegung (C. Grünberg)*, Graz and Zürich, 1973, 177–84; Max Horkheimer, 'Die gegenwärtige Lage der Sozialphilosophie und die Aufgaben eines Instituts für Sozialforschung' (1931), in Max Horkheimer, *Gesammelte Schriften*, vol. 3, Frankfurt am Main, 1988, 20–35, here 30.

20. Kautsky archive, International Institute of Social History, Amsterdam, letter dated 22 October 1909.

21. On the Webbs, see Royden Harrison, 'Sidney and Beatrice Webb', in Carl Levy (ed.), *Socialism and the Intelligentsia, 1880–1914,* London and New York, 1987, 35–89; Lisanne Radice, 'Beatrice und Sidney Webb (1858–1943, 1859–1947)', in Walter Euchner (ed.), *Klassiker des Sozialismus*, vol. II, Munich, 1991, 264–77, 310–12.

22. Eduard Bernstein, *Die Geschichte der Berliner Arbeiterbewegung*, 3 vols, Berlin, 1907–10; Max Nettlau, *Michael Bakunin: eine Biographie*, 3 vols, London, 1895–9; James Guillaume, *L'Internationale*, 4 vols, Paris, 1905–10; reprint: Geneva, 1980. Among other studies of the same type are Anselmo Lorenzo, *El proletariado mili-*

tante, Madrid, 1901; several reprints; Louis Bertrand, *Histoire de la Coopération en Belgique*, 2 vols, Brussels, 1902–3; W.H. Vliegen, *De Dageraad der Volksbevrijding*, 2 vols, Amsterdam, 1905; Robert Grimm, *Geschichte der Berner Arbeiterbewegung*, Bern, 1913. On Bernstein (1850–1932) see Francis L. Carsten, *Eduard Bernstein, 1850–1932: eine politische Biographie*, Munich, 1993; on Nettlau (1865–1944) see Rudolf Rocker, *Max Nettlau: Leben und Werk des Historikers vergessener sozialer Bewegungen*, Berlin, 1978; on Guillaume (1844–1916) see Dorothea Roth, 'James Guillaume', *Schweizerische Zeitschrift für Geschichte*, 15 (1965): 30–86 and Marc Vuilleumier, 'Notes sur James Guillaume, historien de la Première Internationale et ses rapports avec Max Nettlau et Jean Jaurès', *Cahiers Vilfredo Pareto/Revue européenne d'histoire des sciences sociales*, no. 7–8 (1965): 81–109.

23. Georges d'Avenel, *Paysans et ouvriers depuis sept cent ans*, Paris, 1899; Henri Hauser, *Ouvriers du temps passé (XVe-XVIe siècles)*, Paris, 1899.

24. On the Hammonds' work see Teresa Javurek, 'A New Liberal Descent: The "Labourer" Trilogy by Lawrence and Barbara Hammond', *Twentieth Century British History*, 10 (1999): 375–403. See also Henry R. Winkler, 'J.L. Hammond', in Hans A. Schmitt (ed.), *Historians of Modern Europe*, Baton Rouge, 1971, 95–119 and R.H. Tawney, 'J.L. Hammond, 1872–1949', *Proceedings of the British Academy*, 46 (1960): 267–93; reprinted in J.M. Winter (ed.), *History and Society: Essays by R.H. Tawney*, London [etc.], 1978, 229–54.

25. Robert René Kuczynski, *Arbeitslohn und Arbeitszeit in Europa und Amerika, 1870–1909*, Berlin, 1913; Carl von Tyszka, *Löhne und Lebenskosten in Westeuropa im 19. Jahrhundert (Frankreich, England, Spanien, Belgien)*, Munich [etc.], 1914. On Robert René Kuczynski (1876–1947) see Jürgen Kuczynski, *René Kuczynski: ein fortschrittlicher Wissenschaftler in der ersten Hälfte des 20. Jahrhunderts*, Berlin, 1957. In Belgium Louis Varlez (1868–1930) conducted similar research. See his *Les salaires dans l'industrie gantoise*, 2 vols, Brussels, 1901–1904.

26. Georges Haupt, 'Why the History of the Working-Class Movement?', *New German Critique*, no. 14 (1978): 7–27, here 13–14. See also Georges Haupt et al., 'Zwischen Sozialgeschichte und Legitimationswissenschaft', *Jahrbuch Arbeiterbewegung*, 2 (1974): 267–300.

27. For the early history of the IISH see Maria Hunink, *De papieren van de revolutie: Het Internationaal Instituut voor Sociale Geschiedenis 1935–1947*, Amsterdam, 1986. An Italian translation of this book is also now available: Maria Hunink, *Le carte della rivoluzione: l'Istituto Internazionale di Storia Sociale di Amsterdam – nascita e sviluppo dal 1935 al 1947*, Milan, 1998.

28. A serious beginning was made outside Western Europe as well, in the interwar years, with the collection of Western European archives. In 1919 in Stanford, California, the Hoover Institution on War, Revolution and Peace was established (initially in order to collect documents on the causes and consequences of the First World War; and in 1921 in Moscow the Marx-Engels Institute was founded, whose activities definitely extended beyond Marx and Engels.

29. Franz Mehring, *Karl Marx: Geschichte seines Lebens*, Leipzig, 1918; English translation: *Karl Marx: The Story of His Life*, trans. Edward Fitzgerald, London, 1936; Gustav Mayer, *Friedrich Engels in seiner Frühzeit, 1820–1851*, Berlin, 1920 and *Friedrich Engels, Band II: Engels und der Aufstieg der Arbeiterbewegung in Europa*, Berlin, 1933. English version: *Friedrich Engels: A Biography*, London, 1936. On Mehring (1846–1919) see Helga Grebing and Monika Kramme, 'Franz Mehring', in Hans-Ulrich Wehler (ed.), *Deutsche Historiker*, vol. V, Göttingen, 1972, 73–94. On Mayer (1871–1948) see Hans-Ulrich Wehler, 'Gustav Mayer', in Wehler (ed.), *Deutsche Historiker*, vol. II, Göttingen, 1971, 120–32.

30. Ludwig Brügel, *Geschichte der österreichischen Sozialdemokratie*, 5 vols, Vienna, 1922–25; Max Quarck, *Die erste deutsche Arbeiterbewegung: Geschichte der Arbei-*

terverbrüderung 1848/49, Leipzig, 1924; Jan Oudegeest, *De geschiedenis der zelf-standige vakbeweging in Nederland,* 2 vols, Amsterdam, 1926–32; G.D.H. Cole, *A Short History of the British Working Class Movement,* 3 vols, London, 1925–7. On Brügel (1866–1942) see *Autriche. Dictionnaire biographique du mouvement ouvrier international,* Paris, 1971, 60–1; on Quarck (1860–1930) see Franz Osterroth, *Biographisches Lexikon des Sozialismus,* vol. I: Verstorbene Persönlichkeiten, Hannover, 1960, 243; on Oudegeest (1870–1950) see Ger Harmsen, 'Oudegeest, Jan', *Biografisch woordenboek van het socialisme en de arbeidersbeweging in Nederland,* vol. 7, Amsterdam, 1998, 160–7; on Cole (1889–1959) see L.P. Carpenter, *G.D.H. Cole: An Intellectual Biography,* Cambridge, 1973, and Anthony Wright, *G.D.H. Cole and Socialist Democracy,* Oxford, 1979.

31. Several dissertations had already appeared before this, including John Lindgren, *Det socialdemokratiska arbetarpartiets uppkomst i Sverige, 1881–1889,* Stockholm, 1927; G. Hilding Nordström, *Sveriges socialdemokratiska arbetareparti under genombrottsåren, 1889–1894,* Stockholm, 1938, and Tage Lindblom, *Den svenska fackföreningsrörelsens uppkomst och tidigare historia, 1872–1900,* Stockholm, 1938.

32. Edouard Dolléans, *Le Chartisme (1830–1848),* 2 vols, Paris, 1912–13; Dolléans, *Histoire du mouvement ouvrier,* 3 vols, Paris, 1936–54. On Dolléans see *Dictionnaire de biographie française,* vol. 11, Paris, 1967, 449–50.

33. A.J.C. Rüter, *De spoorwegstakingen van 1903: Een spiegel der arbeidersbeweging in Nederland,* Leiden, 1935, reprint Nijmegen, 1973. On Adolf Rüter (1907–65) see Th.J.G. Locher, 'Rüter en zijn werk', in A.J.C. Rüter, *Historische studies over mens en samenleving,* Assen, 1967, ix–xxxiii. See also Johan Frieswijk, 'Rüters spoorwegstakingen nabeschouwd', *Jaarboek voor de geschiedenis van socialisme en arbeidersbeweging 1979,* 287–325.

34. Ivy Pinchbeck, *Women Workers and the Industrial Revolution, 1750–1850,* London, 1930, reprint New York, 1969. On Ivy Pinchbeck (1898–1982) see the entry in *Encyclopedia of Historians and Historical Writing,* London and Chicago, 1999, vol. 2. Several years before Pinchbeck, Alice Clark (1874–1934) had also been a pioneer in the field of British women's history with her *Working Life of Women in the Seventeenth Century,* London and New York, 1919.

35. I.J. Brugmans, *De arbeidende klasse in Nederland in de 19e eeuw* (The Hague, 1925). This study was reprinted many times up until the 1970s.

36. A.L. Morton, *A People's History of England,* London, 1938; reprint London, 1989.

37. Juan Diaz del Moral, *Historia de las agitaciones campesinas andaluzas – Córdoba,* Madrid, 1929; reprints Madrid 1969 and 1973.

38. Ottar Dahl, *Historisk materialisme: historieoppfatningen hos Edvard Bull og Halvdan Koht,* Oslo, 1952.

39. Edvard Bull, *Den Skandinaviske Arbeiderbevegelse 1914–1920,* Kristiania, 1922. Compare Bull's article 'Die Entwicklung der Arbeiterbewegung in den drei skandinavischen Ländern', *Archiv für die Geschichte des Sozialismus und der Arbeiterbewegung,* 10 (1922): 329–61. Thirty years later this statement received international publicity through the work of Walter Galenson, and has been called the Bull-Galenson hypothesis ever since. During the 1970s it became the subject of a lively debate. The debate began with two substantive and sophisticated studies by William M. Lafferty, who provided an alternative explanation involving multiple causes. Walter Galenson, 'Scandinavia', in Galenson (ed.), *Comparative Labor Movements,* New York, 1952, 104–72; Galenson, *Labor in Norway,* Cambridge, MA, 1949; William M. Lafferty, *Economic Development and the Response of Labor in Scandinavia: A Multi-Level Analysis,* Oslo [etc.], 1971; Lafferty, *Industrialization, Community Structure, and Socialism: An Ecological Analysis of Norway, 1875–1924,* Oslo [etc.], 1974. The debate continued in *Tidsskrift for arbeider-*

bevegelse historie, 1976–8. Also see Sten Sparre Nilson, 'Labor Insurgency in Norway: The Crisis of 1917–1920', *Social Science History*, 5 (1981): 393–416, in which he attempts to develop a comprehensive interpretation.

40. The project was coordinated by an International Scientific Committee on Price History. The committee's publications included: Moritz John Elsas, *Umriss einer Geschichte der Preise und Löhne in Deutschland vom ausgehenden Mittelalter bis zum Beginn des neunzehnten Jahrhunderts*, Leiden, 1936; Alfred F. Pribam, *Materialien zur Geschichte der Preise und Löhne in Österreich*, vol. I, Vienna, 1938; William H. Beveridge, *Prices and Wages in England from the Twelfth to the Nineteenth Century*, London, 1939); Earl Jefferson Hamilton, *Money, Prices, and Wages in Valencia, Aragon, and Navarre, 1351–1500*, Cambridge, MA, 1936; and Nicolaas W. Posthumus, *Nederlandsche prijsgeschiedenis*, 2 vols, Leiden, 1943, 1964. Beveridge's (1879–1963) study includes a 'General Introduction' in which the project is described in detail. Other important contributions appeared as well that were not part of the Rockefeller Foundation's project, for instance, François Simiand, *Le salaire, l'évolution sociale et la monnaie*, 3 vols, Paris, 1932, and Ernest Labrousse, *Esquisse du mouvement des prix et des revenues en France au 18ème siècle*, Paris, 1933.

41. On Maitron see the special issue of *Le Mouvement Social*, no. 144 (October–November 1988). Maitron's most important monograph was his *Histoire du mouvement anarchiste en France (1880–1914)*, Paris, 1951. At its completion in 1997 the biographical dictionary consisted of 44 volumes, and is now also available on CD-ROM: *Dictionnaire biographique du mouvement ouvrier français*, Paris, 1964–93, plus Michel Cordillot, Claude Pennetier and Jean Risacher (eds), *Biographies Nouvelles*, Paris, 1997. Maitron directed the project until the 1980s, when Claude Pennetier succeeded him.

   At about the same time as Maitron, John Saville in Britain began work on a comparable (but less massive) project, which continued an intiative of Douglas Cole's. John Saville, 'Dictionary of Labour Movement Biography', *Bulletin*, no. 2 (Spring, 1961): 15–16. See Joyce M. Bellamy and John Saville (eds), *Dictionary of Labour Biography*, 9 vols, London and Basingstoke, 1972–93.

42. Gastone Manacorda, *Il movimento operaio italiano attraverso i suoi congressi: Dalle origini alla formazione del Partito Socialista (1853–1892)*, Rome, 1953; 2nd edn Rome, 1974. For information on 'narrow' Italian labour historiography before 1945, see Enzo Tagliacozzo's pamphlet *Gli studi storici sul movimento operaio in Italia nel cinquantennio 1861–1915*, Pisa, 1937, and Leo Valiani, 'Il movimento socialista in Italia dalle origine al 1921: studi e ricerche del ventennio 1937–1957', in Valiani, *Questioni di storia del socialismo*, Turin, 1958, 13–167.

43. E.g. Giuliano Procacci and Giovanni Rindi, 'Storia di una fabbrica: Le "Officine Galileo" di Firenze', *Movimento Operaio*, New Series, 6 (1954): 5–49; Procacci, 'La classe operaia italiana agli inizi del secolo XX', *Studi Storici*, 3 (1962): 3–76; Procacci, 'Geografia e struttura del movimento contadino della Valle padana nel suo periodo formativo (1901–1906)', *Studi Storici*, 5 (1964): 41–120. See also Procacci's *La lotte di classe in Italia agli inizi del secolo XX*, Rome, 1979, 3–76, and in English his *The Italian Working Class from the Risorgimento to Fascism*, Cambridge MA, 1979.

44. Ernest Labrousse was a committed socialist, including as editor of *Humanité* (1919–25) and editor-in-chief of the SFIO journal *Revue Socialiste*. In the 1950s he left the SFIO and was active in first the PSA and then the PSU. On his trajectory see Pierre Renouvin, 'Ernest Labrousse', in Schmitt, *Historians of Modern Europe*, 235–54; Christophe Charle, 'Entretien avec Ernest Labrousse', *Actes de la recherche en sciences sociales*, no. 32–33 (1980): 111–27; Jean-Yves Grenier and Bernard Lepetit, 'L'expérience historique: A propos de C.-E. Labrousse', *Annales ESC*, New Series, 44 (1989): 1337–60; Pierre Saly, 'Réflexions sur un héritage:

Ernest Labrousse et le marxisme', *Cahiers d'histoire de l'Institut de Recherches Marxistes*, no. 39 (1989): 3–34.

45. Lutz Raphael, *Die Erben von Bloch und Febvre: 'Annales'-Geschichtsschreibung und 'nouvelle histoire' in Frankreich 1945–1980*, Stuttgart, 1994, 139.

46. Asa Briggs and John Saville were influential not only through their own publications but also through three edited volumes, the first of which was intended as a *Festschrift* for G.D.H. Cole (who, however, died just before its publication): *Essays in Labour History*, London [etc.] and New York, 1960); *Essays in Labour History, 1886–1923*, London, 1971; *Essays in Labour History, 1918–1939*, London, 1977.

47. We must content ourselves with an overview of bibliographical essays in the second part of this book. Taken together, these give a good impression of developments since the late 1960s.

48. Eric J. Hobsbawm, 'Labour History and Ideology' (1974), in E.J. Hobsbawm, *Worlds of Labour: Further Studies in the History of Labour*, London, 1984, 1–14, here 6.

49. Raphael Samuel (ed.), *History Workshop: A Collectanea, 1967–1991*, Oxford, 1991.

50. Karl R. Stadler (ed.), *Rückblick und Ausschau: Zehn Jahre Ludwig-Boltzmann-Institut für Geschichte der Arbeiterbewegung*, Vienna, 1978; Karl R. Stadler, 'Arbeitergeschichte und Geschichte der Arbeiterbewegungen in Österreich', in Gerhard Botz (ed.), *Bewegung und Klasse: Studien zur österreichischen Arbeitergeschichte*, Vienna, 1978. On Karl Stadler and the Ludwig-Boltzmann-Institut see Helmut Konrad, 'Nachruf auf Karl R. Stadler', in Rudolf G. Ardelt and Hans Hautmann (eds), *Arbeiterschaft und Nationalsozialismus in Österreich: in memoriam Karl R. Stadler*, Vienna, 1990, 11–26; Gerhard Botz, Hans Hautmann and Helmut Konrad (eds), *Geschichte und Gesellschaft: Festschrift für Karl R. Stadler zum 60. Geburtstag*, Vienna, 1974, 567–71; Gerhard Botz and Christian Broda (eds), *Geschichte als demokratischer Auftrag: Karl R. Stadler zum 70. Geburtstag*, Vienna, 1983, 301–7.

Also important in Austria was the foundation of the Project Team on Labour Movement History in the Ministry of Science (1973). See Helene Maimann, 'Das "Projektteam Geschichte der Arbeiterbewegung" in Wien', *Internationale wissenschaftliche Korrespondenz zur Geschichte der deutschen Arbeiterbewegung*, 11 (1975): 499–500; Josef Ehmer and Albert Müller, 'Sozialgeschichte in Österreich', in Jürgen Kocka (ed.), *Sozialgeschichte im internationalen Überblick: Ergebnisse und Tendenzen der Forschung*, Darmstadt, 1989, 128.

51. The apogee was the special issue of the *Revue européenne des sciences sociales/Cahiers Vilfredo Pareto* in May 1973 (no. 29). See in this issue Marc Vuilleumier, 'Quelques jalons pour une historiographie du mouvement ouvrier en Suisse', 5–35. It also includes an extract from the group's statutes (p. 35).

52. Erich Gruner, *Die Arbeiter in der Schweiz im 19. Jahrhundert: soziale Lage, Organisation, Verhältnis zu Arbeitgebern und Staat*, Berne, 1968.

53. Tuñon de Lara's major work in this period was his *El movimiento obrero en la historia de Espana*, Madrid, 1972, a book of almost a thousand pages. His publications on 'broad' labour history include: *Variaciones del nivel de vida en España*, Madrid, 1965 and *Metodologia de la historia social de Espana*, Madrid, 1973. Biographical information about Tuñon de Lara (1915–97) can be found in José Luis de la Granja and Alberto Reig Tapia, 'Manuel Tuñon de Lara, una trayectoria vital e intelectual', and in José Luis de la Granja and Alberto Reig Tapia (eds), *Manuel Tuñon de Lara: El compromiso con la historia. Su vida y su obra*, Bilbao, 1993, 17–115.

54. Rolande Trempé, *Les mineurs de Carmaux, 1848–1914*, 2 vols, Toulouse, 1971; Michelle Perrot, *Les ouvriers en grève, France, 1871–1890*, 2 vols, Paris, 1974; Yves Lequin, *Les ouvriers de la région lyonnaise dans la seconde moitié du XIXe siècle, 1848–1914*, 2 vols, Lyon, 1977.

55. Yves Lequin, 'Sozialgeschichte à la française', in Jürgen Kocka (ed.), *Sozialgeschichte im internationalen Überblick: Ergebnisse und Tendenzen der Forschung*, Darmstadt, 1989, 163–86, here 173–4.
56. Stefano Merli, *Proletariato di fabbrica e capitalismo industriale: Il caso italiano (1880–1900)*, 2 vols, Florence, 1972–3. See also Franco Livorsi, 'Stefano Merli: lo storico e il socialismo', *Il Ponte*, 51, 12 (December 1995): 75–97; Carlo Carotti, 'Stefano Merli storico, 'militante' ed editore: Un percorso bibliografico', in Luigi Cortesi and Andrea Panaccione (eds), *Il socialismo e la storia: studi per Stefano Merli*, Milan, 1998, 275–98.
57. José Pacheco Pereira, 'L'historiographie ouvrière au Portugal', *Le Mouvement Social*, no. 123 (April-June 1983): 99–109, here 105.
58. Carlos da Fonseca, *História do movimento operário e das ideias socialistas em Portugal*, 4 vols, Mira Sintra, 1979–80.
59. Letter from Lars Olsson to authors, 14 February 2001.
60. Roughly speaking, Ger Harmsen (*1923) has a narrative-institutional perspective, while Theo van Tijn (1927–92) had a structural perspective. On Harmsen see Pim Fortuyn (ed.), *Afscheid van de dialectiek? Rondom het afscheid van Ger Harmsen als hoogleraar*, Nijmegen, 1988; on Van Tijn see Ad Knotter, 'Geschiedwetenschap als engagement: Het perspectief van prof. dr. Th. van Tijn', in Boudien de Vries et al. (eds), *De kracht der zwakken: studies over arbeid en arbeidersbeweging in het verleden*, Amsterdam, 1992, 405–34.
61. See the overview covering the years 1970–82 by Michael Schneider, 'Christliche Arbeiterbewegung in Europa: Ein vergleichender Literaturbericht', in Klaus Tenfelde (ed.), *Arbeiter und Arbeiterbewegung im Vergleich: Berichte zur internationalen historischen Forschung*, Munich, 1986, 477–505.
62. Galenson, *Labor in Norway*; Val R. Lorwin, *The French Labor Movement*, Cambridge, MA, 1954; Maurice F. Neufeld, *Italy: School of Awakening Countries: The Italian Labor Movement in Its Political, Social and Economic Setting from 1800 to 1960*, Ithaca, NY, 1961.
63. John H.M. Laslett et al., 'In Memoriam Robert F. Wheeler', *International Labor and Working-Class History*, no. 13 (May 1978): 3–17; Peter Lösche, 'Nachruf auf Robert F. Wheeler', *Internationale wissenschaftliche Korrespondenz zur Geschichte der deutschen Arbeiterbewegung*, 14 (1978): 1–2.
64. Erich Gruner et al., *Arbeiterschaft und Wirtschaft in der Schweiz 1880–1914*, 3 vols, Zurich, 1988. See also Hans Ulrich Jost's review essay 'Swiss Labour History', *International Review of Social History*, 34 (1989): 485–94.
65. Edvard Bull, Jr. et al. (eds), *Arbeiderbevegelsens historie i Norge*, 6 vols, Oslo, 1985–90. See also the review essay by Fritz Petrick and Michael F. Scholz, 'Norwegian Labour History', *International Review of Social History*, 39 (1994): 93–9.
66. Wolfgang Maderthaner (ed.), *Sozialdemokratie und Habsburgerstaat, 1867–1918*, Vienna, 1988; Anson Rabinbach, *Vom Roten Wien zum Bürgerkrieg: die österreichische Sozialdemokratie 1918–1934*, Vienna, 1989; Manfred Marschalek (ed.), *Untergrund und Exil: Österreichs Sozialisten zwischen 1934 und 1945*, Vienna: Löcker, 1991; Maderthaner (ed.), *Auf dem Weg zur Macht: Integration in den Staat, Sozialpartnerschaft und Regierungspartei*, Vienna, 1992; Heinz Fischer, *Die Kreisky-Jahre, 1967–1983*, Vienna, 1993. Rabinbach's book is the German version of *The Austrian Socialist Experiment: Social Democracy and Austromarxism, 1918–1934*, Boulder, CO, 1985.
67. A summary overview is given in Anders L. Johansson and Lars Magnusson, *LO – andra halvseklet. Fackföreningsrörelsen och samhället*, Stockholm, 1998.
68. On this project as a whole see Gerhard A. Ritter (ed.), *Über das Projekt: Geschichte der Arbeiter und der Arbeiterbewegung in Deutschland seit dem Ende des 18. Jahrhunderts*, Bonn-Bad Godesberg, 1984. The volumes are being published as

their authors complete them. Heinrich August Winkler was the first to complete his share of the work: three volumes on the Weimar Republic (from 1984 on). Jürgen Kocka originally foresaw four volumes on the period 1800–70, of which two have appeared so far. Gerhard A. Ritter and Klaus Tenfelde have finished one volume (out of the three planned) on the years 1871–1918; and a book on the period 1933–9 recently appeared from the pen of Michael Schneider.

69. In Spain, for instance, the shift seems to be less drastic. A new and successful journal of social history with considerable space devoted to labour history was founded there at the Open University (UNED) in Valencia in 1988, and a social history association that devotes considerable attention to labour history has been functioning for a number of years. Our Spanish colleagues evidently need to make up for lost time after the long Franco dictatorship, which, after all, only ended in 1975. They, too, are nonetheless debating labour history's future perspectives. See José Álvarez Junco and Manuel Pérez Ledesma, 'Historia del movimiento obrero. ¿Una segunda ruptura?', *Revista de Occidente*, no. 83 (1982): 19–41, and Ángeles Barrio Alonso, 'A propósito de la historia social, del movimiento obrero y los sindicatos', in German Rueda (ed.), *Doce estudios de historia contemporánea*, Santander, 1991, 41–68.

70. Erich Gruner's efforts in Switzerland seem on balance to have had a negative effect. 'Interest slackened in the history of workers and their organizations after Erich Gruner's monumental collection of material on the period 1880–1914; it seems to have marked something of an end point for the time being, even though great expanses of further work beyond 1914 still remain to be done.' Mario König, 'Neuere Forschungen zur Sozialgeschichte der Schweiz', *Archiv für Sozialgeschichte*, 36 (1996): 395–433, here 397.

71. John Halstead mentions these factors in order to explain the decreased interest in labour history in Britain. See his 'British Labour History After the Collapse of Actually Existing Socialism and in the Postmodern Age', in Bruno Groppo et al. (eds), *Quellen und Historiographie der Arbeiterbewegung nach dem Zusammenbruch des 'Realsozialismus'*, Garbsen, 1998, 83–102, here 85.

72. The Austrian Association for Labour Movement History has gone through a 'cultural turn' since the early 1990s. It has devoted very considerable attention since then to Viennese 'modernity' and popular cultures.

73. This observation is drawn from Schneider, 'Christliche Arbeiterbewegung', 477.

74. On the professionalisation of history see e.g. Doris S. Goldstein, 'The Professionalization of History in Britain in the Late Nineteenth and Early Twentieth Centuries', *Storia della storiografia*, no. 3 (1983): 3–27; Georg G. Iggers, *New Directions in European Historiography: Revised Edition*, Hanover, NH, 1984, 25; Gérard Noiriel, 'Naisance du métier d'historien', *Genèses*, 1 (1990): 58–95.

75. Eric J. Hobsbawm, 'Labour History and Ideology' (1974), in *Worlds of Labour: Further Studies in the History of Labour*, London, 1984, 1–14, here 5.

76. Historian Gustav Bang (1871–1915), for example, a prominent member of Danish social democracy, had specialised in medieval history and history of the nobility. Mogens Rüdiger, *Gustav Bang: historiker og socialdemocrat*, Copenhagen, 1987.

77. Claus Møller Jørgensen, 'Patterns of Professionalization and Institutionalization in Denmark from 1848 to the Present', in Frank Meyer and Jan Eivind Myhre (eds), *Nordic Historiography in the Twentieth Century*, Oslo, 2000, 114–48, here 122–3.

78. The shift took place more slowly not only in countries under dictatorships (such as Spain and Portugal) but also for example in Austria. 'Workers were for a long time emphatically not a subject for academic historical scholarship. True, the first, modest steps towards gathering sources and materials for a "social history of

labour" were taken in the 1950s by Gustav Otruba and Herta Firnberg, former collaborators in the Vienna Seminars on Economic and Cultural History; yet their research was published, not by an academic press, but by the Lower Austrian Chamber of Labour.' Ehmer and Müller, 'Sozialgeschichte in Österreich', 126–7. Dissertations began to appear only in the early 1960s.

79. Bryan D. Palmer, *E.P. Thompson: Objections and Oppositions*, London and New York, 1994, 90–1. Thomas William Heyck (certainly not a 'follower' of Thompson's) noted: 'Of all the English historians who have come to prominence since 1945, the one most likely to be written about a hundred years from now is E.P. Thompson'. Heyck, 'E.P. Thompson: Moralist and Marxist Historian', in Walter L. Arnstein (ed.), *Recent Historians of Great Britain: Essays on the Post-1945 Generation*, Ames: Iowa, 1990, 121–45, here 121.

80. Patricia van den Eeckhout, 'The Quest for Social History in Belgium (1948–1998)', *Archiv für Sozialgeschichte*, 40 (2000): 321–36, places Dhondt in his historical context.

81. Asa Briggs, 'Open Questions of Labour History', *Bulletin* [SSLH], no. 1 (Autumn, 1960): 2–3, here 2. During the discussion that followed this address, Eric Hobsbawm supported Briggs's thrust; he 'protested against the tendency to reduce labour history to the history of labour organisations.' (ibid., 3).

82. Eric J. Hobsbawm, *Labouring Men: Studies in the History of Labour*, London, 1964, vii.

83. Claude Willard, *Les guesdistes: Le Mouvement socialiste en France (1893–1905)*, Paris, 1965.

84. On the Marxist Historians' Group see Eric J. Hobsbawm, 'The Historians' Group of the Communist Party', in Maurice Cornforth (ed.), *Rebels and Their Causes: Essays in Honour of A.L. Morton*, London, 1978), 21–48; Bill Schwarz, 'The People in History: The Communist Party Historians' Group, 1946–56', in Richard Johnson et al. (eds), *Making Histories: Studies in History-Writing and Politics*, London, 1982, 44–95. For the broader context see Raphael Samuel, 'British Marxist Historians, 1880–1980: Part One', *New Left Review*, no. 120 (March-April 1980): 21–96, esp. 42–55; Harvey Kaye, *The British Marxist Historians: An Introductory Analysis*, Oxford, 1984.

85. On this subject see the essays by Winfried Schulze, Irmline Veit-Brause and Jörn Rüsen in Hartmut Lehmann and James Van Horn Melton (eds), *Paths of Continuity: Central European Historiography from the 1930s to the 1950s*, Cambridge [etc.], 1994, and Willi Oberkrome, *Volksgeschichte: Methodische Innovation und völkische Ideologisierung in der deutschen Geschichtswissenschaft, 1918–1945*, Göttingen, 1993, 105–22, 193–4, 196–7, 212, 215. On the *Arbeitskreis* founded by Conze in 1957 see Winfried Schulze, *Deutsche Geschichtswissenschaft nach 1945*, Munich, 1989, 254–65.

86. Georg G. Iggers, 'Comment on Schulze', in Lehman and Van Horn Melton, *Paths of Continuity*, 43–7, here 45.

87. Michelle Perrot, 'The Three Ages of Industrial Discipline in Nineteenth-Century France', in John M. Merriman (ed.), *Consciousness and Class Experience in Nineteenth-Century Europe*, New York and London, 1979, 149–68, here 150.

88. Werner Sombart, 'Studien zur Entwicklungsgeschichte des italienischen Proletariats', *Archiv für soziale Gesetzgebung und Statistik*, 6 (1893): 177–258, 8 (1895): 521–74, and 'Studien zur Entwicklungsgeschichte des nordamerikanischen Proletariats', *Archiv für Sozialwissenschaft und Sozialpolitik*, 21 (1905): 210–36, 308–46, 556–611. The book version of the second series of articles appeared a year later as *Warum gibt es in den Vereinigten Staaten keinen Sozialismus?*, Tübingen, 1906 and was translated into English as *Why is There No Socialism in the United States?*, trans. Patricia M. Hocking and C.T. Husbands, London,

1976. Sombart's Italian study is held up to the light in Ernesto Ragionieri, 'Werner Sombart e il movimento operaio italiano', *Rivista storica del socialismo*, 6 (1960): 329–56. On Sombart see now also Friedrich Lenger, *Werner Sombart 1863–1941: Eine Biographie*, Munich, 1994.

89. Theo Pinkus, 'Die Linzer Internationalen Tagungen der Historiker der Arbeiterbewegung, ITH', *Jahrbuch Arbeiterbewegung*, 1 (1973): 391–3. On the ITH's prehistory, and the central role that Austrian archivist Rudolf Neck (1921–99) played in it, see Herbert Steiner, 'Internationale Tagung der Historiker der Arbeiterbewegung', in Isabella Ackerl, Walter Hummelberger and Hans Mommsen (eds), *Politik und Gesellschaft im alten und neuen Österreich: Festschrift für Rudolf Neck zum 60. Geburtstag*, Munich, 1981, vol. II, 351–8.

90. The ITH proceedings were published regularly under the title *Die Internationale Tagung der Historiker der Arbeiterbewegung*. Well into the 1990s there were also scarcely any substantive criteria used in selecting papers for this publication.

91. Helmut Konrad, 'Die Krise überwunden. Die Linzer Konferenzen der ITH gehen ins vierte Jahrzehnt', *Internationale wissenschaftliche Korrespondenz zur Geschichte der deutschen Arbeiterbewegung*, 30 (1994): 575–8.

92. Among the early attempts were: Walter Kendall, *The Labour Movement in Europe*, London, 1975; Jürgen Kocka (ed.), *Europäische Arbeiterbewegungen im 19. Jahrhundert: Deutschland, Österreich, England und Frankreich im Vergleich*, Göttingen, 1983; Dick Geary, *Labour and Socialist Movements in Europe before 1914*, Oxford [etc.], 1989. For an attempt at a bibliographical inventory (including of studies transcending Europe) see Marcel van der Linden, 'A Bibliography of Comparative Labour History', in Jim Hagan and Andrew Wells (eds), *Australian Labour and Regional Change: Essays in Honour of R.A. Gollan*, Rushcutters Bay, NSW, 1998, 117–45.

93. See, for example, Jan Lucassen and Leo Lucassen, 'Migration, Migration History, History: Old Paradigms and New Perspectives', in Lucassen and Lucassen, *Migration, Migration History, History: Old Paradigms and Perspectives*, Berne [etc.], 1999, 9–38.

94. Works by Haupt published in English are: *Socialism and the Great War: The Collapse of the Second International*, Oxford, 1972, and, posthumously, *Aspects of International Socialism 1871–1914*, trans. Peter Fawcett, preface by Eric Hobsbawm, Cambridge [etc.] and Paris, 1986. A Haupt bibliography has been published in *Le Mouvement Social*, no. 111 (1980): 255–68.

95. Margaret Ramsay Somers, 'Workers of the World, Compare!', *Contemporary Sociology*, 18 (1989): 325–9, here 325.

96. Gisela Bock, 'Women's History and Gender History: Aspects of an International Debate', *Gender & History*, 1 (1989): 7–30, here 10.

97. See e.g. R.A. Leeson, *Travelling Brothers: The Six Centuries' Road from Craft Fellowship to Trade Unionism*, London, 1979; Catharina Lis, Jan Lucassen and Hugo Soly (eds), *Before the Unions: Wage Earners and Collective Action in Europe, 1350–1850*, Cambridge [etc.], 1994; Reinhold Reith, *Lohn und Leistung: Lohnformen im Gewerbe, 1450–1900*, Stuttgart, 1999.

98. See e.g. the exemplary analysis in Josef Mooser, 'Auflösung des proletarischen Milieus: Klassenbindung und Individualisierung in der Arbeiterschaft vom Kaiserreich bis in die Bundesrepublik Deutschland', *Soziale Welt*, 34 (1983): 270–306. André Gorz's book, *Adieux au prolétariat: Au-delà du socialisme*, Paris, 1980, which was published in many languages, was an influential attempt to construct an ideology based on the changes in the working class. For a critical response see Richard Hyman, 'André Gorz and his Disappearing Proletariat', *The Socialist Register 1983*, London, 1983, 272–95. Somewhat later the contrary but very interesting German labour historian Erhard Lucas(-Busemann) (1937–93)

published his book *Vom Scheitern der deutschen Arbeiterbewegung*, Basel and Frankfurt am Main, 1983, in which he sought out issues that the German labour movement had repressed and neglected and pointed out the fatal consequences that this had had.

99. Donald Sassoon, 'Introduction', in Donald Sassoon (ed.), *Looking Left: European Socialism after the Cold War*, London, 1997, 1–16, here 4.

100. The French journal *Les Révoltes Logiques*, published from 1975 to 1981, tried to show through detailed historical case studies that the labour movement and its intellectuals had produced numerous myths that deprived historical workers of their own voices. The central figure in this was Jacques Rancière (*1940), a student and later a harsh critic of Louis Althusser. His most important contribution to labour history is *La nuit des prolétaires*, Paris, 1981. The English version of this book – *The Nights of Labor: The Workers' Dream in Nineteenth-Century France*, trans. John Drury, Philadelphia, 1989 – includes an outstanding introductory essay on Rancière and his group by Donald Reid. Several articles from the milieu around *Les Révoltes Logiques* have been published in translation in Adrian Rifkin and Roger Thomas (eds), *Voices of the People: The Social Life of 'La Sociale' at the End of the Second Empire*, trans. John Moore, London, 1988.

Robert Berdahl et al. established an international historians' and social anthropologists' study group that tried to write 'decentred' history. Alf Lüdtke (*1943) was the study group member who did the most work in labour history. Several of his most important essays were collected as *Eigen-Sinn: Fabrikalltag, Arbeitererfahrungen und Politik vom Kaiserreich bis in den Faschismus*, Hamburg, 1993. See also Marcel van der Linden, 'Keeping Distance: Alf Lüdtke's 'Decentred' Labour History', *International Review of Social History*, 40 (1995): 285–94.

101. Autobiographies were presented in e.g.: Jacques Destray, *La vie d'une famille ouvrière: autobiographies*, Paris, 1971; J. Burnett, *Annals of Labour: Autobiographies of British Working-Class People, 1820–1920*, Bloomington IN, 1974; Wolfgang Emmerich (ed.), *Proletarische Lebensläufe: Autobiographische Dokumente zur Entstehung der zweiten Kultur in Deutschland*, 2 vols, Hamburg, 1974–5; Alfred Kelly (ed.), *The German Worker: Working-Class Autobiographies from the Age of Industrialization*, Berkeley CA [etc.], 1987; Mark Traugott (ed.), *The French Worker: Autobiographies from the Early Industrial Era*, Berkeley CA [etc.], 1993; Mauro Capecchi, *Autobiografia di un operaio comunista, 1913–1967*, Florence, 1997. Edvard Bull pointed out autobiographies' importance for labour history at a very early date in his 'Autobiographies of Industrial Workers: Sources of Norwegian Social History', *International Review of Social History*, 1 (1956): 203–9. One exemplary study based on autobiographies is Mary Jo Maines, *Taking the Hard Road: Life Course in French and German Workers' Autobiographies in the Era of Industrialization*, Chapel Hill and London, 1995.

102. Oral history began its rise in the early 1970s. Among the available overviews are Paul Thompson, *The Voice of the Past: Oral History*, Oxford [etc.], 1978; re-editions in 1988 and 2000; Lutz Niethammer, in collaboration with Werner Trapp, *Lebenserfahrung und kollektives Gedächtnis: Die Praxis der 'Oral History'*, Frankfurt am Main, 1980; reprint Frankfurt am Main, 1985. Good examples of oral labour history are Alfredo Jimenez Nunez, *Biografia de un campesino andalu: la historia oral como etnografia*, Sevilla, 1978; Stephen Humphries, *Hooligans or Rebels? An Oral History of Working-Class Childhood and Youth, 1889–1939*, Oxford, 1981; Lutz Niethammer (ed.), *Lebensgeschichte und Sozialkultur im Ruhrgebiet 1930 bis 1960*, 3 vols, Berlin, 1983–5; Luisa Passerini, *Torino operaio e fascista: una storia orale*, Rome [etc.], 1984 – English version: *Fascism in Popular Memory: The Cultural Experience of the Turin Working Class*, Cambridge [etc.], 1987; Elizabeth Roberts, *A Woman's Place: An Oral History of Working-Class Women, 1890–1940*,

Oxford [etc.], 1984; Selma Leydesdorff, *Wij hebben als mens geleefd: het Joodse proletariaat van Amsterdam, 1900–1940*, Amsterdam, 1985 – English version: *We Lived with Dignity: The Jewish Proletariat of Amsterdam, 1900–1940*, Detroit MI, 1994; Heidi Rosenbaum, *Proletarische Familien: Arbeiterfamilien und Arbeiterväter im frühen 20. Jahrhundert zwischen traditioneller, sozialdemokratischer und kleinbürgerlicher Orientierung*, Frankfurt am Main, 1992.

103. Sara Horrell en Deborah Oxley, 'Work and Prudence: Household Responses to Income Variation in Nineteenth-Century Britain', *European Review of Economic History*, 4 (2000): 27–57.

104. Jan Kok, 'Youth Labor Migration and its Family Setting, The Netherlands 1850–1940', *History of the Family*, 2 (1997): 507–26.

105. Dudley Baines and Paul Johnson, 'In Search of the "Traditional" Working Class: Social Mobility and Occupational Continuity in Interwar London', *Economic History Review*, 52 (1999): 692–713.

106. Dick Geary, 'Working-Class Identities in Europe, 1850s-1930s', *Australian Journal of Politics and History*, 45, 1 (1999): 20–34; Kathleen Paul, *Whitewashing Britain: Race and Citizenship in the Postwar Era*, Ithaca, NY, 1997. A good, but extra-European example of this is the work of the group headed by Erik Olssen, which did research in Caversham, a suburb of Dunedin, an industrial town in New Zealand: E. Olssen, T. Brooking, B. Heenan, H. James, B. McLennan and C. Griffen, 'Urban Society and the Opportunity Structure in New Zealand, 1902–22: the Caversham Project', in *Social History*, 24 (1999): 39–54; T. Brooking, D. Martin, D. Thomson and H. James, 'The Ties that Bind: Persistence in a New World Industrial Suburb, 1902–22', in *Social History*, 24 (1999): 55–73; E. Olssen and H. James, 'Social Mobility and Class Formation. The Worklife Social Mobility of Men in a New Zealand Suburb, 1902–1928', in *International Review of Social History*, 44 (1999): 419–49.

107. See e.g. the overviews in Beate Fieseler and Birgit Schulze (eds), *Frauengeschichte: gesucht, gefunden? Auskünfte zum Stand der historischen Frauenforschung*, Cologne [etc.], 1992; Michelle Perrot (ed.), *Writing Women's History*, Oxford [etc.], 1992; Karin Hausen and Heide Wunder (eds), *Frauengeschichte – Geschlechtergeschichte*, Frankfurt am Main and New York, 1992; Sylvia Dumont et al. (eds), *In haar verleden ingewijd: De ontwikkeling van vrouwengeschiedenis in Nederland*, Zutphen, 1991. See also the thematic special issue of *Differences: A Journal of Feminist Cultural Studies* on 'Women's Studies on the Edge', 9, 3 (Fall 1997).

108. Joan W. Scott, 'Gender: A Useful Category of Historical Analysis', *American Historical Review*, 91 (1985–6): 1,053–75; reprinted in idem, *Gender and the Politics of History*, New York, 1988, 28–50.

109. E.g. Judy Lown, *Women and Industrialization: Gender at Work in Nineteenth-Century England*, Cambridge, 1990; Perry R. Wilson, *The Clockwork Factory: Women and Work in Fascist Italy*, Oxford, 1993; Corrie van Eijl, *Het werkzame verschil: vrouwen in de slag om de arbeid, 1898–1940*, Hilversum, 1994; Gertjan de Groot and Marlou Schrover (eds), *Women Workers and Technological Change in Europe in the Nineteenth and Twentieth Centuries*, London, 1995; Francisca de Haan, *Sekse op kantoor. Over vrouwelijkheid, mannelijkheid en macht: Nederland, 1860–1940*, Hilversum, 1992 – English version: *Gender and the Politics of Office Work, The Netherlands 1860–1940*, Amsterdam, 1998.

110. See e.g. Frances Finnegan, *Poverty and Prostitution: A Study of Victorian Prostitutes in York*, Cambridge [etc.], 1979; Rosemarie Beier, *Frauenarbeit und Frauenalltag im Deutschen Kaiserreich: Heimarbeiterinnen in der Berliner Bekleidungsindustrie, 1880–1914*, Frankfurt am Main and New York, 1983; Karin Walser, *Dienstmädchen: Frauenarbeit und Weiblichkeitsbilder um 1900*, Frankfurt am Main, 1985; Barbara Henkes, *Heimat in Holland: Duitse dienstmeisjes, 1920–1950*, Amsterdam, 1995.

111. E.g. Gro Hagemann, 'Historien om den mannlige arbeiderklassen: Usynlig-gjøring og kjønnsblindhet i arbeiderbevegelsens historie', *Arbeiderhistorie* (1988): 124–51; Mary Lynn Stewart, *Women, Work and the French State: Labour Protection and Social Patriarchy, 1879–1919*, Kingston [etc.], 1989; Karen Hagemann, *Frauenalltag und Männerpolitik: Alltagsleben und gesellschaftliches Handeln von Arbeiterfrauen in der Weimarer Republik*, Bonn, 1990; Jutta Schwarzkopf, 'Gendering Exploitation: The Use of Gender in the Campaign Against Driving in Lancashire Weaving Sheds, 1886–1903', *Women's History Review*, 7 (1998): 449–74; Jane Long, 'The Colour of Disorder: Women's Employment and "Protective" Intervention in the Lead Industry in Victorian England', *Women's History Review*, 7 (1998): 521–46. See also the special issue of the *Årbog for arbejder-bevægelsens historie*, 23 (1993) on 'Køn og klasse'.

112. See e.g. the special issue of *Le Mouvement Social* on 'Travaux de femmes', 105 (1978); Stefan Bajohr, *Die Hälfte der Fabrik: Geschichte der Frauenarbeit in Deutschland, 1914–1945*, Marburg, 1979; Patricia Hilden, *Women, Work and Politics: Belgium, 1830–1914*, Oxford, 1993. Deborah Simonton, *A History of European Women's Work: 1700 to the Present*, London [etc.], 1998, tries to give an overview of some research results.

113. See e.g. Sonya O. Rose, 'Gender Antagonism and Class Conflict: Exclusionary Strategies of Male Trade Unionists in Nineteenth-Century Britain', *Social History*, 13 (1988): 191–208; Keith McClelland, 'Some Thoughts on Masculinity and the "Representative Artisan" in Britain, 1850–1880', *Gender and History*, 1 (1989): 164–177; Dionigi Albera et al., 'I percorsi dell'identità maschile nell'emigrazione', *Rivista di storia contemporanea*, 20 (1991): 69–87; Merry E. Wiesner, 'Wandervogels and Women: Journeymen's Concepts of Masculinity in Early Modern Germany', *Journal of Social History*, 24 (1991): 767–82; Eva Blomberg, *Män i mörker: Arbetsgivare, reformister och syndikalister, Politik och identitet i svensk gruvindustri 1910–1940*, Stockholm, 1995.

114. For an overview see David Roediger, 'What if Labor Were Not White and Male? Recentering Working-Class History and Reconstructing Debate on the Unions and Race', *International Labor and Working-Class History*, 51 (Spring 1997): 72–95.

115. Eric Arnesen, *Waterfront Workers of New Orleans: Race, Class and Politics, 1863–1923*, New York [etc.], 1991.

116. Howard Kimmeldorf and Robert Penney, '"Excluded" By Choice: Dynamics of Interracial Unionism on the Philadelphia Waterfront, 1910–1930', *International Labor and Working-Class History*, 51 (Spring 1997): 50–71.

117. David R. Roediger, *The Wages of Whiteness: Race and the Making of the American Working Class*, London and New York, 1991; Noel Ignatiev, *How the Irish became White*, New York and London, 1995.

118. Jonathan Hyslop, 'The Imperial Working Class Makes Itself "White": White Labourism in Britain, Australia, and South Africa Before the First World War', *Journal of Historical Sociology*, 12 (1999): 398–421.

119. Nancy L. Green, 'Women and Immigrants in the Sweatshop: Categories of Labor Segmentation Revisited', *Comparative Studies in Society and History*, 38 (1996): 411–33.

120. Gérard Noiriel, *Longwy: Immigrés et prolétaires, 1880–1980*, Paris, 1984; Christoph Kleßman, *Polnische Bergarbeiter im Ruhrgebiet 1870–1945: Soziale Integration und nationale Subkultur einer Minderheit in der deutschen Industriegesellschaft*, Göttingen, 1978; Frank Suurenbroek, 'Friezen in Amsterdam: Groepsvorming onder binnenlandse migranten aan het einde van de negentiende eeuw', *Tijdschrift voor Sociale Geschiedenis*, 27 (2000): 325–42; John J. Kulczycki, *The Foreign Worker and the German Labor Movement: Xenophobia and Solidarity in*

the *Coal Fields of the Ruhr, 1871–1914,* Oxford and Providence, 1994; idem, *The Polish Coal Miners' Union and the German Labor Movement in the Ruhr, 1920–1934: National and Social Solidarity,* Oxford and New York, 1997. For a more general account see Lucassen and Lucassen (eds), *Migration, Migration History, History.*

121. Anne Eriksen, 'Kirken, arbeiderne og religionen', *Arbeiderhistorie,* (1994): 4–23; Hugh McLeod, *Religion and the People of Western Europe, 1789–1989,* Oxford and New York, 1997. A fine example of changes in established religion brought about by proletarianisation is given in Timothy Kelly and Joseph Kelly, 'Our Lady of Perpetual Help. Gender Roles and the Decline of Devotional Catholicism', *Journal of Social History,* 32 (1998): 5–26.

122. Carl Strikwerda, *A House Divided: Catholics, Socialists, and Flemish Nationalists in Nineteenth-Century Belgium,* Oxford [etc.], 1997.

123. Hans Jaeger, 'Generationen in der Geschichte: Überlegungen zu einer umstrittenen Konzeption', *Geschichte und Gesellschaft,* 3 (1977): 429–52; Aad Blok et al. (eds), *Generations in Labour History,* Amsterdam, 1989; Paul Ward, *Red Flag and Union Jack: Englishness, Patriotism and the British Left, 1881–1924,* Woodbridge [etc.], 1998; Marcel van der Linden, 'The National Integration of the European Working Classes, 1871–1914', *International Review of Social History,* 33 (1988): 285–311.

124. Victoria de Grazia, with Ellen Furlough (eds), *The Sex of Things: Gender and Consumption in Historical Perspective,* Berkeley CA [etc.], 1996; Gary Cross, 'Consumer History and the Dilemmas of Working-Class History', *Labour History Review,* 62 (1997): 261–74. See also the special issue on 'Class and Consumption' of *International Labor and Working-Class History,* 55 (1999): 71–91, and Joanna Bourke, *Working-Class Cultures in Britain 1890–1960: Gender, Class and Ethnicity,* London and New York, 1994, and the more general work, Paul Nolte, 'Der Markt und seine Kultur – ein neues Paradigma der amerikanischen Geschichte?', *Historische Zeitschrift,* 264 (1997): 329–60.

125. Johan Söderberg, 'Consumption, Gender and Preferences in Sweden, 1920–1965', *Scandinavian Economic History Review,* 46 (1998): 71–84; Mark A. Swiencicki, 'Consuming Brotherhood: Men's Culture, Style and Recreation as Consumer Culture', *Journal of Social History,* 31 (1997–8): 773–808.

126. Charles Tilly (*1929) has become very influential. This US sociologist has himself published works, including (with Edward Shorter) *Strikes in France, 1830–1968,* Cambridge [etc.], 1974. A number of his students have made major contributions, particularly on French nineteenth-century labour history. See e.g.: Ronald Aminzade, *Class, Politics, and Early Industrial Capitalism: A Study of Mid-Nineteenth-Century Toulouse,* Albany, NY, 1981; idem, *Ballots and Barricades: Class Formation and Republican Politics in France, 1830–1871,* Princeton NJ, 1993); Michael P. Hanagan, *The Logic of Solidarity: Artisans and Industrial Workers in Three French Towns, 1871–1914,* Urbana, IL, 1980; idem, *Nascent Proletarians: Class Formation in Post-Revolutionary France,* Oxford [etc.], 1989; Mark Traugott, *Armies of the Poor: Determinants of Working-Class Participation in the Parisian Insurrection of June 1848,* Princeton NJ, 1985. In the course of the 1990s West European labour historians also published some important studies that were strongly influenced by the social sciences, e.g.: Flemming Mikkelsen, *Arbejdskonflikter i Skandinavien, 1848–1980,* Odense, 1992; Gita Deneckere, *Sire, het volk mort: sociaal protest in België, 1831–1918,* Antwerp [etc.], 1997; Don Kalb, *Expanding Class: Power and Everyday Politics in Industrial Communities: The Netherlands, 1850–1950,* Durham, NC, 1997.

127. Gareth Stedman Jones made a big splash with his 'turn', defending his shift to linguistic non-referentialism as a result of 'the gulf between the predictions of the

Marxist explanatory model and the actual assumptions which appear to have guided the activities of ... workers'. Gareth Stedman Jones, *Languages of Class: Studies in English Working Class History, 1832–1982,* Cambridge, 1983, 21. On the context see also Bryan D. Palmer, 'The Eclipse of Materialism: Marxism and the Writing of Social History in the 1980s', *The Socialist Register 1990,* London, 1990, 111–46.

128. Bryan D. Palmer, *Descent into Discourse: The Reification of Language and the Writing of Social History,* Philadelphia PA, 1990, 128.

129. Patrick Joyce, 'The End of Social History?', *Social History,* 20 (1995): 73–91; Geoff Eley and Keith Nield, 'Starting Over: The Present, the Post-Modern and the Moment of Social History', *Social History,* 20 (1995): 355–64; Patrick Joyce, 'The End of Social History? A Brief Reply to Eley and Nield', *Social History,* 21 (1996): 96–8.

130. Dror Wahrman, 'The New Political History: A Review Essay', *Social History,* 21 (1996): 343–54, here 345; Detlev Mares, 'Abschied vom Klassenbegriff?', *Neue Politische Literatur,* 42 (1997): 378–94.

131. F.R. Ankersmit, *History and Tropology: The Rise and Fall of Metaphor,* Berkeley CA [etc.], 1994, 30–1.

132. The Sinologist Steven Sangren's approach may be useful: 'I believe that the traditional Marxian conception of power as control over the means of production is not as anachronistic a formulation as recent academic elaborations upon power would imply, although the scope of what constitutes production should be expanded from its classically materialist conceptualisation to include production of forms of social organization *and* consciousness (including especially representations of the origins and nature of productive power itself). Power as control implies a subject, but subjects may be defined as individuals, as collective institutions (for example, communities, "the state"), or more abstractly, as society understood as an aggregate of such subjectivities and institutions (including, but not limited to, language).' P. Steven Sangren, '"Power" against Ideology: A Critique of Foucaultian Usage', *Cultural Anthropology,* 10 (1995): 3–40, here 26.

133. Ann Curthoys, 'The Three Body Problem: Feminism and Chaos Theory', *Hecate* [Brisbane], 17, 1 (1991): 14–21, here 15.

134. Marcel van der Linden and Jan Lucassen, 'Prolegomena for a Global Labor History', on http://www.iisg.nl/publications/prolegom.pdf; Marcel van der Linden, 'Transnationalizing American Labor History', *Journal of American History,* 86 (1999): 1,078–92; idem, 'Vorläufiges zur transkontinentalen Arbeitergeschichte', *Geschichte und Gesellschaft,* 28 (2002), forthcoming.

135. LabNet List is the discussion list of LabNet. To subscribe, send a mail containing the message SUBSCRIBE LABNET to listserv@iisg.nl. LabNet is moderated by labmod@iisg.nl. For further information, see: http://www.iisg.nl/labnet/index.html.

ISSUES

CHAPTER 2

NEW TRENDS IN LABOUR MOVEMENT HISTORIOGRAPHY

A GERMAN PERSPECTIVE

Jürgen Kocka[1]

Three voices

In late 1993 the *International Review of Social History* published a supplement entitled 'The End of Labour History?' In the introduction Marcel van der Linden observed that labour history was on the defensive. He attributed this to the worldwide collapse of 'socialism' on the one hand and to the diminishing status of work in today's society on the other. The editor expressed the hope that the issue's collection of essays would show ways in which labour history could overcome its current crisis.

In the above issue Carville Earle, of the Department of Geography and Anthropology at Louisiana State University, writes about the splintered geography of labour markets in industrialising America; this article is included to highlight the spatial dimension, traditionally neglected by labour history. Alf Lüdtke discusses 'Polymorphous Synchrony: German Industrial Workers and the Politics of Everyday Life'; this is included to signal that subjective experiences should be given greater weight. Hartmut Zwahr writes on class formation and the labour movement as the subject of a dialectical historiography, in which, as usual, he relates labour and bourgeois history to each other. Gottfried Korff is represented with a contribution entitled 'History of

Symbols as Social History', whose empirical core deals with the history of red flags since the French Revolution, the May-Day festivals since 1890 and the iconography of the clenched fist. This is followed by a contribution by David Roediger on 'Race and the Working-Class Past in the United States: Multiple Identities and the Future of Labour History'. Sonya O. Rose writes about 'Gender and Labour History: The Nineteenth-Century Legacy'. And, lastly, Van der Linden, the editor, seeks to connect household history with labour history ('Working-Class Consumer Power').

The introduction to the issue identifies several other weaknesses of contemporary labour history, two in particular: as a matter for specialists, it isolates itself too much from general history; and it neglects the periphery, the Third World, the world beyond the West.

In the same year (1993) there appeared a collection entitled *Rethinking Labor History: Essays on Discourse and Class Analysis*. This was edited by Lenard R. Berlanstein, a younger historian from the University of Virginia, whose previous work had been on French labour history in particular. His introduction reads like the manifesto for a poststructuralist labour history. The 'new labour history' of the late 1960s, 1970s and early 1980s broke away from the earlier overemphasis on factory workers, he contends, and, for the nineteenth century, put the artisan centre stage. More attention was paid to preindustrial ways of life and mentalities, and their conflict-ridden clash with capitalist modernisation moved historians critical of modernisation to write sympathetic portrayals of proletarianisation. The model of class formation, and hence the notions of the means and relations of production, played a significant role at that time. Even so, workers were not observed exclusively in their workplaces but increasingly attention was paid to their family lives, leisure time and local solidarity and communications structures. Conflicts were at the core of this 'new' labour history, according to Berlanstein. Sociological models played a dominant role, not only those of 'class formation' and 'social protest' but also concepts such as 'rituals' or 'rites of passage'. Leading exponents were E.P. Thompson, Eric Hobsbawm and Charles Tilly, but also Natalie Davis and the early Joan Scott, whose *The Glassworkers of Carmaux* was published in 1974 and highly praised at the time.

But in the 1980s and 1990s this paradigm found itself on the defensive. The 'new labour history' of the 1960s and 1970s had become a respected but slightly stale 'old labour history'. As the crisis of socialism deepened, labour history was also called into question, claims Berlanstein. The class-formation model rapidly lost credibility, not only in the history of the labour movement but also, for instance, in the history of the French Revolution. The view of the primacy of the economic base was replaced by the belief in the autonomy of culture. Moreover, the orientation on human experiences (at the workplace or in terms of social exclusion, for instance), so central to the Thompson tradition and to everyday history, was also gradually called into question, regarded as conventional and replaced by an emphasis on discourse or language – as a system of signs and meanings, constantly in turmoil, but not necessarily related to external reference points such as labour, experience or social inequality. This new linguistic/discursive leaning in research was heavily indebted to Foucault and Derrida. Key exponents were Jacques Rancières (the Gareth Stedman Jones of the 1980s), William H. Sewell, Donald Reid, William Reddy, the later Joan Scott and (to a limited extent) Patrick Joyce. Berlanstein would surely accept the point that these poststructuralist labour historians are few in number and have their implacable critics, including the grand old man Lawrence Stone.

Finally, let me mention an issue of *International Labor and Working-Class History* published in late 1994 under the theme 'What Next for Labor and Working-Class History?'. Its controversial state-of-research debate was launched with a wide-ranging article by Ira Katznelson, the historically orientated sociologist and editor of the widely read collection *Working-Class Formation: Nineteenth-Century Patterns in Western Europe and the United States* (1986). Labour history, he argues, is not really in a crisis. Empirically it has never been better, more broadly based and more differentiated than today. But it has lost its elan, its sense of purpose, its intellectual meaning. Committed young students are moving into other areas of research these days, such as gender history. Labour history is in danger of becoming a lament for disappointed hopes and expectations. 'The cause is gone', he writes. Two factors account for this: first, the emergence of new social movements – focusing on the environment, women's rights, civil rights etc. – which have called into question the prominence of class affiliation and class analysis and prompted the concentration on language; and second, the decline of democratic socialism and then the collapse of dictatorial communism and the consequent questioning of the traditionally influential idea of the 'forward march of labour', in other words the demise of the idea of progress, which had implicitly inspired and guided a considerable part of working-class and labour history.

Katznelson does not wish to draw the poststructuralist conclusion, however, and to abandon the study of contexts in favour of language, discourse and pure meaning. Rather, he urges us to take seriously the institutions, the realm of politics and political ideas and to study the labour movement against the background of government institutions, party-political systems, the welfare state and political theories. Henry Pelling, a rather old-fashioned historian with a predilection for the institutional, is rediscovered.

Incidentally, while Katznelson calls for the rediscovery of politics and its institutions, David Brody, another grand old man of American labour history, calls for a return to industrial relations and the labour process to overcome the current crisis of labour history as well as the labour movement, which in his eyes is caused by the culturalism of many historians and by neoliberal union-bashing policies in contemporary America.

Many other voices could be quoted, but let these three examples suffice. They are not untypical of the recent stock-taking exercises and programmatic articles about working-class and labour history, at least in Western Europe and North America. Common threads are the realisation of a paradigm change, a sense of crisis, and a highly fragmented search for solutions, which range from poststructuralist discourse analysis to a return to conventional institutional history but share a questioning of traditional class-formation analyses. Judging at least from the basic and programmatic declarations of intent that have appeared recently, there is a sense of exhaustion, dissatisfaction with traditions and steady decline, as well as a search for new alternatives.

Practical trends

A rough survey of what is actually produced and of the long-term trends reveals a picture of considerable continuity. It has always been the case that the *Historische Zeitschrift* carried only a few articles on the working class and the labour movement in the broadest sense, while *Geschichte und Gesellschaft* carried many. In every five-year period over the last twenty-five years the former published three to six articles concerned with this field, the latter twenty to thirty. There is no clear downward trend in either publication over this period. The *American Historical Review* and the British *Past and Present* did not publish any fewer articles on the working class and the labour movement in the period 1990–4 compared to 1970–4. Only in the French *Annales* has labour history been further pushed aside in the last twenty years, from what was already a marginal position. The overall impression is one of long-term stability, although there are wide fluctuations in the specifics.

An analysis of the contents of two international journals devoted primarily to labour history, the *International Review of Social History* (published in Amsterdam) and *International Labor and Working-Class History* (published in New York) shows no dramatic changes over the last decade either.

In both journals articles about the West predominate, with the accent on Western Europe in the Amsterdam journal and on North America in the New York journal. With the exception of some tentative but promising efforts in the most recent period (as in the *International Review* in 1995), the main impression is that non-European themes are rarely discussed, and articles on Eastern European themes are even declining in number. Comparative articles remain wholly peripheral, with no more than two every five years.

Two trend shifts are evident. Historical articles on everyday and cultural history are clearly on the increase from the mid-1980s to the mid-1990s, although the primarily political and primarily social articles still account for the lion's share. In the American journal the number of gender-orientated articles has risen somewhat, but remains low. Historical articles with linguistic, discursive or intellectual emphases remain peripheral in both journals, almost negligible in number and with no rising frequency over the last decade.

At least in this respect the programmatic discussion is running well ahead of actual production, and it is by no means clear whether the latter will ever follow the former. It may be, of course, that much new research is still in progress and has not yet reached the point of publication in reputable journals. And since our categorisations and allocations are based solely on the titles of articles, they are very rough and ready. But in any case it is beyond question that the turbulent situation evident in the programmatic articles becomes considerably becalmed when actual output is taken into account. The movements that are diagnosed and debated at the theoretical level appear in weakened form in the empirical work, although they are not wholly absent. On balance the picture is very complex and difficult to reduce to a common denominator.

New emphases

That is why I would like to raise several problems and developments which I consider particularly important, pressing or promising. What is both new and worth pursuing? Where should ideas and research be concentrated? Which blind alleys are best avoided? What questions for working-class and labour history arise from contemporary practical problems, especially with regard to the German experience? The following comments are, of course, highly selective.

Of the challenges faced by traditional working-class and labour history indicated above, that posed by gender history is the most momentous. It is true that gender history sometimes makes rather absurd monopoly-like claims for itself, but I am not concerned with these here. Nor is a gender-historical revolutionisation of social history either imminent or likely in the future. But the (mostly female) representatives of a sophisticated gender history confront the class-based historical approach – which I still defend – with productive challenges, prompting significant modifications to traditional ideas.

For one thing, the gender-historical perspective forces us to address those dimensions of the class-formation process that are not related to gainful employment and jobs. How does one assess to class situation of people who are not permanently engaged in gainful employment (including very many women)? How does one link the history of wage labour and households? Furthermore, a focus on the contributions made by women to the class-formation process opens up long-neglected dimensions, which in recent years have been studied to some extent in relation to the middle class but much less so in relation to the working class. I mean here the role of kinship relations in the development of class-specific networks, the role of friendships and neighbourly relations, the nursing and passing on of 'cultural capital' in the class-formation process. And finally, the gender-historical perspective exposes the labour movement as a men's movement, which manifests itself not only in its programmes and political work, but also in its style and culture. This input helps to make the traditional view of the labour movement both more critical and more realistic. Overall, the problems arising from linking class and gender history have not yet been solved. But the work on these problems promises to produce interesting results.

Less pronounced thus far has been the challenge from the linguistic turn in historical study, specifically in labour history. No one will mourn the fact that its radical variants have hitherto barely made an impression in Germany. After all, the radical representatives of this approach demand that historical reconstruction is restricted to the study of linguistic phenomena. They dismiss the relationship between language and nonlinguistic dimensions of historical reality as either illegitimate or pointless, narrow past reality down to texts, regard only the reconstruction of discourses as possible and worthwhile, and recommend the study of concepts and their meanings only in relation to other concepts and meanings and not in relation to external references. From this standpoint classes appear merely in their linguistic form, as products of discourses, in the medium of language, but not as composites of experiences, interests and structures. This boils down to idealistic reductions, which fail to grasp the past reality and until now have remained the exception even in American historical studies.

The language, rhetoric and discourses of the earlier labour movements are, of course, rewarding objects of study. Anyone who might have forgotten this will be reminded by the representatives of the linguistic turn. It is doubtless wrong to conceive of people's language and concepts merely as derivative variables, as reflexes or dependent manifestations of experiences, interests and underlying structures. Rather, one should acknowledge and take seriously that linguistic formulations, concepts and discourses actively form and inform experiences, that linguistic communications sustain socialisation and justify power structures. It is good that linguistically inspired historians remind us of this. But this was also known from German *Begriffsgeschichte*, contrary to older reductions, which denied the autonomy of language and misjudged it as only a reflex, an epiphenomenon, a mere expression of nonlinguistic reality.

Begriffsgeschichte (conceptual history) has played a fruitful role in labour history for many years. Asa Briggs in Britain and Werner Conze and Reinhart Koselleck in Germany have ensured as much, and many have followed in their footsteps. But it may be that methodological impulses from modern linguistics will lead to further refinements. In my view at least, the language of the labour movement is an as yet insufficiently ploughed field of research. Reconstructing and comparing key concepts, symbols, discourses and rhetorical instruments in the texts may be an important means of eliciting differences, similarities and changes in the experiences and expectations of the labour movement's leaders and spokespeople; of gaining a better understanding of how workers interpreted their reality; of analysing what they had in common as workers, what held them together as a labour movement, what distinguished them from other sections of society, and whom they opposed. This will benefit the study of the intellectual roots of the class-formation process. Even so, it is imperative that researchers constantly examine the dialectical relationship between the linguistic and nonlinguistic dimensions of historical reality and set texts in the context of their origins and effects, which are not sufficiently reflected in the texts themselves.

In 1980 Geoff Eley and Keith Neild published an article entitled 'Why Does Social History Ignore Politics?' in the British journal *Social History*. This first raised a call (which has gradually grown louder and has now become irrepressible) to reincorporate politics, institutions and law again into social history, and hence also into working-class and labour history. What should we make of this?

For one thing, it should be noted that German social historians never marginalised the state and politics as much as their American or British counterparts. So the dramatic appeal to put politics back into history forces an open door as far as German social history, as well as German working-class and labour history, is concerned.

On the other hand, it must be conceded that in Germany too, variants of social history have developed which neglect politics in the sense of institutionalised political activity. This is true of the micro-studies of everyday history, which concentrate so much on the reconstruction of experiences, observations and assimilations on the small scale that they easily lose sight of the overarching structures, including law, state and politics. But I am thinking more of several systematic sociohistorical or class-historical approaches which, while typically keeping a certain distance from crude economism and teleological determinism, still stress the socio-economically defined class situation and the related experiences of work, dependency, conflict and affiliation, then proletarian living conditions (such as family or social life), and finally culture, communications and socialisation, and treat the formation of trade unions, mutual-benefit associations and parties – the politics of the movement – as the last stage, more as a consequence of economics, culture and socialisation and less as an autonomous dimension or a conditioning factor.

In principle I still believe this is a legitimate approach. It seems particularly important in my view to study the political ambitions, activities and institutions *in relation to* economic, social and cultural moments, that is, not in isolation and absolutely, as some people now seem to argue again. But perhaps we should be prepared to rethink the relationship, to be more open to the possibility that the political has greater autonomy and impact. In the case of early working-class and labour history, this would mean interpreting the class-formation process more as one which activists always consciously intended, promoted and influenced by political means. This turns the attention on the goals and the agitation, again on language and rhetoric, on everyday work in the clubs, organisations and local party branches, on class formation as a *project* pursued by active minorities, a project which, insofar as it succeeded, could only succeed because the constellation of economic, social, political and cultural factors was 'right', but still a project, not just a process.

After all, there is much to be said for this approach. In terms of their socio-economic situations, work and life experiences, specific interests and views, wage workers within the labour movement were at all times very different, diverse and heterogeneous. What brought many of them – but always a minority – together in the labour movement was, in addition to the common interests and experiences, the purposive political work of leaders such as Bebel, Lassalle, Tölcke, Liebknecht and thousands of other less well known activists. Class formation was invariably also conscious coalition building on the basis of common goals beyond social and mental fragmentations, through the medium of political activity. The labour movement never grew like a flower out of the fertile soil of economic, social and cultural environmental factors. It was always also a construct.

Such an approach can of course easily lead to new biases, to voluntaristic or anti-structuralist exaggerations. One should guard against that. But socio-economic explanatory paradigms have become sufficiently relativised to call for the rethinking of the relationship between structure and action, and hence the role of politics, also in relation to the history of the labour movement. At least the international debate is pushing in this direction.

Civil society as a vision

The political and intellectual background against which labour history is written has shifted decisively in the last fifteen years or so. Gone is the mixture of radical social critique and modernisation optimism typical of the 1960s and 1970s. Most people these days expect less of the forces of modernisation, emancipation and state intervention than they did then. Postmodern scepticism has in many ways taken the place of modern criticism. Traditional socialist and social democratic reform strategies are failing, it seems, in solving contemporary crises. One need only think of the global ecological crisis, the resurgence of nationalism and return of war in Europe, the indebtedness of governments and the problems of the welfare state in the face of globalisation. The collapse of dictatorial communism in 1989/90 was an act of liberation. But it reinforced the already existing doubts about the socialist faith. The intellectual left has major problems. What are the implications of this for labour history?

As early as the mid-1980s Ralf Dahrendorf spoke of the end of the 'social democratic century'. The debate about the supposed demise of the labour movement flares up time and again. The current problems of the German Social Democratic Party (SPD) appear to confirm this pessimistic view. What are the consequences for labour history?

Western societies are supposedly bereft of vision and utopian ambitions, especially since 1989. This is often argued on the left. It is certainly true that anti-capitalist reform strategies have lost credibility, not because capitalism has proved so perfect and wonderful, but because the concretely applied alternative was discredited as far worse. At the same time, however, the programme of civil society rooted in the late eighteenth-century Enlightenment has until now been neither refuted nor fulfilled. Over the last two centuries it has been constantly developed, amended and revised, not least by social democrats and socialists. Only at a late stage did it address the problem of sexual inequality. Now an ecological overhaul is required. But the ever-changing programme of civil society continues to aim at a sensible coexistence of free citizens, with equal life and participation chances, under constitutional and legal guarantees, without state nannying or harassment, without violence and in emancipation.

Abolishing the market does not help to realise the programme of civil society. Nor can it be reconciled with excessive social and economic differences, however. In other words, it needs the social democratic completion and modification. For without the social democratic extension it would remain a privilege of elites and thus self-contradictory. Its worldwide application has only just begun and at the moment seems by no means assured. The limits of its universalisation are strictly circumscribed on ecological grounds alone; and it will not break out of these unless it undergoes fundamental change. The revolutions of 1989/90 and the collapse of dictatorial communism did not refute this programme. On the contrary. But its development has come to a halt, and is still far from full realisation. The future is, at best, undecided. What does all this have to do with labour history?

The history of the relationship between social democracy and communism as two partly related, partly competing and partly deeply hostile branches of the labour movement seems to me a scientific problem that should be raised again in the new post-1989 constellation. Researchers should try to elucidate even more clearly, on the basis of the history of experiences, mentalities and politics, the differentiation of the socialist labour movement into a democratic and a dictatorial branch. We should also pose the question of why the tradition of the socialist labour movement did not contain sufficient internal safeguards against its anti-liberal and anti-democratic perversion. And on what grounds can one really put social democracy and communism under the same conceptual roof, as parts of a comprehensive 'left', now that the critique of capitalism, which linked them, has lost in historical importance, while the problem of liberal democracy, which separates them, has gained in historical importance?

In my view, the history of the labour movement under the conditions of communist dictatorship is a major research problem that still awaits resolution. And this can only be properly embarked upon conceptually and empirically now that the dictatorships have collapsed. Can and should one classify the communist parties that held power until 1989 as heirs of the labour movement, as they themselves claimed? Or should they be seen as its misbegotten offspring? Did the dictatorship of the Socialist Unity Party (SED) in East Germany not explode, betray and destroy the history of the German labour movement? That is, after all, how it seems at the moment, now that it is apparent how little of a real labour movement survived on the territory of the former 'worker and peasant state'.

After the demise of the communist dictatorships in the East and the fading fascination of democratic socialism in the West, some labour historians have lost the orientation to which they were hitherto explicitly or implicitly wed. Insofar as this was fuelled by the political commitment to the cause of the proletariat or socialism, by the hope of anti-capitalist reforms or even revolutions, the interest in labour-movement themes is doubtless waning. This is noticeable from the falling number of students entering the discipline. This is regrettable. But perhaps this trend offers new opportunities for labour history as an academic discipline, as well. It is freeing itself from its political embrace. The history of the German labour movement is no longer dominated by the struggle between Marxist-Leninist and social-democratic-'bourgeois' interpretations. This has brought about a liberation from outdated notions and enables us to raise new scientific questions. In the past the question was often asked why the labour movement was not more radical during specific phases of its history (such as before 1914, during the First World War or in the early Weimar Republic). Today, however, the question is often asked how the labour movement could become as radical, progressive and adaptable during specific phases of its history as it actually did.

And it is possible to conceive the history of the German labour movement against the background of an unfinished history of civil society.[2] The ambivalent relationship between workers and 'civil' (*bürgerlich*) thus comes to the fore. The partially bourgeois (in the sense of the German '*Bürger*') and the inherent anti-bourgeois elements of the labour movement should be examined, a mixture whose balance shifted over time. In its early phase, from the 1860s until around 1890, the anti-bourgeois features of the German labour movement were prominent not least because the bourgeoisie was weak and the bourgeoisification of society was progressing very slowly. The bourgeoisification of society, culture and politics in the twenty-five years preceding the First World War went hand in hand with a certain dilution of the labour movement's anti-bourgeois features. The deep crisis of the bourgeoisie, bourgeois culture and bourgeois society during and after the First World War in turn went hand in hand with the radicalisation of the anti-bourgeois features of considerable sections of the labour movement, in its radical socialist and then in its communist guise. The renewed consolidation of the bourgeoisie, bourgeois society and bourgeois culture since the 1950s in the western part of Germany, on the other hand, paved the way for a gradual rapprochement between the basic principles of the labour movement and the bourgeoisie.

Let me add a few words on international comparisons. The late Leipzig historian Manfred Kossok wrote in 1990: 'It is surely no coincidence that the countries of deformed socialism did not have a successful "1789"; their people were transformed into "comrades" without having previously been "citizens"'. And indeed, the strength of the labour movement and the extent to which social democratic and communist-dictatorial strands became enmeshed in the twentieth century depended among other factors on the extent of bourgeois penetration of the society in question, that is, on the extent and nature of bourgeois culture and hegemony in the various countries. And the reverse impact of the labour movement on the bourgeoisie should not be neglected in this context either.

At least for the period leading up to the First World War it seems appropriate, on the one hand, to see the German labour movement as part of a society which was more bourgeois (in the sense of *'bürgerlich'*) than the societies of Eastern Europe, where the weakness and under-development of bourgeois lifestyles, rights and constitutions hampered the development of the labour movement while at the same time rad-icalising it and making it more anti-bourgeois; on the other hand, the German labour movement was part of a society which was less bour-geois than the societies of Western Europe, as evidenced by the author-itarian coloration of political life, the strength of pre-bourgeois elites and traditions well into the bourgeois period, the comparatively weak influence and cohesion of the bourgeoisie, and particularly harsh exclu-sion of and discrimination against some groups. These explain the spe-cial characteristics of the German labour movement, such as its early separation from the bourgeois reform movement, its early indepen-dence and size, as well as its opportunity to develop post-bourgeois goals, practices and forms of organisation. The German labour move-ment of the nineteenth and early twentieth century reveals itself as part of a 'medium-strength' bourgeois society, as it were.

On balance, then, the contribution of the social democratic – and to some extent also Christian – labour movement to the gradual real-isation of civil society in Germany is not inconsiderable. We should remember in this context social democracy's commitment to the democratic organisation culture, parliamentary politics, the constitu-tional state, the codification of social relationships, universal education and social justice. Other contributions also deserve mention: the focus on enlightenment, the struggle against anti-Semitism and xenophobia, before 1933 the struggle against fascism in defence of the republic (for which the social democratic labour movement battled, albeit ulti-mately in vain, with greater commitment than most other social forces and political camps). In a country where the strength of liberalism, at least at the national level, declined early and the bourgeoisie was often only half-heartedly committed to the project of civil society, it fell to sections of the labour movement to take on their roles.

The actual realisation, the worldwide dispersal and the requisite internal transformation of the civil-society model will present major tasks for the future. To those looking for left-wing utopias: they can be found in this environment.

Notes

1. This article is based on a paper I presented at the Conference of the Historical Commission of the SPD executive committee, held in Bonn, 15–16 December 1995. I would like to thank Stefan Bresky, Annette Schuhmann and Anne Sudrow for perusing the text and preparing material for the second section. Previously published in *International Review of Social History*, 42 (1997): 67–78.
2. Translator's note: The author uses the concepts *'bürgerlich'* and *'bürgerliche Gesellschaft'*. While 'civil' and 'civil society' are undoubtedly the best translations, the German words carry the connotations of 'bourgeois' or 'middle-class' as well.

Chapter 3

Class and Labour History

Mike Savage

Introduction

It is no easy matter to provide an overview on the relationship between class and labour history, since in the past decade or so both of these subjects have been undergoing a major, frequently critical, rethinking. In some ways this is nothing new. Although for most of the post-Second World War period the concept of class has been central to key debates in labour history, its status has always been contested. There have long been arguments in labour history between, on the one hand, approaches anchored (however loosely) in some form of neo-classical economic theory which tends to be critical of the concept of class (for instance in Britain the work of Musson, or in America the influential Wisconsin school associated with J.R. Commons), and, on the other hand, more radical Marxist versions which emphasise the prime role of class in labour history (for instance the work associated with Eric Hobsbawm[1] and E.P. Thompson[2]). Class was traditionally the central debating point for labour historians and came to occupy strategic prominence in the discipline as a whole. In particular, class was a rallying cry for the majority of labour historians who were critical of neoclassical economic notions and who wanted to adopt a broader, more social-historical and social-scientific approach to the subject.

Today there is a growing sense that labour history is in crisis.[3] This crisis is connected to many things, but in important ways is bound up with growing doubts and uncertainties about the relevance of class analysis itself. For although class continues to be a major debating point in labour history, the terrain has changed. It has been argued that the concept of class actually shares a great deal of intellectual baggage with the neoclassical economic concepts with which it had previously been in dispute.[4] The major debate – at least in Britain – is now not between Marxists and those influenced by neoclassical economic theory, but between those insisting on economic primacy and those championing cultural, textual and linguistic approaches to labour.[5] There is a further political issue here. Whereas class used to be the central rallying cry for those seeking a politically committed labour history, this is less the case today as other 'progressive' political agendas – those associated with feminism, ethnic inequality, ecological issues and other 'new social movements' – have become more prominent. There is now a widespread, almost universal recognition that labour history needs to deal seriously with these issues, but this is no easy matter. It poses major theoretical, as well as political, problems. This trend to 'open up' labour history, to move it more squarely into the ambit of social (rather than economic) history, raises profound questions for the utility of the concept of class. Does the discovery of the salience of gender, ethnicity et cetera serve to discredit the importance of class or can the concept of class be reformulated in such a way that it can be made 'gender-sensitive', 'place-sensitive' and so forth? Is class simply one dimension amongst many which shapes the history of labour, which the careful empirical historian should discuss where relevant? In which case, how can labour history be other than merely descriptive? Further, if the concept of class is lost to labour history, then how can the subject be distinguished from social history, or even just history itself? These are the central questions which labour historians face today and to which there are no straightforward answers. This chapter is a contribution to thinking about – not resolving – this issue.

I should begin by saying that I want to situate my chapter away from one highly visible set of disputes that have taken place in recent years. This is the debate that has been especially marked in British, and to some extent American, circles between those championing the 'cultural turn' and those defending Marxist or neo-Marxist perspectives.[6] Although these debates have produced interesting research along the way, they have to my mind been signally unhelpful in advancing our consideration of the broader issues at stake. There is no doubt that some writers associated with the cultural turn have vilified 'orthodox' labour history in a simple and reductionist way which does not do justice to the complexity of its research.[7] However, it is equally true that there are indeed serious problems in the way the concept of class is frequently used. There is a great need to radically rethink the scope of labour history, and defending the intellectual 'status quo' is not a serious option for those who wish labour history to continue to be a healthy and relevant subject today.[8]

This chapter proceeds in three parts. I begin by discussing some of the theoretical reasons for the current impasse in class analysis, and explain why the concept of class is in need of a radical overhaul. I point to some of the reductionist tendencies inherent in traditional approaches to class and suggest the need to provide a more complex approach focusing on 'class formation'. In the second section I sketch out in more concrete detail what this 'class formation' perspective might entail, examining especially issues concerned with social mobility, historical demography and political mobilisation. In the third section I develop these points further by examining an issue close to my own heart. This concerns the need to think about 'space' and 'place' more seriously in labour history, in order that we deal with the general issue of 'context' more adequately. Here I will endeavour to show that a complex approach to class formation must be anchored in a rich appreciation of the spatial dynamics that affect forms of conflict and political mobilisation, and in the course of making this argument I suggest that we might profitably draw upon 'network analysis'.

Readers will detect that I do not write as an academic historian. Although I have carried out historical research on the cotton textile industry and the Labour movement in Preston, Lancashire in the years between 1880 and 1940,[9] as well as on Slough, in the South-east of England in the 1930s,[10] and have written generally about labour history in Britain,[11] I should emphasise that I write as a maverick historical sociologist with a particular interest in theoretical issues.

Class Analysis at an Impasse?

Marxists and Others

Contemporary doubts about class are related to two developments. One set of problems concerns the changing nature of contemporary politics. Labour history has always drawn upon present political concerns in reflecting on the past, and the contemporary crisis of social democratic politics,[12] and especially the retreat of the trade union movement across many countries, has led to a profound crisis of confidence in labour history. For reasons of space I have little to say directly about these kinds of issues here and instead want to focus on a second set of developments, which concern the intellectual problems concerning the concept of class itself. There is growing uncertainty about some of the core concepts which underpin class analysis.[13] In this section I want to quickly review these intellectual problems in class analysis and suggest some ways of dealing with them.

There are two theoretical roots to sustain class analysis, both of which have come under sustained attack in recent years. Firstly, within the Marxist tradition, the economic basis of class relations has traditionally been seen as the extraction of surplus value, which led to a direct interest in the nature of the labour process, and on the way that the inherent conflict of interests arising out of the relations production led to resistance from workers of both formal and informal kinds and hence created a constant set of tensions between workers and employers. The golden age of this Marxist-influenced labour history was perhaps in the 1970s, when the pioneering work of Hobsbawm and Thompson was developed in the context of Braverman's ideas about deskilling and led to a series of studies exploring the class-based roots of labour organisations and culture in the production process (for example, the work associated with the History Workshop movement, or, in more academic mode, Joyce[14]).

Looking with hindsight from the 1990s, we can identify two main problems with this body of work. The first concerns the growing problematisation of the labour theory of value. This has come under increasing intellectual pressure in recent years. Feminists have shown how it rests on male assumptions about what constitutes 'productive work', as the now forgotten 'domestic labour debate' of the later 1970s indicated all to well. In a different vein, the contemporary growth of white-collar – middle-class – employment has further made it difficult to know how to distinguish those exploited from those who exploit. Manual workers now form a minority of employees in most European countries. Nicos Poulantzas[15] was the last major theorist to defend the distinction between productive and unproductive labour, but his distinctions became hopelessly arbitrary.[16] It is also interesting to note, again from the vantage point of the 1990s, that it is arguably the 'unproductive' white-collar workers, frequently employed by the state, who seem best able to sustain trade union mobilisation, and it seems difficult now to believe that there is a privileged link between (usually male) manual workers in heavy industry and trade unionism and socialist politics.

Subsequent Marxists have indeed come to recognise the difficulty of defending the labour theory of value.[17] But how else to explain the material basis for class divisions? The most important attempt to reformulate the Marxist concept of exploitation has been Wright's use of game theory to conceptualise exploitation as taking place where 'one person's welfare is obtained at the expense of another'.[18] This rather loose definition opens the way to admit all kinds of relationships as being exploitative ones. Wright distinguishes three axes of class exploitation (based around property ownership, organisational hierarchies, and credentialism), which actually converge closely with Weberian ideas.

Before discussing these it is worth mentioning a second problem with Marxist perspectives. It can be argued that the efforts of Hobsbawm and Thompson to recover 'worker's worlds', to contextualise labour institutions in the context of the labour process has, in a curious way, actually undermined itself. It is possible to go beyond Thompson's cautious use of anthropological concepts and suggest an altogether broader, more cultural reading of these worlds, in which case the class focus tends to disappear. And, indeed, recent research excavating the cultural contexts of labour have emphasised the way that many cultural idioms deployed in workplaces make little or no reference to class. This is especially true of American research on European labour history. Much has been written here about the survival of artisanal, 'corporate' and craft-based idioms.[19] There are also studies of the deployment of non-class idioms in the French textile industry,[20] about the populist assumptions underlying British labour culture,[21] and even the way that some forms of work can be analysed through anthropological idioms of purity and filth (Reid on the Paris sewermen,[22] and see generally Joyce[23]). Biernacki[24] has argued that even the cultural meaning of 'labour' and 'work' is fundamentally different in Britain and Germany. Lüdtke's work in German labour history and the 'history of everyday life' movement in general can also be seen to take this interest in work cultures in a direction increasingly divorced from that of social class. These developments all pose difficult questions for the relevance of class for understanding work cultures.

Weberians and Others

It is, of course, mistaken to assume that class analysis depends on Marxist assumptions. It is notable that the past decade has seen a marked resurgence of Weberian class theory in British sociology,[25] and it is important to consider whether this removes the problems encountered within Marxist perspectives. As is well known, Weber adopts a multifaceted approach to social stratification, distinguishing between class, status and party, and rooting class in market relationships. The attractiveness of Weber's approach is that by seeing class as based in market relationships rather than production relationships more narrowly defined, he can operate on the same terrain of neoclassical economics. This could be used to justify a focus on institutions such as trade unions as forces aiming to maximise market position. And indeed classic studies such as that of Turner[26] have in a way worked within a Weberian perspective. However, although Weber's work has become dominant in sociological circles, it has been less important in British labour or social history (Harold Perkin's work is perhaps an exception), though it has been more influential on the German 'historical social science school' associated with Jürgen Kocka.

And there continue to be problems even in Weber's multidimensional rendering of class. One of these is how to theorise the relationship between class and status. If status is regarded as a reflection of class, then the concept of class still leads to a form of economic reductionism (as argued, for instance, by Hindess[27]). This, indeed, is the gist of Lüdtke's criticism of Kocka's focus on 'shared common interests' as the basis for class formation.[28] The sociologists Goldthorpe and Marshall[29] insist that they do not use a deterministic concept of class, since they claim that they are simply interested in examining whether class is revealed to be important or not in empirical research. However, this is hardly a satisfactory resolution to the problem. Historians have rarely tried to use the concept of status seriously, and perhaps the most successful attempt to merge the concepts of class and status is by Bourdieu.[30]

Secondly, one of the inherent problems in Weber's market-based concept of class is the fact that by relating class to life chances he opens up the possibility of there being so many different classes that firm boundaries between them become difficult to draw. In this spirit Roger Penn[31] has argued that the pervasiveness of the skill divide within the British working class, whereby the skilled workers exercised social closure against the unskilled, is such as to undermine the cohesiveness of the working class itself. This Weberian stress can therefore lead towards a denial of class, as in American research in social stratification, for instance in the 'status attainment' tradition championed by Blau and Duncan,[32] whereby inequality is seen as a graded hierarchy with many different levels and without any clear boundaries between such levels. In this perspective, the clear and antagonistic class divisions typically distinguished in Marxist research are regarded as mistaken.

Structural Insecurity

We can see that whether in the Marxist or Weberian tradition the theoretical underpinnings of class theory are in severe difficulties. Two sorts of responses are possible to this. It might be pointed out that there is still no conceptual alternative to class as a means of exploring structurally based unequal economic relationships. The critics of class have not found an alternative way of understanding or explaining social inequality. All they have done is to place the focus elsewhere. Where there have been attempts to explore questions of inequality from non-class paradigms, there has been no resolution to the basic question of where resistance to power comes from (this is an answer which class theorists do have). This is a criticism that can be levelled at the work of Foucault[33] (for all its sophistication), Joyce and others.

Furthermore, I want to suggest an alternative rendering of class theory which might overcome the difficulty of specifying the precise structural base of class relationships.[34] This is to emphasise that the distinctive feature of working-class life lies not exclusively in the labour process (as Marxists might stress) or in the labour market (as Weberians might have it) but in the *structural insecurity* faced by proletarians. The removal of the means of subsistence from workers in capitalist society means that they are forced to find strategies for dealing with the chronic insecurity of everyday life which comes from their being unable to reproduce themselves autonomously and without recourse to other agencies.[35] This formulation allows us to recognise some structural underpinnings of working-class life whilst also pointing to the need to investigate the enormous variety of tactics that workers might adopt to deal with this problem – struggling with their employers, forming cooperative associations, demanding state support, forging neighbourhood support networks and so forth. It is as important to look at the coping strategies used in urban neighbourhoods and within households as at the labour process itself – in this view work as employment need not be seen as the only or even main axis of class.

This formulation allows us to avoid reductionism. The basic fact of chronic insecurity does not mean that any particular form of working-class consciousness or politics develops. It does not mean that workers unite together rather than compete amongst themselves. It emphasises the need to look at the contextual factors which explain how the very general need of workers to deal with insecurity leads to very different sorts of cultural and political outcomes. Key to understanding the variety of actual class cultures and actions which develop in any society is to focus on the complex process of 'class formation'. In thinking about processes of class formation it is possible to draw upon a growing body of work exploring class formation as a fluid, contingent, social process by which stable collectivities may form.[36] The class-formation perspective – which obviously owes its inspiration to E.P. Thompson – is concerned not with reducing mobilisation to class structures, but in exploring the complex mediations between a variety of economic, social and cultural phenomena. It emphatically insists on the contingency of class. There are no guarantees that classes exist as cohesive social collectivities. It is precisely the point of historical research to investigate whether they do and how the boundaries between classes are 'policed'. The theoretical inspiration for this approach can be said to draw eclectically on Marx, Weber, as well as trends in contemporary social theory, such as Giddens's 'structuration' theory. Let me now go on to spell out what this class-formation perspective may entail for labour history.

Class Formation

Social Mobility

There are many ways in which class formation occurs but I want to start with one focus which has been remarkably neglected by social historians: the question of social mobility.[37] Sociologists such as John Goldthorpe have for some years argued that one of the central features of class formation is the process whereby classes become demographically formed entities, that is to say, groups with high rates of self-recruitment and thereby social stability.[38] This insight suggests the need to seriously explore historical processes of social mobility in order to determine how forms of mobility may tend either to accentuate or undermine collective stability.[39] In the past few years it is clear that there has been a considerable growth of historical interest in this topic.[40] The development of the HISMA (Historical International Social Mobility Analysis) network, coordinated by Andrew Miles, Marco van Leeuwen and Ineke Maas, has been of central importance in developing a Europe-wide research initiative in this area.

Let me say a few words about why social mobility is important. There are clear signs that we can learn much about the processes of unionisation and political mobilisation by looking more directly at social mobility processes. Miles's work, for instance, uses marriage register data (which contains information on the occupations of bridegrooms and their fathers) to examine trends in social mobility in England between 1835 and 1914. As well as demonstrating the persistent, massive divide between the middle and working classes in this period (for despite the 'Smilesian myth' of selfimprovement, 90 percent of the sons of manual workers themselves became some form of manual worker), he also demonstrates the complex process of intra-working-class formation. He shows that in the mid-nineteenth century there was a pervasive skill divide within the working class, as the sons of skilled workers tended themselves to follow in their father's trade, whilst the sons of unskilled workers were unlikely to move into skilled ranks (this is in line with Penn's arguments, mentioned above). This pattern is, of course, consistent with the argument that there was a distinct labour aristocracy in Britain in the mid-Victorian period. Miles shows that by 1914, however, there was much more mobility between skilled, semi-skilled and unskilled workers, indicating the demographic formation of the manual working class *as a whole*. This period, of course, was precisely that associated with the development of 'new unionism' (where trade unions became more widespread amongst unskilled workers) and the emergence of the Labour Party as a viable political force.[41]

One issue in this body of work, as in the study of social mobility in general, is the question of gender, and how the social mobility of women is to be analysed in relation to that of men. Miles's work – like that of Goldthorpe – focuses on male occupational mobility. However, we can also learn much about the interface between class and gender by examining the social mobility of women in relation to men and how men's career prospects are related to women's employment. There may be much to be gained by relating class formation to existing research in historical demography, where issues of female employment and family dynamics hold centre stage.[42] Historical demographers, such as Levine,[43] have emphasised how class formation involves the emergence of new family dynamics, as working-class families increase the number of children in order to increase the wage-earning potential of the household. Hanagan's work[44] has begun to relate the study of social mobility to that of family dynamics and spatial mobility in order to chart the emergence of a French proletariat in the years between 1840 and 1880.

There are, however, reasons to be cautious about embracing the sociological approach to social mobility wholesale. Sociologists themselves differ about the best way of researching the subject. Goldthorpe's approach to the study of social mobility focuses on inter-generational (parent – child) male mobility. In recent years sociologists have become more doubtful of the value of this approach, emphasising that it tends to neglect the often complex trajectories people may experience in their work-lives.[45] Goldthorpe's approach to social mobility can lead to an overly structural view of mobility, removed from the 'experience' of individuals. I personally subscribe to the view that there is much to be gained by focusing on intragenerational mobility, and to see class formation as concerned with the creation of 'predictable' occupational routes. By being predictable, such routes can form the context of individuals' expectation and hence shape their awareness, identity and – even – class consciousness. Research I have been carrying out (with Andrew Miles and David Vincent) on career mobility in selected British organisations between 1850 and 1950 suggests an increasing process of social closure in the years between 1890 and 1914. The promotion prospects of manual workers deteriorated in this period (in the railway industry, for instance, it took much longer for firemen to become engine drivers, whilst in the Post Office it became more rare for letter sorters to be promoted into white-collar ranks). On the other hand, middle-class career routes became more formalised, based around incremental salary systems, credentialised systems of entry, and gender demarcation processes whereby women are excluded from employment or confined to subordinate posts as part of the 'white blouse revolution'.[46]

Time

The point I think is worth emphasising is that most occupational studies still tend to focus on labour process at a cross-sectional level and rarely draw attention to the types of career pathways that may have been in existence. There are exceptions here – Matsumura's study of flint glass workers,[47] Daunton's analysis of the different career routes for miners in the North-east as opposed to South Wales,[48] to some extent Sonenscher's study of eighteenth- century French trades.[49] Only rarely are the implications of this point fully developed, however. One recent exception is Lummis's study[50] of the labour aristocracy, which points to the idea of job security as a key factor distinguishing labour aristocrats from other workers. To put this another way, *time* matters. Class formation involves the creation of routinised, typical temporal rhythms and shifts. I recall research I did ten years ago, interviewing workers in a large, American-owned chocolate factory in the South-east of England. This factory had a paternalistic style of management and refused to tolerate trade unions. The workers were, however, well disposed to the company. It became clear that the company's hold over the workers was in part because it operated a compulsory shift system which worked on a ten-day, not weekly, cycle. This shift system made it very difficult for these workers to socialise with other workers, since there was no guarantee that they would enjoy leisure at the weekend. Rather, it made these workers very friendly amongst themselves and helped incorporate them into the culture of the factory. By contrast, if we look at the classic period of the 'formation' of the English working class, it involved the creation of a whole series of temporal rhythms, involving regulated working days, weekend leisure, summer holidays and so forth.[51] Stable classes depend on stable temporalities.

A greater recognition of class formation as a temporally shifting, demographic process – involving family and occupational dimensions – can, I suggest, go some way to alleviating charges of deterministic reductionism levelled against class analysis. But not entirely. We are still left with the tricky question of considering the 'autonomy' of politics from social and economic change. Does demographic class formation 'determine' political class formation? Goldthorpe himself argues political class formation is a separate dimension from demographic class formation. The problem here is that it can be argued that a demographically cohesive class may either be inclined to be politically well organised (by virtue of its cohesion), or by contrast, it may be so insulated from the rest of society that it tends to be inert. The very same points have been discussed in considering the role of spatial processes in class formation. Does a homogeneous occupational community tend to lead to political militancy[52] or to sporadic outbursts of uncoordinated action (as in Kerr and Seigel's idea of the 'isolated mass'), or might it lead more generally to inertia? Some degree of mixing between classes may actually be conducive to forms of radical awareness since people's reference groups are expanded.

This relationship between the 'political' and the 'social' is now so well debated that I cannot hope to offer anything new or interesting here. I will only say that there is a persistent tendency here to pose 'either-or', dichotomous perspectives which only serve to cloud the issues. We can see this clearly, for instance, in the arguments developed by Skocpol and her associates[53] in their criticisms of what they call 'society centred' accounts of political change. They prefer the idea that states themselves have a great deal of autonomy in affecting outcomes. In labour history this idea has been developed by Jonathan Zeitlin[54] in his emphasis on the way that different forms of trade union development, collective bargaining and so forth are linked to state structures, and there are also echoes of these ideas in the generally interesting collection edited by Katznelson and Zollberg.[55]

This is not the place to embark on a full discussion of this body of work.[56] I have, however, argued in this paper that there is little to be gained by developing a 'dualist', 'either-or' framework for studying labour history, or by Skocpol's attempt to construct something she calls a 'society centred' approach: fitting into one over-simple category a whole disparate body of work which sees very different forms of social determination at work. Going back to my earlier remarks concerning the focus on working-class insecurity, it seems possible to recognise – in the spirit of Skocpol – that there is no determinate relationship between the world of everyday, practical struggles to deal with insecurity, and the world of formal political institutions and parties which attempt to mobilise and generalise such actions into social movements and electoral blocs. Nonetheless, we should not assume that political leaders and institutions mobilise people freely and without constraint. The sorts of practical, everyday struggles which people wage to deal with structural insecurity forms a crucial bedrock on which parties may mobilise. There is undoubtedly considerable autonomy for parties to articulate different sorts of practical, everyday issues into more coherent political movements and ideologies, but the most effective appeals mobilise people around issues present in everyday-life situations.

There is a further problem with Skocpol's focus on the nation state. Cronin[57] argues that the emphasis on the national state is in many respects dependent on the nation-based comparative approach adopted by writers such as Skocpol. To put this another way, if we decide that we need to contrast nation states then it is not so surprising that nation states themselves tend to be the most important source of variation. But we should not assume that the nation state is the appropriate unit of analysis. There are also continents, neighbourhoods, cities, villages, trade routes, etc. If we focus on Mann's[58] work, it indicates in an admittedly schematic fashion a more satisfactory attempt to consider the interlinkages between states, classes and other salient social groups, by his notion of looking at societies as 'organised power networks'. In developing this approach I suggest that we need to develop a greater recognition of context in labour history. Here we need to develop an appreciation of the role of space and place.

Bringing in Spatial Networks

Traditionally, labour history has focused on occupations and industries as its object of analysis. Most research has taken the form of case studies of specific trade unions, conflicts, trades or occupations. This tended to lead towards a national focus – on nationally organised unions, or industries.[59] There were, of course, many exceptions, especially where the localisation of economic activities meant that particular regions or cities specialised in particular forms of economic activity. In Britain, one can go back to Asa Briggs's emphasis on the local characteristics of Chartism,[60] to the pioneering work of Hobsbawm – for instance on the London labour market – or Thompson (for instance in 'Homage to Tom Maguire', a study of the West Yorkshire origins of the Labour Party). Nonetheless, despite these examples, it is clear that labour historians tended to neglect the role of space and place in their focus on occupations and industries. In this final section of my chapter I will suggest that a greater spatial sensitivity may allow us to explore the complex linkages between class structures, demographic class formation and forms of political mobilisation in a more sophisticated way.

In the past decade or so, there has been a major growth of interest in local and spatial dimensions of labour history and this has been extremely welcome, and indeed vital, in developing a more sophisticated class analysis. There are numerous reasons for this development. In part it represents a growing awareness of local variations in class formation, even in places with similar industrial structures. In Britain Harrison's[61] edited collection demonstrated that coal-mining

communities differed greatly in different parts of Britain, and this is
a point now extensively developed by Daunton,[62] Gilbert[63] and others. Similar points have been made about local variations in fishing,[64]
textiles[65] and other industries.

There is a further point, raised by Smith,[66] that industrial disputes
are frequently also about community and place[67] (and see also Calhoun[68]). It follows from my theoretical discussion of conceptualising
questions of class around the notion of insecurity that all sorts of
community-based networks and the formation of local identities in
general can become a crucial tool in coping with the insecurity inherent in everyday life. As I have argued elsewhere, class formation is a
spatial process, in which local identities and class identities can merge
and mingle together.[69]

This is, however, a difficult point to develop. For it is clear that
local studies are used in a variety of different ways by various
researchers and there is no consensus about how to do justice to the
complexity of spatial context. Some studies emphasise that local factors – such as local labour markets, urban structure, possibly local
political traditions – determine local political outcomes. This can suggest that national or international dimensions were not important.
This perspective can be found in my study of the labour movement
in Preston, where I pointed to some of the specific features of Preston's local social structure that led to a distinct form of Labour politics in the area: for instance, the way that male concerns over
women's position in the labour market led to a concern to reduce
women's local employment in the years before 1914. Similar kinds of
work can be seen in Tanner's[70] account of local labour politics in
Britain between 1900 and 1914, in Foster's[71] analysis of Oldham,
South Shields and Northampton, Gilbert's comparison of coal-mining settlements in South Wales and the East Midlands, and so forth.

The danger, of course, is that this kind of research simply ends up
as the mirror image of 'national' level historiography. Whereas nation
states might be seen as autonomous spatial units, now localities are.
But like nation states, towns, cities and villages are not self-contained
entities with strong boundaries against the outside world. We need to
recognise spatial fluidity and mobility. Rather than arguing whether
the local or national is more important, as if their respective importance can be weighed up and evaluated, it is better to examine the
complex interconnections between these different spatial levels and to
examine how spatial mediators – people able to move between spatial scales – may come to play a key role in generating forms of political mobilisation. It is, indeed, interesting to note that many of the
occupational groups that played a key role in organising the labour
movement in Britain were groups that routinely travelled between

places, or mediated contact between places. I am thinking particularly of railway workers, who were frequently the bastion of local labour movements in areas where unionised industry was weak,[72] or tramping artisans who enabled craft traditions to be spread between places.[73] I am thinking also of Cooke's[74] emphasis on the way that the development of strong radical traditions in the South Wales coalfield depended not just on the existence of very cohesive mining villages, but also on the creation of elaborate links between different mining villages so that they could coordinate their actions and gain a more general sense of identity.

How do we understand these links between spatial scales? I think there is much to be learnt from some of the ideas developed by American historical sociologists under the rubric of 'network analysis'. In an influential study Mark Granovetter examined how people found jobs.[75] He found that those best able to get jobs were not those with a few, very strong ties, but those with a large number of weak ties. It was these people who had a greater range of contacts and who were most likely to hear of job opportunities. Granovetter's emphasis on the 'strength of weak ties' is an extremely important one. If we extend the logic of his argument, we might stay that political mobilisation does not depend only on the intense identities of militant 'Little Moscows', but also on the existence of 'weak ties' between people in different places. These may come about through migration flows, the spread of print or other media, and so forth.

We still need many more examples of how these network methods might be applied to studying the history of labour. The main example currently to hand is Roger Gould's study of the Paris Commune,[76] which argues that the networks involved in the mobilisation of the commune were based on residential and neighbourhood ties rather than the occupational, class-based ties that had been important in 1848.

Conclusion: Class and Labour History

In this chapter I have sketched out some issues that need to be taken up if we wish to develop a nonreductionist approach to class and labour history. Rather than attempt to 'reduce' forms of industrial and political mobilisation to class dynamics, I argue that it is more important to explore the mediation between structure and agency, between 'class-in-itself' and 'class-for-itself' (to use a well-known adage). This is, of course, a very general statement which few people will disagree with in the abstract. What is more relevant is to indicate what this might really mean for historical research. Here I have three more concrete suggestions.

Firstly, by conceptualising working-class life as being about coping with insecurity we can leave the way open to exploring class in broad, inclusive terms, and we can helpfully focus on the various kinds of coping strategies that workers use. In order to show how these everyday coping strategies may become more generalised (between individuals, households, workplaces, localities etc.) we then need to examine the contexts in which workers' lives are lived. This means seeing both time and space not as backdrops to historical analyses, but as fundamentally implicated in the very process of historical change.

To make this more concrete, time is not simply a 'homogenous empty space' (to paraphrase Walter Benjamin) in which things happen. Instead, time is fundamental to understanding social process.[77] I have suggested that one way of utilising this point in historical research is to pay more attention to social mobility processes – both between and within generations. This will allow us to see history as composed of large-scale historical events along with specific patterns of individual change (and stability). The same point can be made with respect to space.[78]

Notes

1. Eric Hobsbawm, *Labouring Men: Studies in the History of Labour*, London, 1964.
2. E.P. Thompson, *The Making of the English Working Class*, London, 1963. See more generally M. Savage, *Class Analysis and Social Transformation*, Milton Keynes, 2000, esp. chap. 2.
3. See for instance David Howell's editorial in *Labour History Review*, 60, 1 (1995): 2, and the subsequent debate in 60, 3 (1995): 46–53, and *International Review of Social History*, 38 (1993), Supplement 1, 'The End of Labour History?', edited by Marcel van der Linden.
4. E.g., William M. Reddy, *Money and Liberty in Western Europe: A Critique of Historical Understanding*, Cambridge, 1987.
5. This point is especially clear from a reading of the debates in the journal *Social History* between 1990 and 1995 concerning the nature of social history and the status of the concept of class. See esp.: Patrick Joyce, 'The End of Social History?', *Social History*, 20 (1995): 73–91; Geoff Eley and Keith Nield, 'Starting Over: The Present, the Post-Modern and the Moment of Social History', *Social History*, 20 (1995): 355–64; Patrick Joyce, 'The End of Social History? A Brief Reply to Eley and Nield', *Social History*, 21 (1996): 96–8.
6. A cursory reading of the journals *Social History* and *Labour History Review* since 1990 will provide even the casual reader with many examples. Arguably, research in French and German labour history has been more successful at linking together 'structural' and 'cultural' phenomena than is the case in recent English language work (e.g., the work of Michelle Perrot, Alf Lüdtke).
7. E.g., P. Joyce, 'The End of Social History?', *Social History*, 20, (1995): 73–91.
8. Some of Kirk's work runs the risk of reifying and reinforcing these barriers. See e.g., N. Kirk, 'History, Language, Ideas and Post-modernism: a Materialist View', *Social History*, 19 (1994): 221–40.

9. See M. Savage, *The Dynamics of Working Class Politics: The Labour Movement in Preston, 1880–1940*, Cambridge, 1987.

10. See M. Savage, 'Trade Unionism, Sex Segregation and the State: Women's Employment in "New Industries" in Inter-war Britain', *Social History*, 13, (1988): 209–30.

11. See M. Savage and A. Miles, *The Remaking of the English Working Class, 1840–1940*, London, 1994.

12. See e.g., F.F. Piven (ed.), *Labour Parties in Post-Industrial Societies*, Oxford, 1992.

13. See B. Hindess, *Politics and Class Analysis*, Oxford, 1987; R. Crompton, *Class and Stratification: An Introduction to Current Debates*, Oxford, 1993; Reddy, *Money and Liberty in Western Europe*.

14. P. Joyce (ed.), *The Historical Meanings of Work*, Cambridge, 1985.

15. N. Poulantzas, *Classes in Contemporary Capitalism*, London, 1974.

16. Throughout much of the 1980s sociologists became hopelessly bogged down in 'boundary debates' about which occupations fitted into what classes (see e.g., N. Abercrombie and J. Urry, *Capital, Labour and the Middle Classes*, London, 1983). See Crompton, *Class and Stratification*, for an excellent discussion of these issues.

17. E.g., E.O. Wright, *Classes*, London, 1985, and *Class Counts: Comparative Studies in Class Analysis*, Cambridge, 1997. Also G.A. Cohen, *History, Labour and Freedom: Themes from Marx*, Oxford, 1988, and Savage, *Class Analysis and Social Transformation*, chap. 1.

18. Wright, *Classes*, 65.

19. W.H. Sewell, Jr, *Work and Revolution in France: The Language of Labour from the Old Regime to 1848*, Cambridge, 1981; M. Sonenscher, *Work and Wages: Natural Law, Politics, and the Eighteenth-Century French Trades*, Cambridge, 1989.

20. Reddy, *Money and Liberty in Western Europe*.

21. Joyce, *The Historical Meanings of Work*.

22. D. Reid, *Paris sewers and Sewermen: Realities and Representations*, Cambridge, MA,1997.

23. Joyce, *The Historical Meanings of Work*.

24. R. Biernacki, *The Fabrication of Labor: Germany and Britain, 1640–1914*, Berkeley CA, 1995.

25. See e.g., G. Marshall, H. Newby, D. Rose, C. Vogler, *Social Class in Modern Britain*, London, 1988; J. Scott, *Stratification and Power: Structures of Class, Status and Command*, Cambridge, 1996.

26. H.A. Turner, *Trade Union Growth: Structure and Policy, A Comparative Study of the Cotton Unions in England*, Toronto, 1962.

27. Hindess, *Politics and Class Analysis*.

28. See A. Lüdtke, 'Polymorphous Synchrony: German Industrial Workers and the Politics of Everyday Life', *International Review of Social History*, 38, (Supplement 1993): 39–84, esp. 30–40.

29. J.H. Goldthorpe and G. Marshall, 'The promising future of class analysis', *Sociology*, 26 (1992): 381–400.

30. Pierre Bourdieu, *Distinction : A Social Critique of the Judgement of Taste*, London, 1984.

31. Roger Penn, *Skilled Workers in the Class Structure*, Cambridge, 1984.

32. P. Blau and O.D. Duncan, *The American Occupational Structure*, New York, 1967.

33. Foucault's work is also bedevilled by major theoretical problems, notably his tendency to fall back on functionalist arguments. See Axel Honneth's brilliant book, *The Critique of Power: Reflective Stages in a Critical Social Theory*, Cambridge, 1991.

34. This argument is developed at greater length in my book *The Dynamics of Working Class Politics*.

35. The claim here is not that only workers are insecure, for to some degree insecurity is generic to social life in general. It can, however, be argued that both the extent

and scope of insecurity is greater for workers and that the kinds of resources and capacities available to them to deal with it are more restricted (see Savage, *The Dynamics of Working Class Politics*).

36. See generally: Savage and Miles, *The Remaking of the English Working Class*, and Crompton, *Class and Stratification*.

37. There are, of course, exceptions, notably Stephen Thernstrom in the USA and Hartmut Kaelble in Germany.

38. See e.g., J.H. Goldthorpe, *Social Mobility and the Class Structure in Modern Britain*, Oxford, 1980.

39. See M. Savage, 'Social Mobility and Class Analysis: A New Agenda for Social History?', *Social History*, (1994): 69–80.

40. For instance, A. Miles and D. Vincent (eds), *Building European Society: Occupational Change and Social Mobility in Europe 1840–1940*, Manchester, 1993, which includes research on social mobility in most European countries.

41. See the discussion in Savage and Miles, *The Remaking of the English Working Class*.

42. Some interesting general remarks on the possibility of combining household history and labour history can be found in M. van der Linden, 'Connecting Household History and Labour History', *International Review of Social History*, 38, (Supplement 1993): 163–73.

43. D. Levine, *Family Formation in the Age of Nascent Capitalism*, Cambridge, 1977.

44. M. Hanagan, *Nascent Proletarians: Class Formation in Post-Revolutionary France*, Oxford, 1989.

45. See, notably, A. Sorensen, 'Theory and Methodology in Stratification Research', in U. Himmelstrand (ed.), *The Sociology of Structure and Action*, vol. 1: *Sociology from Crisis to Science?*, London, 1986.

46. See A. Miles and M Savage, 'Career Mobility and Class Formation in Britain, 1850–1930', mimeo.

47. T. Matsumura, *The Labour Aristocracy Revisited: The Victorian Flint Glass Makers*, Manchester, 1983.

48. M. Daunton, 'Down the Pit', *Economic History Review*, 34 (1981): 578–597.

49. See especially Chapter 4, Sonenescher, *Work and Wages*.

50. T. Lummis, *The Labour Aristocracy, 1851–1914*, Aldershot, 1994.

51. See generally: G. Cross, *A Quest for Time: The Reduction of Work in Britain and France, 1840–1940*, Berkeley CA, 1989.

52. E.g., S. Macintyre, *Little Moscows: Communism and Working-Class Militancy in Inter-War Britain*, London, 1980.

53. E.g., P.B. Evans et al., *Bringing the State Back in*, Cambridge, 1985; T. Skocpol, *Protecting Soldiers and Mothers: The Political Origins of Social Policy in the United States*, Cambridge MA, 1992; S. Tolliday and J. Zeitlin, *Shop Floor Bargaining and the State: Historical and Comparative Perspectives*, Cambridge, 1985.

54. J. Zeitlin, 'From Labour History to the History of Industrial Relations', *Economic History Review*, 40 (1987): 159–80.

55. I. Katznelson and A. Zollberg, *Working Class Formation: Nineteenth-Century Patterns in Western Europe and the United States*, Oxford, 1986.

56. Although see B. Jessop, *State Theory: Putting the Capitalist State in Its Place*, Oxford, 1990, for some critical remarks.

57. J. Cronin, 'Neither Exceptional nor Peculiar: Towards the Comparative Study of Labour in Advanced Society', *International Review of Social History*, 38, (1993): 59–75.

58. M. Mann, *The Sources of Social Power, Volume 1*, Cambridge, 1986, and *Volume 2*, Cambridge, 1993.

59. See Cronin, 'Neither Exceptional nor Peculiar'.

60. A. Briggs, *Chartist Studies*, London, 1956.

61. R. Harrison, *Independent Collier: The Coal Miner as Archetypal Proletarian*, London, 1978.
62. Daunton, 'Down the Pit'.
63. D. Gilbert, *Class, Community and Collective Action: Social Change in Two British Coalfields, 1850–1926*, Cambridge, 1992.
64. P. Thompson et al., *Living the Fishing*, London, 1983.
65. Joyce, *The Historical Meanings of Work*.
66. D. Smith, 'Tonypandy 1910: Definitions of Community', *Past and Present*, 87, (1980): 158–184
67. This is a point that became particularly clear in Britain during the 1984–5 coal-mining strike, where references to community became legion.
68. C.J. Calhoun, 'The Radicalism of Tradition', *American Journal of Sociology*, 88 (1983): 886–914.
69. See M. Savage, 'Urban History and Social Class: Two Paradigms', *Urban History*, 20 (1993): 61–77.
70. D. Tanner, *Political Change and the Labour Party: 1900–1918*, Cambridge, 1990.
71. J. Foster, *Class Struggle in the Industrial Revolution: Early Industrial Capitalism in Three English Towns*, London, 1974.
72. See the interesting discussion in D. Harvey, *Justice, Nature, and the Geography of Difference*, Oxford, 1997, chap. 1.
73. H. Southall, 'The Tramping Artisan Revisits: Labour Mobility and Economic Distress in Early Victorian England', *Economic History Review*, 44 (1991): 272–296.
74. Ph. Cooke, 'Class Practices as Regional Markers: A Contribution to Labour Geography', in D. Gregory and J. Urry (eds), *Social Relations and Spatial Structures*, London, 1985, 213–241.
75. Mark S. Granovetter, *Getting a Job: A Study of Contacts and Careers*, Cambridge MA, 1974
76. R. Gould, *Insurgent Identities: Class, Community, and Protest in Paris from 1848 to the Commune*, Chicago IL, 1995.
77. See generally: A. Abbott, 'Conceptions of Time and Events in Social Science Methods: Causal and Narrative Approaches', *Historical Methods*, 23 (1990): 140–150; B. Adam, *Time and Social Theory*, Philadelphia PA, 1990.
78. See generally: Harvey, *Justice, Nature, and the Geography of Difference*.

CHAPTER 4

GENDER IN LABOUR AND WORKING-CLASS HISTORY

Eileen Yeo

Once upon a time, actually not very long ago, European working-class and labour history were largely gender-blind. This paper will not linger on the bad old days when the scope of such history embraced, to borrow the splendid title of the Labour Lord Snell's autobiography, *Men, Movements and Myself.* Rather, I want to explore why attention to gender must be a basic part of any analytical grid and then show how viewing everyday life and labour movements through this gendered lens produces new pictures but also new problems. I will first discuss the importance of sex and gender to men, women and history. Then I will cut through what by now should be regarded as gendered territory in different directions. First I will look at horizontal studies which consider gender relations within the working class and within labour movements; and then I will explore more virgin land, where some of my own research lies, by tracking vertical power relations especially between women of different social classes. I wish I could simply board a Eurobus and fly over the whole continent, giving a European overview. But English bustards, as E.P. Thompson used to say, have a limited flying range and all I can do is review trends in Britain and call upon my European colleagues to compare this story with what is going in research in their own countries.

Gender and History

The usual distinction made between sex and gender, which is worth repeating here, is that sex is a biological fact whereas gender is a cultural construct. Sex describes biologically given differences between men and women, gender socially constructed differences. Put more crudely, sex covers the fact that men have penises which ejaculate sperm, and women have vaginas, eggs and wombs and can give birth to children: gender covers all the rest of being a man or woman. More especially, gender relates to ideals and practices of masculinity and femininity which usually interlock together as parts of a cultural system. Often in the past, although certainly not always, the characteristics of masculinity and femininity have been linked in a relationship of binary opposition – the qualities attributed to manliness have been absent from womanliness and vice versa. If women scholars have most insistently called attention to the importance of gender, a sensitivity to gender certainly does not mean only the study of women (although it is never a bad idea to make sure to go beyond the his in history and include the other half of the human race in your inquiry in some form!).

The importance of always taking gender into account has to do with how human beings in the past and present have constructed their identities and thus the perspectives from which they see the world and live (and act) in it. Human identity is a complicated matter, since most people have multiple selves, and many different ways of experiencing their personal sense of self and their social identities or solidarities. In terms of a sense of social belonging, class is one possible basis for felt unity; others that are much discussed at the moment are race, ethnicity, nationality and gender. A key issue for historical study is to illuminate why different groups prioritise different possible collective identities at different moments: why, for example, is class identity seemingly in abeyance at the moment and ethnicity more strongly felt? Whether looking at past or present, however, gender is part of the fundamental bedrock of personal identity. We live and experience ourselves as men and women whether or not we form our primary social allegiances on a gender basis. Conversely, when our social identities are primarily seen in terms of class, race, ethnicity or nationality, we nonetheless experience ourselves at the same time as men and women. One of the groundbreaking studies on gender and class formation, *Family Fortunes*, by Leonore Davidoff and Catherine Hall (which in fact deals, as its subtitle indicates, with 'Men and Women of the Middle Class, 1780–1850'),[1] even asserts that 'class always takes a gendered form'. Certainly the most virulent contemporary ethnicity does: all the factions of the former Yugoslavia officially support models of men as ethnic warriors and women as ethnic reproducer-mothers within an ethnic politics that regards rape as a legitimate tactic of war in order to pollute the enemy's stock or to increase the approved seed![2]

Gender is not only created by cultural ideas but is also formed on the unconscious level of the personality, so psychoanalysis tells us, which fuels desire. Partly for this reason, gender is often implicated in how people experience fear and hope, discontent and longing, indeed in how strongly they are willing to struggle to resist or even challenge powerful social formations. Thus in the early nineteenth century a particularly potent way of representing class exploitation was by imaging it as class rape. In the Ten Hours Movement, some activists like Richard Pilling called attention to the emasculation of unemployed husbands who brought their infants to the factory for mothers to suckle and intimated, too, that, in the factories, foremen and owners could take sexual liberties with the unprotected wives.[3] And yet the key and ubiquitous category of gender does not always marry harmoniously with other categories of identity such as class. The tensions and contradictions which can exist open a vexed area for working-class and labour historians: especially in cases where tactics which seem emancipatory from a class point of view can also be oppressive from a gender perspective.[4]

Horizontal Studies of Gender and Class

These complex analytical and political issues have been added to an already full research agenda on working-class life and labour movements, although it is worth noting that some of the pioneering work, especially by Davidoff and Hall, has been about gender and middle-class formation. The burgeoning research on gender in the working and middle class has moved in at least three directions; one illuminating the importance of gender to the material life of the class, the second establishing the importance of gender to class identity, the third exposing the tensions between class and gender within the same cultural constructions. On the first approach, Davidoff and Hall have uncovered the usually concealed role of women in the launch of the family enterprise, where many women acted as providers of some of the capital, as custodians of the family and friendship networks which provided more of the capital and as workers in the business before the delicate line between public and private widened into a chasm. A range of texts on working-class life, for example by Elizabeth Roberts and Ellen Ross,[5] have emphasised the critical role of women as managers of family survival, who engaged in a myriad of activities which brought money into the household, and which ranged from doing waged work to taking in laundry, to selling cooked food, to accommodating lodgers. Besides this, women took part in elaborate barter and borrowing rituals to secure indispensable goods and services for the family.

Just as important was the way gender featured in the construction of positive class identity. Davidoff and Hall concentrate on the heroic period when women largely cooperated with the project of producing middle-class identity and ascendancy before the mid-nineteenth century moment of feminist revaluation arrived. They argue convincingly that the middle class grounded its moral authority on its responsible Christian family life, with its home-based, pious wife and mother and its provider/protector husband engaged in public commercial, professional or political occupation. What needs more emphasis is how this self-designation was juxtaposed to constructions of the masculinity and femininity of the classes seen as lying above and below. Middle-class ideologues drew a sharp contrast between their group and the barbarous aristocracy with its drinking, gambling, hunting, wenching, duelling men and its vain, idle, frivolous women.[6] The other set of mirrors were the working class, supposedly sunk in ignorance and vice.

In working-class cultures too, when the vision of the good life was evoked, it was often, although not always, in terms of a healthy, secure, independent family life, conditions that became possible only when the family members could be free from exploitation by employers or state authorities. Within this vision, which has sometimes been called the artisan's or industrial worker's view, masculinity was equated with a husband who provided enough to keep his family from having to go to the state (the Poor Law) for help and who thereby protected his family from oppression. Coupled with this masculinity was the femininity of the wife who was a good manager of the family's scant resources (and exhibited all the ingenuity itemised above). Barbara Taylor's *Eve and the New Jerusalem* first called attention to this pairing in the London artisan world and her work has been extended by Anna Clark in *The Struggle for the Breeches: Gender and the Making of the British Working Class*, while Sonia Rose in *Limited Livelihoods* has concentrated on the textile industries and Ellen Ross, in *Love and Toil*, on gender expectations among the East London poor.[7]

But protector/provider masculinity, which featured in trade union wage bargaining and stood at the centre of the demand for a family wage, was also problematic in the way it positioned women in the labour market and, even if unintentionally, sometimes coincided with capitalist priorities. The protector/provider image depended on a view of women as home-based dependents with family and household responsibilities as their primary work and on a gendered view of skill in the workplace. This continually played into the hands of capitalists, who wanted whenever possible to reduce labour costs. Employers defined and treated women, whose income, however small, was always strategic to family survival, as cheap and unskilled labour and left them responsible for all the social costs (like childcare) necessary to their own and their husbands' participation in the labour market. Nancy Grey Osterud has shown how women, who had been highly valued in the family economy, stayed home when their husbands were brought into factory production in the hosiery industry. At home, they were defined as cheap ancillary workers and only when the label stuck were they also brought into factory work.[8] However, since the capitalist labour process always involves a tug of war, Osterud also has indicated how families played the situation to gain whatever possible advantage they could at each new stage.

Of course, working-class masculinity was also equated with prowess at the workplace which extended from strength and skill to collective job control (trade union leverage over the working conditions), nowhere more so than in mining where the fraternity in the face of danger below ground was legendary. Nonetheless there were some industries where conditions of work were so subordinating and trade unionism so weak that the issue of self-respecting masculinity was much more problematic and involved more complex solutions. Important work on docklands and sailor town culture, especially by Pat Ayers and Valerie Burton, is casting light on these issues and showing how many facets come into creating masculinity in these cultures and perhaps all cultures. Writing about Liverpool, Pat Ayers argues that because the casual hiring system of dock work actually pitted men against each other, their solidarities had to be located outside work, in the pub (importantly) and in their religion and ethnicity, e.g., their Irish Catholic men's clubs.[9] In this culture, the superordination or authority in the family also compensated for the relative emasculation at the workplace, an argument made, too, by Valerie Burton about the masculinity of sailor towns. Sailors' myths, as expressed in their popular songs or forebitters, portray themselves as bachelor Jack Tars, or lusty, boozing lads whose intrepidity has to do with boarding any whore, clapped-out or not, and living another day to do a repeat performance. Yet this cultural representation did not coincide with the real situation, which was that sailors had families and indeed families that reproduced the only menfolk willing to go to sea.[10]

In labour movements, the different kinds of masculinity, coupled with their related models of femininity, constrained, sometimes in damaging ways, how women felt they could behave. From the early nineteenth century in Britain there was a powerful cultural offensive coming from above, especially from the evangelical middle class and gentry, which reinforced tendencies already present in working-class culture to confine women to the home; indeed a public women in this period meant nothing more or less than a prostitute. Work on women in movements has been proliferating, first on women in women's movements and increasingly on women in the labour movement.[11] The most recent work is focusing on how women comported and represented themselves in public territory made treacherous by men of their own class as well as by upper-class outsiders, and especially on how they fared in mixed movements with men. A book I am currently editing, called *Radical Femininity,* explores the discursive strategies that women used to navigate dangerous public waters, including a language of militant motherhood which subverted their 'normal' role and asserted that only their public political activism could safeguard the well-being of their families and enable them to resume their household position. As the Chartist women of Newcastle put it: 'We have been told that the province of woman is her home and that the field of politics should be left to men, this we deny: the nature of things renders it impossible.'[12]

The pressures being exerted by the menfolk within the same movement and their inability to prioritise issues of deep importance to women has been under scrutiny in two new studies of turn-of-the-twentieth-century movements indicating the range of options available to women chafed by their gender difficulties. Karen Hunt, in *Equivocal Feminists ... 1884–1911*, explores the problems for feminists who forced a questioning of the Social Democratic Federation's language and culture but never persuaded this first British Marxist organisation to develop even a partly feminist agenda. By contrast, Gillian Scott's work shows how the Women's Co-operative Guild (the women's wing of the British cooperative movement), under the gifted leadership of Margaret Llewelyn Davies between 1896 and 1921, created a feminist politics which held together a movement composed of working-class housewives, who have always been considered the 'unorganisable' constituency, and who had very diverse party political allegiances.[13] European sisters as knowledgeable as Alexandra Kollontai were impressed by this achievement.

The Guild moved in two unifying directions and overarching the two was the concern to disrupt conventional divisions between the public and private spheres. The paid organiser Sarah Reddish knew that

> We are told by some that women are wives and mothers, and that the duties therein involved are enough for them. We reply that men are husbands and fathers, and that they, as such, have duties not to be neglected, but we join in the general opinion that men should also be

interested in the science of government, taking a share in the larger family of the store, the municipality and the State. The WCG has done much towards impressing the fact that women as citizens should take their share in this work.[14]

The first unifying concern was with the self-empowerment for women who were also struggling for political citizenship; this involved learning how to be confident in public, how to hold and chair public meetings, how to write and make public speeches. Secondly, there was the politics of the so-called private sphere over which even working-class men had thrown a thick veil, which concealed terrible suffering to do with marriage, sex and reproduction. The Guild's determination to agitate for changes in the laws concerning divorce, birth control and maternity brought them into open conflict with the Catholic men in the movement who felt these issues to lie beyond the legitimate limits of cooperation's concerns. Taking the penalty for their resoluteness, the women lost a vital subsidy of £400 from the male movement for several years. Significantly, it was when the Guild leadership jettisoned its feminist politics as a vote-loser for the Labour Party and abandoned its democratic structure which had permitted local autonomy, that it prepared the way for a haemorrhage of the membership: 40 percent left between 1938 and 1940.

Vertical Views: Power Relations among Women

Concepts of gender provided one set of pressures operating on women in labour movements: another came from interclass relations between genders and especially relations between women of different classes. There are a number of reasons why this area is the least studied of all: first, the fact that labour and even social history was for a long time man-centred and explored only power relations among men; then when feminists undertook the study of labouring women, it was at first within the political culture of the second-wave Women's Liberation Movement. Here sisterhood was being explored and celebrated, and relations among women were being proposed as intrinsically more nurturing and supportive than those that characterised patriarchal culture (if that was the way you named it), or which characterised late twentieth-century monopoly capitalism (and its proposed socialist replacement as well!). This blanket statement needs qualification, since many British feminist historians were also socialist historians and always made the assumption that conflicting interests could exist among women of different social groups as much as among men.

But of course there are difficulties about locating the class position of women, problems which were identified in the 1970s when it was more fashionable to discuss class.[15] Women have occupied an anomalous position within historical class relations, as they have often been dependent on male kinfolk for material support. Where artisans' wives writing to the *Pioneer* newspaper described themselves as the slaves of slaves, the women kin in the bourgeoisie were also in a dependent position before 1882, given the state of the civil law, which fused wives with husbands, making the husband stand for them both, and given the ideology of separate spheres, which positioned women primarily in the home. The domestic ideology, which received religious, medical and scientific buttressing, made the idea of higher education or paid work for bourgeois women problematic. As William Thompson put it in the *Appeal of One Half the Human Race, Women*, 'a domestic, a civil, a political slave, in the plain unsophisticated sense of the word – in no metaphorical sense – is every married woman'.[16] On the basis of shared oppression, or shared limitation of opportunity, upper-class feminists argued that gender was a key unity, indeed that gender was itself a class. For example, in 1876 the *Englishwoman's Review*, pointing to gender disparity in legal and political rights, declared:

> But there is another sense in which we are justified in talking of women as forming one class, whether in 'the highest, the middle or the humbler ranks of life': a sense in which women whether seamstresses, factory hands, servants, authoresses, countesses or even the women of 'the families of our legislators' do form one common class. There may be every variety of education, thought, or habit; they may differ from each other by nature or by social custom, as much as a prince differs from a peasant, but as long as there is 'class' legislation, so long as the law makes an unsurmountable difference between men and women, women must be spoken of as a separate class. This is the only 'class' legislation remaining in England.[17]

But this statement represented only one point of view in a critical area of disagreement, where positions were continually shifting in dynamic situations, about whether class unity was to be prioritised over gender or vice versa. On the whole, so far in historical struggle women in less powerful social groups, including racial and ethnic as well as class groups, have tended to prioritise social solidarity over gender solidarity. But this has not universally been the case in the past and it remains an open question for the future.[18]

Partly perhaps because of the anomalies of women's position within historical classes, their cross-class relations have been complex and riddled with contradiction. At all times both the differences and similarities between groups are present to be experienced and mobilised. Thus women have clearly acted in ordinary capitalist ways as employers of other women, most spectacularly in the case of domestic servants, the largest occupational group of women from the mid-nineteenth century onwards. And yet this employment took place in the home of the employer, which could allow space for a more fleshed-out emotional interaction than bare cash nexus and lead to friendship, at least with upper servants.

Women's Languages of Power

Besides being involved in employer/employee relations, women from different classes interacted in suffrage movements, in women's trade unions, and in the philanthropic or social work which burgeoned from the late eighteenth century onward. In all these areas, women used a range of discursive strategies which mediated relations between them. I am using the term 'discourse' to mean a powerful system of meanings or knowledge which is not just to be found in written texts but is embodied in actual social institutions and social relations. I am using 'language' to mean a patterned system of images, often existing in binary opposition, which convey a pecking order of value and thus serve either to dignify or devalue people depending upon where they are placed in the contrast.[19] Women used a number of contradictory languages/discourses which seemed to offer supportiveness and solidarity but could equally operate to cement hierarchy and inequality of power. I will spend the rest of this chapter exploring three such languages, namely, of motherhood, of sisterhood and of women workers united. I could as easily add other languages too, like the language of citizenship.

Motherhood

Languages of motherhood were prevalent in scientific philanthropy, which was then professionalised into scientific social work at the turn of the twentieth century. I have written elsewhere about how middle-class women trying to move into the public sphere remodelled the hallowed image of married motherhood in the home by creating a vision of a virgin social mother who did nurturing social work in the public sphere and introduced a home influence into it.[20] But three different and sometimes incompatible kinds of motherhood were operating here, which I have called disciplining, protecting and empowering. The disciplining and the protective faces of motherhood both assumed clients who were either children at risk, adolescent girls in sexual danger or adult working-class women (mothers or workers) who were incapable of acting on their own behalf because so ground down or victimised by their life circumstances. In these cases social workers tended, whether they intended this or not, to infantilise the client (even if she was adult) and to operate political strategies of advocacy, rather than empowering poor women to act and speak in their own right (write!). These tendencies were most pronounced in the social work emanating from the Charity Organisation Society, the Anglican Church, the Ladies' Sanitary Association and some women's social settlements, notably the Women's University Settlement in Bermondsey, which played a pioneering role in developing social work training.

Working-class women could utilise and appreciate the material benefits that might accrue from this kind of social work. But they also resented any infantilising attitude, as evidenced by testimony contrasting the Mothers' Meetings laid on by the social work agencies above and the Women's Co-operative Guild:

> I used for a short time to attend a Mothers' Meeting, and did so more from a point of duty than anything, but after joining the Guild I did not feel to have the patience to listen to the simple childish tales that were read at the former, and did not like to feel we had no voice in its control. There is such a different feeling in speaking of trials and troubles to Guilders (where they are real) than to speak to the Ladies of the Mothers' Meeting. You know that they (the Guilders) have a fellow feeling being all on an equality.[21]

The kinds of social motherhood being operated by scientific philanthropy before 1914 often contained a dominative power relation between social worker and client which could undercut other rhetoric about skilling for citizenship. Helen Bosanquet, activist and ideologue of the Charity Organisation Society in the early-twentieth century, was quite convinced that working-class women deserved the vote and yet her texts were saturated with the disciplining and punitive rhetoric that went along with evaluating cultural difference as cultural deficiency.[22]

Interestingly, Margaret Llewelyn Davies, who eventually became General Secretary of the Women's Co-operative Guild and came from a background similar to that of many later nineteenth-century women social servants, was seen by Guildswomen as an empowering mother. Her conscious strategy was to skill women for citizenship and where possible to enable women to speak for themselves. Thus when asked to supply evidence to the Royal Commission on Divorce and Matrimonial Causes, she solicited testimony from Guildswomen and presented this unprecedented response instead. By contrast the estimable ladies of the Mothers' Union spoke on behalf of their members, which Davies regarded with real disdain. On the occasion of Davies' retirement, testimonials flooded in from Guildswomen, including one from Eleanor Hood of Enfield, who recalled her first attempt at public speaking and portrayed Davies as the epitome of the empowering mother:

> I was almost frightened to death, but when I stood up to speak I saw your face in the audience, and the different expressions that passed over it were an inspiration to me, when you smiled or clapped I went on with a fresh heart, and when you congratulated me at the end, I made up my mind to do all I could to merit your confidence in me. And I am not the only one who has to thank you for showing them what they are capable of doing, over and over again.[23]

Sisterhood

The rhetoric of sisterhood, which featured in the early socialist movement, in the anti-slavery campaign, in interactions between English reformers and colonialised people and in religious discourse, was also prevalent in the political and industrial women's movements at the turn of the twentieth century. It has been conspicuous in women's liberation movements ever since.[24] But here again the discourse could presume and foster either equality or inequality. There can be sisters whose supportiveness empowers other women to develop their potential: the Chartist women often called upon their 'sisters and fellow countrywomen' to take action; the encouraging Margaret Llewelyn Davies was called 'a loving big sister'. On the negative side, there can also be more overweening big sisters who, often without any deliberate intention, confirm the underdevelopedness of their little sisters, not least by constructing the junior siblings as suffering, overburdened little sisters who need not only to be protected but to be represented by bigger sisters in command of more cultural resources of education and time. This is a difficult area because the bigger sisters often genuinely mean well and offer valuable assistance; but the help can also sometimes be experienced as oppressive rather than enabling by its recipients. Emily Pethwick conflated motherhood and sisterhood language, revealing an uncomfortable tension between attitudes of protectiveness and superiority (especially in the last line), in her description of girls' clubs, aimed at young women workers:

> Surely the girl of 15, 16, 17 years needs the happy shelter of home with its individual care and sympathetic companionship. Every girls' club can be that to its members. Every club I know has its 'Mother', who is always at home there, and whose special work is the knowledge of the girls individually, through sympathy, resource, and patience ... [M]any an educated girl coming into the club for even an hour a week is doing the part of the elder sister by giving of her very best to the girls, whether the gift be laughter or learning ... The club leaders have

a unique opportunity of getting at the facts ... They know, too, what the workers want, which is often more than either the workers themselves or their rulers know.[25]

Within the turn-of-the-century women's movements, it was common to presume a spiritual or theological or religious equality but to think that socially divided circumstances made it impossible, at least in the near future, to give working-class women agency. Many of the arguments not only justifying women's suffrage, but more especially women's suffrage on the same basis as that of propertied men, was built on the foundation of this kind of argument. By this means women would be politically enabled to act on behalf of their ground-down poor sisters.

Women Workers

Perhaps the language that might seem to be of most immediate interest to labour historians would be the language conflating all women as workers. This was first in evidence in the midcentury Langham Place feminist moment and was also salient in analyses and policies of the Fabian Women's Group before the First World War, and then surfaced again in second-wave women's liberation movements. The prospectus for the *English Women's Journal*, the first feminist journal to be produced entirely by women, presented itself as a 'working women's journal':

> In the term 'Working Women' it is intended to include all women who are actively engaged in any labours of brain or hand, whether they be the wives and daughters of landed proprietors, devoted to the well-being of their tenantry, or are to be classed among the many other labourers in the broad field of philanthropy; – whether they belong to the army of teachers, public or private, or to the realms of professional artists; or are engaged in any of those manual occupations by which multitudes of British women, at home and in the colonies, gain their daily bread.[26]

The later Fabian women's version acknowledged that the employment experiences of middle- and working-class women had been diametrically different during the Industrial Revolution: middle-class women were removed from the labour market and working-class women increasingly exploited there. But the task now was to build a united women's movement on the foundation of common aspirations to combine useful paid work with motherhood.[27]

But here, too, difficult issues surfaced about hierarchy within the world of women workers. Leaving aside the mid-century proposals for unity which presumed a two-track line of advance, one for 'manual workers' and another for professional women: thus within the

Langham Place employment services there was segregation into these two categories. The situation at the turn of the twentieth-century was more complex, not least because women's trade unions were difficult to sustain and effort increasingly went towards pressing for and then operating legislative protection, for example, via health and safety law and via Trade Boards (later called Wages Councils). Although women did not become capitalists on any large scale, educated women moved into professional employment, where, partly to remain 'womanly' (in the eyes of women as well as men), they took supervisory charge of other women workers or dealt with women and children as their primary professional clientele, in medicine or social work, for example. In the civil service, women reached the higher grades, according to Meta Zimmeck, only in this kind of supervisory capacity over the burgeoning army of women telegraphers and clerical workers in the Post Office and other government departments.[28] Social work as a profession received enormous government support during the First World War, when 'welfare officers' were installed to oversee women workers in munitions and other heavy industry. The whole area of a presumed unity between women as workers is riddled, on closer inspection, with the tensions that bedevil (or bewitch!) the relationship between the professional/managerial class and the lower-paid working class – which has complicated relations among women as well as relations among men.[29]

Whither class and gender in this coming period? The restructuring of the British economy seems to be delivering a feminisation of all paid work. Many industries are being destroyed, like shipbuilding, coal-mining, steel-making and the railways, which were traditional bastions of 'male' jobs, or, put more accurately, work on the better conditions that unionised men historically struggled for and won for themselves. Since equal opportunities battles are still being waged on all levels of employment hierarchies, it is again tempting to argue the unity of all women workers. And yet, the inequalities of power among working women also exist at the same time that they have the common experience of being denied an equality with some men. These complexities of class and gender in horizontal, diagonal and vertical directions need to be recognised before they can be moved beyond.

Notes

1. L. Davidoff and C. Hall, *Family Fortunes: Men and Women of the English Middle Class, 1780–1850*, London, 1987, 13.

2. Maya Korac, 'Women in the Balkan Wars', in Ken Coates (ed.), *Peace Register: Drawing the Peace Dividend*, Bertrand Russell Foundation, Nottingham, 1993; also her 'Understanding Ethnic-National Identity and its Meaning: Questions from Women's Experience', *Women's Studies International Forum*, vol. 18, 4–5, (Summer 1995).

3. 'Richard Pilling's Defence', in F. O'Connor (ed.), *The Trial of Fergus O'Connor and 58 Other Chartists on a Charge of Seditious Conspiracy at Lancaster, 1842*; A. Clark, *Women's Silence, Men's Violence: Sexual Assault in England 1770–1845*, London, 1987, 93–7.

4. For debates on class and gender, see A. Phillips, *Divided Loyalties: Dilemmas of Sex and Class*, London, 1987; S. Alexander, *Becoming a Woman and Other Essays in 19th and 20th-Century Feminist History*, London, 1994.

5. E. Roberts, *A Woman's Place: An Oral History of Working-Class Women, 1890–1940*, Oxford, 1984. For women's networks, see E. Ross, 'Survival Networks: Women's Neighbourhood Sharing in London before World War One', *History Workshop*, 15, (Spring 1983).

6. Davidoff and Hall, *Family Fortunes*, 21; the attack on aristocratic femininity is pervasive in Mary Wollstonecraft, *A Vindication of the Rights of Woman* (1792), Harmondsworth, 1992; for constituting identity vis-à-vis the working class see E. Janes Yeo, *The Contest for Social Science: Relations and Representations of Gender and Class*, London, 1996, chap. 3.

7. B. Taylor, *Eve and the New Jerusalem: Socialism and Feminism in the Nineteenth Century*, London, 1983; A. Clark, *The Struggle for the Breeches. Gender and the Making of the British Working Class*, London, 1995; also her 'The Rhetoric of Chartist Domesticity: Gender, Language and Class in the 1830's and 1840's', *Journal of British Studies*, vol. 31, 1 (1992): 62–88; S. Rose, *Limited Livelihoods: Gender and Class in Nineteenth-Century England*, Berkeley CA, 1992; E. Ross, *Love and Toil: Motherhood in Outcast London, 1870–1918*, New York, 1993.

8. N. Grey Osterud, 'Gender Divisions and the Organization of Work in the Leicester Hosiery Industry', in A. John (ed.), *Unequal Opportunities: Women's Employment in England, 1800–1918,* Oxford, 45–68.

9. Pat Ayers, *The Liverpool Docklands: Life and Work in Athol Street* (Liverpool, 1988).

10. Valerie Burton, "The Work and Home Life of Seafarers with Special Reference to the Port of Southampton, 1871–1921", PhD thesis, University of London, 1988.

11. Dorothy Thompson, 'Women and Nineteenth-century Radical Politics', in J. Mitchell and A. Oakley (eds), *The Rights and Wrongs of Women,* Harmondsworth, 1977; D. Thompson, *The Chartists: Popular Politics in the Industrial Revolution*, Aldershot, 1984; David Jones, 'Women and Chartism', *History*, vol. 68 (1983); and most recently and thoroughly, J. Schwarzkopf, *Women in the Chartist Movement*, London, 1991; E. Janes Yeo (ed.), *Radical Femininity: Women's Self-Representation in British Social Movements*, Manchester, 1998.

12. 'Address of the Female Political Union of Newcastle', *Northern Star*, 9 February 1839; also the Birmingham Female Political Union, *The Charter*, 10 November 1839.

13. Karen Hunt, *Equivocal Feminists: the Social Democratic Federation and the Woman Question, 1884–1911*, Cambridge, 1996; Gillian Scott, '"As a War Horse to the Drum Beat": Representations of Working-class Femininity in the English Women's Co-operative Guild, 1880s-1940s', in Yeo, *Radical Femininity*; also her forthcoming book on the Guild to be published by Taylor and Francis.

14. Sarah Reddish, 'Organiser's Report. Annual Report of the Women's Co-operative Guild', *Co-operative Congress Report*, 1894, 58.

15. A. Kuhn and A. Wolpe, *Feminism and Materialism: Women and Modes of Production*, London, 1978; L. Sargent (ed.), *Women and Revolution: A Discussion of the Unhappy Marriage of Marxism and Feminism*, London, 1981.

16. W. Thompson, *Appeal of One Half the Human Race, Women*, (1825), London, 1983, 67.

17. *Englishwoman's Review*, May 1876, 200.

18. Significantly, working-class women have tended to organise on women's issues within a mixed-sex movement, whether that movement was Owenite socialism early in the nineteenth century, or the cooperative movement at the beginning of the next. But socialist women like Hannah Mitchell, fed up with the reluctance of labour men to focus gender issues at the turn of the twentieth century, did begin to prioritise work in the women's suffrage movement over activity in labour movements: H. Mitchell, *The Hard Way Up: The Autobiography of Hannah Mitchell, Suffragette and Rebel*, ed. G. Mitchell, London, 1977, 126, 149, 175, 179.

19. For a more extended discussion of discourse and language, see my *Contest for Social Science*, intro.

20. Eileen Janes Yeo, 'Social Motherhood and the Sexual Communion of Labour in British Social Science, 1850–1950', *Women's History Review*, vol. 1, 1 (1992): 755; also my *Contest for Social Science*, chap. 5.

21. Women's Co-operative Guild, *Life as We Have Known It*, ed. M. Llewelyn Davies, (1931), London, 1975, 40.

22. I discuss her at greater length in *Contest for Social Science*, chap. 9.

23. E. Hood to M. Llewelyn Davies, 5 October 1921, Women's Co-operative Guild Collection, vol. 8, 46–7, London Library of Political Science.

24. For the rhetoric of the anti-slavery movement, e.g., a pendant of 1826 picturing a female slave and inscribed, 'am I not a woman and sister' and for pleas for British women to get involved in India and raise 'their Eastern sisters to their own level', see V. Ware, *Beyond the Pale: White Women, Racism and History*, London, 1992, 71,130; R. Feuer, 'The Meaning of "Sisterhood". The British Women's Movement and Protective Labor Legislation, 1870–1900', *Victorian Studies*, vol. 31, 2 (1988), assumes rather than interrogates the concept of sisterhood; however, G. Holloway, 'A Common Cause? Class Relations in the Women's Industrial Movement, 1870–1920', Ph.D. thesis University of Sussex, 1995, explores the issues in perceptive ways. I shall be doing further writing to illuminate the contested nature of sisterhood.

25. E. Pethwick, 'Working Girls' Clubs', in W. Reason (ed.), *University and Social Settlements*, London, 1898, 110, 113.

26. C. Mitchell, *The Newspaper Press Directory ... 1858*, quoted in J. Rendall, '"A Moral Engine?" Feminism, Liberalism and the *English Woman's Journal*', in J. Rendall (ed.), *Equal or Different? Women's Politics 1800–1914*, Oxford, 1987, 115.

27. See, e.g., M. Atkinson, *The Economic Foundations of the Women's Movement*, Fabian Tract no. 175, (June 1914): 15–18.

28. M. Zimmeck, 'Strategies and Strategems for the Employment of Women in the British Civil Service, 1919–1939', *Historical Journal*, vol. 27 (1984): 904–5.

29. John and Barbara Ehrenreich provide the most useful analysis of these tensions in their article on 'The Professional Managerial Class', which is reprinted with critical responses in P. Walker (ed.), *Between Capital and Labour*, Hassocks, 1979.

CHAPTER 5

ETHNICITY AND LABOUR HISTORY

WITH SPECIAL REFERENCE TO IRISH MIGRATION

John Belchem

Ethnicity

Ethnicity, a form of cultural belonging, is a relatively recent addition to the conceptual vocabulary of history and the social sciences: its first recorded use in the *Oxford English Dictionary* is 1953. For the most part, it has been deployed negatively, applied only to the 'other', to migrant and minority groups: in Britain, for example, Englishness has been assumed as a superior non-ethnic norm over and above the 'ethnic' characteristics of others.[1] While such usage may be traced back to the Greek *ethnos,* a synonym of gentile, my approach is more historical and inclusive. Whether through ascription, affective preference or participant primordialism, ethnic identities are relational, constructed in sociohistorical dialogue between dominant and subordinate groups. Put bluntly, there can be no ethnic 'other' without an ethnic 'us'.[2] Thus, while giving a voice to the other, to previously excluded marginal and minority groups, a focus on ethnicity (as on gender) should also encourage critical deconstruction of dominant formations. Furthermore, ethnicity combines affect with material interest. As such, it may offer the labour historian new understanding of the space between socio-economic context and cultural representation.

Until goaded by feminism and postmodernism, labour historians were reluctant to consider identities other than class. Among the gamut of 'multiple identities', ethnic affiliation now commands attention. The end of history has ushered in the era of ethnicity: in the absence of ideological confrontation, ethnic cleavage and conflict have provoked the horrors of genocidal 'ethnic cleansing'. At the domestic level, the development of the postindustrial service society has exposed the problem of the underclass, a deprived and disadvantaged residuum composed for the most part of ethnic minority groups. Unwilling and/or unable to abandon decaying inner-city areas for new patterns of decentralised employment and consumption, these ethnic minority groups have fallen (whether through choice or constraint) into double dispossession. To the consternation of neoclassical economists and policy makers, immobility is the preferred option. A form of cultural (and segregated) security, the community bonds of ethnicity preclude movement outward and upward, away from the 'internal colony' and its culture of poverty.[3]

Although sociological analysis tends not to look back beyond recent postcolonial in-migration, such ethnic 'visibility' has a long history. Irish migrants, the underclass of early industrialisation, were the focus of concern in discussion of the 'Condition of England' question in the 1830s and 1840s. In one of the foundation texts, *The Moral and Physical Condition of the Working Classes ... in Manchester* (1832), James Kay, an advocate of social reform at the national level, mobilised prejudices against the Irish to construct an image of the 'nation' from which they were excluded.[4] Thereafter, Irish migrants were kept in their place (as a valuable if not indispensable economic presence)[5] by an ethnic identity which was as much imposed upon them as constructed by themselves. Whether in Britain or America, they were to be cast as the internal 'other' against whom the host identity or 'ethnicity' was defined and confirmed.[6]

Ideas about the Irish

Irish migrants are an interesting case study. According to functional analysis, migrant labour needs to be not only a quantitative addition (to allow expansion of production when lack of domestic labour might impose constraint) but also a qualitatively different source of supply (low-level labour prepared to accept conditions below normal standards).[7] In the case of the Irish, there were no legal, linguistic, pigmentary or other means of distinguishing and defining them as alien and hence more exploitable: in this respect, their position would seem more favourable than that of 'German' Poles on the Ruhr, let alone that of later 'guestworkers', illegal immigrants or colonial migrants from a distant 'dark' continent.[8] Furthermore, as David Fitzpatrick has observed, Irish migrants were unusually well-tailored for the role of servicing other people's industrial revolutions (allowing Ireland itself to remain 'green', an emerald isle relatively unpolluted by industrialisation). Young unmarried adults with an even sex balance, they left home without question, entering the labour markets of their new lands of residence with low expectations of comfort and without the burden of accompanying dependents – the age selectivity, sex balance and low return-home rates distinguish the Irish from other 'moving Europeans'.[9] Bred to migrate, they readily withstood the 'shocks' of displacement, displaying 'coping capacities', which the Chicago School, Oscar Handlin and other pioneer investigators of the 'uprooted' failed to appreciate.[10] Given such favourable 'human capital' factors for industrial development – not least their readiness to speak English and to undertake tasks which native workers preferred not to do – why did the Irish encounter prejudice in their new lands of residence?

Ethnic stereotyping provided the requisite labelling to facilitate labour market segmentation. Through 'ethnic' portrayal of 'Paddy' as drunken and feckless, fit only for the most menial physical labour, Irish migrants were kept confined to the bottom of the labour market. The stereotype soon entered the 'common sense' of lowly native workers, enabling them to exercise options, to lift themselves above the least desirable occupations. Thereafter, a harsh self-fulfilling logic prevailed: set off from society by the type of work they did, the Irish were identified with the roughest of rough labour, performed by the lowest of the low. Stigmatised by ethnic stereotype as more suited to strenuous work than their Anglo peers, Irish migrants endured a rationalisation of labour exploitation reminiscent, Peter Way notes, of the assertion that blacks were built to work under a broiling sun or in fetid rice swamps.[11]

The gender implications of this stereotyping merit deconstruction. As the heaviest and hardest manual labour was undertaken by Irish migrants and blacks, physical abilities were at a discount in the construction of mainstream working-class masculinity. Emphasis was placed on craft skill and discipline. This construction, with its emphasis on masculine 'property in skill', was subsequently adopted (and privileged) by labour history, which has tended to idealise such artisan culture as the plebeian prototype of working-class consciousness.[12] Conflict over skill and control of production has dominated the conventional narrative, closing off the real history from below, the struggle over material conditions which preoccupied women, the unskilled and ethnic migrant communities.

At this level of struggle and survival, ethnicity can prove a functional means of mobilising resources. As Weber suggested, ethnicity exists in direct relationship to its usefulness as a mechanism of group formation and mobilisation. Whereas classes in the Marxian sense must develop their sense of identity, forms of organisation and culture *ab initio*, ethnic groups can call upon their sense of ethnicity and their forms of ethnic bonding as a resource. From the outset, as John Rex notes, they are 'ethnics-for-themselves'. There can be rapid progress from ethnic identity (factors which distinguish one communal group from another) to ethnic identification (consciousness of the significance of these factors). Awareness of ethnic category leads readily through participation in ethnic network and ethnic association to ethnic community. Given this facility, ethnic forms of collective association and mutuality can reach into parts untouched by the class-based movements privileged in conventional labour history.[13]

However, there are problems in applying such functional resource mobilisation theory. For the Irish migrants of the nineteenth century, the necessary components of ethnic affiliation – a common proper name; a myth of common ancestry; shared historical memories; elements of common culture; link with a homeland; and a sense of solidarity – were not all in place, ready for instant activation. As suggested above, ethnic identity, a sense of Irishness, developed only through the complex interaction of ascription and affiliation. Migration may have helped to construct an 'imagined' national identity, to superimpose a wider 'invented' affiliation upon traditional and instinctive subnational loyalties, but it was a delayed and interactive process within which host labelling was an important factor.

Chain Migration

As the Irish diaspora evinces, chain migration replaced local and circular forms to become the dominant migration system in nineteenth-century Europe, facilitating long-distance movement from densely populated peripheral areas – particularly Ireland, Italy and the Polish provinces – to core industrial and commercial regions.[14] Working through family networks, social connections and regional solidarities, chain migration involved social arrangements with people already at a destination, who characteristically helped newcomers to find jobs and housing, thereby protecting them from disorientation, dislocation and anomic behaviour. The initial mechanics of chain migration preserved old subethnic allegiances, functioning along lines of clan, county and regional filiations. In the 'paddy camps' of Lowell, Massachusetts, workplace loyalties to specific foremen were based upon clan/family/regional ties simply transferred across the briny ocean. Beyond the workplace, each camp maintained a distinct physical appearance based on regional provenance, as in 'the Acre', fiercely-defended territory of migrants from south-west Ireland. Faction fighting, indeed, was transplanted with undiminished vigour: 'Far-ups' and 'Far-downs' adapted the intimidatory tactics of the agrarian secret societies to defend territory and jobs in urban-industrial America. In the shanty camps of canal construction, rivalry between Corkonians and Connaughtmen was the axis around which existence was ordered, subsets which created social solidarity but more profoundly led to dissonance in the canaller community.[15]

Such fierce rivalries notwithstanding, combatants were perceived by resident Americans as one and the same, Irish. Continually labelled in this way, migrants began to take an inverted pride in their 'Irishness'. Life in America, Patrick Ford later observed, elevated the Irish out of 'the littleness of countyism into the broad feeling of nationalism'.[16] The development of networks and associations above the region, clan and faction, however, depended on a number of factors. Here I wish briefly to highlight two: the presence of an Irish middle class, and the role of the Catholic Church.

The Irish Middle Class

Previously neglected, the middle-class presence in the Irish diaspora has gained attention through revisionist interest in what Roy Foster has called 'Micks on the make'.[17] Some middle-class migrants favoured 'ethnic fade', distancing themselves from all things Irish to effect the quickest route to economic success and assimilation. A significant number, however, having identified their best interests (or market niche) in servicing the migrant community, chose to accentuate their Irishness. They exercised an important influence over their less fortunate fellow-countrymen, encouraging them to abandon transience, faction fighting and other behaviour which conformed to host labelling, and to adopt instead a transregional national or ethnic 'Irish' pride in themselves. Once implanted, ethnic associational culture provided a means by which successful Irish-Americans could guard against social radicalism while keeping a check on violent inflexions of nationalism. Sponsored by the Irish-American middle class, Irish organisations sought to attract blue-collar workers to a programme of Celtic cultural ethnicity, promoted in a manner which conformed to the norms and values of the host society.[18] At the same time, middle-class women in the ethnic community acted as 'social housekeepers': class status, female activism and mutual aid were interwoven, Donna Gabaccia notes, as they 'used their "brooms" simultaneously to sweep away native-born competitors, to guarantee their own status, and to promote ethnic group survival'.[19] The Irish example confirms recent comparative research: throughout late nineteenth-century Europe, ethnic associations 'tended to be related to social class, to be bids for group leadership'.[20]

In large migrant enclaves, there was considerable internal stratification, but socio-economic success was often legitimised through ethnic leadership, both cultural and political. Merchants, professionals, publicans and tradesmen provided an influential and respected leadership cadre for ethnic action in Liverpool, where the 1841 census recorded 49,639 Irish-born, some 17.3 percent of the population. In expectation of nationalist revolution in Ireland in 1848, shipping agents, doctors and tradesmen revivified the Ribbonite culture of secrecy to penetrate deep into the migrant community, establishing a network of clubs in sympathetic pubs, temperance hotels and private houses.[21] Throughout the nineteenth century upward mobility into the 'ethnic' middle class was generally topped off by political leadership. Biographical details of the Irish National Party councillors in Liverpool show three major groups: lawyers, doctors and other professionals whose practices covered the Irish community; traders who prospered and/or diversified as they took responsibility for the Liverpool end of business with Ireland; and shopkeepers and others who attended to the daily needs of the Liverpool-Irish. This last group contained some genuine 'rags to riches' stories, entrepreneurs who made their fortune supplying basic pleasures within the ethnic enclave – for example, J. Clancy who began as a 'hotel boots' and then developed a lucrative tobacconist business, worth over £25,000 on his death; and 'Dandy Pat' Byrne who started work as a dock labourer, before acquiring a string of public houses.[22]

The Role of the Catholic Church

Australia

In Australia, where the Irish were by far the largest ethnic minority, constituting about 25 percent of all immigrants from 1788 to the early twentieth century, the middle class held back from 'Irish' mobilisation until prompted into action by the Catholic Church. Originally in the control of English Benedictines, the church underwent 'hibernicisation' to cater for the Irish influx. Cardinal Moran hastened the process by championing Irish Home Rule, trusting that its attainment would greatly improve the status and standing of Catholic Australians. Once blessed by the hierarchy, Irish associational culture emerged from relative obscurity to attract the temporal resources (and secular aspirations) of successful Irish immigrants. Ideals of colonial success and loyalty readily harmonised with hopes for Ireland (as for Australia) as an independent dominion within the British empire.[23]

Despite its exclusive and integrative beginnings, Catholic-led ethnic culture developed in a radical direction. Dismayed by Protestant conservative reaction against Catholic claims at the time of federation, Moran gave his blessing to the Australian Labor Party. Sectarian strife was not long delayed, provoked by Archbishop Mannix's radical advocacy of Catholic (and workers') claims during the frenzied atmosphere of the First World War. Mannix became the hero of working-class Catholics – and the arch-villain of patriotic established Protestants (in whose ranks Irish Protestant immigrants were well represented) – as he led the successful anti-conscription campaign of 1916, upholding the cause of the Irish rebellion while he condemned the capitalist war, Australian society and anti-Catholic discrimination.

Under Mannix, Irishness became a characteristic not of the Irish-born but of the Catholic worker, of those who fared least well in the Australian narrative of material advance. For all their 'ordinariness and normality' as Australians, Irish Catholics lagged behind others in reaping the rewards. Stirred into recognition of their relative deprivation by Mannix's rhetoric, the Irish Catholic working class were drawn into a rich and overlapping pattern of assertive associational culture, embracing the Labor Party branch and parish-based sporting and welfare societies. Mannix had succeeded in fusing religious, ethnic and class identities, but in a manner detrimental to the wider projection of the Australian labour movement. Seen from outside, such developments undermined the carefully-constructed nonsectarian image of the Australian Labor Party. Labour was stigmatised as Irish and Catholic, and hence un-Australian. This potent sectarian backlash persisted well into the 1920s, by which time, however, nationalist associational culture had reverted to its low Australian norm as the Irish cause lost direction and identity.[24] Henceforth, Irishness was expressed in an informal and domestic manner: while eschewing specific ethnic associations in the public sphere, Irish-Australians delighted in giving Irish names to their homes. In the interwar Australian city, identity and affiliation tended to be determined by locality – the symbols of local pride were as likely to be the local football ground, town-hall steeple, pub or bookmaker as the Catholic Church – but the incidence of intra-marriage, street crime and gang behaviour (the 'larrikin push') suggested an Irish 'apartness'.[25] Some Irish-Australians played up to the image by constructing a 'culture of poverty', which eschewed the Australian ethic of individual material advancement in favour of the communality and solidarity available only at the bottom of the social (but not spiritual) scale.[26]

England

Throughout the Irish diaspora, ethnic and religious identity were interwoven, a symbiotic relationship which 'made Irish, catholic, and catholic, Irish'. Catholic cultural provision was the immediate priority in areas of high Irish migration in Britain. Walker's study of Dundee shows how the church created 'an entire way of life based upon the parish church, school and church-hall', a 'community within a community' in which 'religious, political, economic, educational and recreational elements were so fused as to form a culture from which total withdrawal was unlikely'.[27] In Liverpool, the church, spurred by competition from Irish pubs offering various forms of convivial, bibulous and nationalist culture, decided to offer its own 'cradle to grave' range of welfare and recreational provision. Liverpool's north end emerged as a distinctively Irish – and Catholic – community in which new churches with Irish priests became the centre of associational life, encouraging the tendency to residential propinquity. In these dockland parishes, the benefits reached down to casual labourers and their families, bad risks excluded from the ranks of organised labour whose actuarial calculations of collective mutuality precluded such 'moral hazards' and 'adverse selection'. By the late nineteenth century there was a flourishing local 'Vereinskatholizismus', to use the German term for the multiplication of organisations designed to meet the special needs – spiritual, economic and recreational – of every identifiable group within the Catholic population.[28]

While primarily concerned with spiritual salvation, or rather the prevention of leakage from the faith, such Catholic welfare provision sought also to prepare the poor for assimilation and citizenship. However, by imparting 'respectable' values within a self-enclosed network of charity and collective mutuality, Catholic social policy served to underline Catholic apartness. Indeed, as in Australia, it may well have engendered a dependency culture or an inverse pride in poverty and destitution. In Liverpool, as in Dundee, poverty was rationalised by the conflation of religious adherence and ethnic affiliation.[29] Sanctified by Catholicism, poverty became the proud hallmark of being genuinely Irish.

America

In America, Catholic culture promoted a more positive image. At the outset, it often offered no more than defensive segregation, a 'comfort station' (in Lawrence McCaffrey's terminology) or safe haven from 'Know-Nothing' and other forms of nativist prejudice. Self-defence, however, developed into self-assertion. Within the interlocking network of parish institutions, Irish migrants, heavily Catholic and working class, gained a new confidence and identity which soon enabled them to stand forward against Yankee prejudice, discrimination and intolerance as proud Irish-Americans. Some, indeed, sought a more integrated form of hyphenated identity, placing themselves at the head of other Catholic ethnic groups as the leaders of Catholic America. The Knights of Columbus, which emphasised Catholic and American loyalties over narrowly Irish ones, proved very popular with successful second-generation 'lace-curtain' Irish-Americans.[30]

With varying degrees of success, Catholic culture served to mediate socio-economic, gender and other tensions within the ethnic community. Church-based culture offered considerable opportunities and space for women. Parish facilities enabled Irish-American women to band together in instrumental manner, less for 'fraternal' recreational, social or political pursuits than for economic and religious purposes. Such instrumentalism was encouraged by nuns, sisterhoods who offered a national network of social services for Irish-American women, providing training schools and employment services, houses of refuge and shelter, medical facilities and day nurseries. Trusting to heighten the spirituality of immigrant women and their daughters, the Sisters of Mercy helped them to acquire economic self-sufficiency.[31]

For Irish migrant women, Catholic sodalities and other forms of associational culture served to complement the two key components of the ethnic community: kinship ties (which in the migrant context more nearly resembled peer groups than lineages) ; and neighbourliness. Constructed in this way, ethnic communities should not be studied in terms of the conventional distinction between private and public. Ethnic associational culture operated within an enlarged private space shared by men and women: the public sphere was further off, beyond a boundary which some married women were perhaps never to cross. Significantly, once the public associational framework began to decline (along with patterns of neighbourhood residence), the maintenance of 'symbolic' ethnicity came to depend more on women. An optional lifestyle, ethnicity became domesticated, a residual matter of family festivals, stories, tales and the socialisation of children.[32]

As the Irish experience attests, generational tensions probably caused as much conflict as gender or class differences within the ethnic community. Such problems were compounded when the ethnic culture of pioneer migrants was challenged or repudiated not only by their settler descendants but by later arrivals (a different generation) from the homeland. Here there is a need for comparative research on Irish-Australia and Irish-America: unlike the latter, the former was not replenished and redefined by continuing stem migration, by successive waves of newcomers from the homeland. Emmons's work on Butte, Montana has shown how generational tensions pulled the Irish apart, jeopardising their control of this high-wage, hard-rock mining town. The key underground workers, an 'ethno-occupational aristocracy', manipulated Irish organisations (most notably the Ancient Order of Hibernians, the Clan-na-Gael, and the Irish-dominated Miners Union) to safeguard their privileges and security, rigorously excluding their transient fellow-countrymen who showed no interest in steady employment and home ownership. The next generation, however, aspired higher: sons preferred to cross the collar gap, abandoning the mines and exclusively Irish forms of associational culture. Wages and security were later put at risk when Butte's disposable labour force was swollen by the arrival of a new generation of Irish immigrants. Imbued with Larkinite social radicalism, they joined together in class alliance with disadvantaged ethnic groups to mount a fundamental challenge to the cosy ethnic/corporate/union world of the settled Irish workers.[33]

Field of Study

By focusing on Irish migrants, this chapter has highlighted some of the structural strengths and weaknesses of ethnic mobilisation. This is not to suggest that ethnic communities should be studied in isolation: such an approach would tend simply to confirm their marginalisation. As stated at the outset, ethnicity must be studied as fluid and relational, part of the sociohistorical dialogue – along with class, gender and other vocabularies – between dominant and subordinate groups. Until recently, labour historians tended to regard ethnicity as divisive and dysfunctional, a hindrance to working-class collectivism. Perspectives are changing to suggest a positive or symbiotic relationship between ethnicity and class. An element of competition remains implicit in some postmodernist accounts which highlight the bewildering array of choice for individuals as ethnic and class identities, protean forms of consciousness devoid of anterior meaning, were continually contested, redefined and repackaged.[34] With the de-centring of class, however, historians have come to appreciate the salience of ethnic affiliation. Ethnicity is recognised either as a functional and inclusive alternative to exclusive class-based forms of collective behaviour, or as a proactive force, an essential preliminary to the construction of wider class-based attitudes and structures.[35]

Class formation in America is now understood as ethnocultural and segmented, a cumulative interethnic and intergenerational process. Building upon their ethnic networks, Irish-Americans contributed much to the American house of labour. Elevated to supervisory status and union leadership in steel mills, iron foundries, anthracite mines and railroad yards, Irish-American blue-collar workers were disproportionately concentrated in the best-paid and most highly-unionised trades by 1900, placed in charge of the new unskilled labour force recruited from Eastern and Southern Europe.[36] No longer the target of nativist prejudice, the 'black' Irish had become white, boosted by the 'uplifting effect' of subsequent waves of 'foreign' in-migration. Old stereotypes were abandoned along with pseudo-scientific taxonomies. No longer portrayed as physically different, Paddy and Bridget were recast as Maggie and Jiggs in a comedy of suburban middle-class manners, where Irish-Americans were applauded as role models, as suitable intermediaries to acculturate the new wave of European immigrants.[37] As union leaders (and urban political bosses), Irish-Americans may have constructed some interethnic solidarity among the 'not-yet-white ethnics'. As workplace culture brokers for the white American mainstream, however, they implanted dominant 'ethnic' attitudes, thereby ensuring the spread of racist stereotyping and prejudice. Originally an ethnic minority, the Irish were to contribute much to 'Americanisation from the bottom up'.[38]

Notes

1. Catherine Hall, "'From Greenland's Icy Mountains ... to Africa's Golden Sand": Ethnicity, Race and Nation in Mid-Nineteenth Century England', *Gender and History*, 5 (1993): 212–30.
2. For an introduction to the vast amount of theoretical and conceptual writing on ethnicity, see J. Hutchinson and A.D. Smith (eds), *Ethnicity*, Oxford, 1996. As the Project Director conceded, research funded by the European Science Foundation on 'Comparative Studies on Governments and Non-dominant Ethnic Groups in Europe, 1850–1940' concentrated on ethnic minorities, see F.M.L. Thompson, 'Series Preface', in M. Engman, F.W. Carter, A.C. Hepburn and C.G. Pooley (eds), *Ethnic Identity in Urban Europe*, Aldershot, 1992, xix. See also, Richard Williams, *Hierarchical Structures and Social Value: The Creation of Black and Irish Identities in the United States,* Cambridge, 1990.
3. M. Cross, 'Introduction: Migration, the City and the Urban Dispossessed', in M. Cross (ed.), *Ethnic Minorities and Industrial Change in Europe and North America,* Cambridge, 1992; M. Hechter, *Internal Colonialism*, London, 1975, xv.
4. Mary Poovey, 'Curing the "Social Body" in 1832: James Phillips Kay and the Irish in Manchester', *Gender and History*, 5 (1993): 196–211.
5. J.G. Williamson, 'The Impact of the Irish on British Labor Markets During the Industrial Revolution', *Journal of Economic History*, xlvi (1986): 693–720.
6. For the political aspects of this process, see John Belchem, 'Nationalism, Republicanism and Exile: Irish Emigrants and the Revolutions of 1848', *Past and Present*, 146 (1995): 103–35. See also, Dale T. Knobel, *Paddy and the Republic: Ethnicity and Nationality in Antebellum America*, Middletown CT, 1986.
7. Stephen Castles, 'Migrants and Minorities in Post-Keynesian Capitalism: the German Case', in Cross (ed.), *Ethnic Minorities*, 36–54.

8. R.C. Murphy, *Guestworkers in the German Reich: a Polish Community in Wilhemian Germany*, New York, 1983; Ulrich Herbert, *A History of Foreign Labor in Germany, 1880–1980*, Ann Arbor MI, 1990.

9. David Fitzpatrick, *Irish Emigration, 1801–1921*, Dublin, 1984, 32.

10. For a useful introduction to historiographical developments, see David Ward, *Poverty, Ethnicity and the American City, 1840–1925*, Cambridge, 1989, chap. 6; and Leo Lucassen, 'The Gulf between Long Term and Short Term Approaches in Immigration: A Reassessment of the Chicago School's Assimilation Concept', paper presented to the 'European Social Science History Conference', Noordwijkerhout, 9–11 May 1996.

11. Peter Way, *Common Labour: Workers and the Digging of North American Canals, 1780–1860*, Cambridge, 1993, 90.

12. David Roediger, 'Race and the Working-class Past in the United States: Multiple Identities and the Future of Labour History', *International Review of Social History*, 38 (1993): Supplement, 135–7; Anna Clark, *The Struggle for the Breeches: Gender and the Making of the British Working Class*, Berkeley CA, 1995, 25.

13. John Rex, 'Ethnic Mobilisation in Multi-cultural Societies', in J. Rex and B. Drury (eds), *Ethnic Mobilisation in Multi-Cultural Europe*, Aldershot, 1994, 3–12. See also J. Rex, D. Joly and C. Wilpert (eds), *Immigrant Associations in Europe*, Aldershot, 1987; and A.C. Hepburn, 'Ethnic Identity and the City', in Engman et al., *Ethnic Identity in Urban Europe*, 1–9.

14. Leslie Page Moch, *Moving Europeans: Migration in Western Europe since 1650*, Bloomington IN, 1992.

15. Brian Mitchell, *The Paddy Camps: The Irish of Lowell, 1821–61*, Urbana IL, 1988; Way, *Common Labour*, 192–9. See also George W. Potter, *To the Golden Door: The Story of the Irish in Ireland and America*, Boston MA, 1960, chap. 32; David Montgomery, 'The Irish and the American Labor Movement', in D.N. Doyle and O.D. Edwards (eds), *America and Ireland, 1776–1976*, Westport, 1980, 206–9; and R.S. Wilentz, 'Industrializing America and the Irish: Towards the New Departure', *Labor History*, 20 (1979): 582.

16. Quoted in T.N. Brown, *Irish-American Nationalism*, Philadelphia and New York, 1966, 21.

17. Roy Foster, 'Marginal Men and Micks on the Make: The Uses of Irish Exile c.1840–1922', in *Paddy and Mr Punch*, London, 1995, 281–305.

18. D.B. Light Jr, 'The Role of Irish-American Organizations in Assimilation and Community Formation', in P.J. Drudy (ed.), *The Irish in America: Emigration, Assimilation and Impact*, Cambridge, 1985, 113–42.

19. Donna Gabaccia, *From the Other Side: Women, Gender and Immigrant Life in the U.S., 1820–1990*, Bloomington IN, 1994, 92.

20. Hepburn, 'Ethnic identity and the City', 4.

21. John Belchem, '"Freedom and Friendship to Ireland": Ribbonism in Early Nineteenth-century Liverpool', *International Review of Social History*, 39 (1994): 33–56; and *idem*, 'Liverpool in the Year of Revolution: the Political and Associational Culture of the Irish Immigrant Community in 1848', in John Belchem (ed.), *Popular Politics, Riot and Labour: Essays in Liverpool History, 1790–1940*, Liverpool, 1992, 68–97.

22. Biographical details can be obtained from the appendices of C.D. Watkinson, 'The Liberal Party on Merseyside in the Nineteenth Century', unpublished Ph.D. thesis, University of Liverpool, 1967; and B. O'Connell, 'The Irish Nationalist Party in Liverpool, 1873–1922', unpublished M.A. thesis, University of Liverpool, 1971.

23. As well as the classic study, Patrick O'Farrell, *The Irish in Australia*, Kensington, NSW, 1986, see also C. McConville, 'Emigrant Irish and Suburban Catholics: Faith and Nation in Melbourne and Sydney', unpublished Ph.D. thesis, University of Melbourne, 1984, 301–19.

24. Frank Farrell, 'J.H. Scullin, the Irish Question and the Australian Labor Party', in C. Kiernan (ed.), *Australia and Ireland 1788–1988,* Dublin, 1986, 156–69.
25. S. Alomes, 'Culture, Ethnicity and Class in Australia's Dominion Period, 1900–39', in Kiernan (ed.), *Australia and Ireland, 1788–1988,* 189–90. McConville, 'Emigrant Irish and Suburban Catholics', chap. 7.
26. O'Farrell, *The Irish in Australia,* 299.
27. W.M. Walker, *Juteopolis: Dundee and its Textile Workers, 1885–1923,* Edinburgh, 1979, 55, 122, 129.
28. John Belchem, 'The Immigrant Alternative: Ethnic and Sectarian Mutuality among the Liverpool Irish during the Nineteenth Century', in O. Ashton, R. Fyson and S. Roberts (eds), *The Duty of Discontent: Essays for Dorothy Thompson,* London, 1995, 231–50. See also H. McLeod, 'Building the "Catholic Ghetto": Catholic Organizations 1870–1914', in W.J. Sheils and D. Wood (eds), *Studies in Church History: Voluntary Religion,* Oxford, 1986, 411–44.
29. W.M. Walker, 'Irish Immigrants in Scotland: their Priests, Politics and Parochial Life', *Historical Journal,* 15 (1972): 649–67.
30. Lawrence J. McCaffrey, *Textures of Irish America,* Syracuse NY, 1992, 47–88. See also the local studies in T.J. Meagher (ed.), *From Paddy to Studs: Irish-American Communities in the Turn of the Century era,* New York, 1986.
31. H. Diner, *Erin's Daughters in America: Irish Immigrant Women in the Nineteenth Century,* Baltimore MD, 1983, chap. 6.
32. Gabaccia, *From the Other Side,* 121–3.
33. D.M. Emmons, *The Butte Irish: Class and Ethnicity in an American Mining Town, 1875–1925,* Urbana IL, 1989, chap. 3–7.
34. Such is the approach adopted in Steven Fielding, *Class and Ethnicity: Irish Catholics in England, 1880–1939,* Buckingham, 1993.
35. John Belchem, 'The Irish in Britain, United States and Australia: Some Comparative Reflections', in Patrick Buckland and John Belchem (eds), *The Irish in British Labour History,* Conference Proceedings in Irish Studies, 1, Liverpool, 1992, 19–28.
36. D.N. Doyle, 'The Irish and American Labour, 1880–1920', *Saothar: Journal of the Irish Labour History Society,* 1 (1975): 42–53.
37. K. Donovan, 'Good old Pat: an Irish-American Stereotype in Decline', *Éire-Ireland,* 15 (1980): 6–14; and J.J. Appel, 'From Shanties to Lace Curtains: the Irish Image in *Puck,* 1876–1910', *Comparative Studies in Society and History,* 13 (1971): 365–75. See also, Noel Ignatiev, *How the Irish Became White,* New York, 1995.
38. J.R. Barrett, 'Americanization from the Bottom Up: Immigration and the Remaking of the Working Class in the United States, 1880–1930', *Journal of American History,* 79 (1992): 996–1020.

CHAPTER 6

THE ROLE OF RELIGION IN SOCIAL AND LABOUR HISTORY

Patrick Pasture

Some readers may find it surprising to find here,[1] in an overview of the state of labour and working-class history in Europe, a chapter on religion and Christian workers' organisations. Indeed social historians, in particular labour historians on the European continent (though France and Italy seem to a certain extent to be an exception to this trend), usually focus almost exclusively on Marxist-socialist or social-democratic labour movements and adopt an outspoken secularist perspective. Consequently, they tend to overlook or, rather, to underestimate the role of religion as well as of the church(es) in modern, industrial societies.[2]

In the last fifteen to twenty years, however, this situation seems to have altered fundamentally. Religion has moved onto the agenda of social history and is increasingly perceived as a basic dimension of life in industrial societies, offering a source of inspiration and identification. The role of the churches has also been reassessed, and in particular the social and political activity of Christian lay militants. This development is expressed in a growing number of studies devoted to Christian workers' organisations, which were largely neglected in traditional labour and working-class historiography. Rather than provide an account of the 'state of the art' in the form of a simple review of the literature regarding these Christian working-class organisations, I would like to assess this (in my view) fundamental shift in perception and to outline some particular developments in social history – as well as in the sociology of work and in political science –

that I consider to be of general importance and particularly relevant for labour historians. I begin my account with the renewed interest in the Christian labour movement, but subsequently expand the scope of my contribution to remarkable parallel developments not only in the study of labour history, but in the study of the social history of the churches, the welfare state, and working-class cultures. The geographical focus of my attention is (Western) Europe, but I choose not to exclude some American authors studying European history who appear particularly relevant.[3]

The Increase of Studies on Christian Workers' Organisations

My first observation is that since circa 1980 a great number of studies have been dedicated to Christian labour organisations, which existed in most Central and Western European countries.[4] The German scholar Michael Schneider's was one of the first, in 1982 – an impressive monograph on the German Christian trade unions between 1894 and 1933 – even if there were already many detailed local studies available.[5] Many other publications have followed since then, not only on Germany but also regarding France, Italy, Austria, the Netherlands, Belgium and Spain.[6] Much emphasis has been given to these movements' political orientation and to their relationship with Christian democracy.

Political Catholicism and Christian democracy, the latter movement in some ways closely related to the Christian labour movement (though the exact nature of that relationship can vary considerably), have evoked similar interest in recent years as well.[7] Some studies focus especially on the relationship between workers and Catholic or Christian democratic parties.[8] A related subject which also receives particular attention is so-called 'Left Catholicism', a collective term used to describe different movements in the 1940s and 1950s that reached out beyond the (perceived) closed Catholic community, in the political as well as in the philosophical and apostolic fields, and eventually associated themselves with socialism or even Marxism.[9] In the context of this chapter, left Catholic initiatives in the apostolic field, such as the worker priests and the *Mouvement Populaire des Familles* and *Action Catholique Ouvrière*,[10] are perhaps most relevant, because they directly involved Catholic workers. As Martin Conway rightly observed, left Catholicism as a cultural and political movement merely concerned urban intellectuals.[11]

As part of increased attention to working-class culture in general, which dates from the early 1980s, several studies have recently been devoted to cultural associations of Catholic workers in the nineteenth and twentieth centuries as well, particularly in Germany and Belgium.[12] Special mention has to be made of studies of Christian working-class women and of Christian women's movements in general, which usually include the former.[13] Incidentally, it is noteworthy that all these studies deal with Catholic and hardly any with Protestant workers, though this may be beginning to change.[14]

It is not only the number of publications that should be noted, but also their nature, that is, their quality as well as the will to take the Christian workers' movement seriously. In this context I would like to refer to the 'professionalisation' of organisational research. Most studies on the history of social organisations, of whatever kind, were conducted in the past by people from these organisations themselves, often for commemorative purposes, and seldom by professional historians with more academic ambitions. The studies I refer to are, by contrast, written by scholars attached to university research units, some admittedly sympathetic – some even overly sympathetic – some outspokenly critical or even negative.[15] In a number of cases such studies were commissioned and even (partly or wholly) subsidised by a Christian workers' organisation, but sometimes they were financed from scholarly research funds.[16] We can also observe on the side of the Christian workers' organisations a desire for 'academic quality' and a commitment to respect the researcher's autonomy, which nevertheless goes along with the need for a 'relationship of trust' (which, incidentally, is beneficial for the scholars as well, if only to get free access to private archives).[17] If everyone sticks to the basic rules of the game, this can be a 'win-win' situation. In general, one may conclude that the major studies on Christian workers' organisations that have been produced in this way are critical and meet high standards of scholarship.[18] The most important negative aspect of this kind of research, in my view, is not so much the danger of censorship or a lack of objectivity or even of legitimacy, but rather that it engenders a more traditional and conservative historiography and that it risks compartmentalising labour history.[19]

Most recent research, however, has escaped from this institutional perspective. It has become more common to adopt a comparative approach that includes mainly Catholic and socialist working-class movements and cultures; certainly this offers the most promising perspectives.[20] Recent general overviews of the labour movement tend to include Christian workers' organisations more than before,[21] even if the above-mentioned monographs are often not yet taken into account. Incidentally, studies focusing on gender issues have no tendency towards underestimating Christian working-class women, perhaps even the opposite.[22] Recent studies on industrial relations and business history at the sidelines of labour history also no longer include hidden 'discriminations' as in the past.[23]

Nevertheless, the increased attention to Christian workers' organisations is somewhat surprising. In most classic studies about the labour movement they were ignored. This is, of course, understandable. It was – and often still is – widely believed that religious practice as well as the churches' social and political influence have declined rapidly since the eighteenth century, especially among the working class. In addition, the churches, at least until the very end of the nineteenth century, according to a widespread prejudice, showed little interest in the social question. Moreover, the churches and denominational social organisations were reputed to be reactionary and anti-modern by their very nature. Socialism, on the contrary, was considered to be in the vanguard of modernity; at least on the European continent it also adopted a clear anti-clerical if not anti-religious stance.[24] In turn, Christian workers' organisations, especially the Christian trade unions, were considered hardly anything other than 'yellow unions' dominated by the employers, or were reproved for breaking working-class unity and weakening the force of labour – incidentally, as Carl Strikwerda rightly observed, a presumption that is seldom seriously debated.[25] Christian unions usually remained small, though they were more widespread than generally supposed, while in some specific regions their range could extend quite far, especially if one also takes into account their political weight.

The more fundamental reasons why Christian labour organisations often were ignored are mainly the paradigm of labour unity and the myth of secularisation, which represents religion as opposed to modernity and progress. These fundamental presuppositions have been put in question.

The Secularisation Thesis Reconsidered

From the early 1980s onwards the interpretation of the changes in the position of the church in society in terms of secularisation, i.e., the decline of the churches' public role as well as the decline in church attendance, seen as an inevitable characteristic of modernity, has been questioned. Several British scholars in particular have launched a vigorous attack on the secularisation thesis and argued that in any case secularisation theory is inadequate to describe the complex relationship between religion and modernity.[26] This debate has focused on the presumed dechristianisation, i.e., the decline in church involvement and in participation in religious activities on the individual level. But secularisation also means the relegation of religion to the private sphere and, more specifically, the churches' diminishing relevance for society and politics.[27]

Dechristianisation in the Nineteenth and Twentieth Centuries?

Twenty years before the Anglo-Saxon so-called 'revisionist' church historiography challenged the secularisation thesis, French historians inspired by the Annales School, with its interest in quantitative history, concluded that in the nineteenth and twentieth centuries there was no unilinear decline in church activity, and no proof that dechristianisation was directly linked to industrialisation and urbanisation, even if workers in general from the late nineteenth century onwards tended to become alienated from the established churches.[28]

The causes of this alienation were a subject of considerable debate. Gérard Cholvy and Yves-Marie Hilaire made a decisive argument against the accepted wisdom that it was because of the 'association between the chuch and capital' or the hostility of the working class towards religion, as had been suggested by Pierre Pierrard among many others. Drawing on the extensive available statistics for France, Cholvy and Hilaire especially highlighted the complexities of the social geography and legacies of the preindustrial past.[29] German scholars investigating popular cultures in Wilhelmine Germany also observed that in some industrialising areas, such as the Saar and Ruhr valleys, industrialisation and modernisation did not necessarily cause a decline in religious involvement. On the contrary, they sometimes provoked, in the words of Klaus-Michael Haltmann, a 'new attractiveness of Heaven'.[30] By using refined historical statistics as well as oral history, British so-called 'revisionist' historians demonstrated that between 1840 and 1900 in British cities – and among the working class in particular – church attendance *grew* considerably. A decline set in later, while religious values and habits remained strong at least until 1940.[31] According to the leading comparative church historian Hugh McLeod, in his own view trying to overcome the dichotomy between so-called 'orthodox' and 'revisionist' approaches to secularisation, the most distinctive feature of urban – and therefore also largely working-class – religion in the nineteenth and early twentieth century may not have been secularisation, but rather the high level of antagonism between rival sects and between believers and non-believers.[32] The German historian Olaf Blaschke recently labelled the nineteenth century in Germany as 'a second confessional era', after the sixteenth century.[33]

At least among church historians, this debate seems to have been settled in favour of a more nuanced approach to the role of church and religion in modern societies. The 'secularisation of the European mind' (in Owen Chadwick's words) was paralleled – if not preceded – by a revaluation of the strictly religious sphere in the eighteenth century and engendered a counter-offensive by the churches.[34] The Réveil movement in the 1840s (among Catholics as well as among Protestants), for example, produced an increase in popular devotion, social education and charity, changing the very notion of religiosity as well as the churches' social focus (emphasising at first the countryside as well as the petty bourgeoisie and middle classes).[35] It resulted in an intensification of popular belief which appealed to the 'heart' rather than to the 'head' (Ralph Gibson) – and apparently to women more than men as well: from the mid-nineteenth century onwards, religious practices underwent a remarkable 'feminisation'. Even more remarkably, through religious orders and congregations the Catholic Church (it would be interesting to look for parallels among Protestants) offered women opportunities for social mobility as well.[36] Incidentally, the observation that religious practice differed considerably between men and women is nothing new, but it was not considered to undermine the secularisation thesis, quite the contrary – an interpretation which is obviously difficult to maintain.

From the mid-nineteenth century onwards until circa 1960, but with great regional variations and temporary setbacks, most of Europe was very profoundly religious. Even Catholicism in the first decades of the twentieth century was, in the words of Martin Conway, 'emphatically not a religion in decline'; on the contrary it 'fully recovered a mood of self-confident optimism'.[37] The working class was part of this, or developed a strongly anti-clerical subculture, in which, however, quasi-religious rites were cultivated and socialism presented itself as an alternative religion (see below).

Christians and the Social Question

Even before the mid-nineteenth century, the social question became a subject of intellectual debate among prominent Christians, which was discussed at universities and seminaries, in special conferences and journals, on an international scale. In accordance with the line of thought laid out by Ernst Troeltsch (1865–1923), historians' attention has focused on the role of Catholics.[38] Even without reference to this classic of the sociology of religion, there exists an important literature on the (pre-)history and development of Catholic social doctrine. Only recently historians have begun to acknowledge the existence of Protestant and even Lutheran social thinking and practice, in particular in Germany.[39]

The success of Catholic apostolic and moral associations and workers' leagues in some regions paved the way for the later development of Christian workers' movements, though the exact nature of the relationship needs to be further investigated.[40] In the course of the nineteenth century, the churches, in particular in North-western Europe, modified their strategy towards the working class and recognised the importance of the social question and the necessity of social action – be it as a defence against socialism or even from the perspective of a *reconquista*. The so-called 'turn of the church to the people' around 1891,[41] however, in practice remained restricted mainly to Catholics – although a very similar development occurred among Dutch Calvinists – and to countries where the church was on the defensive in an open state-church conflict; clearly it was part of and subordinated to a political perspective. As Stathis Kalyvas forcefully argued, if political circumstances changed, this social and political strategy was easily abandoned and replaced by another, much less socially orientated policy, and one which gave the hierarchy full authority.[42]

It should be emphasised that, paradoxically, the social orientation of the Catholic and Calvinist Churches was not so much initiated by so-called 'liberal' Christians who accepted the principles of liberal democracy, but often by *certain* anti-modern, 'intransigent', 'conservative' or even 'fundamentalist' Christians – ultramontane Catholics or anti-revolutionary Calvinists.[43] An emphasis on these origins of Christian democracy and the Christian workers' movement characterised much research in the 1980s and 1990s, especially in France, Germany and Belgium.[44] However, scholars working on Christian trade unions have observed that the early Christian unions originated from authentic workers' responses.[45] Nevertheless, the church(es)' strategic reorientation, when implemented, may have fostered the conditions for the development of Christian democracy and a Christian workers' movement. In both interpretations in practice the hierarchy mainly recovered a nonclerical but primary anti-socialist lay movement, since these initiatives were not initiated by the church leadership but by the laymen or lower clergy and definitely not from a pure religious perspective.[46] The Lutheran and Orthodox Churches hardly witnessed such an evolution at all. While the development of a specific Protestant-Lutheran social practice has been underscored in recent studies,[47] it seems obvious that the Lutheran churches in general did not support the formation of explicitly Christian emancipatory workers' organisations; and Lutheran workers in Germany and, probably to a lesser extent, in the Netherlands remained outside the organised working class or joined nonconfessional unions.[48] This difference can be ascribed to the Lutheran and Orthodox Churches' conception of the separation between the spiritual and temporal worlds as well as to their close relations with the state – whereby the Orthodox Church considers the church as subordinate to the state. The Catholic and Calvinist Churches, on the contrary, stress the significance of religious values for the secular world.[49]

It should be noted that relations between the Christian labour movement and the churches were never very smooth. Notorious was the so-called *Gewerkschaftsstreit* in Germany, opposing the Catholic workers' associations (*Fachabteilungen*) of Berlin to the interconfessional Christian trade unions (mainly consisting of Catholics as well, however) which developed mainly in the industrial basins of the Rhine and Ruhr.[50] But many countries experienced their own version of the *Gewerkschaftsstreit*, and the Christian labour movement had to fight its way to recognition in the Christian community, particularly by the Lutheran churches and Catholic episcopacy. Recognition of the tension, not to say the divide between the churches and Christian workers' movements (particularly the trade unions), has been one of the most important features of the research done since the early 1980s. Except for the Dutch Catholic workers' movement, which was by far the most clerical and submissive to the church's authority,[51] one can even speak of a kind of 'anti-clericalism' within the Christian labour movement, which appeared clearly in disputes like the ones with 'Catholic Action' in Belgium and France in the 1920s and 1930s, and after the Second World War in the often negative attitudes of the Christian labour movement, the unions in particular, towards worker priests.[52] Moreover, the church hierarchy in the different countries and regions took very different and even radically opposed stances towards social commitment in general and towards Christian workers' organisations in particular (which is particularly true for the so-called 'universal' Catholic Church). As several authors have argued, this is essential to understanding the development as well as, in some cases, the non-formation of a Christian workers' movement and its position in the religious community.[53]

Secularisation and Politics

Nevertheless, the social and even political action of laymen was also perceived as a church activity and therefore altered the very notion of what should be considered apostolic action.[54] From this perspective one can also question the churches' loss of social and political influence, since at least part of it was recovered. In large parts of Europe the anti-clerical offensive of the 1860s and 1870s gave way to the creation of relatively closed Catholic and, to a lesser extent, Protestant subcultures (also called 'pillars') (alongside similar closed socialist communities).[55] From this perspective the church fully engaged in political action – supporting or, as I have already mentioned in this article, combating Catholic and Christian democratic parties. Nevertheless, and notwithstanding the fact that its demise has been predicted again and again, Christian democracy after the Second World War developed into 'the most successful Western political force since 1945'.[56] It could only do so by exercising a strong appeal to the popular, working classes. Even if at the time of writing the Christian

Democrats are no longer in government in Germany, the Netherlands and Belgium, this should not too easily be attributed to secularisation. After all, they have dominated the political scene in these countries for decades and other political movements – like social democracy – have shrunk remarkably as well. Undoubtedly, the causes of their present disarray are complex and it may once more be premature to sound their death knell.[57] More fundamentally, however, pillarisation did not prevent secularisation; as Stathis Kalyvas recently argued, it may even have contributed to it.[58] Even so, the laicisation of Catholic (workers') organisations in the postwar era should not always be attributed to dechristianisation, but rather to changing views within the Catholic community regarding the role of the church in society. [59] This could be described as a 'protestantisation' – or, better, 'Lutheranisation' – of Catholic social and political practice, whereby the Catholic Church accepted the separation of the temporal and the spiritual in a way that is in fact very similar to the Lutheran approach to church-state relations.

Secularisation theory, at least in its primitive form, received its final *coup de grâce* with what, most inadequately, has been labelled the 'comeback of religion', i.e., the fact that (post)modern society, by generating chaos, isolation and a general sense of non-belonging as well as a loss of perspective, paradoxically (!) offers new incentives for religious belief.[60] The success (in Europe quite relative, however)[61] of religious sects and so-called New Religious Movements in the West is only one example of a far more generalised phenomenon, which includes the widespread eclectic combination of different religious elements in a personal but 'unproblematic' *Weltanschauung*. Some observers even diagnosed a massive return to the traditional churches in the public sphere in the 1980s (though one can, to say the least, seriously question the relevance of the many public appearances of Pope John Paul II, at least – again – to European Catholics).[62] Samuel Huntington describes the main political world conflict in the late twentieth century in terms of a clash of civilisations, which he considers to be fundamentally religious in nature.[63] The European integration process also underscores the immense diversity of the old continent and the persistent importance of regional ethnic and religious collective identities.[64] Finally, the experience of non-European industrial societies, where modernisation and industrialisation do not seem to lead to the same decline of religion as in the West, challenges the universalist assumptions of the secularisation thesis.[65]

Secularisation and Modernity

Questioning of secularisation theory can be considered part of a larger phenomenon in which the nature of modernity, of which secularisation is considered to be a main feature, is reassessed. The traditional concept of modernity is rooted in the values of the Enlightenment and French Revolution – assuming a unilateral growth through technological progress towards an ideal, by definition rational and secular society.[66] According to many contemporary scholars this modernity has come to an end, or entered a new phase: postmodernism. In postmodern society not only is there more room for religious experiences, but the paradigm change has stimulated a new interest in religious phenomena – the very questioning of secularisation theory may be considered an illustration of this development.[67] Following the Belgian-Dutch sociologist Staf Hellemans, we may expand on this observation so as to put 'traditional', industrial modernity in question as well.[68] In the theory of 'reflexive modernisation' attention is given to counter-modernisation, which is essential to modernisation itself. As Eric Hobsbawm and Theo Ranger showed in their seminal volume, the 'invention of tradition' is also part of modernity.[69] According to the main protagonists of this theory, Ulrich Beck and Anthony Giddens, modern industrial society has a potential for continuous self-destruction and renewal, and can give rise to 'many modernities'. In fact, anti-modern criticism is an essential feature of modernity.[70]

These observations may fundamentally alter the perception of church and religion. Returning to the classic insights of Max Weber, Danièle Hervieu-Léger, for example, stresses the continuities and parallels between modernity and Judaism and Christianity, and shows how the logic of rationality and progress *opens up* ways for religion to develop. At the same time, religious values in modern times infiltrate the secular realm.[71] The idea of a break with the preindustrial and 'traditional' Christian past, incidentally not only in this context, can no longer be maintained.[72] Hellemans pleads for a new study of how religion(s) modernise(s) from an anti-modernist perspective.[73] The apparent contradiction between modernity and anti-modernism, which has puzzled so many historians and sociologists dealing with (in particular) the Catholic social movement and the development of Catholic social action, may be overcome in this context.[74]

Of course, this perception of church and religion also alters the perception of social and political movements that identify themselves with them, especially since these movements have been considered the vectors of the modernisation of Christianity in the nineteenth century. This becomes apparent in studies such as Carl Strikwerda's masterful *A House Divided*, in which this American scholar offers a detailed and insightful comparison of the rise of Christian and socialist workers' movements in three major Belgian cities. In this book, earlier prejudices towards the Christian labour movement have totally disappeared. Strikwerda clearly shows how, in particular in Ghent, the Christian labour movement developed 'modern' bureaucratic structures and a modern outlook, expressed for example in a more positive attitude towards contemporary technologies than its socialist competitor.[75]

In any case it may be concluded that the general theory of secularisation as a consequence of social differentiation, socialisation and rationalisation,[76] the idea of a universal and inevitable process – central features of modernity in the old paradigm – is being replaced by a much more flexible theoretical framework. This allows for contingency, for regional as well as social variation, for divergent trajectories (for secularisation as well as religious renewal and changing conceptions about the role and function of the churches), and for very complex and diverse relations between churches, denominations and modern states.[77]

The Turn-around of Pillarisation Theory

Another illustration of the deep transformation that has occurred in historical perceptions of the significance of religion in modern society is what has happened to the theory of pillarisation ('verzuiling') in Belgium and the Netherlands. Pillarisation was, roughly stated, considered for decades to be a reactionary strategy of the Catholic Church to protect its followers from the dangers of socialism and modernity. However, due to the comparative work in the late 1960s of political scientists such as Stein Rokkan, Arend Lijphart and Hans Daalder, it came to be recognised that pillarisation could have a certain value in stabilising deeply divided political democracies as they existed in some smaller European countries, such as Belgium, the Netherlands, Austria and Switzerland ('consociational democracy').[78] The pillars, and in particular the Catholic pillar, also appeared much less homogenous and monolithic than earlier portrayals had suggested. Later on, some social historians observed similarities between Dutch pillarisation and existing subcultures, and not only religious ones, in other European countries.[79]

In a decisive synthesis, Staf Hellemans has analysed pillarisation as a general process that occurred among different political families (social democrats, communists, and to a lesser extent liberals and nationalists) and that took place in most European countries, including France, Germany and Italy. By developing into large and mutually integrated networks of organisations, social movements structured the changing environment and adapted to mass society.[80] Therefore pillarisation should not be seen as opposed to, but as characteristic of modernisation.[81] As for Catholic pillarisation, it is now acknowledged that it developed despite the church (the hierarchy) and was not initiated by it.[82] Recently questions also arose with respect to the exclusiveness of the closed subcultures, in particular among the working class.[83] It is hard to imagine a more radical shift of perception, since we are confronted here with an intellectual turn-around of 180 degrees![84]

However, with these observations we have strayed quite a bit from our initial observation: increased and fundamentally modified attention to Christian labour organisations.

Multiple Identities and the Changed Class Perspective

This heightened attention is also related to the recognition of multiple identities, of pluralism, within the working class, which resulted from the growing interest in social history and in workers' daily lives – of which Marxist historians such as E.P. Thompson and Eric Hobsbawm were forerunners – but also from the decline of the concept of class, together with Marxism in general, as a primary frame of analysis.[85] It seems clear that the unity of the working class served as a powerful metaphor not only for labour activists themselves but for labour historians as well. Today, partly because of the diminishing importance of industrial workers and growing differentiation among employees at the end of the twentieth century, the idea of a homogenous working class with one major common concern seems obsolete. This is reflected in the present perception of the past as well.

The postmodern world-view, especially after the 'end of ideology' and the fall of the Berlin Wall, discredits portrayals of homogenous ideological movements and instead emphasises diversity, pluralism, and multiple identities. In a major historical-sociological study, Bernhard Ebbinghaus (building on earlier work of Stein Rokkan on political party formation) has linked the formation of the labour movement to several major cleavages in industrial society and not only, or even primarily, to the labour-capital cleavage. This gives way to an extremely fragmented overall picture of working-class organisation and of the origins of its development.[86] No longer the unity, but the diversity of the working class and its social organisation has a central place in today's social history.

The interest in 'history from below' and everyday life, as well as the demise of the predominance of the unitary class perspective, have led contemporary researchers to investigate the multiplicity of experience in workers' lives. At the same time, the importance of 'cultural' dimensions and divisions has come to the fore. For many, religion is one of these.[87] Indeed, religion remained part of workers' lives in many areas of Europe[88] even when they joined anti-clerical, socialist organisations, and even when, for numerous reasons, they distanced themselves from the established church. Therefore, knowing 'why people go to church is at least as important to understand as why they go on strike' (as James Barett has said).[89] Especially in this context it may be necessary to distinguish between established church practices and popular religious expressions. However, one should emphasise the meaning of these religious practices – of those that were abandoned as much as of those that were maintained – because their significance can vary considerably depending on denomination, social geography, class, gender and time. Therefore, the whole context of religious belief and practice as well as non-belief and non-practice should be assessed.

But religion was not only a part of certain working-class cultures; it also contributed to the formation of a distinct class identity and to specific political behaviour, though these differed from the socialist vision(s) of class.[90] Christian democracy as well as the Christian labour movement in particular reject the class struggle and stress the organic character of society, in which each particle has its own place and function which gives each social group a positive value as well. Contrary to the traditional (i.e., older) view of society held by conservative church authorities – in fact until the twentieth century – Christian workers' organisations, in particular the Young Christian Workers (JOC) founded by the Belgian priest (later Cardinal) Joseph Cardijn, emphasised the human value of the worker, trying to give him – or her, since there was also a branch for young working girls – not only self-esteem but a clear class consciousness as well, which included the moral obligation to stand up for one's own rights.[91]

Incidentally, religious identity often acted as a marker for national and other identifications as well.[92] It is fascinating to see how different identifications influence each other and create distinctive collective identities. Some of the most interesting studies in recent labour history focus on workers with complex identities and competing allegiances (class, nation, race and gender as well as religion).[93] Such studies also challenge other traditional assumptions in labour and working-class history, such as the working class's alleged internationalism or egalitarianism, particularly regarding race and gender.[94] The gender perspective is particularly relevant here, since religious as well as bourgeois and also increasingly working-class values in the nineteenth and the first half of the twentieth century emphasised distinct gender roles. Incidentally, such reappraisals of old research paradigms corroborate social scientific evidence on the 'sociocultural conservatism' of working-class culture.[95]

Religion survived in the working class, though certainly its significance changed considerably. But it should no longer come as a surprise that religion, even in so-called 'secularised' Western societies, contributed considerably to the establishment and development of modern welfare states. This has become quite clear from new research on the development of the welfare state, which has also undergone a real (and generally acknowledged) 'paradigm shift' since 1990.

Christian Democracy and the Welfare State

The best-known example of this paradigm shift is undoubtedly the ground-breaking publication of the Danish political economist Gösta Esping-Andersen, *The Three Worlds of Welfare Capitalism*,[96] though there were some predecessors like John D. Stephens who, as early as 1979, considered Christian democracy to be an important factor in understanding the nature and development of welfare states.[97] This change in perspective, of course, follows from the increased interest in the origins and development of the welfare state, which was perceived in the 1980s and 1990s as being in deep crisis. However, until 1990 the formation and development of the welfare state, in particular in social and political sciences, were mainly described in functional-materialist terms as an outcome of modernisation, the product of 'the logic of industrialism', or, in a Marxian analysis, as a condition for capitalist growth; at most religion was considered a lasting historical effect but not an active factor.

In opposition to such functional-materialist theories, some scholars have suggested that political democracy was a necessary condition or that welfare reforms were primarily the result of the collective action of the social democratic labour movement. In that view the Scandinavian welfare states appear as the ideal, i.e., most modern, societies. However, by analysing and comparing the structure and the nature of welfare arrangements, Esping-Andersen discovered three major and clearly distinct welfare state regimes, each characterised by very different social security institutions, social benefit distribution patterns, and ways of de-commodification ('the degree to which individuals, or families, can uphold a socially acceptable standard of living independently of labour market participation'), with very different outcomes regarding social stratification as well: [98] (1) the social democratic welfare states in the Scandinavian countries; (2) Anglo-Saxon liberal schemes; and (3) conservative-corporatist regimes. The latter are characterised by their generous but passive welfare provisions. In explaining the different welfare state regimes, Esping-Andersen highlights the long-lasting impact of historical legacies, in particular preindustrial church-state relations, the industrialisation process itself and its consequences for social stratification, family patterns, and the trajectories of political representation and democratisation. In this respect he particularly emphasises the importance of Catholicism and absolutism. Though his research is not of a historical nature, his conclusions have far-reaching historical implications and have consequently given way to new historical-sociological studies of the welfare state.

It is, of course, in this perspective that his work is relevant here. It raises new and fundamental questions regarding the role of religion and of Christian social organisations in modern society. American sociologists have moved in the same direction by investigating the influence of Catholicism as a political culture on the development of welfare states, social infrastructure, and unionisation.[99] Feminist critics of Esping-Andersen have emphasised other aspects of welfare state regimes – which partly resulted in different clusters of welfare states – but in general also recognised the importance of the denominational factor in developing welfare provision, in particular in family policy.[100] From a similar point of view the classic Weberian thesis of the importance of religion for capitalist development, including the origins and development of the welfare state, is being taken up again.[101] The approach of Esping-Anderson and Van Kersbergen has also inspired further historical research into the role of Christian social movements, in particular in the Netherlands.[102] In the end Christian religions and sociopolitical movements appear as important factors, alongside one other.[103]

However, Christian democracy may not be considered as just the political face of Catholicism, and not only because this would mean a manifest underestimation of Protestant contributions. The Dutch political scientist Kees van Kersbergen, a former pupil of Esping-Andersen at the European University Institute in Florence, has argued that Christian democratic social and political organisations managed to transcend Catholic social teachings about solidarity and charity. Even if his representation of Catholic social doctrine may be subject to discussion, the development of a proper Christian democrat social practice, departing at times considerably from the official teachings of the church, is evident from many examples.[104] It is this so-called 'little tradition' of social capitalism that provides the core of Christian democratic welfare policy. It emphasises the fundamental social rights attributed to the individual, leading to demands for social justice and state intervention. Its intellectual sources vary from democracy itself to traditionalism, religious conservatism and the writings of religious theoreticians as well as the 'grand tradition' of the churches. Therefore Christian democracy, in Van Kersbergen's view, needs to be distinguished from traditional conservatism as well.[105] In this context he stresses the importance of the working class: 'Without the working class – or perhaps formulated more accurately – without substantial working-class support, there can be no Christian Democracy.'[106] In his eyes, Christian democracy not only pursues a middle way between capitalism and socialism, but also is, and perhaps more, about reconciliation and harmonising conflicting interests. Incidentally, that makes a precise assessment of its nature and concrete forms rather difficult, since 'the precise configurations of social capitalism become historically contingent, although societal accommodation and the integration of demands of the working class are always at the heart of the package. ... This is why social capitalist nations vary among themselves and yet, taken as a group, can be distinguished from the other models of affiliating the market, the state and the family'.[107]

The reorientation of the study of the welfare state has also favoured an increased interest in its origins in general and in particular in private social care and charity as organised by Christian social organisations.[108] In this way church history and social history, which tended traditionally to have little or no contact, converge. Christian charities were omnipresent before the development of state services, but sometimes remained important alongside and even as part of the organised welfare state, most visibly in Belgium.[109] They 'reappeared' in a significant way in the 1970s and 1980s.[110] Incidentally, thanks to the pioneering work of Jochen-Christoph Kaiser in Germany, this perspective has highlighted the role not only of Catholics but also of Protestants.[111]

Observations similar to those concerning the development of social security schemes and welfare state regimes can be made regarding industrial relations and (neo-)corporatism, though here the shift of perspective is probably less pronounced. But in fact here too the predominance of functionalist or Marxist and social democratic perspectives has yielded to a more complex approach that highlights different 'state traditions' in which the churches' historical heritage is a major factor alongside others, including, of course, the heritage of social democracy.[112]

Conclusions

I have argued throughout this article that a fundamental shift has occurred in the labour and social historian's perception of the role of church and religion in the construction of modern society in the West. This new perception is characterised by a greater recognition of their role in the development of (Western) European industrial societies, in particular the socio-economic organisation of the welfare state that protects individual citizens from the hazards of the capitalist free market. Research paradigms marked by Marxian and secularist premises have become obsolete; the new, 'postmodern', perceptual framework which now 'pre-structures' historians' scholarly approach has led to the discovery of a (relatively) 'new' working class, with multiple identities, including religion and church allegiance.

As indicated above, labour and working-class history could investigate further the reality of religious life in (local) working-class communities. Notwithstanding much talk about the importance of the *histoire des mentalités, Alltagsgeschichte*, and 'history from below', there is still much research to be done on the popular religion of the working classes and the remarkable survival of some religious rites, such as 'rites of passage', even in secular worlds. In doing so, one should adopt an open and reflective stance towards 'religious' expressions, assessing their meaning in their local, denominational, gendered and chronological contexts. Paraphrasing Callum Brown, one of the most radical advocates of the revisionist stance towards the secularisation thesis, one may conclude that 'it is through the historian's treatment of popular religion during the process of urban growth and change that we need to approach a revision of social history'.[113]

Regarding Christian workers' organisations, much research has been done already, though a catch-up operation is needed for Central and Eastern European countries where, at least in some areas, Christian social action once flourished. However, the focus of research should quickly move on from the political and trade union movement to educational and cultural associations and their role in the formation and persistence of religious sensitivities and orientations. This should certainly also include family and women's movements. Such sociocultural confessional organisations acted in secularised trade union environments as well, as was the case in postwar Germany and Italy in particular. But also where Christian trade unions or political workers' leagues existed, the realm of cultural associations could extend further towards non-unionised workers or even workers who joined socialist (or liberal) unions or voted for parties other than the Christian democrats, as was the case in Wilhelmine and Weimar Germany.[114] In this way, a link can be made between collective action and mentality, including politics, and individual experiences.

Individual and collective biographies of Christian workers and labour leaders could offer a very interesting approach to demonstrating concretely the changing meanings of religious practices and content, as well as different motivations for political and social commitment. In such an approach, one should include the rise of anticlericalism, the formation of quasi-religions or 'religions without God', and the transformation of religious rites and values in secular (even secularist) contexts.[115] Perhaps in that case one would need to enlarge the concept of religion and adopt a Geertzian approach, which considers religion as a cultural system, a set of symbols and collective representations of society.[116] Personally, however, I would prefer to consider social movements as *'churches* without God', eventually developing secular rites. The term religion in my view should be restricted to an ideology or *Weltanschauung* referring to the supernatural.[117] In any case it seems likely to me that such a perspective would dramatically alter the interpretation of the nature of the cultural changes that accompanied, or rather were part of, the establishment and development of modern industrial society – and of today's 'postmodern' society as well.

Notes

1. This article was first presented at the international conference *The State of Labour and Working Class History in Europe*, International Institute of Social History, Amsterdam/ Rotterdam, 17 – 18 February 1997. I wish to thank Jan de Maeyer, Bruno Duriez, Hans-Ulrich Jost, Staf Hellemans, Emiel Lamberts, Michael Schneider, Klaus Tenfelde, Marcel van der Linden, Johan Verberckmoes and Vincent Viaene, as well as the many participants in the lively discussion at the conference, for their comments on earlier versions of this text. Of course the author alone remains responsible for the ideas expressed.

2. See e.g., I. Katznelson and A.R. Zolberg (eds), *Working-Class Formation: Nineteenth Century Patterns in Western Europe and the United States*, Princeton NJ, 1986; E. Hobsbawm, *Workers: Worlds of Labour. Further Studies in the History of Labour*, New York, 1984; J. Kocka (ed.), *Europäische Arbeiterbewegung im 19. Jahrhundert*, Göttingen, 1983; W. Kendall, *The Labour Movement in Europe*, London, 1975. A similar observation in W. Spohn, 'Religion and Working-Class Formation in Imperial Germany, 1871–1914', *Politics and Society*, XIX, 1 (1991): 71–108; C. Strikwerda, 'Catholic Working-Class Movements in Western Europe', *International Labor and Working-Class History*, 34 (Fall 1988): 70–85 (review article in this special issue on *Religion and the Working-Class*) and, in a different context, J. Winter, *Sites of Memory, Sites of Mourning: The Great War in European Cultural History*, Cambridge, 1995, 119.

3. History still largely being a national discipline, this overview is inevitably incomplete, and what studies are dealt with not only depends on my subjective choice, but is also due to my incomplete knowledge of the national historiography of the different countries, which is largely in other languages than English. The historical literature in the Mediterranean and Scandinavian countries, as well as Eastern Europe, is in practice completely left out of this presentation.

4. For an overview of what is left of those movements see P. Pasture, *Christian Trade Unionism in Europe since 1968: Tensions between Identity and Practice*, Aldershot, 1994. For historical overviews see P. Pasture, *Histoire du syndicalisme chrétien international. La difficile recherche d'une troisième voie*, Paris, 1999; S.H. Scholl (ed.), *150 années de mouvement ouvrier catholique*, Brussels, 1961.

5. M. Schneider, *Die christlichen Gewerkschaften 1894–1933*, 'Politik und Gesellschaftsgeschichte' 10, Bonn, 1982; M. Schneider, 'Christliche Arbeiterbewegung in Europa. Ein vergleichender Literaturbericht', in K. Tenfelde (ed.), *Arbeiter und Arbeiterbewegung im Vergleich. Berichte zur internationalen historischen Forschung; Historische Zeitschrift*, Sonderheft 15, Munich, 1986, 477–505.

6. The major titles (published since circa 1985 and not included in Schneider, 'Christliche Arbeiterbewegung in Europa') include for Austria: L. Reichhold, *Geschichte der christlichen Gewerkschaften Österreichs*, Vienna, 1987; for Belgium: E. Gerard and P. Wynants (eds), *Histoire du mouvement ouvrier chrétien en Belgique*, KADOC-Studies 16, Leuven, 1994, 2 vols.; P. Pasture, *Kerk, politiek en sociale actie. De unieke positie van de christelijke arbeidersbeweging in België (1944–1973)*, HIVA-reeks 14, Leuven/Apeldoorn 1992; for France: P. Pierrard, *L'Église et les ouvriers en France (1840–1940/1940–1990)*, Paris, 1984/ 1991; M. Branciard, *Histoire de la CFDT. Soixante-dix ans d'action syndicale*, Paris, 1990; M. Launay, *La CFTC. Origines et développement 1919–1940*, Paris, 1986; F. Georgi, *L'invention de la CFDT 1957–1970. Syndicalisme, catholicisme et politique dans la France d'expansion*, Paris, 1995; G. Groux and René Mouriaux, *La CFDT*, Paris, 1989; for Germany: E.D. Brose, *Christian Labor and the Politics of Frustration in Imperial Germany*, Baltimore MD, 1985; W. Patch, *Christian Trade Unions in the Weimar Republic, 1918–1933: The Failure of 'Corporate Pluralism'*, New Haven CT/ London, 1985; W. Schroeder, *Katholizismus und Einheitsgewerkschaft. Der Streit um den DGB und der Niedergang des Sozialkatholizismus in der Bundesrepublik bis 1960*, Bonn, 1992; for Italy: A. Ciampani, *La buona battaglia. Giulio Pastore e i cattolici sociali nella crisi dell' Italia Liberale*, Milan, 1990; S. Zaninelli (ed.), *Il sindacalismo bianco tra guerra, dopoguerra e fascismo (1914–1926)*, Milan, 1982; S. Agòcs, *The Troubled Origin of the Italian Catholic Labor Movement, 1878–1914*, Detroit MI, 1988; for the Netherlands: J. van Meeuwen, *Lijden aan eenheid. Katholieke arbeiders op zoek naar hun politiek recht (1897–1929)*, Hilversum, 1998; J. Roes (ed.), *Katholieke arbeidersbeweging. Studies over KAB en NKV in de economische en politieke ontwikkeling van Nederland na 1945*, KDC Bronnen en studies 13, Baarn, 1985; J. Peet, P. Mertens (coll.), and J. Roes (ed.), *Katholieke arbeidersbeweging*, vol. II: *De KAB en het NKV in de maatschappelijke ontwikkeling van Nederland na 1945*, KDC Bronnen en Studies 25, Baarn, 1993; for Spain: C.M. Winston, *Workers and the Right in Spain, 1900–1936*, Princeton NJ, 1985; Comparative: P. Pasture, 'Diverging Paths: The Development of Catholic Labour Organisations in France, The Netherlands and Belgium since 1945', *Revue d'histoire ecclésiastique*, LXXXVIII, 1 (1994): 54–90; Pasture, *Christian Trade Unionism in Europe since 1968*. See also the titles quoted in notes 12 and 20.

7. The main titles include M. Conway, *Catholic Politics in Western Europe, 1918–1945*, London/ New York, 1997; E. Lamberts (ed.), *Christian Democracy in the European Union (1945–1995)*, KADOC-Studies 21, Leuven, 1997; S.N. Kalyvas, *The Rise of Christian Democracy in Europe*, Ithaca NY/ London, 1996; M. Conway and T. Buchanan (eds), *Political Catholicism in Europe, 1918–1965*, Oxford, 1996; J.-D. Durand, *L'Europe de la Démocratie chrétienne*, Brussels, 1995; D. Hanley (ed.), *Christian Democracy in Europe: A Comparative Perspective*, London/ New York, 1994; J. Witte Jr (ed.), *Christianity and Democracy in Global Context*, Boulder CO, 1993; R. Papini, *The Christian Democrat International*, 'Religious Forces in the Modern Political World', Lanham, 1997; H. Portelli and Th. Jansen (dir.), *La démocratie chrétienne, force internationale*, Coll. Recherches de Politique Comparée, Nanterre, 1986. See also B. Ebbinghaus, 'The Siameses Twins: Citizenship Rights, Cleavage Formation and Party-Union Relations in Western Europe', in Ch. Tilly (ed.), 'Citizenship, Identity and Social History', *International Review of Social History*, Supplement 3, (1996): 51–90. Ebbinghaus stresses the importance of Christian democracy for Christian unions, while I would argue that the social movement – not restricted to unionism – *precedes* the party formation.

8. In this respect the work of Emmanuel Gerard on the Catholic Party in Belgium has to be noted, in particular *De Katholieke Partij in crisis. Partijpolitiek leven in België, 1918–1940*, Leuven, 1985 (and many other studies by this author). Other

titles include B. Béthouart, *Des syndicalistes chrétiens en politique (1944–1962)*. *De la Libération à la Ve République*, Villeneuve d'Ascq (Nord), 1999 for France; Schroeder, *Katholizismus und Einheitsgewerkschaft* and F. Neuhaus, *DGB und CDU*. *Analysen zum bilateralen Verhältnis von 1982 bis 1990*, Köln, 1996 regarding Germany; and Van Meeuwen, *Lijden aan eenheid* regarding the Netherlands.

9. It is impossible here to enumerate all the literature on this subject. For a recent overview: G.-R. Horn and E. Gerard (eds), Left Catholicism, 1943–1955: Catholics and Society in Western Europe at the Point of Liberation, Leuven, 2001.

10. These movements were mainly active in Francophone countries, especially France, Switzerland and Belgium. Among the most interesting studies on the subject I mention two older publications: J. Debès, *Naissance de l'Action Catholique Ouvrière*, Paris, 1982; R. Wattebled, *Stratégies catholiques en monde ouvrier dans la France d'après-guerre*, Paris, 1990 (see also the volumes edited by Gerard and Wynants, *Histoire du mouvement ouvrier chrétien en Belgique*, and Pasture, *Kerk, politiek en sociale actie*, for Belgium). On the theological background of these developments in France see E. Fouilloux's masterful *Une église en quête de liberté: la pensée catholique française entre modernisme et Vatican II, 1914–1962*, Paris, 1998.

11. M. Conway, 'Left Catholics in Europe in the 1940s: Elements of an interpretation', Paper presented at the international seminar *Left Catholicism in Western Europe in the 1940s and 1950s*, Leuven 28 – 29 May 1999.

12. Apart from many regional studies see e.g., G. Klein, *Der Volksverein für das katholische Deutschland 1890–1933. Geschichte, Bedeutung, Untergang*, Veröffentlichungen der Kommission zur Zeitgeschichte – Reihe B, 75, Paderborn, 1996; Dirk H. Müller, *Arbeiter – Katholizismus – Staat. Der Volksverein für das katholische Deutschland und die katholischen Arbeiterorganisationen in der Weimerer Republik*, Bonn, 1996; C. Haffert, *Die katholischen Arbeitervereine Westdeutschlands in der Weimarer Republik*, Essen, 1994. For Belgium see the studies in Gerard and Wynants (eds), *Histoire du mouvement ouvrier chrétien en Belgique*.

13. E.g., A. de Decker, *Vormingswerk in vrouwenhanden*, vol. 1: *De voorgeschiedenis van de KAV (1892–1924)*, and A. de Decker and R. Christens, vol. 2: *De geschiedenis van de KAV vóór de Tweede Wereldoorlog (1920–1940)*, Leuven/ Amersfoort, 1986–8; B. Sack, *Zwischen religiöser Bindung und moderne Gesellschaft. Katholische Frauenbewegung und politische Kultur in der Weimarer Republik (1918/19–1933)*, Münster, 1998.

14. See note 38.

15. The studies of Gerard and Roes quoted in note 6 were commissioned by the Christian labour movement, but have clear academic ambitions. Launay and Reichhold appear very 'sympathetic' to their subject, to say the least. Patch, *Christian Trade Unions*, is very critical of Schneider's rather negative stance towards the German Christian trade unions. See also Strikwerda, 'Catholic Working-Class Movements in Western Europe' (review article).

16. As was the case with my own research on the history of the Christian labour movement in Belgium and the international Christian trade unions, which benefited from grants from the Belgian National Fund for Scientific Research.

17. In this respect it is worth observing with Karel Dobbelaere that attention to 'quality' has become a key value of the Belgian Christian social organisations, and probably elsewhere as well (particularly in Germany and the Netherlands). K. Dobbelaere, 'Professionalization and Secularization in the Belgian Catholic Pillar', *Japanese Journal of Religious Studies*, VI, 1–2 (1979): 39–64; K. Dobbelaere and J. Billiet, 'Les changements internes au pilier catholique en Flandre: d'une catholicité d'Église à une chrétienté socioculturelle', *Recherches sociologiques*, XIV, 2 (1983): 141–84; L. Voyé, 'From Institutional Catholicism to "Christian Inspiration". Another Look at Belgium', in W.C. Roof, J.W. Caroll and D.A. Roose

(eds), *The Post-War Generation and Established Religion. Cross-Cultural Perspectives*, Westview, 1995, 191–206.

18. Good examples of this kind of studies are the titles of J. Roes, and E. Gerard and P. Wynants (eds) quoted in note 6, as well as the study of the Dutch Protestant union of industrial and food workers by A. Bornebroek, *De strijd voor harmonie. De geschiedenis van de Industrie- en Voedingsbond CNV, 1896–1996*, Amsterdam, 1996.

19. A similar observation is made by M.L. Anderson, 'Piety and Politics: Recent Work on German Catholicism', *Journal of Modern History*, LXIII, 4 (December 1991): 715.

20. D. Kalb, *Expanding Class: Power and Everyday Politics in Industrial Communities: The Netherlands, 1850–1950*, Durham, 1997; C. Strikwerda, *A House Divided – Mass Politics and the Origins of Pluralism: Catholicism, Socialism and Flemish Nationalism in Nineteenth Century Belgium*, Lanham, 1997; G. Bedani, *Politics and Ideology in the Italian Workers' Movement: Union Development and the Changing Role of the Catholic and Communist Subcultures in Postwar Italy*, Oxford/ Providence, 1995; H.-W. Frohn, *Arbeiterbewegingskulturen in Köln, 1890–1933*, Düsseldorfer Schriften zur Neueren Landesgeschichte und zur Geschichte Nordrhein-Westfalens 45, Essen, 1997; H. Rosenbaum, *Proletarische Familien. Arbeiterfamilien und Arbeiterväter im frühen 20. Jahrhundert zwischen traditioneller, sozialdemokratischer und kleinbürgerlicher Orientierung*, Frankfurt am Main, 1992; C. Rauh-Kühne, *Katholisches Milieu und Kleinstadtgesellschaft. Ettlingen, 1918–1939*, Geschichte der Stadt Ettlingen, Sigmaringen, 1991. Müller, *Arbeiter – Katholizismus – Staat* is also part of a comparative project which includes socialist and Catholic working-class subcultures.

21. E.g., B. Ebbinghaus, 'Labour Unity in Union Diversity: Trade Unions and Social Cleavages in Western Europe, 1890–1989', Unpublished Ph.D. thesis, European University Institute, Florence, 1993; J. Sagnes (dir.), *Histoire du syndicalisme dans le monde des origines à nos jours*, Toulouse, 1994; S. Berger and D. Broughton (eds), *The Force of Labour: The Western European Labour Movement and the Working Class in the Twentieth Century*, Oxford/ Washington D.C., 1995; F. Guedj and S. Sirot (dir.), *Histoire sociale de l'Europe. Industrialisation et société en Europe occidentale 1880–1970*, Histoire, culture et sociétés, Paris, 1998.

22. E.g., C. van Eijl, *Maandag tolereren we niets meer: vrouwen, arbeid en vakbeweging 1945–1990*, Amsterdam, 1997. See also below regarding welfare state research.

23. E.g., M. Nolan, *Visions of Modernity: American Business and the Modernization of Germany*, New York/ Oxford, 1994.

24. Hobsbawm, *Workers: Worlds of Labour*, 33–48.

25. Strikwerda, *A House Divided*, 322 (note 117).

26. S. Bruce (ed.), *Religion and Modernization: Sociologists and Historians Debate the Secularization Thesis*, Oxford, 1992 provides a survey of this debate in the English-speaking world in the early 1990s (with contributions by Callum Brown, Hugh McLeod, Robin Gill and Bryan R. Wilson, et al.); P. van Rooden, *Religieuze regimes. Over godsdienst en maatschappij in Nederland, 1570–1990*, Amsterdam, 1996. However, similar statements were made much earlier by French church historians: e.g., G. Cholvy and Y.-M. Hilaire, *Histoire religieuse de la France contemporaine*, vol. 3: *1930–1988*, Bibliothèque historique Privat, Toulouse, 1988, 484–95 (conclusion). A recent summary of the anti-secularisation theory can be found in P.L. Berger (ed.), *The Desecularisation of the World: Resurgent Religion and World Politics*, Ethics and Public Policy Center, Washington/ Grand Rapids, 1999 and in the special issue of *Sociology of Religion*, LX, 3 (Fall 1999): *The Secularization Debate*, William H. Swatos, (ed.).

27. José Casanova, *Public Religions in the Modern World*, Chicago IL, 1994, 211; K. Dobbelaere, 'Secularization: A Multi-dimensional Concept', *Current Sociology*,

XXIX, 2 (1981): 3–213. There is no evidence, however, that these three meanings of secularisation are interdependent, what lies at the basis of many misunderstandings. As argued further in the text, it may well be that a retreat of the churches from the public sphere engenders a revitalisation of religious life. On this subject see especially the essay by J. de Maeyer and S. Hellemans, 'Katholiek reveil, katholieke verzuiling en dagelijks leven', in J. Billiet (ed.), *Tussen bescherming en verovering. Sociologen en historici over zuilvorming*, KADOC-Studies 6, 1988, 171–200. I will return to the question of the relation to modernity later in this text.

28. E.g., F. Boulard and J. Rémy, *Pratique religieuse urbaine et régions culturelles*, Paris, 1968. G. Cholvy and Y.-M. Hilaire, *Histoire religieuse de la France contemporaine*, vol. 2: *1880–1930*, Toulouse, 1986, 184, however, observe that just a minority of the working class dechristianised totally, usually unchristianised immigrants. Étienne Fouilloux has presented a particularly insightful overview on the French historiography on the church(es) and the working class at the conference *Chrétiens et ouvriers*, Roubaix, 13 to 15 October 1999. In English compare the nuanced data and comments of T. Kselman, 'The Varieties of Religious Experience in Urban France', in H. McLeod (ed.), *European Religion in the Age of Great Cities, 1830–1930*, London / New York, 1994, 165–90.

29. Cholvy and Hilaire, *Histoire religieuse*, vol. 2, esp. 178–85. Compare Pierrard, *L'Église et les ouvriers*. As for the wealth of edited quantitative material see especially *L'observation quantitative du fait religieux. Colloque de l'Association Française d'Histoire Religieuse Contemporaine*, Centre d'Histoire … Université Charles-de-Gaulle, Lille III, 1992; F. Boulard et al., *Matériaux pour l'histoire religieuse du peuple français (1800–1960)*, 2 vols, éditions de l'EHESS/ FNSP/ CNRS, Paris, 1982–7. See also R. Gibson, *A Social History of French Catholicism, 1789–1914*, London, 1989.

30. Kl.-M. Haltmann, 'Die neue Attractivität des Himmels. Kirche, Religion und industrielle Modernisierung', in R. van Dülmen (ed.), *Industriekultur an der Saar. Leben und Arbeit in einer Industrieregion 1840–1914*, Munich, 1989, 248–57. This author has made this point in several publications, e.g., in '"Aus des Tages Last machen sie ein Kreuz des Herrn …?" Bergarbeiter, Religion und sozialer Protest im Saarrevier des 19. Jahrhunderts', in W. Schieder (ed.), 'Volksreligiosität in der modernen Sozialgeschichte'; *Geschichte und Gesellschaft*, Sonderheft 11, (1986): 154–84. More generally see W.K. Blessing, 'Reform, Restauration, Rezession. Kirchen, Religion und Volksreligiosität zwischen Aufklärung und Industrialisierung', in W. Schieder, *Volksreligiosität*, 97–122. See further Cl. Hiepel, '"Zentrumsgewerkverein" oder autonome Interessenvertretung? Zur Frühgeschichte des Gewerkvereins christlicher Bergarbeiter im Ruhrgebiet', in H.-J. Kaiser and W. Loth (eds), *Soziale Reform im Kaiserreich. Protestantismus, Katholizismus und Sozialpolitik*, Konfession und Gesellschaft, Stuttgart/ Berlin/ Köln, 1997, 155–73; O. Blaschke, 'Das 19. Jahrhundert: Ein Zweites Konfessionelles Zeitalter?', *Geschichte und Gesellschaft*, XXVI, 1 (2000): 38–75; H. Lehman (ed.), *Säkularisierung, Dechristianisierung, Rechristianisierung im neuzeitlichen Europa: Bilanz und Perspektiven der Forschung*, Göttingen, 1997; J. Sperber, *Popular Catholicism in Nineteenth Century Germany: Society, Religion and Politics in Rhineland-Westphalia, 1830–1880*, Princeton NJ, 1984. A. Liedhegener, *Christentum und Urbanisierung. Katholiken und Protestanten in Münster und Bochum, 1830–1933*, Veröffentlichungen der Kommission der Zeitgeschichte, Reihe B, Forschungen 77, Paderborn, 1997 confirmed earlier observations that Catholic practice diverged considerably from Protestant evangelical practice.

31. The most outspoken examples are C.G. Brown, 'The Mechanism of Religious Growth in Urban Cities: British Cities Since the Eighteenth century', in McLeod

(ed.), *European Religion*, 239–62, and Brown, 'A Revisionist Approach to Religious Change', in Bruce (ed.), *Religion and Modernization*, 31–58.

32. McLeod, *Piety and Politics*, 201–9 (esp. 208). This author has developed this thesis in several publications, e.g., in *Religion and the People of Western Europe, 1789–1989*, Oxford/ New York, 1997, 75ff. (orig. 1981); 'Introduction', in McLeod (ed.), *European Religion*, 1–39; *Religion and Society in England*. A new comparative volume by the same author on secularisation in Western Europe, 1848–1914, is forthcoming. S.J.D. Green, *Religion in the Age of Decline. Organisation and Experience in Industrial Yorkshire, 1870–1920*, Cambridge, 1996 also tries to clear away the discussion between 'orthodoxy' and 'revisionism' regarding the secularisation thesis.

33. Blaschke, 'Das 19. Jahrhundert'.

34. To mention only a few review articles which give a survey of the literature: C. Ford, 'Religion and Popular Culture in Modern Europe', *Journal of Modern History*, LXV, 1 (March 1993): 152–75; Anderson, 'Piety and Politics'; D. Blackbourn, 'The Catholic Church in Europe: A Review Article', *Comparative Studies in Society and History*, XXXIII, 4 (1991): 778–90; De Maeyer and Hellemans, 'Katholiek reveil, katholieke verzuiling en dagelijks leven'; McLeod, 'Introduction'.

35. L. Hölscher, 'Secularisation and Urbanisation in the Nineteenth Century: An Interpretative Model', in McLeod (ed.), *European Religion*, 263–88; De Maeyer and Hellemans, 'Katholiek reveil'.

36. See the literature quoted in note 34 and esp. C. Langlois, *Le catholicisme au féminin*, Paris, 1983; C. Langlois, 'Féminisation du catholicisme', in J. Le Goff and R. Rémond (dir.), *Histoire de la France religieuse*, vol. 3: Ph. Boutry et al., *XVIIIe-XIXe siècles*, Paris, 1991, 292–310; Gibson, Social History of French Catholicism; Kl.-M. Haltmann, 'Ultramontanismus und Arbeiterbewegung im Kaiserreich. Überlegungen am Beispiel des Saarriviers', in W. Loth (ed.), *Deutscher Katholizismus im Umbruch zur Moderne*, Konfession und Gesellschaft, 3, Stuttgart, 1991, 76–94.

37. Conway, 'Introduction', 5–6.

38. Compare E. Troeltsch, *The Social Teaching of the Christian Churches*, Chicago IL, 1976, 2 vols (orig. 1912).

39. In this respect the role of the research programme *Konfession und Gesellschaft* of the University of Marburg (Germany) should be emphasised (http://staff-www.uni-marburg.de/~kaiserj). Jochen-Christian Kaiser, one of the main protagonists of this debate, offers an overview of the literature in his article 'Le rôle du facteur religieux dans le travail social aux XIXe et XXe siècles en Allemagne. Bilan de la recherche', in I. von Bueltzingsloewen and D. Pelletier (eds), *La charité en pratique. Chrétiens français et allemands sur le terrain social: XIXe et XXe siècles*, Presses Universitaires de Strasbourg, 1999, 19–32. Also the Ruhr University of Bochum is developing a similar programme. See also the pioneering volume of K. Elm and H.-D. Lock (eds), *Seelsorge und Diakonie in Berlin. Beiträge zum Verhältnis von Kirche und Großstadt im 19. Jahrhundert*, Veröffentlichungen der Historischen Kommission zu Berlin 74, Berlin/New York, 1990; W.R. Ward, *Theology, Sociology and Politics: The German Protestant Social Conscience, 1890–1930*, Bern, 1979; Ward, 'Guilt and Innocence: The German Churches in the Twentieth Century', *The Journal of Modern History*, 68 (June 1996): 398–426; G. Brakelman, 'Evangelischer Sozialtheoretiker vor dem Problem der Gewerkschaften', in F. von Auer and F. Segbers (eds), *Sozialer Protestantismus und Gewerkschaftsbewegung. Kaiserreich – Weimarer Republik – Bundesrepublik Deutschland*, Köln, 1994, 17–38. (Compare, however, Josef Kaiser's review of the volume in which Brakelman's article appeared, in *Internationale Wissenschaftliche*

Korrespondenz zur Geschichte der deutschen Arbeiterbewegung, XXXI, 3 (1995): 433–4). For the Netherlands, see G.J. Schutte (ed.), *De arbeider is zijn loon waardig*. *Honderd jaar na Rerum Novarum en Christelijk Sociaal Congres 1891*. *De ontwikkeling van het christelijk-sociaal denken en handelen in Nederland 1891–1914*, Den Haag, 1991.

40. The exact relationship between the Catholic apostolic and moral associations and workers' leagues and the Christian workers' movements is not always that clear. The question will be discussed at an international conference on the comparative history of the Christian labour movement in Amsterdam, in January 2001 (organisation: IISH and University of Leuven).

41. E. Lamberts (ed.), *Een kantelend tijdperk. De wending van de Kerk naar het volk in Noord-West-Europa – Une époque en mutation. Le catholicisme social dans le Nord-Ouest de l'Europe – Ein Zeitalter im Umbruch. Die Wende der Kirche zum Volk im nordwestlichen Europa (1890–1910)*, KADOC-Studies 13, Leuven University Press, 1992 discusses this change of strategy of the Catholic Church in Belgium, the Netherlands, Germany and Northern France.

42. Cf. Kalyvas, *The Rise of Christian Democracy*, passim.

43. The classic formulation of this paradox (for the Catholic world) is J.-M. Mayeur, 'Catholicisme intransigeant, catholicisme social, démocratie chrétienne', *Annales ESC*, XXII (1972): 483–99; E. Poulat, 'Pour une nouvelle compréhension de la démocratie chrétienne', *Revue d'histoire ecclésiastique*, LXX (1975): 5–38. Recently, Vincent Viaene ('Belgium and the Holy See from Gregory XVI to Pius IX (1831–1859): Catholic Revival, Society and Politics in 19th Century Europe', Unpublished Ph.D. dissertation, Katholieke Universiteit Leuven, 1999) has made an insightful and innovating assessment of the notions of 'intransigentism' (intransigence) and 'transigentism' ('transigence') as well as ultramontanism and liberal Catholicism and their interrelations, which are of capital importance in this context.

44. The ultramontane origin of Christian democracy in Belgium was already observed in 1959 by Karel van Isacker, *Averechtse democratie. De gilden en de christendemocratie in België, 1875–1914*, Antwerp, 1959. The thesis has influenced much research. See e.g., the impressive biography of one of the founders of the Belgian Christian labour movement by Jan de Maeyer, *Arthur Verhaegen 1847–1917. De rode baron*, KADOC-Studies 18, Leuven, 1994. Durand, *L'Europe de la démocratie chrétienne*, however, rightly stresses the distinction between the intransigent stance and Christian democracy. On this subject, see also the comments of Emmanuel Gerard, 'Christen-democratie in België tussen 1891 en 1945. De archeologie van de Christelijke Volkspartij', *Trajecta*, II (1993): 154–75. For Germany see Loth (ed.), *Katholizismus*, esp. Haltmann, 'Ultramontanismus und Arbeiterbewegung'.

45. Pasture, *Histoire du syndicalisme chrétien international*; C. Hiepel, *Arbeiterkatholizismus an der Ruhr. August Brust und der Gewerkverein christlicher Bergarbeiter*, Konfession und Gesellschaft, Stuttgart, 1999; Strikwerda, *A House Divided*.

46. Pasture, *Histoire du syndicalisme chrétien international*; Kalyvas, *The Rise of Christian Democracy*.

47. See note 38.

48. See Schneider, *Die christlichen Gewerkschaften* and even Auer and Segbers (eds), *Sozialer Protestantismus und Gewerkschaftsbewegung*, which attempts to underline the positive attitude of Protestants towards trade unionism (see esp. the article of Traugott Jähnichen, 'Der Evangelisch-soziale Kongress vor der Gewerkschaftsfrage', 113–28); for the Netherlands P.E. Werkman, ' "Een groot werk en een kleine kracht". De organisatie van Lutherse mannen in Nederland 1897–1981', in *Voorlopers en dwarsliggers*. Cahier over de geschiedenis van de christelijk-sociale

beweging 2, Amsterdam/ Utrecht, 1998, 45–78. On closer examination, however, important differences existed within the Lutheran churches. See e.g., H. Otte, "More Churches – More Churchgoers": The Lutheran Church in Hanover between 1850 and 1914', in McLeod, *European Religion*, 90–118. More generally see Spohn, 'Religion and Working-Class Formation in Imperial Germany'; Schneider, *Christliche Gewerkschaften*; H. McLeod, 'Protestantism and Workers in Imperial Germany'.

49. Compare Troeltsch, *The Social Teaching of the Churches*. Some studies on Christian democracy also emphasise the different attitudes of different Christian denominations towards social and political action. See e.g., Conway, 'Introduction' in Conway and Buchanan, *Political Catholicism in Europe*, 1–33; M.P. Fogarty, *Christian Democracy in Europe, 1820–1953*, London, 1957; J.H. Whyte, *Catholics in Western Democracies: A Study in Political Behaviour*, Dublin, 1981; S. Hellemans, 'Zuilen en verzuiling in Europa', in U. Becker (ed.), *Nederlandse politiek in historisch en vergelijkend perspectief*, Amsterdam, 1993, 121–50; J. Madeley, 'Politics and Religion in Western Europe', in G. Moyser (ed.), *Politics and Religion in the Modern World*, London, 1991, 28–66. For Scandinavia, see J. Madeley et al., 'Politics and the Pulpit: the Case of Protestant Europe', in S. Berger (ed.), *Religion in West European Politics*, London, 1982, 149–71. In the Netherlands one has to distinguish between the Dutch Reformed Churches, which remained very reticent towards trade union action, and the Reformed Church in the Netherlands. See Schutte (ed.), *De arbeider is zijn loon waardig*. Liedhegener, *Christentum und Urbanisierung* recently also underlined the importance of the differences in theology between denominations for their relations with modernity.

50. On the *Gewerkschaftsstreit* see the studies of Schneider, Brose and Patch in note 6. In my book *Histoire du syndicalisme chrétien international* I present an overview of the conflicts between unions and churches in most European countries.

51. Pasture, 'Diverging Paths' and *Histoire du syndicalisme chrétien international*.

52. See E. Gerard, 'L'épanouissement du mouvement ouvrier chrétien (1904–1921)', in Gerard and Wynants, *Histoire du Mouvement ouvrier chrétien en Belgique*, vol. I, 114–73; P. Pasture, 'Redressement et expansion (1944–1960)', in ibid., vol. I, 246–301; Pasture, *Kerk, politiek en sociale actie*.

53. See e.g., for Spain: Winston, *Workers and the Right in Spain* and F. Lannon, *Privilege, Persecution and Prophecy: The Catholic Church in Spain, 1875–1975*, Oxford, 1987. In general see Kalyvas, *The Rise of Christian Democracy* (which includes further references) and P. Pasture and E. Lamberts, 'Il sindicalismo cristiano'. Compare also the literature quoted in notes 40 and 48.

54. Hölscher, 'Secularisation and urbanisation'.

55. Kalyvas, *The Rise of Christian Democracy in Europe*; S. Hellemans, *Strijd om de moderniteit. Sociale bewegingen en verzuiling in Europa sinds 1800*, KADOC-Studies 10, Leuven, 1990; Hellemans, 'Zuilen en verzuiling in Europa'; H. Righart, *De katholieke zuil in Europa. Het ontstaan van verzuiling onder katholieken in Oostenrijk, Zwitserland, België en Nederland*, Meppel/ Amsterdam, 1986; H. McLeod, 'Building the "Catholic Ghetto": Catholic Organisations 1870–1914', in W.J. Sheils and D. Wood (eds), *Voluntary Religion*, Studies in Church History 23, Oxford, 1986, 411–44; E.L. Evans, 'Catholic Political Movements in Germany, Switzerland, and The Netherlands: Notes for a Comparative Approach', *Central European History*, VIII (1984): 91–119.

56. Kalyvas, *The Rise of Christian Democracy in Europe*, 2.

57. For opposing views on the future of Christian democracy see David Hanley, 'The Future of Christian Democracy in Europe', in D. Hanley (ed.), *Christian Democracy in Europe*, 212–14 and Lamberts (ed.), *Christian Democracy in the European Union*.

58. Speaking about Catholic parties, Kalyvas argues that they finally became antagonistic to the church, first 'by competing with the church for the right to represent the same constituency and by underlying its hierarchical structure, and second, by redefining Catholicism in a way that eliminated most of its religious content'. Kalyvas, *The Rise of Christian Democracy in Europe*, 258 (and passim). Though I do not question the second observation, I consider this rather as an expression of internal secularisation but not as a cause. In my opinion Kalyvas gives no evidence to prove a causal relation (but see my next observation in the text).

59. Pasture, 'Diverging Paths'.

60. Martin, 'Remise en question'; D. Hervieu-Léger and G. Davie, 'Le déferlement spirituel des nouveaux mouvements religieux', in Davie and Hervieu-Léger (eds), *Identités religieuses en Europe*, 269–89. The emergence of new religious movements, however, does not necessarily contradict the secularisation thesis. See e.g., S. Bruce, *Religion in the Modern World: From Cathedrals to Cults*, Oxford, 1996.

61. P.B. Clarke, 'Introduction: Change and Variety in New Religious Movements in Western Europe, c. 1960 to Present', in E. Arneck and P.B. Clarke, *New Religious Movements in Western Europe: An Annotated Bibliography*, Westport CT / London, 1997, xvii-xliii; Hervieu-Léger and Davie, 'Le déferlement spirituel'.

62. D. Westerlund (ed.), *Questioning the Secular State: The Worldwide Resurgence of Religion in Politics*, London, 1996; J. Casanova, *Public Religions in the Modern World*, Chicago/ London, 1994; Bruce, *Religion in the Modern World;* M. Juergensmeyer, *The New Cold War?: Religious Nationalism Confronts the National State*, Comparative Studies on Religion and Society 5, Berkely/ Los Angeles, 1993.

63. S. Huntington, *The Clash of Civilizations and the Remaking of the World Order*, New York, 1996.

64. G. Davie, 'Contrastes dans l'héritage religieux de l'Europe', and J.-C. Willaime, 'Les religions et l'unification européenne', in Davie and Hervieu-Léger (eds), *Identités religieuses en Europe*, 43–63 and 291–313; S. Zetterholm (ed.), *National Cultures and European Integration: Exploratory Essays on Cultural Diversity and Common Policies*, Oxford/ Providence, 1994. (An opposite perspective is to be found in M. Wintle (ed.), *Culture and Identity in Europe: Perceptions of Divergence and Unity in Past and Present*, Aldershot, 1996.)

65. P.L. Berger, 'The Desecularisation of the World: A Global Overview', in Berger (ed.), *The Desecularisation of the World*, 1–18. Berger, however, considers Europe to be the 'exception', where secularisation indeed is a useful concept, at least since the 1960s. For a challenging alternative interpretation of the dechristianisation/secularisation of Western Europe see D. Hervieu-Léger, *La religion pour mémoire*, Paris, 1993; G. Davie, 'Europe: The Exception that Proves the Rule?', in Berger (ed.), *The Desecularisation of the World*, 65–83, and G. Davie, *Religion in Modern Europe: A Memory Mutates*, Oxford, 2000.

66. An authorative definition of modernity by Stuart Hall refers to the following defining features of modern societies: the dominance of secular forms of political power in defined territorial boundaries; a monetarised exchange economy; the decline of the traditional social order and the appearance of a dynamic social and sexual division of labour; and the decline of the religious world-view and the rise of a secular and materialist culture. S. Hall, 'Introduction', in S. Hall and B. Gieben (eds), *Formations of Modernity*, Understanding of Modern Societies vol. 1, Cambridge, 1992, 6. On the relationship between modernisation theory and the social history of religion see also J. Sperber, 'Kirchengeschichte or the Social and Cultural History of Religion?', *Neue Polnische Literatur*, XL, 1 (1998): 13–35, and K.-E. Löhne, 'Katholizismus-Forschung', *Geschichte und Gesellschaft*, XXVI, 1 (2000): 128–70 (review article).

67. On the relevance of postmodernism for the sociological study of religion see the volume edited by Kieran Flanagan and Peter C. Jupp, *Postmodernity, Sociology and Religion*, Basingstoke, 1996, esp. the introduction (1–13) and the articles of David Lyon, 'Religion and the Postmodern: Old Problems, New Prospects', 14–29, and James A. Bedford, 'Postmodernity, High Modernity, and New Modernity: Three Concepts in Search of Religion', 30–47 (contains a very critical assessment of the work of Z. Bauman, A. Giddens, U. Beck and E. Gellner on religion and postmodernity).

68. S. Hellemans, *Religieuze modernisering*, Katholieke Theologische Universiteit te Utrecht, 1997.

69. E. Hobsbawm and T. Ranger (eds), *The Invention of Tradition*, Past and Present Publications, Cambridge, 1983 (see in particular the introduction, 'Inventing Traditions' by E. Hobsbawm, 1–15); Hellemans, *Religieuze modernisering*, 24–5; E. Poulat, *Eglise contre bourgeoisie. Introduction au devenir du catholicisme actuel*, Tournai, 1977, 242.

70. See esp. U. Beck, *The Reinvention of Politics: Rethinking Modernity in the Global Social Order*, Cambridge, 1997, chap. 2; U. Beck, A. Giddens and S. Lash, *Reflexive Modernisation: Politics, Society and Aesthetics in the Modern Social Order*, Cambridge, 1994.

71. D. Hervieu-Léger, 'La religion des européens: modernité, religion, sécularisation', in Davie and Hervieu-Léger (eds), *Identités religieuses en Europe*, 9–23. See also D. Hervieu-Léger, *Vers un nouveau christianisme? Introduction à la sociologie du christianisme occidental*, Paris, 1982, and *La religion pour mémoire*, Paris, 1992. A similar point, but from a different perspective, is made in A. Vergote, *Modernité et christianisme: interrogations critiques réciproques*, Paris, 1999.

72. Hervieu-Léger, 'La religion des européens'; Blackburn, 'The Catholic Church in Europe'.

73. Hellemans, *Religieuze modernisering*.

74. See e.g., Arbeitskreis für Kirchlichen Zeitgeschichte, Münster, 'Katholiken zwischen Tradition und Moderne. Das katholische Milieu als Forschungsausgabe', *Westfälische Forschungen*, XLIII (1993): 588–654; Liedhegener, *Christentum und Urbanisierung*; I. von Bueltzingsloewen and D. Pelletier, 'Modernité des chrétiens-sociaux', *Vingtième siècle. Revue d'histoire*, 53 (1997): 156–7 (report on the conference *Pratiques chrétiennes sur le terrain social. France – Allemagne XIX-XXe siècle*, Göttingen, 30 to 31 mai 1996); Cl. Langlois, 'Le catholicisme au XIXe siècle. Entre modernité et modernisation', *Recherches de science religieuse*, LXXIX, 3 (1991): 326–36, but also the conclusion of Cholvy and Hilaire, *Histoire religieuse*, vol. II, 485–495. Compare the ambivalent way in which Urs Altermatt describes the Catholic social movement as 'Antimodernismus mit modernen Mitteln' (*Katholizismus und Moderne. Zur Sozial- und Mentalitätsgeschichte der Schweizer Katholiken im 19. und 20. Jahrhundert*, Zürich, 1989, 49) or K. Gabriel, 'Ein Amalgam aus Tradition und Modernität', in *Christentum zwischen Tradition und Postmoderne*, Freiburg i. Breisgau, 1992, 16 (examples quoted in Hellemans, *Religieuze modernisering*, 10).

75. Strikwerda, *A House Divided*, about technology: 292–3.

76. R. Wallis and S. Bruce, 'Secularisation: The Orthodox Model', in Bruce, *Religion and Modernization*, 8–29.

77. See in particular the recent literature quoted in note 26. The secularisation thesis, however, still finds fervent supporters, of whom Karel Dobbelaere and Bryan Wilson probably are the most distinguished. See e.g., K. Dobbelaere, 'Religion in Europe and North America', in R. de Moor (ed.), *Values in Western Societies*, Tilburg, 1995, 1–30, and 'Church Involvment and Secularization: Making Sense of the European Case', in E. Barker, J.E. Beckford and K. Dobbelaere (eds), *Sec-*

ularization, Rationalism and Sectarianism: Essays in Honour of Bryan R. Wilson, Oxford, 1993, 19–36 (it should be noted, however, that Dobbelaere limits the scope of his argument to the last decades).

78. There is a (highly critical) review of the Dutch and Belgian literature on pillarisation in S. Hellemans, *Pleidooi voor een internationale en tegen een provincialistische benadering van verzuiling*, Rapport 1990/1, KU Leuven, 1990. Incidentally, these ideas show remarkable resemblances with those of Maria Rainer Lepsius, 'Parteiensystem und Sozialstruktur. Zum Problem der Demokratisierung der deutschen Gesellschaft', in Gerhard A. Ritter (ed.), *Deutsche Parteien vor 1918*, Köln, 1973, 56–80. As Wilhelm Damberg observed, the theoretical and empirical research about these phenomena in the Netherlands – and I would add also in Belgium – is 'much further developed than in Germany'. W. Damberg, *Abschied von Milieu? Katholizismus im Bistum Münster und in den Niederlanden, 1948–1980*, Veröffentlichungen der Kommission der Zeitgeschichte, Reihe B Forschungen 79, Paderborn, 1997, 26. Two recent overviews of the pillarisation debate are Michael Wintle, 'Pillarisation, Consociation, and Vertical Pluralism in the Netherlands Revisited: A European View' and J.C.H. Blom, 'Pillarisation in Perspective', *West European Politics*, XXIII, 3 (July 2000) 139–52, 153–64.

79. E.g., W. Damberg, 'Kirchliche Zeitgeschichte Westfalens, der Schweiz, Belgiens und der Niederlande. Das Katholische Beispiel', *Westfälische Forschungen*, XLII (1992): 445–56; H. McLeod, 'Protestantism and the Working Class in Imperial Germany', *European Studies Review*, XII, 3 (July 1982): 323–43, and 'Building the Catholic 'ghetto''; U. Altermatt, 'Katholische Subgesellschaft. These zum Konzept der "katholischen Subgesellschaft" am Beispiel des Schweizer Katholizismus', in K. Gabriel and F.X. Kauffmann (eds), *Zur Soziologie des Katholizismus*, Mainz, 1980, 145–65; R. Steininger, *Polarisierung und Integration. Eine vergleichende Untersuchung der strukturellen Versäulung der Gesellschaft in den Niederlanden und in Österreich*, Meisenheim am Glan, 1975; Spohn, 'Religion and Working-Class Formation', 111. See also Whyte, *Catholics in Western Democracies* and Fogarty, *Christian Democracy in Western Europe*. See also K. Tenfelde, 'Historische Milieus – Erleblichkeit und Konkurrenz', in M. Hettling and P. Nolte (eds), *Nation und Gesellschaft in Deutschland. Historische Essays*, Munich, 1996, 247–68; W. Loth, 'Integration und Erosion. Wandlungen des katholischen Milieus in Deutschland', in Loth (ed.), *Deutscher Katholizismus im Ubruch zur Moderne*, 266–81; H. Mooser, 'Das katholische Milieu in der bürgerlichen Gesellschaft. Zum Vereinswesen des Katholizismus im späten Deutschen Kaiserreich', in O. Blachke and F.M. Kuhlemann (eds), *Religion im Kaiserreich. Milieus – Mentalitäten – Krisen*, Religiöse Kulturen der Moderne, vol. 2, Gütersloh, 1991, 59–92; Spohn, 'Religion and Working-Class Formation'.

80. Hellemans, *Strijd om de moderniteit*; Hellemans, 'Zuilen en verzuiling in Europa'. The idea of viewing pillars as social movements and thus as part of modernity was, to my knowledge, first suggested by J.E. Ellemers, 'Pillarization as a Process of Modernization', *Acta Politica*, XIX, 1 (1984): 129–44. See also D. Blackbourn, 'Progress and Piety: Liberals, Catholics and the State in Bismarck's Germany', in D. Blackbourn, *Populists and Patricians: Essays in Modern German History*, London, 1987, 143–67; Ebbinghaus, *Labour Unity in Union Diversity*. We look forward to the results of the current comparative study of pillarisation by Elisabeth Fix (Mannheimer Zentrum für Europäische Sozialforschung, University of Mannheim).

81. It is precisely this observation that led Hellemans to reassess the notion of modernity as described above (Hellemans, *Religieuze modernisering*, 36, note 10). A similar point regarding recent German studies about 'Milieus' is made by Sperber, 'Kirchengeschichte', 15.

82. Kalyvas, *Christian Democracy in Europe*; Hellemans, *Strijd om de moderniteit*; Righart, *De katholieke zuil in Europa*. This observation also dovetails remarkably with Van Kersbergen's comment concerning the development and importance of Catholic social doctrine: 'It was, however, the "little" tradition of social capitalism that has provided the Christian-Democratic movements in Western Europe with a social concern and with a more practical theory of social policy and modern politics. Social capitalism has managed to go beyond medieval ideas on charity in spite of rather than thanks to the social teaching of the church'. K. van Kersbergen, *Social Capitalism: A Study of Christian Democracy and the Welfare State*, London/ New York, 1995, 228.

83. P. Pasture, 'Belgium: Pragmatism in Pluralism', in Pasture, Verberckmoes and De Witte (eds), *The Lost Perspective?*, vol. 1, 91–135; Spohn, 'Religion and Working-Class Formation', esp. 112.

84. Most recently, Dutch scholars in particular have tended to abandon the concept of pillarisation, arguing that it has become too vague and therefore useless as an analytical tool. E.g., Meeuwen, *Lijden aan eenheid*, 16–19. In Germany, however, the concept of sociocultural 'Milieus' recently witnessed a renaissance: e.g., T. Adam and W. Bramke (eds), *Milieukonzept und empirische Forschung*, Komparativ – Leipziger Beiträge zur Universalgeschichte und vergleichenden Gesellschafts-forschung, XI, 2, Leipzig, 1999; Klaus Tenfelde, *Milieus, politische Sozialisation und Generationenkonflikte*, Bonn, 1998.

85. The concept of 'multiple identities' seems to me to have been popularised in labour history by E.P. Thompson, *Worlds of Labour*.

86. Ebbinghaus, *Labour Unity in Union Diversity*; Ebbinghaus, 'From Ideology to Organization: The Transformation of Political Unionism in Western Europe', in Pasture, Verberckmoes and De Witte (eds), *The Lost Perspective?*, vol. 2, 28–59. See also, but to a much lesser extent, S. Berger, 'European Labour Movements and the European Working Class in Comparative Perspective', in Berger and Broughton (eds), *The Force of Labour*, 245–61.

87. An early example in S. Yeo, *Religion and Voluntary Organisations in Crisis*, London, 1976. An excellent overview of this shift in this context is Ford, 'Religion and Popular Culture'. See also the contributions of Jürgen Kocka and Mike Savage elsewhere in this volume.

88. See H. McLeod, *Religion and the People of Western Europe*, 1789–1970, Oxford, 1981 (1997), 118–37.

89. Quoted in K. Geiger, A. Grossman and R. Horowitz, '[Report of the] 1994 Social Science History Association [Conference]', *International Labor and Working-Class History*, 48 (Fall 1995): 162.

90. The significance of religion for the politics of the early labour movement was of course a major theme in Britain, but this perspective largely remained confined to British labour and working-class history and did not spread to the European continent. This literature is discussed in H. McLeod, *Religion and the Working Class in Nineteenth-Century Britain*, Studies in Economic Social History, London/ Basingstoke, 1984.

91. Spohn, 'Religion and Working-Class Formation'; P. Pasture, 'Où sont les travailleurs d'antan? La perception de la classe ouvrière par le mouvement ouvrier chrétien belge dans la période d'après-guerre', in J. Deniot and C. Dutheil (dir.), *Métamorphoses ouvrières*, Logiques sociales, Paris, 1995, vol. 2, 225–37. Though there exist numerous books and articles on the JOC, the movement (which spread over Europe and even over the whole world) still awaits a historical-critical study.

92. This idea is crucial to P. Joyce, *Visions of the People: Industrial England and the Question of Class*, Cambridge, 1991.

93. This idea shows some similarities with the anthropological notions of 'primordial attachments' or sentiments found in the work of Clifford Geertz and others (e.g., C. Geertz, 'The Integrative Revolution: Primordial Sentiments and Civil Politics in the New States', in C. Geertz, *The Interpretation of Cultures: Selected Essays*, London, 1993 (orig. 1963), 255–310). However I do not see why nation or even race or ethnicity should be regarded as more 'primordial' than class. I consider all collective identities as 'constructed', based upon common experiences and perceptions (and therefore I prefer the notion 'constructed' to 'imagined').

94. Recent examples include P. van Duin, 'Proletarian Prejudices: The Impact of Ethnic and Racial Antagonism on Working-Class Organization 1830–1930', in W.R. Garscha and C. Schindler (eds), *Arbeiterbewegung und nationale Identität*, ITH-Tagungsberichte 30, Vienna, 1994, 55–95; S. Fielding, *Class and Ethnicity: Irish Catholics in England, 1880–1939*, Themes in Twentieth Century, Buckingham/ Philadelphia, 1993; J.J. Kulczycki, *The Foreign Worker and the German Labor Movement: Xenophobia and Solidarity in the Coal Fields of the Ruhr, 1871–1914*, Oxford/ Providence, 1994; Kulczycki, *The Polish Coal Miners' Union and the German Labor Movement in the Ruhr, 1902–1934: National and Social Solidarity*, Oxford/ New York, 1997; L. Mees, 'Nationalismus und Arbeiterbewegung im Spanischen Baskenland zwischen 1876 und 1923', *Geschichte und Gesellschaft*, XX, 3 (1994): 364–84; C.M. Prelinger, *Charity, Challenge and Change: Religious Dimensions of the Mid-Nineteenth Century Women's Movement in Germany*, Contributions on Women's Studies 75, Westport CO, 1987. See also S. Berger and A. Smith (eds), *Nationalism, Labour and Ethnicity, 1870–1939*, Manchester/ New York, 1999; P. Pasture and J. Verberckmoes (eds), *Working Class Internationalism and the Appeal of National Identity: Historical Dilemmas and Current Debates on Western Europe*, Oxford, 1998; H. Gruber and P. Graves (eds), *Women and Socialism, Socialism and Women: Europe Between the Two World Wars*, New York, 1998; Ford, 'Religion and Popular Culture'.

95. See S.M. Lipset's famous thesis, 'Democracy and Working-Class Authoritarianism', *American Sociological Review*, IV (1959): 482–501, further developed in the publications of C.P. Middendorp and H. de Witte. See H. de Witte and P. Scheepers (eds), *Ideology in the Low Countries: Trends, Models and Lacunae*, Assen, 1999.

96. G. Esping-Andersen, *The Three Worlds of Welfare Capitalism*, Cambridge, 1990.

97. J.D. Stephens, *The Transition from Capitalism to Socialism*, London, 1979; P. Flora and J. Alber, 'Modernization, Democratization and the Development of Welfare States in Western Europe', in P. Flora and A.J. Heidenheimer (eds), *The Development of Welfare States in Europe and America*, New Brunswick/ London, 1990, 37–80. Van Kersbergen, *Social Capitalism*, 24, gives some other references. Good overviews of the literature are provided by Van Kersbergen, *Social Capitalism*, 6–30, and A. Hemerijck, 'Welfare State Development, European Integration and the Lost Perspective of Inclusive Unionism', in Pasture, Verberckmoes and De Witte, *The Lost Perspective?*, vol. 2, 107–36.

98. Esping-Andersen, *Three Worlds*, 37.

99. F. Castles and D. Mitchell, 'Worlds of Welfare and Families of Nations', in F. Castles (ed.), *Families of Nations: Patterns of Public Policy in Western Democracies*, Aldershot, 1993; E. Huber, C. Ragin and J.D. Stephens, 'Social Democracy, Christian Democracy, Constitutional Structure, and the Welfare State', *American Journal of Sociology*, IC, 3 (Nov. 1993): 711–49; J. Misra and A. Hicks, 'Catholicism and Unionization in Affluent Postwar Democracies: Catholicism, Culture, Party and Unionization', *American Sociological Review*, 59 (April 1994): 304–26.

100. J. Bussemakers and K. van Kersbergen, 'Gender and Welfare States: Some Theoretical Reflections', in D. Sainsbury (ed.), *Gendering Welfare States*, London,

1993, 8–25; S. Pedersen, *Family, Dependence and the Origins of the Welfare State: Britain and France*, Cambridge, 1993; Castles and Mitchell, 'Worlds of Welfare and Families of Nations'; J. Misra, 'Mothers or Workers? The Value of Unpaid Labour and Welfare State Regimes', Unpublished Paper, University of Georgia, [1996]; S. Lessenich and I. Ostner, 'Die institionelle Dynamik "dritter Wege" – Zur Entwicklung der Familienpolitik in "katholischen" Wohlfahrtstaaten am Beispiel Deutschlands und Frankreichs', in F.X. Kaufmann (ed.), *Sozialpolitik im französisch-deutschen Vergleich*, Schriften der Sektion Sozialpolitik der Deutschen Gesellschaft für Soziologie 1, Wiesbaden, 1996, 780–803.

101. See e.g., L. Heerma van Voss, 'The Embarrassment of Poverty: Why Do the Proverbial Welfare States Border on the North Sea?', in A. Knotter, B. Altena and D. Damsma, *Labour, Social Policy and the Welfare State*, Amsterdam, 1997, 17–33. See also D. van Damme, *Armenzorg en de staat. Comparatief-historische studie van de origines van de moderne verzorgingsstaat in West-Europa (voornamelijk achttiende tot begin negentiende eeuw)*, Gent, 1990. The importance of the religious factor and differences between denominations, in medieval and early modern Europe, are of course major themes in social history, but ones I do not deal with in this article.

102. M. Hertogh, *'Geene wet, maar de Heer!'. De confessionele ordening van het Nederlandse sociale-zekerheidsstelsel (1870–1975)*, 's Gravenhage, 1998; J. Roebroek and M. Hertogh, *'De beschavende invloed des tijds': twee eeuwen sociale politiek, verzorgingsstaat en sociale zekerheid in Nederland*, 's Gravenhage, 1998. I am currently preparing a comparative study on the impact of Christian social movements on the development of welfare states in Europe from 1860 to 1960.

103. E.g., in M.H.D. van Leeuwen, 'Trade Unions and the Provision of Social Welfare in the Netherlands, 1910–1960', *Economic History Review*, L, 4 (1997): 764–91; R.H. Cox, *The Development of the Dutch Welfare State: From Workers' Insurance to Universal Entitlement*, Pittsburgh, 1993.

104. Van Kersbergen, *Social Capitalism*, 192 ff. See also Kalyvas, *The Rise of Christian Democracy*, and Pasture, *Kerk, politiek en sociale actie*, chap. 4.

105. Lamberts, 'General Conclusions' in Lamberts (ed.), *Christian Democracy in the European Union*, stresses the parallelisms between Christian democracy and conservatism. For Van Kersbergen, Christian democracy partly originates in conservative and traditional ideologies, but has other sources as well, *Social Capitalism*, 205–28.

106. Van Kersbergen, *Social Capitalism*, 207. Apparently, however, in Austria Christian democracy developed without much attention to the workers. See J.W. Boyer, *Political Radicalism in Late Imperial Vienna: Origins of the Christian Social Movement, 1848–1897*, Chicago, 1991, and Boyer, *Culture and Political Crisis in Vienna: Christian Socialism in Power, 1897–1914*, Chicago, 1995.

107. Van Kersbergen, *Social Capitalism*, 231. See also H.E.S. Woldring, *De christendemocratie: een kritisch onderzoek naar haar politieke filosofie*, Utrecht, 1996.

108. I. von Bueltzingsloewen and D. Pelletier, 'Introduction', and Pelletier, 'Les pratiques charitables françaises' in Bueltzingsloewen and Pelletier (eds), *La charité en pratique*, 9–17 and 33–47; S. Kott, 'Vers une historiographie européenne de l'état social? Recherches récentes sur les cas français et allemand au XIXe siècle', *Archiv für Sozialgeschichte*, XXXV (1995): 445–56.

109. In Belgium the trade unions and mutual help societies (*mutualités*), in which Christian organisations hold a majority position, have a predominant role in the payment and organisation of social security, especially in unemployment and health insurance respectively.

110. See e.g., M.H.D. van Leeuwen, 'Opbloei van de charitas na 1965', in J. van Gerwen and M.H.D. van Leeuwen (eds), *Studies over zekerheidsarrangementen:*

risico's, risicobestrijding en verzekeringen in Nederland vanaf de Middeleeuwen, Amsterdam/ Den Haag, 1998, 759–806.

111. Kaiser, 'Le rôle du facteur religieux dans le travail social'; 'Einleitung des Herausgeber', in Kaiser and Loth (eds), *Soziale Reform im Kaiserreich*, 9–18.

112. C. Crouch, *Industrial Relations and European State Traditions*, Oxford, 1993.

113. The original quotation runs as follows: 'it is through the historian's treatment of the working classes during the process of urban growth and change that we need to approach the revision of the social history of modern (British) religion'. Brown, 'The Mechanism of Religious Growth', 241.

114. Loth, 'Integration und Erosion'.

115. See particularly Spohn, 'Religion and Working-Class Formation'; J.E. Smith, *Quasi-Religions: Humanism, Marxism and Nationalism*, Themes in Comparative Religion, Basingstoke, 1994; C. Lane, *The Rites of Rulers, Ritual in Industrial Society: The Soviet Case*, Cambridge, 1981; S. Yeo, 'A New Life: the Religion of Socialism in Britain, 1883–1896', *History Workshop*, 4 (Autumn 1977): 5–56. Noteworthy in this respect is also Erhard Lucas' remarkable essay on the significance of 'religion' in its broadest sense for the history of the German labour movement: E. Lucas, *Vom Scheitern der deutschen Arbeiterbewegung*, Basel/ Frankfurt, 1983 (thanks to Klaus Tenfelde for drawing my attention to this booklet).

116. C. Geertz, *The Interpretation of Cultures: Selected Essays*, London, 1993, 87–125 (orig. publ. 1966); P. Berger, *The Sacred Panoply: Elements of a Sociological Theory of Religion*, New York, 1969. Such an approach to nineteenth-century religion is promoted by Thomas Kselman (e.g., *Death and the Afterlife in Nineteenth-Century France*, Princeton NJ, 1993; Kselman, 'The Variations of Religious Experience'). The International Conference of Labour Historians, 'Rituals, Myths and Symbols – The Labour Movement Between Religion and Popular Culture', Linz, 9 – 13 September 1997, fits remarkably well in this perspective.

117. Cf. A. Vergote, *Religion, Belief and Unbelief. A Psychological Study*, Leuven, 1997 (offers in my opinion the best assessment of the religious phenomenon). One overview of different approaches to and definitions of religion is J.G. Platvoet and A.L. Molendijk (eds), *The Pragmatics of Defining Religion: Contexts, Concepts and Contests*, Studies in the History of Religions, Numen Book Series 84, Leiden, 1999.

CHAPTER 7

TWO LABOUR HISTORIES OR ONE?

Alice Kessler-Harris

Critique and Applause

Laments over the poor health of scholarship in labour history have continued now on both sides of the Atlantic for many years. In the USA, the field is depicted as being 'on the defensive', chastened by accusations of fragmentation and its failure to develop a 'synthesis' that can explain the American past. Discontent is reflected in the repeated calls to labour historians to produce a labour history that utilises class relations to speak to the meaning of US political processes and ideas. Some, like Ira Katznelson, have attributed our failure to achieve such a synthesis to the 'mutual suspicion and disdain' held by two groups of seemingly irreconcilable labour historians: 'those grounded in Marxism and ancillary socialist traditions and those nourished by various postmodern turns, including the multi-layered emphasis on discourse, power, and identity'.[1] I confess to some puzzlement over this phenomenon, for in my view the territorial markers laid out by many of the practitioners of labour history do not so much identify obstacles in the path of intellectual synergy as create them.

There is much to applaud. The numbers of books published in the field continues unabated; the North American Labor History Conference, born in 1979 and revivified in 1990, expands apace; and, as I write, a new national Labor and Working Class History Association is in the process of nominating its first slate of officers. There is more. Many traditional political historians protest that social history, by which they often mean the history of ordinary folk, has permeated the professional associations and dominates its journals. At the same time, several journals have joined the now venerable *Labor History* to expand the intellectual and geographical boundaries of the field. *International Labor and Working-Class History*; *Radical History Review*; and *Labour/Le Travail* have redefined the meaning of working-class history and increasingly US scholars of labour have inched out of their insularity to engage issues raised by South Asian, Australian and European (particularly British) scholars. Efforts to think about history comparatively are still in their early stages.[2] They promise exciting results. So exciting, in fact, that part of me wants to act on the slogan we used to shout in 1960s anti-war demonstrations: let's just declare victory and go home.

The voices that mourn confusion and division are just as loud in Europe as they are in the United States, and just as contested. Jürgen Kocka describes the current mood as one of 'exhaustion, dissatisfaction with traditions and steady decline'. In his view, this is largely brought on by the declining authority of labour and social democratic parties and in their transformation into representatives of more centrist, or less class-conscious positions. Michael Savage speaks about a labour history in crisis – one that is bound up with questions about the relevance of class analysis. Their voices echo a sharp divide between the advocates of poststructuralist explorations of language and those who cling to materially rooted explanations. And yet the substance of much new work, including the chapters in this volume, suggests a healthy new effort at integration that transcends arguments that pit a postmodern mode against Marxian dicta.

Collectively, these chapters suggest that the sources of discontent among European labour historians lie in the failure of the field to come to terms with several interrelated issues. These include challenges to old notions of class and class formation; gender, race and ethnicity as political factors; the threat to the contemporary labour movement posed by the global market; and poststructural theory. Individually, each essay seeks an opportunity to bridge the chasm created by rigid uses of class and narrow definitions of materialism by making use of new analytic categories whose absence has constrained the range of labour history. In some sense, then, each essay is an effort to expand the capacious possibilities of our field rather than a sign of confusion. The authors infuse categories like worker, production and consciousness with a broader range of meanings as they reshape them to accommodate households, neighbourhoods and communities. In their hands, we begin to see how gender, race and ethnicity serve as access routes to a transnational analysis of labour by fostering visions of shared identity and purpose across national borders. These papers suggest, in other words, something of how the tropes of the postmodern might serve less to obstruct synthesis than to facilitate new meanings of class so that it becomes once again a usable category.

Positions

I want to make a case for this optimistic projection for the field of labour history by speaking to how some of the papers in this collection, as well as other recent works, move us in this new direction. I suggest that the search for identity and the use of some form of linguistic analysis are both crucial to this process. But I do not pose them as alternatives to a class analysis. Rather, I argue that by focusing on the creation of social identities, the new labour history provides a promising pathway into expanding class, and a helpful way of rejuvenating class analysis. It can also tell us much about how community and political consciousness are shaped in ways that deeply influence the global market place.

My position in this respect differs tangentially from that of Jürgen Kocka. Kocka acknowledges the influence of language and identity, particularly gendered identity, in opening new topics to debate and in enriching understandings of categories like production. Yet far from conceiving these as vital opportunities for labour historians, he draws comfort from the paucity of articles in the leading journals that deal with new arenas and from recognizable continuities with Marxian and Weberian frameworks. I ask, instead, what happens when we allow the insights that accrue from embracing what is sometimes labelled as a paradigm shift to enter our work. I believe that only when we begin to imagine class as both process and identity, infused with a variety of other processual identities, will we be able to imagine a labour history for the future. Far from seeing that shift as the source of fragmentation in historical interpretation – a negative and dispiriting phenomenon that undermines the efforts of scholars to find continuities – I detect in it unifying forces that are potentially inspiring to those who seek synthesis.

In this respect, Michael Savage comes closer. Savage identifies a new division in our field, with advocates of class as the central analytical category for labour history on one side, and, on the other, those who seek and find explanation in such new social movements as feminism, ethnicity and ecology. One side maintains the value of an empirical history rooted in the workplace and everyday life; the other locates itself in the tropes of gender, culturalism and the postmodern. Savage backs off from a sharp distinction, suggesting instead that lines might more fruitfully be drawn elsewhere: between those who argue for a history in which the structure of capitalism (including industrial relations and workplace culture) determines consciousness and therefore class identification, and those who understand capitalism in its more complex dimensions as including what we might call 'social being'. This latter, Savage argues, engages issues of identity like job security and leisure and through them yields clues to the politics of class formation.

If more rigid definitions of class challenge labour historians to write histories of working people in an environment where the forward march of labour has been halted, more fluid definitions yield the much more formidable (though perhaps less depressing task) of wielding class constructively. The two approaches differ not only in their usage of class but in their assessment of how class is formed and in the ingredients of class formation as well. They are united by their agreement about the centrality of class consciousness to political culture. In this respect both deserve the mantle of labour history. Still, what appear to some labour historians as 'trends', accommodated within a versatile labour history that continues to rotate around working men and the positions of their families in the marketplace, are perhaps more usefully captured as an effort to renegotiate the content of class in ways consistent with traditional definitions yet at the same time more supple and more amenable to explaining historically-specific class formations.

Pessimism

A look at some of the problem areas in recent work moves us in that direction. Scholars on both sides of the Atlantic share the pessimism engendered by a steady decline of the labour movement. In the United States, organised labour represents less than 15 percent of all public and private workers; it is routinely portrayed as a 'special interest' in political circles. In Europe, the practical restraints of a global market, as well as a newly pervasive ideology of free enterprise, have eroded the ability of working people to elect governments that protect their well-being. The growing irrelevance of workers and their institutions to contemporary politics has called into question a teleology of progress embedded in both liberal and Marxian theories, creating what Savage calls 'a profound crisis of confidence' among labour historians. Both Savage and Kocka note that the declining authority of labour has shaken labour history to its core. Their concern echoes that of American labour historians, whose distress has led them recently to become the leading elements of a 'teach-in' movement on the value of trade unions, and to join with trade union leaders to create an organisation called Scholars and Writers for Social Justice.

If doubts about labour's relevance have disrupted scholarly efforts to portray workers and their unions as the sparks of class struggle, methodological challenges have undermined the capacity of labour historians to speak confidently about the content of class and class formation.[3] Class, as Savage notes, 'was the central rallying cry for those seeking a politically committed labour history'. And yet now he wonders whether 'the salience of gender, ethnicity, etc. serve to discredit the importance of class' or whether the concept can be reformulated. Savage in the end ducks this question in favour of a theory of economic insecurity – which indirectly incorporates both gender and ethnicity without abandoning class. Kocka is less generous. He seems to argue that newer explorations of group consciousness widen the chasm between social history and politics, and protests the efforts of scholars eager to infuse the unwieldy insights of gender and post-structuralism into the field even as he acknowledges their contributions to invigorating and extending the boundaries of labour history. Dismissing what he calls 'the rather absurd monopoly-like claims' that gender sometimes makes for itself, and savouring the failure of the linguistic turn to make much of an impact, he suggests that these challenges will be readily incorporated without changing the shape of a labour history in which class constitutes the central analytical force.

Optimism

But some of the essays in this collection reveal how new and richer meanings for class and class formation can emerge from these seemingly peripheral positions to enrich the meaning of labour history. Because each presents a more complicated portrait of the relationship of working people to politics and culture, these pieces are, in total, informed by a more encompassing view of class. At the same time, they offer a fuller view of emerging consciousness and engagement that speaks to issues of class formation – one that implicitly shakes off a rigid insistence on its relationship to production and incorporates the possibilities of relations of consumption. Taken together, they reveal the workings of a more complex sense of identity than labour historians have traditionally allowed. John Belchem, for example, tells us that his focus on ethnicity is meant to enable 'a critical deconstruction of dominant formations'. Eileen Yeo identifies gender as a key aspect of identity construction and then leaps from it to examine the perspectives from which working people 'see the world and live and act in it'. Patrick Pasture challenges the received wisdom about the irrelevance of religion to explore the role of the religious ideal in modernity.

Like other recent work, these essays are profoundly political even where their analysis is not driven by institutions (as it sometimes is in Belchem's work, for example) and does not rotate around the state. They promise to reveal something of the relationship of ordinary people to political culture. And they speak effectively to relationships of power, illuminating on the one hand the creation of consciousness, and on the other, the ways political decisions emerge. Their eagerness to embrace the idea that individuals develop consciousness out of multiple forms of identity produced in arenas that are both inside and outside the workplace, suggests a complex and layered conception of class as a source of political behaviour, and one far more usable in a world where fewer and fewer workers produce goods; most workers identify themselves as middle class; and where consumption (which is defined as leisure) has become far and away the primary object of work for most workers.

A more capacious understanding of class enables a usage of power (some might call this Foucaultian) and politics independent of institutions; it provides access to notions like civil society and citizenship that have only recently become the province of historians and are still bound to liberal political theory. Granted that such usages tend to decentre the structures of capitalism and their relationship to workers, they also have the advantage of providing new ways to reconstruct the politics of ordinary people. They are especially useful for describing how different people imagine themselves as political creatures, members of civil society, and active participants. A notion of class as a process that emerges from layered and complicated identities has fuelled a new usage of conceptions of citizenship, especially among historians of late nineteenth- and twentieth-century labour. Read as active participation, rather than as the distribution of formal rights, the idea of citizenship has become an access route into understanding the relationship of workers to the state. The recent work of David Montgomery, for example, argues that as nineteenth-century free-market entrepreneurs took greater control over the mechanisms of state regulation, workers attempted to protect community welfare by exercising political pressure. Glenda Gilmore's explorations of middle-class African-Americans in the late nineteenth century reveals the particular patterns that emerged in one community when racial restrictions constrained efforts to draw on class privilege. Joanne Goodwin's analysis of political struggles among middle-class women speaks to the ways in which gendered and class-derived conceptions of order and virtue negatively affected the lives of poor and working-class women.[4]

Citizenship and Consciousness

A citizenship rooted in historical circumstance rather than in abstract ideals can more readily be imagined as a process. In addition to endowing individuals and groups with positive and negative rights and freedoms, it opens up for examination questions of how ordinary people situate themselves with respect to national ideals like liberty, equality and freedom, and what forces create change. In the United States, for example, the relationship of women to liberty is mediated by ethnic and racial constraints; but just as male members of certain ethnic and racial groups possesses differential relationships to liberty, so no woman possess the same relationship to it as white men. The locations of particular men and women with respect to rights and freedoms foster and/or inhibit various forms of participation in the polity such as voting, public demonstrations, or trade union organising. But exactly how do racial and gendered location participate in class formation? We can answer that question by utilising language to provide access to subjective experience and to uncover individual perceptions of agency. Without entering the debate about the historical nihilism of poststructuralism, I would argue, along with many of my colleagues, that insofar as the linguistic turn enhances the explanatory power of concepts like identity and citizenship, it will continue to be one among many methods on which we will rely. If citizenship is a historical process, the dynamics of which is engaged by power, then one task of the historian is surely to explore how a variety of factors reshape its meanings in different historical circumstances. Political scientists and sociologists have tried to do this by looking at power resources and state structures. Their methods beg underlying questions of how groups are constituted and particularly of the consciousness and identity that produces them. They have not, in my judgement, overcome the need for a set of analytic categories that makes sense of individual and group pressures for change. A gendered and racialised conception of class fills that need. Why not, then, seize 'identity' as a way of deconstructing the meaning of class and turning it into a more discerning category of analysis?

The work of a large number of historians of working people has already demonstrated the value of a variety of conceptions of identity in opening up the meaning of consciousness.[5] Among these papers, John Belchem's essay provides a case in point, suggesting some of its rich possibilities by applying this new view of consciousness to working-class life in Ireland. Irish ethnic identities, he tells us, were constructed on both sides of the Atlantic. They are 'relational, constructed in historical dialogue between dominant and subordinate groups'. In the piece reprinted here, Belchem eloquently reveals how

Irish identity in the USA becomes saturated with Catholicism, how kinship ties, perpetuated and imagined by women, influenced political participation, and how generational change re-formed identity in new and more complex ways. Though every sentence of his chapter contains some allusion to how these shifts altered economic circumstance, he stops short of conceiving class as a part of the changing phenomena he describes. Rather, he tells us towards the end of the chapter that 'generational tensions probably caused as much conflict as gender or class differences within the ethnic community'. The statement cries out for integration. For he seems to have beautifully suggested the ways in which class consciousness has changed as its generational and gendered content have shifted meaning. His own work makes far more sense if we imagine identities bound into a sheaf that measures class formation.

Belchem prefigures and participates in some recently published work that reflects the spirit of David Roediger's pioneering work on the emergence of a white wage-earning consciousness in the USA. For Roediger, the white working class constructed its identity in significant part out of the desire to differentiate itself from nonwhite people and thus to mark its privileges. In his view, all workers were raced, some differently from others. The idea that race is actively constructed, not least by the white folks who benefit from it in relation to nonwhites and by different ethnic groups to position themselves closer to whiteness, has since been picked up by other historians and social scientists. American labour historians have taken for granted not merely the privileges that accrued to whiteness and the effects of such privileges in constructing the labour force but the limits they imposed on consciousness. These include collusion among white men across class lines in the interest of racial privilege, and of all men across gendered lines in the interest of gender privilege.[6] Belchem does not pursue this insight, offering instead his own notion that relations of domination can be seen through the activity of particular forms of ethnicity.

Identity and Gender

It is no accident that American labour historians perceive race as a constitutive element of class conflict or that issues of race and empire have begun to enter the work of British historians. In the USA, we can trace much of the initiative back to W.E.B. Dubois, whose work on Reconstruction was long neglected by the mainstream, and has now been resurrected to reveal the boundaries that historicised racial identities differently imposed on the expectations of black and white workers. Only recently has a younger generation of labour historians begun to explore the political meanings of combined black and working-class identity. Partially inspired by the work of Herbert Gutman (who perhaps more than anyone else introduced E.P. Thompson to America) and his students and by that of Alexander Saxton, as well as by a generation of postmodern theorists of diasporic consciousness, this new work has become the linchpin of a generation of transformative insight into the role of black identity on political consciousness.[7] The work of Elizabeth Clark-Lewis and that of Tera Hunter in exploring the relationship of black women domestic workers to work and family comes instantly to mind. Like historians Robin Kelley, Brenda Stephenson and Stephanie Shaw, they reveal how fundamentally racialised and gendered identities shaped the incorporation of black workers into the labour force and participated in constructing the modes by which they could participate in their own communities and the larger polity.[8]

Conceived as issues of identity and therefore as constitutive of the creation of consciousness, the reach of gender, race and ethnicity extend far beyond their role in helping to construct the labour market. I am struck in this respect with the way in which recent explorations have melded religion into newly problematised notions of class. Belchem hints at the continuing role of Catholicism in Irish working-class identity. His work buttresses vivid portraits painted by African-American historians like Evelyn Brooks Higginbotham. Higginbotham has persuasively demonstrated the many functions that the church membership of black women serves, including shaping middle-class identity, bridging class identities among African-Americans, and providing access to political activity.[9] In this context, Patrick Pasture offers a welcome argument for more explicitly introducing religion into the collective identities we consider when we think about 'cultural dimensions and divisions' in the lives of workers. Pasture warns of the complexity of thinking about the meaning of religion in its broader context. Thus, the continuing importance of religious practices, rites and rituals, as well as of spiritual commitments, form one gatepost, but the political organisations that pursue religious objectives another. Anyone who has explored the rise of the welfare state can point to examples of public and private extensions of religious identity as sources for justifying or rationalising state power.

Such efforts to disclose the powerful impact of multiple forms of identity on economic behaviour should encourage us to believe that its role in constructing class is more than a function of presentism. The evidence presented here suggests that class might well be conceived as more than 'one possible basis for felt unity'. Without trying to assign priorities, this seems to me to be nowhere more true than in the case of gender, for there is no more crucial nor more universal

system of social relations, no more fundamental element in the construction of identity. To paraphrase Joan Scott, if there is no gender
without class, there is no class that is not always already gendered.[10]
We already know that masculinity plays a continuing role in how
labour markets are constructed, and that social relationships of gender deeply influence political and economic policies of many different
kinds. To pretend that a history of workers, their institutions, their
culture, or their politics can be written without exploring how a gendered power dynamics plays itself out in particular ways (even if all
the action is among men) seems to me to be utter folly.

Eileen Yeo's essay in this volume demonstrates how leaving gender
out of this nexus impoverishes it. I am grateful to her for once again
reminding us that historians who have imposed gendered definitions
of wage-work, production and the household as though they were
timeless, have distorted the world-views of those who performed
these activities at other times.[11] Each of the other authors in this book
makes a similar acknowledgement: an encouraging recognition of
how fully and how quickly gender has become imbricated in our
notions of class. Yeo builds on these recognitions to move us from the
structural to the poststructural. Viewing gender as one of the ways
that 'human beings have constructed their identities' and thus as one
of the 'perspectives from which they see the world and act in it', Yeo
attempts in this paper to unfold some of the ways in which relationships among women cross class lines, as well as the ways in which gender functions within class, and class functions across gender lines. Her
historiographical excursions into these arenas review some of the
many ways in which historians of labour have reconstructed the mul-
tiply gendered identities from which men and women perceive their
worlds, and suggest how their actions might have been influenced.

Her examples might have included American parallels. The one
that comes most instantly to mind is that of Mary Blewett, whose
study of mid-nineteenth-century Lynn, Massachusetts, shoemakers
indicated how their marital status and relationships to family influenced the meaning of equality and constrained or encouraged political activity rooted in its different meanings.[12] Yeo also remarks on the
salience of relational identity construction. Class-based feminine
identities emerge in relation to class-based masculine identities. Feminine and masculine identities similarly shape class and class expectations. Thus the language of work is rooted in a shifting sense of class
and gender identities that are inseparable and are captured by such
concepts as skill, providerhood, family wage, housewife and women's
place. For a working-class woman to reimagine herself outside these
conceptions, even in the presence of other women, was, as Yeo's own
work and the work of others demonstrates, extraordinarily difficult.

And yet many labour historians continue to treat gender and class as analytically separable categories. For example, Ira Katznelson, whose work on class formation I very much admire, apologises in a footnote to an important book he edited, for the 'lack of consideration of family and gender relations'.[13] And though he, like Jürgen Kocka in this collection, recognises that this leads to some important omissions, neither of them entertains the possibility (so persuasively demonstrated in Davidoff and Hall's *Family Fortunes*) that our view of how classes emerge and come to consciousness might in fact alter if we fully incorporated the gendered perspectives of the men and women whose activities we are attempting to comprehend. Kathleen Canning's recent study of German textile workers beautifully argues the case for dismantling linear views of class formation. Using the language of mostly women workers, she reveals how their family positions led them to understand their class positions differently.[14] Her work forcefully suggests that introducing gender does not merely enrich our understanding of class: in helping us to see how men and women of different classes experience their lives and construct a sense of self, it exposes how men and women relate to each other within and beyond racial/ethnic lines, inside and outside the workplace and the household. Understanding how those dynamics work is one of the great opportunities of our generation.

Masculine and Linguistic

If studying wage-earning women did not sufficiently reveal this, recent work on masculinity has enormously enhanced our understanding of power relations in the workplace and in the household.[15] In the workplace, the privileges of white masculinity have far exceeded all others, and it is difficult to imagine the construction of class identity in which masculinity is not deeply imbricated. Male work cultures, the policing of apprenticeships and admission to crafts, the formation of trade unions, regulation of women's labour – all these and more reflect the privileges of masculinity. Their salience in producing working-class community is not in doubt. In the household, whether viewed as a site of production or consumption, class identity is equally produced along with and inseparably from relations of patriarchal domination and subordination.[16] Just how different kinds of households produce different kinds of identity, ideology and political consciousness has recently become the subject of study. My favourite example is Earl Lewis's *In Their Own Interests,* which effectively demonstrates how racialised and gendered households maintain and reproduce class identities.[17]

Perhaps there are better tools than those of linguistic analysis to illuminate the issue of identity. I know of none. Psychologists, political scientists and sociologists have thought about identities in other and more particular ways. Freudians describe it as 'overdetermined' actions or behaviour that seem to be the consequences of multiple, layered and interleaved causes. It seems foolhardy, then, to dismiss the advantages of poststructuralism, particularly in exploring what we have come to know as 'agency'. That term first entered my vocabulary through the work of Edward Thompson as a way to describe how the actions of working people were consciously employed. But the poststructural moment has provided it with its most useful incarnation, weaving together the idea that ordinary people develop identities out of their own experiences and then act on them. It is corollary and precursor to the idea that we, as historians, need to access what some have called the 'subjective sense of self' – to sort out how people might have imagined their own worlds. Together these ideas have opened the sphere of 'alterity' – the notion that identity is imagined and subjectivity developed relationally, and that all of these concepts are therefore best understood by examining not merely their explicit content but by looking at the contradictory meanings of which they are constituted. In these quite specific respects, I find the turn to language not only useful but essential to an exploration of identity, and believe that in exploring the history of the working class it constitutes the kind of breakthrough that will enable us (perhaps has already enabled us) to hear the voices of the formerly silent.

To acknowledge that we can use language to access forms of gendered and racial identity (that mimic class) does not require us to embrace all of the extremes of postmodernism. Here I ally myself with those, like Kocka and Savage, who reject what seem to be patterns of historical nihilism. But at its simplest, language provides a vocabulary that, in focusing on the centrality of subjectivity, concedes diffuse sites of power. It also offers a path into identity that makes room for the social perceptions or culture of ordinary people and enables us to see how their behaviour mattered. In this sense, the linguistic turn can be profoundly political. It provides, for example, a deeper meaning to notions of consciousness, as it enables us to move beyond mentalites. In his pioneering essay on working-class formation, Katznelson refused to talk about consciousness, turning instead to 'disposition' – a word that embodies action in thought, that captures motivation, interaction and practical outcome. I like the sensibility with which, in this respect and in others, he tries to disengage from a language that is fraught with the weight of old ideological battles. And yet he might never have replaced consciousness with 'disposition' had he not searched for a word that carried both social meaning and more power to connect to action, than consciousness has come to imply.

Instead of a New Labour History

Like other historians, I am reluctant to give up the dramatic narratives that labour history has made possible in the past: narratives of ideologies realised; of strikes won; of political unity realised or squandered. But while these have made possible a sort of synthesis, they have done so at the cost of romanticisation, omission and distortion; now that the forward march of labour seems to have been halted, at the price of teleological confusion – if not despair as well. We have much to gain by abandoning a hopeless quest for a new 'new Labour History', especially if we pursue instead the complex notion of class towards which Labour History seems to be slowly stumbling. Among the advantages of that course, four are immediately apparent.

First, a more capacious view of class opens possibilities for a fully interdisciplinary stance among labour historians. This is true both in the way those of us who think about labour history engage with our field, and in terms of the capacity of the field to make use of other disciplinary insights. When Thompson first introduced the notion of time-work discipline as a way of organising labour, he noted its capacity to yield solidaristic self-perceptions among workers. Recently some historians have paid attention to leisure as an object of class struggle, as well as a vehicle for developing a consumer mentality and undermining class loyalties. Others have explored the multiple meanings of nineteenth- and early-twentieth-century corporations to develop company towns. They have served as incentives to company loyalty as well as sources of solidarity. In the 1950s, modern corporations began to loosen bonds of place in order to undermine working-class community. Concern with space opens new agendas: Karen Sawislak's work on the aftermath of the Great Chicago Fire, for example, tells us something about the ways in which boundaries of class and community were constructed. As Michael Savage suggests, the permeable boundaries of space and place still require exploration.[18] And in this respect the work of geographers like David Harvey and Neil Smith, who have challenged finite notions of urban space, is worth the attention of labour historians.

Second, it opens possibilities for comparative work by disrupting national histories and yielding new options for developing comparative frameworks both within industrialised societies and across time and culture with societies that are only now in the process of industrialising. Once again Belchem's work is important, revealing the intersection between how identities are imposed and how they are claimed. Belchem suggests the uses of identity for creating images of nation. Recent studies of the Black Atlantic and the Black diaspora confirm their value and at the same time caution us to acknowledge their limits by revealing how race and ethnicity participate in diffusing national identity.[19] Feminism has had a similar two-edged value. Solidarity among women across international borders benefits from common engagement in such projects as protective labour legislation for women only. Yet the same enterprises engendered national pride and fostered nationalism among women within nations, sometimes undermining solidaristic class commitments.[20] Studies of migration and mobility in transnational context offer equally powerful possibilities, as witnessed by the work of British labour historians who have identified intangible sources of identification with power and privilege that extend beyond the particular benefits of a capitalist nexus. In this view imperialism relies on a complicated effort to persuade workers to identify as British, rather than as workers.

Third, more capacious explorations of class will help us overcome the narrowness of politics and institutions and to think more broadly in terms of 'meaning systems'. We can acknowledge the successful efforts of labour movements in most industrial countries to achieve welfare states and their roles in perpetuating generous benefits. At the same time we remain aware of how welfare states were differently shaped by concerns to protect racial privilege, group interests, or particular visions of family life. These interests have often been the focus of cross-class alliances among women in the 'vertical relationships' to which Eileen Yeo calls our attention. Tracing them reveals, for example, how gender, like race, has functioned as a cross-cutting category, explaining particular forms of legislative change, accounting for its relative acceptability at certain moments, and producing new definitions of what constitutes politics.

Fourth, an expanded view of class exposes the contents of citizenship, and some of the processes, as well as the meaning of civil society. For example, the meaning of rights in work has become a central question for American labour historians. Contrasts between classical political rights and those conceived and imagined by workers reveals the forces of masculinity in shaping workplace expectations. Classical political rights, as Norwegian political theorist Jon Elster notes, 'are negative, in the sense that they protect the individual from interference by others or by the state'.[21] The right to work, in contrast, was a positive right, enforceable not by legal mandate, but implicit in the expectations inspired by an emergent nineteenth-century democratic decision-making process and closely tied to gender. The distinguished Swedish social theorist, Walter Korpi, calls such rights 'proto-rights'.

They are rights generally not enforceable by state power, but 'norm-based' and socially reinforced.[22] And yet, what was no right in the legal framework nevertheless constituted a deeply rooted gendered prerogative and one of the fundamental sources of citizenship under liberal theory. A wide variety of political theorists have chimed in to reinforce the idea that without economic independence, vested for most people in claims to jobs, and acknowledged as the social right to work if not as a claim to a particular job, political participation remains a chimera.[23] The idea resonated in the lives of American workers, as witnessed by American labour leader Samuel Gompers' blunt pronouncement before Congress in 1898: 'a declaration of political liberty which does not involve an opportunity for economic independence is a delusion'.[24] But if democratic citizenship was closely tied to earning then limits on rights to work constrained not merely the power to support one's family, but one's relationship to civil life as well.

The sum of these explorations is, finally, to enrich the meaning of class. Like Jürgen Kocka and most of my fellow labour historians, I do not want to abandon it. I believe that people come to conscious-ness (or develop dispositions) through their relations to production *and* consumption; through their locations in workplaces and house-holds. The social elements of location are at least as important as structural elements in developing consciousness; and the process of developing these relations cannot be conceived independently of a variety of other relations that may include ethnicity, race, nationality and religion, and most certainly gender. Herein lies the source of my optimism. If the old labour history allowed the possibilities of explanatory narratives that spoke to working-class achievements, the new allows a more complex exposure to the workings of class and its meanings for historically specific formations. As labour historians, we need to seize this day, not resist it.

Notes

1. Ira Katznelson, 'The "Bourgeois Dimension": A Provocation About Institutions, Politics and the Future of Labor History', *International Labor and Working-Class History*, 46, (Fall, 1994): 14; for access to some of this material, see as well, Jerry Lee Lembcke, 'Labor History's "Synthesis Debate": Sociological Interventions,' *Science and Society*, 59, (Summer, 1995): 137–73; the special issue of the *International Review of Social History*, 38 (1993); the special issue of *International Labor and Working-Class History*, 46, (Fall, 1994).
2. Some recent efforts include George Frederickson, *The Comparative Imagination: On the History of Racism, Nationalism, and Social Movements*, Berkeley CA, 1997; Helmut Gruber and Pamela Graves (eds), *Women and Socialism, Socialism and Women: Europe Between the Two World Wars*, New York, 1998; and Ulla Wikander,

Alice Kessler-Harris and Jane Lewis, *Protecting Women: Labor Legislation in Europe, Australia and the United States,* Urbana, 1995.

3. In addition to the European sources that Kocka cites, see the volume that captured the growing discontent in the USA: Carroll Moody and Alice Kessler-Harris (eds), *Perspectives on American Labor History: The Problem of Synthesis* , DeKalb IL, 1990.

4. David Montgomery, *Citizen Worker: the Experience of Workers in the United States with Democracy and the Free Market during the Nineteenth Century,* New York, 1993; Glenda Elizabeth Gilmore, *Gender and Jim Crow: Women and the Politics of White Supremacy in North Carolina, 1896–1920,* Chapel Hill, 1996; Joanne L. Goodwin, *Gender and the Politics of Welfare Reform: Mothers' Pensions in Chicago, 1911–1929,* Chicago, 1997.

5. It has been particularly valuable in opening up arenas of Southern US labour history. See especially Jacquelyn Hall et al., *Like a Family: The Making of a Southern Cotton Mill World,* Chapel Hill NC, 1987; Michelle Brattain, *The Politics of Whiteness: Race, Workers and Culture in the Modern South,* Princeton NJ, 2001; Julie Saville, *The Work of Reconstruction: From Slave to Wage Laborer in South Carolina, 1860–1870,* New York, 1994; and see Margaret Creighton and Lisa Norling (eds), *Iron Men, Wooden Women: Gender and Seafaring in the Atlantic World, 1700–1920,* Baltimore MD, 1996.

6. David Roediger, *The Wages of Whiteness: Race and the Making of the American Working Class,* London, 1991; Matthew Frye Jacobson, *Whiteness of a Different Color: European Immigrants and the Alchemy of Race,* Cambridge MA, 1998; Neil Foley, *The White Scourge: Mexicans, Blacks and Poor Whites in Texas Cotton Culture,* Berkeley CA, 1997; Karen Brodkin, *How Jews Became White Folks and What that Says about Race in America,* New Brunswick, NJ, 1998; Anne McClintock, *Imperial Leather: Race, Gender and Sexuality in the Colonial Contest,* New York, 1999.

7. Herbert S. Gutman, *The Black Family in Slavery and Freedom,* New York, 1983, and Gutman, *Work, Culture and Society in Industrializing America: Essays in American Working-Class and Social History,* New York, 1976; Alexander Saxton, *The Indispensable Enemy: Labor and the anti-Chinese Movement in California,* Berkeley CA, 1971; and Saxton, *The Rise and Fall of the White Republic: Class Politics and Mass Culture in Nineteenth Century America,* London, 1990.

8. Elizabeth Clark-Lewis, *Living In, Living Out: African American Domestics and the Great Migration,* New York, 1996; Tera W. Hunter, *To Joy My Freedom': Southern Black Women's Lives and Labors after the Civil War,* Cambridge, 1997; Stephanie Shaw, *What a Woman Ought to Be and Do:Black Professional Women Workers During the Jim Crow Era,* Chicago IL, 1996; Robin D. G. Kelley, *Hammer and Hoe: Alabama Communists During the Great Depression,* Chapel Hill NC, 1990.

9. Evelyn Brooks Higginbotham, *Righteous Discontent: The Women's Movement in the Black Baptist Church, 1880–1920,* Cambridge MA, 1993; and see Melinda Chateauvert, *Marching Together: Women of the Brotherhood of Sleeping Car Porters,* Urbana, IL, 1998.

10. Joan Wallach Scott, 'Women in the Making of the English Working Class', in J.W. Scott, *Gender and the Politics of History,* New York, 1988, 68–92.

11. The breakthrough book was Leonore Davidoff and Catherine Hall, *Family Fortunes: Men and Women of the English Middle Class, 1780–1850,* Chicago IL, 1987; for more on gender and class relationships see L. Davidoff, *Worlds Between: Historical Perspectives on Gender and Class,* London, 1995; Catherine Hall, *White, Male and Middle Class: Explorations in Feminism and History,* New York, 1992; and Sally Alexander, *Becoming a Woman and other Essays in 19th and 20th Century Feminist History,* London, 1994.

12. Mary H. Blewett, *Men, Women, and Work: Class, Gender and Protest in the New England Shoe Industry, 1780–1910,* Urbana IL, 1988.

13. Ira Katznelson, 'Working-Class Formation: Constructing Cases and Comparisons', in Ira Katznelson and Aristide Zolberg (eds), *Working-Class Formation: Nineteenth Century Patterns in Western Europe and the United States*, Princeton NJ, 1986, 4.

14. Kathleen Canning, *Languages of Labor and Gender: Female Factory Work in Germany, 1850–1914*, Ithaca NY, 1996. Some equally disruptive essays appear in Laura Frader and Sonya O. Rose (eds), *Gender and Class in Modern Europe*, Ithaca NY, 1996.

15. Ava Baron, 'An "Other" Side of Gender Antagonism at Work: Men, Boys and the Remasculinization of Printers' Work, 1830–1920', in *Work Engendered: Toward a New History of American Labor*, Ithaca NY, 1991; Patricia Cooper, *Once a Cigar Maker*, Urbana IL, 1991; Marianne Clawson, *Constructing Brotherhood: Class, Gender and Fraternalism*, Princeton NJ, 1989.

16. See especially Dana Frank, *Purchasing Power: Consumer Organizing, Gender, and the Seattle Labor Movement, 1919–1929*, New York, 1994; Marcel van der Linden, 'Connecting Household History and Labour History', *International Review of Social History*, 38 (Supplement, 1993): 163–73.

17. E. Lewis, *In Their Own Interests: Race, Class and Power in Twentieth Century Norfolk Virginia*, Berkeley CA, 1991.

18. Karen Sawislak, *Smoldering City: Chicagoans and the Great Fire, 1871–1874*, Chicago IL, 1995; intriguing explorations of the importance of space have begun to occupy the energies of historians. See for example Savage in this volume, and Katznelson, 'The "Bourgeois Dimension"', 36. For efforts to think about space and class in the language of the new geography, see Brian Roberts, *American Alchemy: The California Gold Rush and the Middle Class Culture*, Chapel Hill NC, 2000. On leisure and the labour movement, see especially the works of Benjamin Hunnicutt, *Work Without End: Abandoning Shorter Hours for the Right to Work*, Philadelphia PA, 1988, and *Kellogg's Six-Hour Day*, Philadelphia PA, 1996.

19. Paul Gilroy, *The Black Atlantic: Modernity and Double Consciousness*, Cambridge, 1993; Sidney Lemelle and Robin D. G. Kelley (eds), *Imagining Home: Class, Culture and Nationalism in the African Diaspora*, London, 1994.

20. See especially Susan Pedersen, *Family, Dependence and the Origins of the Welfare State: Britain and France, 1914–1945*, New York, 1993; and Wikander et al., *Protecting Women*.

21. Jon Elster, 'Is There (or should there be) a Right to Work?', in Amy Gutmann (ed.), *Democracy and the Welfare State*, Princeton NJ, 1988, 56.

22. The idea is most clearly articulated in Walter Korpi, 'The Institutionalization of Citizenship: Class, Gender, and Citizenship Rights', paper delivered at the conference on 'The Welfare State at the Crossroads', Balsta, Sweden, 12–14 June, 1998.

23. See especially T.H. Marshall, *Citizenship and Social Class and other Essays*, Cambridge, 1950, 15, 17; Judith Shklar, *American Citizenship: The Quest for Inclusion*, Cambridge MA, 1991; Shklar argues that a presumption of the right to work has existed since Jacksonian times: 98–99 and chap. 2; Helga Hernes, *Welfare State and Woman Power: Essays in State Feminism*, Oslo, 1987; Hege Skejeie, 'Ending the Male Political Hegemony: Changes in Party Politics, 1970–90', in *Den Poitiske betydningen av Kjonn: En Studie av Norsk Topp Politik*, Institutt for Samfunnsforskning, Oslo, 1992, 144–82; and Ruth Lister, 'Women, Economic Dependency and Citizenship', *Journal of Social Policy*, 19 (October, 1990): 445–67.

24. Testifying before Congress in 1898: Stuart Kauffman et al. (eds), *The Papers of Samuel Gompers*, IV, Urbana IL, 1991, 498.

CHAPTER 8

PARADIGM LOST?
THE FUTURES OF LABOUR HISTORY

Janaki Nair

The steady dissolution, or at least weakening, of a unitary, even transcendent, concept of class as it has structured labour history has often been met with dismay, and to a lesser extent by cautious optimism. The impetus for the radical interrogation of the basic unit of labour history – the identity of workers acting in the interests of their class – has sprung from at least two identifiable sources. On the one hand, there is increasing recognition of identities that had long been subsumed under, or considered an unnecessary distraction to, the category of 'working class', which is at once a *structural location* arising out of the specific way in which capitalism has organised relations of production, and, following E.P. Thompson's monumental *The Making of the English Working Class*, a *relationship* that is negotiated and renegotiated on economic as well as cultural terrain. This recognition of other identities was prompted, not just by the 'retreat of trade unionism' but by the reorganisation of the field of political struggles to include those relating to the status of women, to ethnic and religious identities and to the political importance of region and space. The new political challenges had important resonances in the field of labour history, especially since, as E.J.Hobsbawm has pointed out, labour history is 'by tradition a highly political concept'.[1]

If the admission of new subjects of history and agents of historical change has refashioned the field of labour history at one end, a questioning of the categories relating to the meanings of work and working-class organisation has also been enabled by the burgeoning of social history, which has opened up new objects of enquiry, including the politics of everyday life. The quotidian life of workers has revealed much about the 'classness' of workers – and even more about the lack of it – than had been suspected. Yet the risks, if they may be so called, of focusing on these questions were soon more than apparent: the 'micro event', even on the shop floor, which may have been dismissed as inconsequential in narratives that staged the confrontations between labour and capital, has thrown cleavages between workers into sharp and unrelenting focus.[2]

These micro registers of social and cultural history have also turned attention away from the familiar dialectic between the leaders and the led, and from quantifiable historical material relating to unions, their strength, or the volume and scale of workers' collective actions against their employers. The pioneering work of Michelle Perrot (*Workers on Strike, France 1870–1891*) and others notwithstanding, a strong focus on collective actions such as strikes has yielded space to studies of riots, intraethnic rivalries and antagonisms between workers themselves. Often, quite contrary evidence to the heroic unity of workers has emerged from histories of the daily life of workers, since it is most often here that the workings of gender, religion or ethnicity may be more scrupulously observed.

May we then conclude that the theoretical 'tyranny' of class has met a just end? If so, what might the futures of labour history be once the primacy of class as the structuring identity is destabilised? The four articles by Mike Savage, Eileen Yeo, Patrick Pasture and John Belchem discuss the ways in which the analytical category of class has been interrogated by other categories such as gender, ethnicity or religiosity in the field of European labour historiography. There is agreement among all four authors that the more orthodox, unified notion of class, and therefore labour history, was inadequate in making sense of the complex ways in which the working class negotiated life under capitalism. Capitalism did indeed tear down certain kinds of barriers but there were serious limits to the 'levelling' achieved by the capitalist workplace. It is rather well known that there were divisions within the workforce based on religion, race or gender that were actively exploited, deepened and strengthened, rather than effaced, under capitalism. Class identities were much more contingent and negotiated identities than have been admitted by the more orthodox historians.

Yet, as all these papers attempt to show, there were important ways in which the identities of religion, gender or ethnicity were elements in the emerging self-definition of workers, although these identities could remain aligned with or disjunct from class identity. John

Belchem's discussion of the Irish diaspora clearly demonstrates that both a strengthened unionism and a fragmented working class could be the outcome of a well-developed Irish Catholic working-class culture. Patrick Pasture, while admitting that the Christian democratic movement in parts of Europe resulted from intense anti-socialism, proposes that the contemporary welfare state is an important and direct legacy of these movements.

Nevertheless, a discussion of these identities takes class as its starting point. Labour history must continue the negative-critical task of interrogating the concept of 'working class' inaugurated, among others, by Joan Scott in her 'Women in *The Making of the English Working Class*' which, despite its title, argued for much more than just an additive approach.

Such interrogations had long since begun in places beyond Europe. Glorious traditions of artisanal protest, as they were transformed into workers' collective actions in Europe, have found few parallels in, say, the North American, Indian or African context, due to the enduring influence of ethnic, religious or regional divisions. Labour historians of these regions have necessarily confronted the question of this fragmented heritage to conclude that it may well be the European, rather than the non-European, that is marked by 'exceptionalism'. How successful have recent efforts been in extending or challenging the framework of class analysis and, further, in denaturalising the category of 'working class'? Does the attempt to distance oneself from the 'foul smell of economism' inevitably lead to a labour history that is merely 'descriptive' rather than analytical, a history that then becomes indistinguishable from the broader genre of social history, as Mike Savage seems to fear?

There is no doubt that the categories of race, ethnicity or gender have long had some *descriptive* value even in European history before they were admitted as important categories of *analysis*. Thus the manliness of skilled work or the marked subalternity of the Irish labourer in early industrial capitalism were amply evident not only to contemporary observers such as Friedrich Engels but also to historians such as E.P.Thompson or John Rule. The challenge then has been to refashion labour history by deploying the categories analytically. Each of these papers not only attempts to provide an evaluation of the historiographical refashioning but also proposes certain alternative readings. In the rest of this chapter I shall discuss these contributions separately while drawing attention to their areas of overlap.

Rethinking Labour History

Mike Savage's chapter addresses the general crisis of labour history by beginning with a useful summary of challenges to both the Marxist and the Weberian notions of class. Nevertheless Savage concludes that there is no alternative theoretical framework to that of class in understanding 'unequal economic relationships'. Instead of either a focus on 'labour process' or 'labour markets' that characterise the Marxist and Weberian studies respectively, Savage proposes 'the structural insecurity of workers' as a way of opening the field of labour history to include not just 'the structural underpinnings of working-class life' but the range of tactics that workers might evolve in their struggle for survival. This, he feels, opens the way to understanding the 'contingency of class'.

Savage may be quite right in arguing that there is no alternative to class in analysing *economic* relationships, but he does not justify the need to retain the primacy of the economic in working-class lives. This, after all, is what those attentive to contending identities have been at pains to establish, namely that the primacy of class is not a historical given, so that in both political movements and analytical studies, a unitary notion of class has long been a way of suppressing or denying other legitimate worker identities. At the same time, giving up what William Reddy has so evocatively called 'paycheck fetishism' does not necessarily deny that the antagonism between labour and capital is a structural, and not episodic, antagonism. Indeed, Savage's proposed alternative may well be read as a sternly Marxist reading of working-class life, for the 'chronic insecurity' of working-class life was what Marx referred to in his famous characterisation of the worker as being free in the 'double sense, that as a free individual he can dispose of his labour power as his own commodity and that on the other hand he has no commodity for sale i.e., he is rid of them'.[3] It is not very clear how Savage's formulation represents a *theoretical* advance on this, although the benefits in terms of making labour history a more inclusive field are evident.

Savage moves on to favour a notion of class formation over labour process, an emphasis that will enable historians to trace the social mobility of workers between different class positions. The author, importantly, points to the ways in which the class position of workers is contingent on a range of familial (non-workplace) strategies, especially to what he characterises as a 'temporally shifting demographic process'. Nothing illustrates this point better than John Belchem's article, which suggests that the position of a group of workers, such as Irish-American immigrants, can be dramatically transformed over time so that the proverbial underdog of the labouring classes comes to occupy the upper end of the scale vis-à-vis new entrants to the labour market. But these once more refer to intraclass differences that do not in fundamental ways restructure the relationship between different classes.

What then of the articulation between social formations and political processes? Here Savage makes an assertion about the importance of space, especially as it adds to our understanding of the experience of class, and more properly of class politics. In this section, Savage rightly cautions against the valorisation of the 'local' that could either merely mirror or (equally problematic) deny the importance of the 'national'. Yet the example that he approvingly cites (Roger Gould's 1995 study of the Paris Commune) raises important questions. If residential and neighbourhood ties were important to the Paris Commune, it was at a specific historical conjuncture: there were other historical junctures, such as 1848, when the specificities of place were transcended and occupational class-based ties were more important. The spatial perspective must then account for both the possibilities.

Savage certainly opens up the debate surrounding the primacy of class even while he tacitly acknowledges that the field has already been refashioned, by the challenges of gender, for instance. But to what extent is the study of gender in working-class history to be confined to the question of 'family dynamics', as Savage suggests, and with what consequences?

Gender and Class

It is a sign of the increasing attention paid to women in labour and social history today that all the four chapters here make specific reference to the importance of women in class formation or the formation of religious and ethnic identities.

Eileen Yeo's article focuses exclusively on the category of women although her canvas is broad and not confined to the question of working-class women alone. Yeo's article begins with a general, if somewhat well-known, summary of the meaning of 'gender' which is not reducible to the female sex, but thereafter the discussion is closely focused on the position of women in British historiography. The specific attention to women in an article that promises to look at 'gender' is a slippage that is disturbingly common. There is brief reference to the ways in which trade unionism and working-class identity was contingent on a certain notion of masculinity but this is not sustained throughout the piece.

However, Yeo provides a useful overview of recent work on the middle class, especially as it is contingent on family life, and she also delineates the ways in which certain social movements – namely the Co-operative Guild or the suffrage movement – constructed the working-class woman. This is important especially in emphasising that 'woman' cannot be an alternative meta-category to class, and in stressing that there is a certain irreducibility to class identity within gender categories, just as gender hierarchies challenge the notion of class solidarity.

Surprisingly absent from this account are the conditions of women in the workforce or in the trade union movement. This silence seems to signal a tacit agreement with the formulation that while men's identities are forged out of their work experiences, women's identities are primarily formed in the non-work spheres. Yet how do we make sense of the massive presence of women in the European workforce, which has not necessarily translated into a presence in trade unions or in collective class action? It is here that the complicity of union official and labour historian stands unmasked, for both have denied gender differences in the name of class unity. Yet there is recent work that charts successful challenges posed by women workers to trade unions. Kathleen Canning's work on German social democracy has shown that there were definite attempts by women trade unionists to recast trade union politics so that 'weibliche Eigenart', female specificities, were taken into account. There was an attempt to 'feminise' trade unions, and make them more responsive to women's needs, moves that were bitterly resisted and even resented by male trade unionists.[4] A similar moment is referred to by Yeo in her description of the feminist demands on the cooperative movement.

However, the heavy emphasis here on the construction of working-class women by the middle class obscures from view several other levels of analysis. There is little on what Yeo promises will be a delineation of 'diagonal studies between men from one class and women from another'. One wonders, for instance, whether the problems arising from the upper-class women's mobilisation of working women were substantially different from male mobilisation, and if so in what ways? Was not a certain paternalism a characteristic of male upper/middle-class mobilisation of men too? Indeed, would that not be a necessary part of the dynamics between leaders and the led in most situations?

Yeo's article seems to blur the distinctions between the descriptive and analytical uses of 'gender' as a category. For instance, the increasing feminisation of paid work that Yeo points to in conclusion, while true in a descriptive sense, provides no guarantees that women will hereafter find a more prominent place in labour history. While Yeo stresses the important point that the category of woman has not, and indeed cannot, become a unitary category to replace class, she leans quite heavily on the 'languages of power' in order to highlight hierarchies between women. There are strong limits to linguistic analysis once we move beyond studies of mobilisation of women in political campaigns to the structure of the workplace, questions of wages or conditions of work. Also, such analytical tools may be somewhat inadequate in demonstrating the continued salience of class as it intersects with gender identities, especially in making sense of those multi-class initiatives that do succeed in at least temporarily sealing the ranks, whether for revolutionary reasons or for defending community religious or ethnic identity.

Subaltern Religiosities

Patrick Pasture points to a significant reassessment of the role of religion that is under way in European historiography. It is today better recognised that religiosities were an important site of workers' self-definition where they both came to terms with, and to a lesser extent, challenged the capitalist work process. Anthropological studies of workers have been more willing to acknowledge the formative influence of religion in workers' lives. Thus Michael Taussig and June Nash, among others, have done pioneering work on the interface between Catholicism, the devil and commodity production in Latin America. But such assessments of the role of religion were not unknown in European historiography. One need only recall Thompson's brilliant disquisition on the meaning of Methodism in England and other chiliastic movements as well. Methodism was not merely a ruling-class tool for controlling the paroxysms of workers but in turn a resource for unexpected new solidarities to emerge.

Pasture's strong focus is on Christian democracy, which is unique to Europe and arose from a desire to combat socialism. It would be unwise, suggests Pasture, to ignore one of the most important legacies of the Christian democratic movement today, namely the welfare state. The attribution of welfare state ideologies to the terrors posed by Bolshevism are somewhat well known, but the direct link between these ideologies and the Christian democrats is less well known. Although this is not spelt out in great detail, Pasture's account is richly suggestive of a link between church and state that frustrates any commonsensical view about modernity producing increased 'secularisation'. But the reference to the 'collective actions of the social democratic movement' are too cryptic, and not adequately spelt out. Further, only in passing does Pasture refer to other forms of subaltern religiosity that would be relevant to the labour historian, namely 'rites of passage' that persist within secular modernity.

As in the articles by John Belchem and Mike Savage, Pasture briefly refers to the 'feminisation of religion', especially of popular Catholicism, which offered women important roles in the construction of religious identity. But here again the reference is too fleeting, although there is clearly a rich vein of secondary sources that may be profitably consulted.

Unlike the other authors, Pasture proposes something close to the radical heterogeneity of identities as a solution to the neglect of religion in working-class history. In his piece, religion figures largely as a long-standing absence in historiography that can be easily redressed by admitting the radical heterogeneity of workers' identities. Such an approach could only be nurtured at the expense of a more critical engagement with religiosity as it constructed the experience of certain groups at specific historical junctures. The Irish were among the rather well-known ethnic labouring communities of Europe, marked in their subalternity by their regional, religious and class positions, as John Belchem's article outlines.

The Ethnicity of Class

There are several points at which Belchem's assessment of the Irish-American and Irish-Australian immigrant communities intersects with the focus of the other chapters. Like Eileen Yeo, Belchem's article also emphasises the importance of including the Irish middle class in any attempt at understanding the meaning of ethnicity in immigrant labouring communities. Neglected by most historians, the middle-class Irish immigrants, and particularly the women, were shapers and defenders of the corporate Irish identity. In his discussion of the upward mobility of the lower class, Irish migrant Belchem touches on the theme that Savage foregrounds regarding the importance of social mobility within working-class communities.

But what is more interesting in Belchem's article is his delineation of the ambiguities inherent in any such ethnic self-definition, since it was often quite closely linked to the claims of the working class for better working conditions, though in ways that were sometimes resented by the mainstream labour movement. In contrast to Savage, Belchem also cites instances when the stereotype of chronic Irish poverty was actively deployed by those who chose to refuse avenues of social mobility.

Furthermore, and even more interesting, is Belchem's suggestion that the equation between Irish ethnicity and subalternity was not always stable, since by 1900 'the black Irish had become white' in America, serving as the role models for the new wave of immigrants who replaced the Irish at the bottom of the pile. Although this did not in any way place the Irish in an exploitative relationship *vis-à-vis* the other working-class communities, there were hierarchies that developed over time, though rarely stable or enduring.

The construction of Irishness, and more properly Catholicism, turned most crucially on the work of women, so that 'the maintenance of "symbolic" ethnicity came to depend more on women'. This is by far the most detailed outline of the links between religiosity/ethnicity and women of all the articles here, though most of them have gestured towards such a link. But even Belchem, unwittingly perhaps, reasserts the familiar pairing of women with household/community and men with work. Indeed the realm of work processes, work cultures and regimes seem, to have disappeared as a focus of analysis and only rarely figures as an element in the new directions that have been proposed for labour historians. Each of the authors makes a reasonably persuasive case for the inclusion of other elements – space, religion, gender and ethnicity – but only rarely are these portrayed as reconstituting the category of class. What then is the future of labour history, and how may it be distinguished from the more inclusive genre of social history?

All the articles are agreed that a teleological historical enterprise is no longer tenable. But there is less unanimity on what theoretical framework – or paradigm – can take the place of the older reliance on class. Perhaps this is the reason why the authors more than once fall back on the term 'complex' as a way of characterising the field of labour history today. Such a description does not adequately serve as a new paradigm. We might ask: does this vast body of work to which these articles refer add up to a more nuanced reading of class, or does it successfully destabilise the concept of class itself?

Clearly, the search for newer 'objective categories' of analysis is rather sterile: any new paradigm must, as Kian Tajbaksh has suggested, focus instead on the *failure* of any single identity 'to unify the heterogenous social elements into a self-presence or identity'.[5] The question of working-class identity may then be traced in 'terms of *the separation between workplace, community and home*' rather than seeking a class unity in these disparate spaces.[6] This would in no way undo the importance of class as a category of analysis, but would certainly not privilege it over other identities, and would enable a fuller account to be given of the relationships between contradictory elements that are at play at given historical junctures.

Notes

1. E.J. Hobsbawm, 'Labour History and Ideology', *Journal of Social History* (1974): 371–81.
2. For a recent example of a reading of race and gender relations on the shop floor, using a Christmas incident, see Kevin Boyle, 'The Kiss: Racial and Gender Conflict in a 1950s Automobile Factory', *The Journal of American History*, (September 1997): 496–523.
3. Karl Marx, *Capital*, vol. 1, trans. Ben Fowkes, New York, 1977, 272.
4. Kathleen Canning, 'Gender and the Politics of Class Formation: Rethinking German Labour History', *American Historical Review*, 97, 3 (June 1992): 736–68.
5. Kian Tajbaksh, 'History of a Subject or the Subjects of History? (Or: Is a Labour History Possible?)', *Studies in History*, 11, 1 (1995): 143–62, esp. 162.
6. Ibid., 160.

REFERENCES

MAIN WEST EUROPEAN LABOUR HISTORY PERIODICALS, 1911–2000

Originally Issued by	Journal
(Germany/Austria)	*Archiv für die Geschichte des Sozialismus und der Arbeiterbewegung/Grünbergs Archiv* (1911–1930)
Arbetarnas Kulturhistoriska Sällskap (Stockholm)	*Notitser* (1926/27–1962) → *Årsboken* (1963–1969)
International Institute of Social History (Amsterdam)	*International Review for Social History* (1936–1940) *Bulletin* (1936–40; 1951–1955) → *International Review of Social History* (1956–)
Biblioteca Feltrinelli (Milan)	*Movimento Operaio* [New Series] (1949–1956)* → *Annali* (1958–)
Institut français d'histoire sociale (Paris)	*Bulletin Annuel* (1949–1952) → *L'Actualité de l'histoire* (1953–1960) → *Le Mouvement Social* (1960–)
Sociaal Historische Studiekring (Amsterdam)	*Mededelingenblad* (1953–1974) → *Tijdschrift voor Sociale Geschiedenis* (1975–)
Centro Ligure di Storia Sociale (Genova)	*Movimento operaio e contadino in Liguria* (1955–1958) → *Movimento operaio e socialista in Liguria* (1959–1961) → *Movimento operaio e socialista* (1962–1990) → *Ventesimo Secolo* (1991–)

Originally Issued by	Journal
(Italy)	*Rivista storica del socialismo* (1958–1967; 1969)
Society for the Study of Labour History (Sheffield)	*Bulletin* (1960–1989) → *Labour History Review* (1990–)
Verein für Geschichte der Arbeiterbewegung (Vienna)	*Archiv: Mitteilungsblatt des Vereins für Geschichte der Arbeiterbewegung* (1961–1984) → *Archiv: Jahrbuch des Vereins für Geschichte der Arbeiterbewegung* (1985–1996) → *Dokumentation* (1989–)
Institut für Sozialgeschichte (Friedrich-Ebert-Stiftung) (Bonn-Bad Godesberg)	*Archiv für Sozialgeschichte* (1961–)
Historische Kommission (Berlin)	*Internationale wissenschaftliche Korrespondenz zur Geschichte der deutschen Arbeiterbewegung* [*IWK*] (1965–)
Scottish Labour History Society	*Journal of the Scottish Labour History Society* (1969–1984)
Arbetarnas Kulturhistoriska Sällskap and Arbetarrörelsens arkiv (Stockholm)	*Arbetarrörelsens årsbok* (1970–1983)
Sällskapet för studier i arbetarrörelsens historia (Lund)	*Arkiv för studier i arbetarrörelsens historia* (1971–)
Selskabet til forskning i arbejderbevægelsens historie (Copenhagen)	*Årbog for arbejderbevægelsens historie* (1971–1994) *Meddelelser om forskning i arbejderbevægelsens historie* (1973–1981) → *Arbejderhistorie: meddelelser om forskning i arbejderbevægelsens historie* (1982–1994) → *Arbejderhistorie: tidsskrift for historie, kultur och politik* (1995–)
(Germany)	*Jahrbuch Arbeiterbewegung* (1973–1978, 1981–1983) → *Soziale Bewegungen* (1984–1986)
Irish Labour History Society/Cumann Stair Saothair na hÉireann	*Saothar: Journal of the Irish Labour History Society* (1974–)

Originally Issued by	Journal
Society for the Study of Welsh Labour History	*Llafur: The Journal of the Society for the Study of Welsh Labour History* (1974–)
(Netherlands)	*Jaarboek voor de geschiedenis van socialisme en arbeidersbeweging* (1976–1980) → *Bulletin Nederlandse Arbeidersbeweging* (1983–1995)
Arbeiderbevegelsens arkiv og bibliotek (Oslo)	*Tidsskrift for arbeiderbevegelsens historie* (1976–1986) → *Arbeiderhistorie* (1987–)
Instituto de Estudios Laborales y de Seguridad Social (Madrid)	*Estudios de Historia Social* (1977–1991)
Arbetarrörelsens Arkiv och Bibliotek (Stockholm)	*Meddelande* (1977–1984) → *Arbetarhistoria* (1985–)
(Germany)	*Archiv für die Geschichte des Widerstandes und der Arbeit* (1980–)
Association pour l'étude de l'histoire du mouvement ouvrier (Lausanne)	*Cahiers d'histoire du mouvement ouvrier* (1984–)
Bibliothèque de documentation internationale contemporaine (BDIC) (Paris-Nanterre)	*Matériaux pour l'histoire de notre temps* (1985–)
Institut zur Erforschung der europäischen Arbeiterbewegung (Bochum)	*Mitteilungsblatt* (1987–)
Fondazione Giacomo Brodolini (Milan)	*Socialismo Storia* (1987–1991, 1993–1994)
(Group of Finnish labour history institutions and associations)	*Työväentutkimus* (1987–)
Insitituto de la Historia Social UNED (Valencia)	*Historia Social* (1988–)
(Germany)	*Beiträge zur Geschichte der Arbeiterbewegung* (1990–)**
Institut d'histoire sociale (Nanterre)	*Cahiers d'histoire sociale* (1993–)

Originally Issued by	Journal
Archief en Museum van de Socialistische Arbeidersbeweging [Amsab – Instituut voor sociale geschiedenis] (Ghent)	*Brood en Rozen: Tijdschrift voor de geschiedenis van sociale bewegingen* (1996–)
(Britain)	*Historical Studies in Industrial Relations* (1996–)

→ Continued as ...
* Published since 1949, but Feltrinelli's responsibility since 1952.
** Published since 1959 in the GDR; since 1990 an all-German periodical.

BIBLIOGRAPHICAL ESSAYS ON THE DEVELOPMENT OF WEST EUROPEAN LABOUR HISTORY, 1965–2000

General and Cross-country

Seppo Hentilä and Hannes Saarinen (eds), *Forskningsläget inom arbetarrörelsens historia i Norden. Material från det första nordiska seminaret för forskning rörande arbetarrörelsens historia*, Helsingfors: University of Helsinki, 1974.

Klaus Tenfelde (ed.), *Arbeiter und Arbeiterbewegung im Vergleich. Berichte zur internationalen historischen Forschung*, Munich: Oldenbourg, 1986, 896 pp. This volume includes a number of relevant essays:

- Klaus Tenfelde, 'Sozialgeschichte und vergleichende Geschichte der Arbeiter', 13–62.
- Hermann Wellenreuther, 'Forschungen zur Geschichte der Arbeiter in Deutschland, England und Nordamerika im 18. Jahrhundert: Der Arbeitsmarkt', 63–99.
- Albert Eßer, 'Die Lohn-Preis-Entwicklung für landwirtschaftliche Arbeiter in Deutschland, England und Nordamerika im 18. Jahrhundert', 101–36.
- Hartmut Kaelble, 'Arbeiter und soziale Ungleichheit in Westeuropa 1850–1930', 137–78.
- John Breuilly, 'The Labour Aristocracy in Britain and Germany 1850–1914: A Review Article', 179–226.
- Geoffrey Crossick, 'The Petite Bourgeoisie in Nineteenth-Century Europe: Problems and Research', 227–77.
- David F. Crew, 'Class and Community. Local Research on Working-Class History in Four Countries' [USA, Great Britain, France, Germany], 279–336.

- Vernon Lidtke, 'Recent Literature on Workers' Culture in Germany and England', 337–62.
- Dick Geary, 'Protest and Strike: Recent Research on "Collective Action" in England, Germany, and France', 363–87.
- Peter Schöttler, 'Syndikalismus in der europäischen Arbeiterbewegung. Neuere Forschungen in Frankreich, England und Deutschland', 419–75.
- Michael Schneider, 'Christliche Arbeiterbewegung in Europa. Ein vergleichender Literaturbericht', 477–505.
- Hans-Gerhard Husung, 'Arbeiterschaft und Arbeiterbewegung im Ersten Weltkrieg: Neue Forschungen über Deutschland und England', 611–64.
- Einhart Lorenz, 'Neuere Forschungen zur Geschichte der Arbeiterbewegung in Norwegen und Schweden', 711–79.

Søren Federspiel, 'Forskningsoversigt: den internationale fagbevægelses historie til 1914 med hovedvægt på fagforeningsinternationalen', *Årbog for arbejderbevægelsens historie*, 16 (1986): 183–99.

Brigitte Studer and Berthold Unfried, 'At the Beginning of a History: Visions of the Comintern After the Opening of the Archives', *International Review of Social History*, 42 (1997): 419–46.

Austria

Elisabeth Dietrich, 'Zur Sozial- und Zeitgeschichtsforschung in Österreich. Ausgewählte Publikationen und aktueller Stand (1984–1988)', *Archiv für Sozialgeschichte*, 29 (1989): 341–84.

Belgium

Bernard Dandois, 'Dix ans d'histoire sociale en Belgique (1960–1969)', *Le mouvement social*, no. 71 (1970): 83–101.

Jean Puissant, 'L'Historiographie du mouvement ouvrier', *Revue de l'Université Libre de Bruxelles*, 1–2 (1981): 175–92.

Denise de Weerdt, 'Een terugblik op een terugblik. Geschiedschrijving van 100 jaar socialistische partij', *Belgisch Tijdschrift voor Nieuwste Geschiedenis*, 16 (1985): 507–21.

Patricia van den Eeckhout and Peter Scholliers, 'Social History in Belgium: Old Habits and New Perspectives', *Tijdschrift voor Sociale Geschiedenis*, 23 (1997): 147–81.

Guy Vanschoenbeek, 'Arbeid adelt. De arbeidersaristocratie als verklaring voor het reformisme in de arbeidersbeweging', *Belgisch Tijdschrift voor Filologie en Geschiedenis*, 76 (1998): 1021–61.

Patricia van den Eeckhout, 'The Quest for Social History in Belgium (1948–1998)', *Archiv für Sozialgeschichte*, 40 (2000): 321–36.

Britain

Robert G. Neville and John Benson, 'Labour in the Coalfields (II)', *Bulletin* [SSLH], no. 31 (Autumn 1975): 45–59. See also: J.E. Williams, 'Labour in the Coalfields', *Bulletin* [SSLH], no. 4 (Spring 1962): 24–32.

Anthony Sutcliffe, 'Working-Class Housing in Nineteenth-Century Britain: A Review of Recent Research', *Bulletin* [Society for the Study of Labour History, hereafter: SSLH], no. 24 (Spring 1972): 40–50.

Sidney Pollard, 'Englische Arbeiterkultur im Zeitalter der Industrialisierung: Forschungsergebnisse und Forschungsprobleme. Ein bibliographischer Aufsatz', *Geschichte und Gesellschaft*, 5 (1979): 150–66.

Ken Worpole, 'Forskningen i arbejderklassens historie i England og Wales i dag', *Årbog for arbejderbevægelsens historie*, 10 (1980): 235–43.

J.S. Hurt, 'Education and the Working Classes', *Bulletin* [SSLH], no. 30 (Spring 1975): 42–54; no. 31 (Autumn 1975): 20–44; no. 43 (Autumn 1981): 22–39.

Royden Harrison, 'The Last Ten Years in British Labour Historiography', *Historical Papers* [Canadian Historical Association] (1980): 212–27.

Victor Bailey, 'Crime, Criminal Justice and Authority in England', *Bulletin* [SSLH], no. 40 (Spring 1980): 36–46.

Alan J. MacKenzie, 'The Communist Party of Great Britain', *Bulletin* [SSLH], no. 44 (Spring 1982): 23–41.

Barbara Bush, 'Forgotten Comrades: Black Colonial Labour and the Development of Anti-Colonialism in the Interwar Years', *Bulletin* [SSLH], no. 45 (Autumn 1982): 26–31.

Alan Booth, 'The Labour Party and Economics between the Wars', *Bulletin* [SSLH], no. 47 (Autumn 1983): 36–42.

Peter Stead, 'British Society and British Films', *Bulletin* [SSLH], no. 48 (Spring 1984): 72–75.

John Young, 'Idealism and Realism in the History of Labour's Foreign Policy', *Bulletin* [SSLH], no. 50 (Spring 1985): 14–19.

Sue Lawrence, 'Municipal Socialism, Municipal Trading and Public Utilities', *Bulletin* [SSLH], 52/1 (April 1987): 46–53.

Arthur McIvor, 'Political Black Listing and Anti-Socialist Activity Between the Wars', *Bulletin* [SSLH], 53/1 (Spring 1988): 18–26.

Susana Tavera García, 'La condición de la clase obrera inglesa, 1780–1850: un debate', *Historia Social*, no. 2 (1988): 144–56.

Roy Church, Quintin Outram and David N. Smith, 'Towards a History of British Miners' Militancy', *Bulletin* [SSLH], 54/1 (Spring 1989): 21–36.

Henry Baldwin, 'Labour History in Britain: A Survey', in: Raimund Löw (ed.), *Historiographie der Arbeiterbewegung in Frankreich und Grossbritannien*, Vienna and Zurich: Europaverlag, 1989, 69–97.

Arbeiterschaft und Arbeiterbewegung in Großbritannien: Forschungsstand und Perspektiven der Forschung. Special issue of *Mitteilungsblatt* [Bochum], no. 11 (1991) including:
- Arthur McIvor, 'Die Forschung zur Geschichte der Arbeiterschaft und der Arbeiterbewegung in England: Ein Überblick über die jüngsten Entwicklungen', 14–58.

- Conan Fischer and William Knox, 'Geschichte der Arbeiterschaft und der Arbeiterbewegung in Schottland: Die Geschichtsschreibung der letzten zwanzig Jahre', 59–84.
- Deian Rhys Hopkin, 'Die soziale, wirtschaftliche und politische Historiographie des modernen Wales', 85–110.

Neil Evans, 'Writing the Social History of Modern Wales: Approaches, Achievements and Problems', *Social History*, 17 (1992): 479–92.

Mike Savage, 'Social Mobility and Class Analysis: A New Agenda for Social History?', *Social History*, 19 (1994): 69–79.

Keith Neild, 'A British Debate. Under the Sign of the Social: Bringing Politics Back In?', *Tijdschrift voor Sociale Geschiedenis*, 23 (1997): 182–97.

John L. Halstead, 'British Labour History After the Collapse of Actually Existing Socialism and in the Postmodern Age', in: Bruno Groppo et al. (eds), *Quellen und Historiographie der Arbeiterbewegung nach dem Zusammenbruch des 'Realsozialismus'*, Garbsen: Calenberg Press, 1998, 83–102.

Denmark

Gerd Callesen, 'Zur Geschichte der dänischen Arbeiterbewegung', *Archiv für Sozialgeschichte*, 12 (1972): 628–48.

Steen Bille Larsen, 'Mellem partihistorie og socialhistorie. Nogle sider af historieskrivningen om dansk arbejderbevægelse efter 1945', *Årbog for arbejderbevægelsens historie*, 7 (1977): 194–207.

Niels Finn Christiansen, 'Social- og fagforeningshistorieforskning i 1930'erne', *Årbog for arbejderbevægelsens historie*, 8 (1978): 211–23.

Flemming Ibsen and Henning Jørgensen, 'Temaer og problemer i nyere danske fagforeningsundersøgelser', *Årbog for arbejderbevægelsens historie*, 8 (1978): 224–51.

Gerd Callesen et al. (eds), *'Fremad og aldrig glemme': Ti års forskning i arbejderbevægelsens historie: status og perspektiver*, Copenhagen: SFAH, 1981.

Hans Chr. Johansen, 'Trends in Modern and Early Modern Social History Writing in Denmark after 1970', *Social History*, 8 (1983): 375–81.

Svend Åge Andersen, 'Arbejderhverdag og arbejdersubjektivitet: henimod en arbejderhistorie "fra neden". Nye tendenser i arbejderforskning', *Årbog for arbejderbevægelsens historie*, 15 (1985): 197–269.

Niels Ole Højstrup Jensen et al. (eds), *Fremad – ad nye veje. Bidrag til diskussionen om arbejderhistorien i 1990'erne*, Copenhagen: SFAH, 1990.

Finland

Maurice Carrez, 'L'Historiographie ouvrière en Finlande', *Le Mouvement Social*, no. 133 (1985): 81–92.

Forschungen zur Arbeiterschaft und Arbeiterbewegung in Finnland. Special issue of the *Mitteilungsblatt* [Bochum], no.12 (1992) including:

- Pertti Haapala, 'Von der Legitimationswissenschaft zur Gesellschaftsgeschichtsschreibung: Traditionen und Paradigmen der finnischen Arbeitergeschichte', 13–17.

- Pauli Kettunen, 'Die alte Arbeiterbewegung "unter dem Polarstern" in neuer Sicht', 18–26.
- Marja Rantala, 'Von der Klassen- zur Rahmen- und Sammelpartei: Die Geschichtsschreibung über die Sozialdemokratische Partei (nach 1918)', 27–33.
- Kimmo Rentola, 'Nur noch als Vergangenheit lebendig: Zur Forschung über die Geschichte des finnischen Kommunismus', 34–41.
- Risto Reuna, 'Abseits und verspätet, aber nicht zu spät: Zur Forschung über die finnische Gewerkschaftsbewegung', 42–51.
- Tero Tuomisto, 'Hartes Geld für die politische Arbeit: Zur Erforschung der Wirtschaftstätigkeit der Arbeiterbewegung', 52–57.
- Maria Lähteenmäki, 'Spät "entdeckt", aber immerhin: Die Arbeiterinnen als Forschungsgegenstand', 58–62.
- Timo Holmalahti, 'Industriearbeit und Lebensweise: Die Arbeiterkulturforschung in Finnland', 63–72.
- Simo Laaksovirta, 'Verbindungen der Tradition und Geschichte zum heutigen Leben aufzeigen: Arbeitermemoiren und Arbeitertraditionsforschung heute', 73–83.

Seppo Hentilä, 'Arbeitergeschichte aus finnischer Sicht', in Bruno Groppo et al. (eds), *Quellen und Historiographie der Arbeiterbewegung nach dem Zusammenbruch des 'Realsozialismus'*, Garbsen: Calenberg Press, 1998, 109–26.

France

Michelle Perrot and Jean Maitron, 'Sources, institutions et recherches en histoire ouvrière française', *Le mouvement social*, no. 65 (1968): 121–61.

Volker Hunecke, 'Die Pariser Kommune von 1871', *Neue Politische Literatur*, 19 (1974): 83–108.

Michelle Perrot, 'The Strengths and Weaknesses of French Social History', *Journal of Social History*, 10 (1976): 166–77.

'Histoire ouvrière, histoire sociale (table ronde)', *Le Mouvement Social*, no. 100 (July-September 1977): 45–80.

Michael Seidelin, 'Fransk fagbevægelses historie frem til 1914 i lyset af den nyeste forskning', *Årbog for arbejderbevægelsens historie*, 8 (1978): 273–85.

Andrew Lincoln, 'Through the Undergrowth: Capitalist Development and Social Formation in Nineteenth-Century France', in Raphael Samuel (ed.), *People's History and Socialist Theory*, London [etc.]: Routledge & Kegan Paul, 1981, 255–67.

Jacques Rancière, '"Le Social": The Lost Tradition in French Labour History', in Raphael Samuel (ed.), *People's History and Socialist Theory*, London [etc.]: Routledge & Kegan Paul, 1981, 267–72.

Heinz-Gerhard Haupt, 'Außerbetriebliche Situationen und Erfahrungen von französischen Arbeitern vor 1914: einige Ansätze in der französischen Forschung', *Archiv für Sozialgeschichte*, 22 (1982): 491–513.

Danielle Tartakowsky, 'L'historiographie du Parti communiste français: nouveau bilan, bibliographie', *Cahiers d'histoire de l'institut de recherches marxistes*, no. 23 (1985): 81–110.

Ivan Avakoumovitch, 'Le PCF dans l'optique des chercheurs anglo-améri-
cains, 1970–1984', *Cahiers d'histoire de l'institut de recherches marxistes*,
no. 23 (1985): 111–23.

Heinz-Gerhard Haupt, 'Forschungen zur neueren Sozialgeschichte Frankreichs: neue Ansätze und Ergebnisse', *Archiv für Sozialgeschichte*, 27
(1987): 483–98.

Franz Pichler, 'Zur Transformation der französischen Arbeiterklasse:
Diskussion und Forschungsergebnisse', *Archiv: Jahrbuch des Vereins für
Geschichte der Arbeiterbewegung*, Vienna, 1987, 115–24.

Raimund Löw, 'Probleme und Stand der Forschung zur Geschichte der
Arbeiterbewegung in Frankreich', in Raimund Löw (ed.), *Historiogra-
phie der Arbeiterbewegung in Frankreich und Grossbritannien*, Vienna and
Zurich: Europaverlag, 1989, 9–41.

Berthold Unfried, 'Geschichte und aktuelle Tendenzen der französischen
Arbeiterhistoriographie', in Raimund Löw (ed.), *Historiographie der
Arbeiterbewegung in Frankreich und Grossbritannien*, Vienna and Zurich:
Europaverlag, 1989, 43–67.

Antoine Prost, 'What Has Happened to French Social History?', *Historical
Journal*, 35 (1992): 671–9.

Berthold Unfried in collaboration with Françoise Blum, 'Entwicklungsten-
denzen der französischen Arbeiterhistoriographie', *Mitteilungsblatt*
[Bochum], no.14 (1993): 30–57.

Jean-Louis Robert, 'The Social Group: Three Approaches to Social History', *Tijdschrift voor Sociale Geschiedenis*, 23 (1997): 198–208.

Bruno Groppo, 'L'évolution récente de l'historiographie du mouvement
ouvrier en France', in Bruno Groppo et al. (eds), *Quellen und Historiographie der Arbeiterbewegung nach dem Zusammenbruch des 'Realsozialismus'*, Garbsen: Calenberg Press, 1998, 83–102.

Germany

Ursula Ratz, 'Von der Opposition zur staatlichen Mitverantwortung: Zur
Geschichte der deutschen Arbeiterbewegung', *Neue Politische Literatur*,
14 (1969): 508–20.

Ursula Ratz, 'Zur Sozialgeschichte der deutschen Arbeiterbewegung: Lokal-
und Regionalstudien', *Neue Politische Literatur*, 15 (1970): 343–53.

Volker Ullrich, 'Emanzipation durch Integration? Zur Kritik der bürgerlichen Geschichtsschreibung über die Arbeiterbewegung bis 1914', *Das
Argument*, no. 75 (1972): 104–47.

John A. Maxwell, 'On American Studies of the German Labor Movement,
1848–1933', *Archiv für Sozialgeschichte*, 14 (1974): 593–609.

Christoph Butterwege, 'Zur Typologie sozialdemokratischer Parteihistori-
ographie', *Sozialistische Politik*, no. 37–38 (1976): 139–66.

Ursula Ratz, 'Zwischen Anpassung und Systemkritik: Zur Geschichte der
deutschen Arbeiterbewegung', *Neue Politische Literatur*, 21 (1976):
208–16.

Dieter Kramer, 'Forschungsbericht: Literatur zur Kultursoziologie der
Arbeiter', *Zeitschrift für Volkskunde*, 71 (1975): 88–103 and 73 (1977):
246–61.

Dieter Emig and Rüdiger Zimmermann, *Arbeiterbewegung in Deutschland: Ein Dissertationsverzeichnis = Internationale wissenschaftliche Korrespondenz zur Geschichte der deutschen Arbeiterbewegung*, 13, 3 (1977).

Hannes Heer, Dirk Hemje-Oltmanns and Volker Ullrich, 'Organisationsgeschichte oder Geschichte der "eigentlichen Arbeiterbewegung"? Zu neueren Veröffentlichungen über die Geschichte der deutschen Arbeiterbewegung', *Das Argument*, no. 106 (1977): 860–80.

Detlev Peukert, 'Zur Regionalgeschichtsschreibung der Arbeiterbewegung', *Das Argument*, no. 110 (1978): 546–65.

Klaus Tenfelde, 'Wege zur Sozialgeschichte der Arbeiterschaft und Arbeiterbewegung. Regional- und lokalgeschichtliche Forschungen (1945–1975) zur deutschen Arbeiterbewegung bis 1914', *Geschichte und Gesellschaft*, 4 (1978, Supplement): 197–255.

Jürgen Kocka, 'Theory and Social History: Recent Developments in West Germany', *Social Research*, 47 (1980): 426–57.

Ursula Ratz, 'Zur Ideologie- und Organisationsgeschichte der Sozialdemokratie: Neue Arbeiten über die deutsche Arbeiterbewegung', *Neue Politische Literatur*, 25 (1980): 475–84.

Klaus Tenfelde and Gerhard A. Ritter, 'Einleitung', in Tenfelde and Ritter, *Bibliographie zur Geschichte der deutschen Arbeiterschaft und Arbeiterbewegung 1863 bis 1914. Berichtszeitraum 1945 bis 1975,* Bonn: Neue Gesellschaft, 1981, 37–132.

Dieter Kramer, 'Forskning om arbejderkultur fra Forbundsrepublikken Tyskland. En oversigt over de nyere tendenser', *Årbog for arbejderbevægelsens historie*, 11 (1981): 250–63.

Gustavo Corni, 'Systemkrise, Arbeiterbewegung und der Weg zum Sozialismus: Das Ende der Weimarer Republik in der italienischen Diskussion der 70er Jahre', *Neue Politische Literatur*, 26 (1981): 226–36.

Michael Schneider, 'Kirche und soziale Frage im 19. und 20. Jahrhundert, unter besonderer Berücksichtigung des Katholizismus', *Archiv für Sozialgeschichte*, 21 (1981): 533–53.

Ursula Ratz, 'Arbeiterbewegung und Sozialpolitik: Neuerscheinungen zur Geschichte der Arbeiterbewegung und Sozialpolitik in Deutschland', *Neue Politische Literatur*, 27 (1982): 304–18.

Volker Ullrich, 'Die deutsche Arbeiterbewegung im ersten Weltkrieg und in der Revolution von 1918/19: Anmerkungen zu neueren Veröffentlichungen', *Neue Politische Literatur*, 27 (1982): 446–62.

Jürgen Kocka, ' Klassen oder Kultur. Durchbrüche und Sackgassen der Arbeitergeschichte', *Merkur*, 36 (1982): 955–65. [Plus: Martin Broszat, 'Plädoyer für Alltagsgeschichte. Eine Replik auf Jürgen Kocka', *Merkur*, 36 (1982): 1244–48.]

Sidney Pollard, 'Current German Economic and Social History: Attitudes to Hermeneutics and Objectivity', *South African Historical Journal*, 16 (1984): 6–25.

William L. Patch, Jr., 'German Social History and Labor History: A Troubled Partnership', *Journal of Modern History*, 56 (1984): 483–98.

Dieter Langewiesche, '"Arbeiterkultur": Kultur der Arbeiterbewegung im Kaiserreich und in der Weimarer Republik. Bemerkungen zum

Forschungsstand', *Ergebnisse: Zeitschrift für demokratische Geschichtswissenschaft*, 26 (1984): 9–23.

John C. Fout, 'Current Research on German Women's History in the Nineteenth Century', in: John C. Fout (ed.), *German Women in the Nineteenth Century: A Social History*, New York: Holmes & Meier, 1984, 3–34.

Klaus Tenfelde, 'Schwierigkeiten mit dem Alltag', *Geschichte und Gesellschaft*, 10 (1984): 376–94.

Ursula Ratz, 'Arbeiterbewegung zwischen Protest und Reform', *Neue Politische Literatur*, 29 (1984): 205–20.

Volker Ullrich, 'Zwischen Alltag und Organisation: Neue Beiträge zur Geschichte der Arbeiter und Arbeiterbewegung', *Neue Politische Literatur*, 30 (1985): 252–71.

Jens Flemming, 'Die vergessene Klasse: Literatur zur Geschichte der Landarbeiter in Deutschland', in Klaus Tenfelde (ed.), *Arbeiter und Arbeiterbewegung im Vergleich. Berichte zur internationalen historischen Forschung*, Munich: Oldenbourg, 1986, 389–418.

Johannes Klotz, 'Neuere Literatur zur Geschichte der Arbeiterbewegung in Deutschland', *Neue Politische Literatur*, 31 (1986): 21–53.

Klaus Tenfelde, 'Die Sozialgeschichte der Arbeiter zwischen Strukturgeschichte und Alltagsgeschichte', in Wolfgang Schieder and Volker Sellin (eds), *Sozialgeschichte in Deutschland*, vol. 4, Göttingen: Vandenhoeck & Ruprecht, 1987, 81–107.

Dieter Langewiesche, 'The Impact of the German Labor Movement on Workers' Culture', *Journal of Modern History*, 59 (1987): 506–23.

Gerhard A. Ritter, 'Probleme der Erforschung von Arbeiterschaft und Arbeiterbewegung in Deutschland vom Ende des 18. Jahrhunderts bis zum Ersten Weltkrieg', *Tel Aviver Jahrbuch für deutsche Geschichte*, 16 (1987): 369–97.

Ursula Ratz, 'Perspektiven über Karl Kautsky: Neuerscheinungen zur Geschichte der Arbeiterbewegung anläßlich des 50. Todestages des "Chefideologen"', *Neue Politische Literatur*, 33 (1988): 7–24.

Roger Fletcher, 'History from Below Comes to Germany: The New History Movement in the Federal Republic of Germany', *Journal of Modern History*, 60 (1988): 557–68.

Marina Cattaruzza, 'Arbeiterkultur, Arbeiterbewegungskultur, männliche Kultur', *Neue Politische Literatur*, 34 (1989): 256–77.

Geoff Eley, 'Labor History, Social History, *Alltagsgeschichte*: Experience, Culture, and the Politics of the Everyday: a New Direction for German Social History', *Journal of Modern History*, 61 (1989): 297–343.

Ulrich Herbert, 'Arbeiterschaft im "Dritten Reich": Zwischenbilanz und offene Fragen', *Geschichte und Gesellschaft*, 15 (1989): 320–60.

Hans Manfred Bock, 'Anarchosyndikalismus in Deutschland. Eine Zwischenbilanz', *Internationale wissenschaftliche Korrespondenz zur Geschichte der deutschen Arbeiterbewegung*, 25 (1989): 293–358.

Carola Lipp, 'History as Political Culture: Social History vs. *Alltagsgeschichte* – A German Debate', *Storia della storiografia*, 17 (1990): 66–100.

Matthias Frese, 'Kooperation und Konflikt: Neuere Studien zu den Gewerkschaften in der Weimarer Republik', *Neue Politische Literatur*, 36 (1991): 405–49.

John Breuilly, 'Von den Unterschichten zur Arbeiterklasse: Deutschland 1800–1875', *Geschichte und Gesellschaft*, 20 (1994): 251–73.

Karl Ditt, 'Fabrikarbeiter und Handwerker im 19. Jahrhundert in der neueren deutschen Sozialgeschichtsschreibung: Eine Zwischenbilanz', *Geschichte und Gesellschaft*, 20 (1994): 299–320.

Dieter Nelles, 'Syndikalismus und Unionismus: Neuere Ergebnisse und Perspektiven der Forschung', *Internationale wissenschaftliche Korrespondenz zur Geschichte der deutschen Arbeiterbewegung*, 31 (1995): 348–56.

Mary Nolan, 'Rationalization, Racism, and *Resistenz*: Recent Studies of Work and the Working Class in Nazi Germany', *International Labor and Working-Class History*, no. 48 (Fall 1995): 131–51.

Jürgen Kocka, 'Social History in Germany', *Tijdschrift voor Sociale Geschiedenis*, 23 (1997): 137–46.

Ireland

Francis Devine and Emmet O'Connor, 'Labour and Irish History', *Saothar*, 10 (1984): 3–8.

Emmet O'Connor, 'A Historiography of Irish Labour', *Labour History Review*, 60/1 (Spring 1995): 21–34.

Emmet O'Connor, 'Reds and the Green: Problems of the History and Historiography of Communism in Ireland', *Science and Society*, 61 (1997): 113–18.

Italy

Aris Accornero, 'Per una nuova fase di studi sul movimento sindicale', *Annali Istituto Giangiacomo Feltrinelli*, 16 (1974): 1–105.

Volker Hunecke, 'Die neuere Literatur zur Geschichte der italienischen Arbeiterbewegung', *Archiv für Sozialgeschichte*, 14 (1974): 543–92, and 15 (1975): 409–51.

Viggo Bank Jensen, 'Italien: oversigt over forskning i italienske arbejdskampe efter 2. verdenskrig', *Årbog for arbejderbevægelsens historie*, 9 (1979): 257–74.

Alberto Caracciolo, 'Between Tradition and Innovation: Italian Studies in Modern Social History', *Social Research*, 47 (1980): 404–25.

Fabio Fabbri, 'Studi recenti sulla cooperazione italiana', *Italia contemporanea*, 33 (1981): 77–83.

Renato Giusti, 'Economia e società in Italia nell'età delle riforme', *Archivio storico italiano*, no. 139 (1981): 289–322.

Stefano Privato, 'La cultura del movimento operaio', *Italia contemporanea*, 33 (1981): 103–7.

Maurizio Virli, 'Socialismo e cultura', *Studi Storici*, 22 (1981): 179–97.

Gaetano Arfé, 'La storiografia del movimento socialista in Italia', in: *Prampolini e il socialismo riformista: Atti del convegno di Reggio Emilia, ottobre 1978*, 2 vols, Rome: Mondoperaio, 1979–81, I, 1–17 (plus debates: 19–161).

Giulio Sapelli, 'Zur Erforschung der Probleme der Arbeiter in der Fabrik um die Wende vom 19. zum 20. Jahrhundert in Italien', *Archiv für Sozialgeschichte*, 21 (1981): 399–426.

Ivano Granata, *Il socialismo italiano nella storiografia del secondo dopoguerra*, Bari: Laterza, 1981.

C. Natoli, 'Il socialismo italiano tra le due guerre: bilancio e prospettivi di ricerca', *Italia contemporanea*, (December 1982): 53–85,

Ivano Granata, 'Il socialismo riformista italiano e la storiografia', *Storia della storiografia*, 8 (1985): 133–53.

Leonardo Rapone, 'Il socialismo italiano dall'antifascismo alla repubblica in alcuni studi recenti', *Studi Storici*, 31 (1990): 213–34.

Claudio Natoli, 'Il socialismo italiano nella crisi dello Stato liberale', *Passato e Presente*, no. 32 (1994): 135–49.

Adriano Ballone, 'Storiografia e storia del PCI', *Passato e Presente*, no. 33 (1994): 129–46.

Maurizio Ridolfi, 'Ripensare la storia del socialismo', *Studi Storici*, 35 (1994): 111–27.

Claudo Venza, 'Historiografia italiana del movimiento obrero: una nota y unas publicaciones recientes', *Historia Social*, no. 28 (1995): 143–9.

David Bidussa, 'Storia e storiografia sul movimento operaio nell'Italia del secondo dopoguerra. Gli anni della formazione (1945–1956)', in Luigi Cortesi and Andrea Panaccione (eds), *Il socialismo e la storia: studi per Stefano Merli*, Milan: Franco Angeli, 1998, 183–230.

The Netherlands

John Gerber, 'Working Class Historiography in the Netherlands, 1960–1975', *International Labor and Working-Class History*, no. 10 (1976): 28–34.

Marcel van der Linden and Jan Lucassen, 'Social History in the Netherlands', *Tijdschrift voor Sociale Geschiedenis*, 23 (1997): 209–23.

Norway

Einhart Lorenz, 'Zur Geschichte der norwegischen Arbeiterbewegung', *Archiv für Sozialgeschichte*, 13 (1973): 574–99.

Knut Kjeldstadli, 'Fagbevegelsens historie i Norge – en litteraturveiledning', *Årbog for arbejderbevægelsens historie*, 8 (1978): 252–8.

Einhart Lorenz, 'Arbeiterklasse und Arbeiterbewegung in Norwegen: Ein Literaturbericht', *Archiv für Sozialgeschichte*, 21 (1981): 630–656.

Ingar Kaldal, 'Från arbetare i politiken till politiken i arbetet? Arbetslivsforskning i Norge', *Arbetarhistoria*, no. 52 (1989): 25–30.

Portugal

José Pacheco Pereira, 'L'historiographie ouvrière au Portugal', *Le Mouvement Social*, no. 123 (April-June 1983): 99–109.

Spain

Manuel Tuñon de Lara, 'Historia del movimiento obrero en España (Un estado de la cuestion en los diez ultimos años)', in: Manuel Tuñon de

Lara (ed.), *Historiografia Española contemporanea. X Coloquio del Centro de Investigaciones Hispánicas de la Universidad de Pau: Balance y resumen*, Madrid: Siglo XXI, 1980, 231–49.

Jean-Louis Guereña, 'La recherche en histoire ouvrière en Espagne: Approche bibliographique', *Le Mouvement Social*, no. 128 (July-September 1984): 113–25.

Pere Gabriel, 'Historiografia reciente sobre el anarquismo y el sindicalismo en España, 1870–1923', *Historia Social*, no. 1 (1988): 45–54.

Feliciano Montero, 'Catolicismo social en España: Una revisión historiográfica', *Historia Social*, no. 2 (1988): 157–64.

Ángeles Barrio Alonso, 'A propósito de la historia social, del movimiento obrero y los sindicatos', in German Rueda Hernanz (ed.), *Doce estudios de historia contemporánea*, Santander: Universidad de Cantabria, 1991, 41–68.

Javier Paniagua, 'Una gran pregunta y varias respuestas. El anarquismo español: desde la politica a la historiográfia', *Historia Social*, no. 12 (1992): 31–57.

M. Pilar Salomón, 'Poder y ética: balance historiográfico sobre anticlericalismo', *Historia Social*, no. 19 (1994): 113–28.

Pere Gabriel, 'A vueltas y revueltas con la historia social obrera en España: historia obrera, historia popular e historia contemporánea', *Historia Social*, no. 22 (1995): 43–53.

Alejandro Tiana Ferrer, 'Movimiento obrero y educación popular en la España contemporánea', *Historia Social*, no. 27 (1997): 127–44.

Carme Molinero and Pere Ysàs, 'La historia social de la época franquista: una aproximación', *Historia Social*, no. 30 (1998): 133–54.

Sweden

Lars Björlin, 'Politik och historia. Kring den socialdemokratiska historieskrivningen', *Meddelande från Arbetarrörelsens Arkiv och Bibliotek*, no. 2–3 (1977): 2–33.

Bo Stråth, 'Recent Developments in Swedish Social History of the Period Since 1800', *Social History*, 9 (1984): 77–85.

Tom Olsson, 'Uppsvinget. Forskningen om den svenska fackföreningsrörelsen till 1979', *Arbetarhistoria*, no. 31–32 (1984): 39–45.

Klas Åmark, 'Från kaos till ordning. Forsking på 80-talet', *Arbetarhistoria*, no. 31–32 (1984): 46–57.

Lars Olsson, 'Från socialhistoria till samhällshistoria: Arbetarhistorisk forskning', *Arbetarhistoria*, no. 41 (1987): 3–8.

Lars Olsson, 'Swedish Working-Class History', *International Labor and Working-Class History*, no. 35 (1989): 61–80.

Forschungen zur Arbeiterschaft und Arbeiterbewegung in Schweden. Special issue of the *Mitteilungsblatt* [Bochum], 10 (1990), including:
- Lars Edgren and Lars Olsson, 'Die schwedische Forschung zur Geschichte der Arbeiterschaft', 8–28.
- Gunnel Karlsson, 'Ein roter Streifen am Horizont: Untersuchung zu den Frauen in der Arbeiterbewegung', 29–42.
- Lars Björlin, 'Die Forschung über die schwedischen Arbeiterparteien in den 70er und 80er Jahren: einige Hauptzüge', 43–57.

- Klas Åmark, 'Das schwedische Modell. Die Gewerkschaftsbewegung der Arbeiter und die Zusammenarbeit zwischen den Tarifpartnern auf dem schwedischen Arbeitsmarkt', 58–73.
- Marion Leffler, 'Die Bildungseinrichtungen der schwedischen Arbeiterbewegung: Hintergründe und Forschungsübersicht', 74–89.

Rolf Torstendahl, 'Social History at the End of the 1980s', *Storia della storiografia*, no. 18 (1990): 29–35.

Klaus Misgeld and Klas Åmark (eds), *Arbetsliv och arbetarrörelse: Modern historisk forskning i Sverige*, Stockholm: Arbetarrörelsens arkiv och bibliotek, 1991.

Martin Grass, 'Arbeiterschaft und Arbeiterbewegung in Schweden: Forschungsübersicht', in Bruno Groppo et al. (eds), *Quellen und Historiographie der Arbeiterbewegung nach dem Zusammenbruch des 'Realsozialismus'*, Garbsen: Calenberg Press, 1998, 127–9.

Switzerland

Marc Vuilleumier, 'Le Mouvement ouvrier en Suisse pendant et après la première guerre mondiale: bilan historiographique', *Le Mouvement Social*, 84 (1973): 97–126.

Bernard Degen, 'Arbeiterinnen, Arbeiter und Angestellte in der schweizerischen Geschichtsschreibung', in *Geschichtsforschung in der Schweiz: Bilanz und Perspektiven*, Basel: Schwabe, 1992, 79–91.

Marc Vuilleumier, 'Historiographie et histoire du mouvement ouvrier', in *Guido Pedroli 'storico': quale storia?* Bellinzona: Casablanca, 1993, 41–57.

Brigitte Studer and François Valloton (eds), *Histoire sociale et mouvement ouvrier: Un bilan historiographique 1848–1998 / Sozialgeschichte und Arbeiterbewegung: Eine historiographische Bilanz 1848–1998*, Lausanne and Zurich: Editions d'en bas and Chronos Verlag, 1997. This volume includes:

- Hans Ulrich Jost, 'L'historiographie du mouvement ouvrier suisse: sous l'emprise de l'histoire des vainqueurs', 21–31.
- Bernard Degen, 'Arbeiterbewegung und Politik in der Geschichtsschreibung', 33–60.
- Brigitte Studer, 'Genre, travail et histoire ouvrière', 63–88.
- Jakob Tanner, 'Klassenkämpfe, industrielle Beziehungen und Konsumbewegung', 91–105.
- Rudolf Jaun, 'Arbeit, Arbeitslosigkeit und Arbeitsrecht', 107–16.
- Mario König, 'Die Angestellten neben der Arbeiterbewegung: Aufstieg und Niedergang einer Forschungsthematik', 119–35.
- Charles Heimberg, 'Culture ouvrière et vie quotidienne: vers de nouvelles perspectives de recherches sur le mouvement ouvrier', 137–52.
- Charles Heimberg, 'La question de l'immigration', 155–61.
- Gabriele Rossi, 'Bibliografia del movimento operaio: Ticino', 163–83.
- Cinoptika, 'Cinéma et mouvement ouvrier', 187–222.

Marc Vuilleumier, 'Remarques à propos de l'historiographie du mouvement ouvrier en Suisse', *Cahiers d'histoire du mouvement ouvrier*, no. 16 (2000): 143–51.

BIBLIOGRAPHIES OF WEST EUROPEAN LABOUR HISTORIOGRAPHY, 1965–2000

General and Cross-country

Theo Pinkus et al., 'Bibliographien zur deutschsprachigen Arbeiterbewegung', *Jahrbuch Arbeiterbewegung*, 2 (1974): 334–8.

Victor F. Gilbert, *Labour and Social History Theses: American, British and Irish University Theses and Dissertations in the Field of British and Irish Labour History, Presented between 1900 and 1978*, London: Mansell, 1978.

Vilém Kahan, *Bibliography of the Communist International (1919–1979)*, vol. I, Leiden [etc.]: Brill, 1985.

Barry Taylor, *Society and Economy in Early Modern Europe, 1450–1789: A Bibliography of Post-War Research*, Manchester and New York: Manchester University Press, 1989.

Karin Hofmeester, 'Bibliography', in Marcel van der Linden and Jürgen Rojahn (eds), *The Formation of Labour Movements 1870–1914: An International Perspective*, Leiden [etc.]: Brill, 1990, vol. II, 701–81.

Karin Hofmeester et al., *De ontwikkeling van arbeidersbewegingen in internationaal vergelijkend perspectief. Een geannoteerde bibliografie*, Amsterdam: Stichting beheer IISG, 1990.

Marianne Bagge Hansen and Gerd Callesen, *Foreign Language Literature on the Nordic Labour Movements*, Copenhagen: Arbejderbevægelsens Bibliotek og Arkiv, 1992.

Lidewij Hesselink, 'The History of Dock Labour: An Annotated Bibliography', in Sam Davies et al. (eds), *Dock Workers: International Explorations in Comparative Labour History, 1790–1970*, 2 vols, Aldershot [etc.]: Ashgate, 2000, II, 781–822.

Bruno Groppo and Bernard Pudal, 'Historiographies des communismes français et italien', in Michel Dreyfus et al. (eds), *Le siècle des communismes*, Paris: Ed. de l'Atelier, 2000, 67–81.

Austria

Herbert Steiner, *Bibliographie zur Geschichte der österreichischen Arbeiterbewegung*, vol. I (1867–1918), vol. II (1918–1934), vol. III (1934–1945), Vienna [etc.]: Europaverlag, 1962, 1967, 1970.

Helene Maimann in collaboration with Roswitha Böhm, *Arbeitergeschichte und Arbeiterbewegung: Dissertationen und Diplomarbeiten in Österreich, 1918–1979*, Vienna: Österreichischer Bundesverlag, 1978.

Belgium

Denise de Weerdt, *Socialisme en socialistische arbeidersbeweging in België. Bibliografie van werken en tijdschriftartikels, verschenen sedert 1944*, 2 vols, Brussels: Emile Vandervelde Instituut, 1979.

Reinhard Schiffers, 'Die sozialgeschichtliche Forschung zum Industriezeitalter in Belgien', *Vierteljahrschrift für Sozial- und Wirtschaftsgeschichte*, 67 (1980): 22–80.

Britain

Ian MacDougall, *An Interim Bibliography of the Scottish Working Class Movement and Other Labour Records Held in Scotland*, Edinburgh: Society for the Study of Labour History: Scottish Committee, 1965.

I. Wagner, *Labour Party Bibliography*, no place: Labour Party, 1967.

A. Potts and E.R. Jones, *Northern Labour History: A Bibliography*, London: The Library Association, 1981.

Harold Smith, *The British Labour Movement to 1970: A Bibliography*, London: Mansell, 1981.

W.H. Chaloner and R.C. Richardson, *Bibliography of British Economic and Social History*, Manchester and Dover, NH: Manchester University Press, 1983.

Owen Ashton, Robert Fryson and Stephen Roberts, *The Chartist Movement: A New Annotated Bibliography*, London and New York: Mansell, 1995. [See also: J.F.C. Harrison and Dorothy Thompson, *Bibliography of the Chartist Movement, 1837–1976*, Sussex: The Harvester Press and New Jersey: Humanities Press, 1978.]

Denmark

Jens Christensen, 'Kommenteret bibliografi til den danske arbejderklassen og bevægelses historie', *Den jyske historiker*, no. 13 (1978): 139–236.

Hans Rohr Christoffersen, *Fremdsprachige Literatur über die dänische Arbeiterbewegung: Eine Bibliographie*, Copenhagen: Arbejderbevægelsens Bibliotek og Arkiv, 1983.

Jens Erik Kofoed Pedersen, *Arbejderhistorie i Danmark: En litteraturoversigt*, Copenhagen: Arbejderbevægelsens Bibliotek og Arkiv, 1992.

'Bibliography' in Flemming Hemmersam (ed.), *'To Work, to Life or to Death': Studies in Working Class Lore*, Copenhagen: SFAH, 1996, 262–92.

Finland

Mervi Kaarninen, *Työväen bibliografia I: Opinnäytteet 1978–1987*, Helsinki: Työväenperinne-Arbetartradition, 1988.

Pekka Kaarninen, *Työväen bibliografia II: Artikkeliaineistoa 1978–1987*, Helsinki: Työväenperinne-Arbetartradition, 1989.

Pekka Kaarninen, *Työväen bibliografia III: Historiikit 1978–1990*, Helsinki: Työväenperinne-Arbetartradition, 1992.

France

Leon A. Dale, *A Bibliography of French Labor with a Selection of Documents on the French Labor Movement*, New York: Augustus M. Kelley, 1969.

Robert Brécy, *Le Mouvement syndical en France, 1871–1921. Essai bibliographique*, 1963; 2nd edn, Paris: Ed. du Signe, 1982.

Robert Le Quillec, *La Commune de Paris: Bibliographie Critique, 1871–1997*, Paris: Ed. La Boutique de l'Histoire, 1997.

Germany

Hans Manfred Bock, 'Bibliographischer Versuch zur Geschichte des Anarchismus und Anarcho-Syndikalismus in Deutschland', *Jahrbuch Arbeiterbewegung*, 1 (1973): 295–334.

Eckhard Tramsen, *Bibliographie zur geschichtlichen Entwicklung der Arbeiterjugendbewegung bis 1945, insbesondere in Deutschland*, Frankfurt am Main: Roter Stern, 1973.

Dieter Dowe, *Bibliographie zur Geschichte der deutschen Arbeiterbewegung, sozialistischen und kommunistischen Bewegung von den Anfängen bis 1863*, Bonn: Verlag Neue Gesellschaft, 1976.

Dieter Emig and Rüdiger Zimmermann, *Arbeiterbewegung in Deutschland: Ein Dissertationsverzeichnis = Internationale wissenschaftliche Korrespondenz zur Geschichte der deutschen Arbeiterbewegung [IWK]*, 13, 3 (1977).

Hans-Josef Steinberg, *Die deutsche sozialistische Arbeiterbewegung bis 1914: Eine bibliographische Einführung*, Frankfurt am Main and New York: Campus Verlag, 1979, XI, 379 pp.

Klaus Günther and Kurt Thomas Schmitz, *SPD, KPD/DKP, DGB in den Westzonen in der Bundesrepublik Deutschland 1945–1975. Eine Bibliographie*, Bonn: Verlag Neue Gesellschaft, 1980.

Kurt Klotzbach, *Bibliographie zur Geschichte der deutschen Arbeiterbewegung 1914–1945*, 3rd edn, Bonn: Verlag Neue Gesellschaft, 1981, 394 pp.

Bert Andréas, *Ferdinand Lassalle – Allgemeiner Deutscher Arbeiterverein. Bibliographie ihrer Schriften und der Literatur uber sie 1840 bis 1975*, Bonn: Verlag Neue Gesellschaft, 1981.

Klaus Tenfelde and Gerhard A. Ritter (eds), *Bibliographie zur Geschichte der deutschen Arbeiterschaft und Arbeiterbewegung 1863–1914. Berichtszeitraum 1945–1975*, Bonn: Verlag Neue Gesellschaft, 1981.

Christoph Stamm, *Regionale Fest- und Gedenkschriften der deutschen Arbeiterbewegung*, Bonn: Verlag Neue Gesellschaft, 1987.

Ireland

Deirde O'Connell, 'A Bibliography of Irish Labour History, 1973–1977', *Saothar*, 5 (1979): 97–108.

Mary E. Flynn, 'Ten Year Retrospective Bibliography of Irish Labour History, 1963–1972', *Saothar*, 14 (1989): 143–57.

Mary E. Flynn, 'A Retrospective Bibliography of Irish Labour History, 1960–1972', *Saothar*, 16 (1991): 144–58.

Italy

Bibliografia del socialismo e del movimento operaio italiano, 6 vols, Rome: E.S.M.O.I., 1962–91.

Aldo Agosti et al., *Il movimento sindacale in Italia: rassegne di studi 1945–1969*, Turin: Einaudi, 1970.

The Netherlands

Ger Harmsen, *Idee en beweging. Bibliografiese aanwijzingen bij de studie en het onderzoek van de geschiedenis van socialisme en arbeidersbeweging in Nederland*, Nijmegen: SUN, 1972.

Ger Harmsen and Joost Wormer, 'Bibliografie van de geschiedschrijving van het Nederlandse communisme', in Cor Boet et al., *Van bron tot boek: Apparaat voor de geschiedschrijving van het communisme*, Amsterdam: IPSO and Stichting beheer IISG, 1986, 133–73.

Supplement: Margreet Schrevel and Gerrit Voerman, 'Geschiedschrijving over het Nederlandse communisme: een aanvullende bibliografie, 1986–1996', in Schrevel and Voerman (eds), *De communistische erfenis: bibliografie en bronnen betreffende de CPN*, Amsterdam: Stichting beheer IISG/DNPP, 1997, 139–59.

Bert Freriks, 'Bibliografie van de PSP', in Paul Denekamp, Bert Freriks and Gerrit Voerman (eds), *Sporen van pacifistisch socialisme: Bibliografie en bronnen betreffende de PSP*, Amsterdam: Stichting beheer IISG/DNPP, 1993, 9–36.

Maarten Brinkman, *Honderd jaar sociaal-democratie in boek en tijdschrift: Bibliografie van de geschiedenis van de SDAP en de PvdA, 1894–1994*, Amsterdam: Stichting beheer IISG, 1994.

Merijn van der Vlist, *Bibliografie arbeiders en arbeidersbeweging Nederland, 1800–1940. Een geannoteerde bibliograie van publicaties verschenen in de jaren 1970–1994*, Amsterdam: Stichting beheer IISG, 1999.

Norway

Arbeiderbevegelsen i Norge. En bibliografi, Oslo: Arbeiderbevegelsens Arkiv, 1979.

Spain

E. Giralt i Raventós et al. (eds), *Bibliografia dels moviments socials a Catalunya, País Valencià i les illes*, Barcelona: Ed. Lavinia, 1972.

Renée Lambaret and Luis Moreno Herrero, *Movimientos Obreros y Socialistas (Chronologia y Bibliografia): España, 1700–1939*, vol. I, Madrid: Ed.

Jucar, 1985. [First part of a revised and enlarged edition of: Renée Lamberet, *Mouvements ouvriers et socialistes (Chronologie et bibliograhie): L'Espagne, 1750–1936*, Paris: Editions Ouvrières, 1953.]

Rosa Maria Capel and Julio Iglesias de Ussel, *Mujer Española y sociedad: bibliografía (1900–1984)*, Madrid: Solana, [1985].

Aurelio Martin Nájera, *Fuentes para la historia del PSOE y de las Juventudes Socialistas de España, 1879–1990*, 2 vols, Madrid: Editorial Pablo Iglesias, 1991.

Sweden

Gunnar Olofsson, 'Arbetsmarknad och strejker i Sverige – en kommenterad litteraturlista', *Årbog for arbejderbevægelsens historie*, 9 (1979): 233–41.

Lars Ekstrand, 'Lokal facklig verksamhet och studiet av den svenska fackföreningsrörelsen', *Årbog for arbejderbevægelsens historie*, 10 (1980): 226–34.

Grete Solberg, *En bibliografi över folkrörelseforskning 1930–1978*, Stockholm: Delegation för folkrörelseforskning, 1981.

Karin Bergenfalk, Birgit Parding and Johan Selme, 'Memoarer, biografer ... Personer i arbetarrörelsen. En bibliografi', *Arbetarhistoria*, no. 39–40 (1986): 41–60.

Birgit Parding, in collaboration with Ann Kristin Forsberg, *Svensk arbetarrörelse – en litteraturförteckning*, Stockholm: Tidens Förlag, 1989.

Marie Hedström, 'Bibliography', in Klaus Misgeld, Karl Molin and Klas Åmark (eds), *Creating Social Democracy: A Century of the Social Democratic Labor Party in Sweden*, University Park, PA: Pennsylvania State University Press, 1992, 456–78. (Titles in English, German and Spanish: 456–61, and titles in Scandinavian languages: 461–78.)

Switzerland

'Mille titres en histoire sociale suisse', in Brigitte Studer and François Valloton (eds), *Histoire sociale et mouvement ouvrier: Un bilan historiographique 1848–1998*, Lausanne and Zurich: Editions d'en bas and Chronos Verlag, 1997, 307–64.

BIOGRAPHICAL DICTIONARIES

General and cross-country

Hubert Dethier and Hubert Vandenbossche (eds), *Woordenboek van Belgische en Nederlandse vrijdenkers*, 2 vols, Brussels: Centrum voor de studie van de Verlichting, 1979, 1982.

Vladimir Muñoz, *Anarchists: A Biographical Encyclopaedia (Series I)*, trans. Scott Johnson, New York: Gordon Press, 1981.

Branko Lazitch, in collaboration with Milorad M. Drachkovitch, *Biographical Dictionary of the Comintern*, New, revised and expanded, Stanford, CA: Stanford University Press, 1986.

David Nicholls and Peter Marsh (eds), *A Biographical Dictionary of Modern European Radicals and Socialists*, vol. I: 1780–1815, Brighton: Harvester, 1988.

A. Thomas Lane (ed.), *Biographical Dictionary of European Labor Leaders*, 2 vols, Westport, CT: Greenwood Press, 1995.

Aldo Agosti (ed.), *Enciclopedia della sinistra europea nel XX secolo*, Rome: Riuniti, 2000.

Austria

Yvon Bourdet et al. (eds), *Autriche. Dictionnaire biographique du mouvement ouvrier international*, Paris: Editions Ouvrières, 1971.

Belgium

Jean Neuville (ed.), *Dictionnaire biographique des militants du mouvement ouvrier en Belgique. Tôme 1 A-B* [Histoire du Mouvement Ouvrier en Belgique, vol. 12], Brussels: Editions Vie Ouvrière, no date.

Britain

Joyce M. Bellamy and John Saville (eds), *Dictionary of Labour Biography*, nine vols, London and Basingstoke: Macmillan, 1972–93.

William Knox (ed.), *Scottish Labour Leaders, 1918–1939: A Biographical Dictionary*, Edinburgh: Mainstream Publishing, 1984.

Joyce Bellamy et al. (eds), *Grande-Bretagne. Dictionnaire biographique du mouvement ouvrier international*, 2 vols, Paris: Editions Ouvrières, 1979 and 1986.

Joseph O. Baylen and Norbert J. Gossman (eds), *Biographical Dictionary of Modern British Radicals, 1770–1914*, 3 vols, New York [etc.]: Harvester Press, 1979–88.

Olive Banks (ed.), *The Biographical Dictionary of British Feminists*, vol. I: 1800–1930; vol. II: A Supplement, 1900–1945, Brighton: Harvester, 1985 and 1990.

France

Jean Maitron (ed.), *Dictionnaire biographique du mouvement ouvrier français*, 44 vols, Paris: Editions Ouvrières, 1964–97.
* R. Dufraisse et al. (eds), *Première Partie, 1789–1864.*
* M. Egrot and J. Maitron (eds), *Deuxième Partie, 1864–1871.*
* H. Dubief et al. (eds), *Troisième Partie, 1871–1914.*
* J. Maitron and C. Pennetier (eds), *Quatrième Partie, 1914–1939.*
* Michel Cordillot, Claude Pennetier and Jean Risacher (eds), *Biographies Nouvelles.*

Jean Bennet (ed.), *Biographies de personnalités mutualistes (XIXe et XX siècles)*, Paris: Mutualité Française, 1987.

Thierry Maricourt (ed.), *Dictionnaire des auteurs prolétariens de langue française de la Révolution à nos jours,* Amiens: Encrage, 1994.

Geneviève Poujol and Madeleine Romer (eds), *Dictionnaire biographique des militants. XIXe-XXe siècles*, Paris: L'Harmattan, 1996.

Jacques Julliard and Michel Winock (eds), *Dictionnaire des intellectuels français,* Paris: Ed. du Seuil, 1996.

Germany

Franz Osterroth, *Biographisches Lexikon des Sozialismus*, vol. I: Verstorbene Persönlichkeiten, Hannover: J.H.W. Dietz Nachf., 1960.

Geschichte der deutschen Arbeiterbewegung: Biographisches Lexikon, Berlin [GDR]: Dietz, 1970.

Wilhelm Heinz Schröder, *Sozialdemokratische Reichstagsabgeordnete und Reichstagskandidaten, 1898–1918: Biographisch-statistisches Handbuch,* Düsseldorf: Droste, 1986.

Jacques Droz (ed.), *L'Allemagne. Dictionnaire biographique du mouvement ouvrier international*, Paris: Editions Ouvrières, 1990.

Simone Barck et al. (eds), *Lexikon sozialistischer Literatur: Ihre Geschichte in Deutschland bis 1945*, Stuttgart and Weimar: J.B. Metzler, 1994.

Wilhelm Heinz Schröder, *Sozialdemokratische Parlamentarier in den deutschen Reichs- und Landtagen, 1867–1933: Biographien, Chronik, Wahldokumentation*, Düsseldorf: Droste, 1995.

Italy

Franco Andreucci and Tommaso Detti (eds), *Il movimento operaio italiano: dizionario biografico, 1853–1943*, five vols plus index volume, Rome: Editori Riuniti, 1975–79.

The Netherlands

P.J. Meertens et al. (eds), *Biografisch woordenboek van het socialisme en de arbeidersbeweging in Nederland*, eight vols, Amsterdam: Stichting beheer IISG, 1986–2000.

Bert Freriks, 'Biografische literatuur over 101 PSP-ers', in Paul Denekamp, Bert Freriks and Gerrit Voerman (eds), *Sporen van pacifistisch socialisme: Bibliografie en bronnen betreffende de PSP*, Amsterdam: Stichting beheer IISG/DNPP, 1993, 37–53.

Norway

Jakon Friis and Trond Hegna (eds.), *Arbeidernes leksikon*, 6 vols, Oslo: Arbeidermagasinets forlag, 1932–6.

MULTIPLE-COUNTRY SURVEYS OF WEST EUROPEAN LABOUR HISTORY

Walter Galenson (ed.), *Comparative Labor Movements,* New York: Prentice Hall, 1952, xiv + 599pp. West European chapters: Britain (Allan Flanders), France (Val R. Lorwin), Germany (Philip Taft), Italy (John Clarke Adams), Scandinavia (Walter Galenson).

Adolf Sturmthal, *Unity and Diversity in European Labor: An Introduction to Contemporary Labor Movements,* Glencoe, IL: The Free Press, 1953, 237pp. Mainly focuses on Austria, Britain, France, Germany, Italy, Norway.

Ludwig Reichhold, *Europäische Arbeiterbewegung,* 2 vols, Frankfurt am Main: Knecht, 1953, xiv + 391 and viii + 340pp.

Carl Landauer, *European Socialism: A History of Ideas and Movements from the Industrial Revolution to Hitler's Seizure of Power,* 2 vols, Berkeley CA: University of California Press, 1959, 1,894pp.

Wolfgang Abendroth, *Sozialgeschichte der europäischen Arbeiterbewegung,* Frankfurt am Main: Suhrkamp, 1965, 190pp. English translation: *A Short History of the European Working Class,* trans. N. Jacobs and B. Trench, London: New Left Books, 1972, 204pp.

Alfredo Gradilone, *Storia del sindacalismo,* 7 vols, Milan: Giuffre, 1957–69, iv + 335; viii + 507; xii + 488; iv + 454; xii + 510; viii + 450; vi + 399pp. West European countries covered: Belgium, Britain, Denmark, Finland, France, Germany, Italy, The Netherlands, Norway, Sweden.

Jürgen Kuczynski, *Die Geschichte der Lage der Arbeiter unter dem Kapitalismus,* 43 vols, Berlin: Tribüne, 1960–72. West European studies focus on Britain (5 vols), France (3 vols), Germany (20 vols).

Adolf Sturmthal and James G. Scoville (eds), *The International Labor Movement in Transition: Essays on Africa, Asia, Europe, and South America,* Urbana IL and London: University of Illinois Press, 1973, x + 294pp. West European chapters: France (François Sellier), Germany (Peter Lösche), The Netherlands (Jan Pen).

Leo Michielsen, *Geschiedenis van de Europese arbeidersbeweging*, 4 vols, Ghent: Frans Masereel Fonds, 1973–80, 1,105pp. Covers Austria, Belgium, Britain, France, Germany, Italy, The Netherlands.

Walter Kendall, *The Labour Movement in Europe*, London: Allen Lane, 1975, 456pp. Chapters on Belgium, Britain, France, Germany, Italy, The Netherlands.

Charles L. Bertrand (ed.), *Revolutionary Situations in Europe, 1917–1922: Germany, Italy, Austria-Hungary*, Montreal: Interuniversity Centre for European Studies, 1977, xi + 251pp. Country chapters on Austria-Hungary (Istvan Deak; Miklos Molnar), Germany (Robert F. Wheeler; Allan Mitchell), Italy (Adrian Littleton; Alan Cassels).

Colin Crouch and Alessandro Pizzorno (eds), *The Resurgence of Class Conflict in Western Europe Since 1968*, 2 vols, London and Basingstoke: Macmillan, 1978. Vol. I (National Studies) xxiv + 349pp. West European chapters: Belgium (Michel Molitor), Britain (Colin Crouch), France (Pierre Dubois et al.), Germany (Walther Müller-Jentsch and Hans-Joachim Sperling), Italy (Ida Regalia et al.), The Netherlands (Tinie Akkermans and Peter Grootings).

Marilyn J. Boxer and Jean H. Quataert (eds), *Socialist Women: European Socialist Feminism in the Nineteenth and Early Twentieth Centuries*, New York: Elsevier, 1978, x + 260pp. West European chapters: Austria (Ingrun Lafleur), France (Marilyn J. Boxer), Germany (Jean H. Quataert), Italy (Claire LaVigna).

W.A Paterson and H.A. Thomas (eds), *Social Democratic Parties in Western Europe*, London: Croom Helm, 1978, 444pp. Chapters on Austria (Melanie A. Sully), Belgium (Xavier Mabille and Val R. Lorwin), Britain (Lewis Minkin and Patrick Seyd), Denmark (Alastair H. Thomas), Finland (Ralf Helenius), France (Byron Criddle), Germany (William E. Paterson), Ireland (Andrew Orridge), Italy (David Hine), The Netherlands (Steven B. Wolinetz), Norway (Knut Heidar), Portugal and Spain (Jonathan Story), Sweden (Richard Scase).

William E. Paterson and Kurt Th. Schmitz (eds), *Sozialdemokratische Parteien in Europa*, Bonn: Verlag Neue Gesellschaft, 1979, xi + 332pp. Chapters on Austria (Alfred Pfabigan), Belgium (Xavier Mabille and Val R. Lorwin), Britain (Peter J. Byrd and William E. Paterson), Denmark (Alastair H. Thomas), Finland (David Arter), France (Gerhard Kiersch), Germany (Kurt Thomas Schmitz), Greece (Karl-Hermann Buck), Ireland (Andrew Orridge), Italy (Karl-Hermann Buck), The Netherlands (Steven B. Wolinetz), Norway (Knut Heidar), Portugal (Jonathan Story), Spain (Lothar P. Maier), Sweden (Karl Kuhn), Switzerland (Raimund E. Germann).

Gilles Martinet, *Sept Syndicalismes*, Paris: Seuil, 1979, 247pp. West European countries covered: Britain, France, Germany, Italy, Sweden.

George S. Bain and Robert Price, *Profiles of Union Growth: A Comparative Statistical Portrait of Eight Countries*, Oxford: Blackwell, 1980, xiv + 177pp. West European countries covered: Britain, Denmark, Germany, Norway, Sweden (1890s – 1970s).

Dick Geary, *European Labour Protest, 1848–1939,* London: Croom Helm, 1981, 191pp. Focuses on Britain, France, Germany.

[Alain Brossat and Raimund Löw (eds),] *Profils de la social-démocratie européenne,* Paris: P.E.C. La Brèche, 1982, 430pp. Chapters on Austria (Raimund Löw), Britain (Julian Atkinson and Alan Freeman), France (Jacques Kergoat), Germany (Günter Minnerup), Italy (Antonio Moscato), Portugal (Francisco Louça), Spain (Mariano Fernandez Enguita), Sweden (Gert-Inge Johnsson and Tom Gustafsson).

Anders Kjellberg, *Facklig organisering i tolv länder* [Trade-Union Organising in Twelve Countries], Lund: Arkiv förlag, 1983, 338pp. West European countries covered: Austria, Belgium, Britain, Denmark, France, (West) Germany, Italy, The Netherlands, Norway, Sweden. Period: 1930–75.

Adolf Sturmthal, *Left of Center: European Labor Since World War II,* Urbana, IL: University of Illinois Press, 1983, xv + 302pp. Focuses mainly on Britain, France, Germany, Italy.

Jürgen Kocka (ed.), *Europäische Arbeiterbewegungen im 19. Jahrhundert: Deutschland, Österreich, England und Frankreich im Vergleich,* Göttingen: Vandenhoeck & Ruprecht, 1983, 169pp. Chapters on Austria (Helmut Konrad), Britain (Sidney Pollard), France (Heinz-Gerhard Haupt), Germany (Dieter Dowe).

Alice H. Cook, Val R. Lorwin and Arlene Kaplan Daniels (eds), *Women and Trade Unions in Eleven Industrialized Countries,* Philadelphia PA: Temple University Press, 1984, xiii + 327pp. West European chapters: Britain (Val R. Lorwin and Sarah Boston), Denmark (Brita Foged et al.), Finland (Elina Haavio-Mannila), France (Margaret Maruani), Germany (Alice H. Cook), Ireland (Deborah Schuster King), Italy (Bianca Beccalli), Norway (Harriet Holter and Bjørg Aase Sørensen), Sweden (Gunnar Qvist et al.).

Ira Katznelson and Aristide R. Zolberg (eds), *Working-Class Formation: Nineteenth-Century Patterns in Western Europe and the United States,* Princeton, NJ: Princeton University Press, 1986, viii + 470 pp. Includes chapters on France (William H. Sewell, Jr.; Michelle Perrot; Alain Cottereau) and Germany (Jürgen Kocka; Mary Nolan).

Hans A. Schmitt (ed.), *Neutral Europe between War and Revolution 1917–23,* Charlottesville: University Press of Virginia, 1988, ix + 257pp. Country chapters on Belgium and Luxemburg (Hans A. Schmitt), Denmark (Carol Gold), The Netherlands (Erik Hansen), Norway (Sten Sparre Nilson), Spain (Gerald H. Meaker), Sweden (Steven Koblik), Switzerland (Heinz K. Meier).

Maurizio Degl'Innocenti (ed.), *Il movimento cooperativo nella storia d'Europa,* Milan: Franco Angeli, 1988, 331pp. West European chapters: Belgium (Jean Puissant), Britain (Malcolm Hornsby), France (Yves Saint-Jours), Germany (Dieter Dowe; Klaus Novy), Italy (Fabio Fabbri; Maurizio Degl'Innocenti).

Dick Geary (ed.), *Labour and Socialist Movements in Europe before 1914,* Oxford [etc.]: Berg, 1989, vi + 278pp. Chapters on Britain (Gordon Phillips), France (Roger Magraw), Germany (Dick Geary), Italy (John A. Davis) and Spain (Paul Heywood).

Jelle Visser, *European Trade Unions in Figures,* Deventer and Boston: Kluwer, 1989, 254pp. Covers Austria, Britain, Denmark, France, Germany, Italy, The Netherlands, Norway, Sweden, Switzerland from the First World War until the mid-1980s.

Marcel van der Linden and Jürgen Rojahn (eds), *The Formation of Labour Movements, 1870–1914: An International Perspective,* 2 vols, Leiden [etc.]: Brill, 1990, xxi + 785pp. West European chapters: Austria (Siegfried Mattl), Belgium (Daisy E. Devreese), Britain (Richard Price), Denmark (Gerd Callesen), France (Jacques Kergoat), Germany (Klaus Tenfelde), Italy (Franco Andreucci), The Netherlands (Henny Buiting), Norway (Einar A. Terjesen), Spain (Santiago Castillo), Sweden (Birger Simonson), Switzerland (Hans Ulrich Jost).

Marcel van der Linden and Wayne Thorpe (eds), *Revolutionary Syndicalism: An International Perspective,* Aldershot: Scolar Press, 1990, xi + 260pp. West European chapters: Britain (Joseph White), France (Barbara Mitchell), Germany (Hans Manfred Bock), Italy (Charles L. Bertrand), The Netherlands (Marcel van der Linden), Portugal (Bernhard Bayerlein and Marcel van der Linden), Spain (Antonio Bar), Sweden (Lennart K. Persson).

Stephen Salter and John Stevenson (eds), *The Working-Class and Politics in Europe and America, 1929–1945,* London and New York: Longman, 1990, vi + 287pp. West European chapters: Austria (Tim Kirk), Britain (John Stevenson), Finland (David Kirby), France (Roger Magraw), Germany (Stephen Salter), Italy (Paul Corner), Spain (Martin Blinkhorn).

Michel Launay, *Le Syndicalisme en Europe,* Paris: Imprimerie nationale, 1990, 504pp. Covers all West European countries.

Stephen Padgett and William E. Paterson, *A History of Social Democracy in Postwar Europe,* London and New York: Longman, 1991, xii + 290pp.

Paul Misner, *Social Catholicism in Europe: From the Onset of Industrialization to the First World War,* New York: Crossroads, 1991, x + 362pp. Focuses on Austria, Belgium, France, Germany, Italy.

Chris Wrigley (ed.), *Challenges of Labour: Central and Western Europe 1917–1920,* London [etc.]: Routledge, 1993, x + 300pp. West European chapters: Austria (Hans Hautmann; Elisabeth Dietrich), Britain (John Foster, Chris Wrigley), France (Roger Magraw; John Horne), Germany (Dick Geary; Martin H. Geyer; Wolfram Wette), Italy (Giuseppe Berta; Piero Melograni).

Perry Anderson and Patrick Camiller (eds), *Mapping the West European Left,* London: Verso, 1994, 276pp. Chapters on Britain (Peter Mair), Denmark (Niels Finn Christiansen), France (George Ross and Jane Jenson), Germany (Stephen Padgett and William E. Peterson), Italy (Tobias Abse), Norway (Lars Mjøset et al.), Spain (Patrick Camiller), Sweden (Jonas Pontusson).

Stefan Berger and David Broughton (eds), *The Force of Labour: The Western European Labour Movement and the Working Class in the Twentieth Century,* Oxford and Washington, DC: Berg, 1995, xvi + 286pp. Chapters on Britain (Chris Williams), France (Susan Milner), Germany (Stefan

Berger), Italy (Tobias Abse), The Netherlands (Lex Heerma van Voss), Spain (Angel Smith), Sweden (James Fulcher).

Marcel van der Linden (ed.), *Social Security Mutualism: The Comparative History of Mutual Benefit Societies,* Berne [etc.]: Peter Lang Academic Publishers, 1996, 706pp. West European chapters: Austria (Wolfgang Maderthaner), Belgium (Paule Verbruggen), Britain (David Neave), Finland (Jouko Jaakkola), France (Michel Dreyfus), Germany (Gunnar Stollberg), Ireland (John Campbell), Italy (Luigi Tomassini), The Netherlands (Jacques van Gerwen and Jan Lucassen), Portugal (Carlos da Fonseca), Spain (Santiago Castillo), Sweden (Birger Simonson), Switzerland (Hans Ulrich Jost).

Donald Sassoon, *One Hundred Years of Socialism: The West European Left in the Twentieth Century,* London and New York: I.B. Tauris, 1996, xxv + 965pp.

Donald Sassoon (ed.), *Looking Left: European Socialism after the Cold War,* London and New York: I.B. Tauris, 1997, x + 198pp. West European chapters: Britain (Colin Leys), France (François Hincker), Germany (Thomas Meyer), Greece (Vassilis Fouskas), Italy (Giulio Sapelli), Spain (Paul Kennedy).

Helmut Gruber and Pamela Graves (eds), *Women and Socialism – Socialism and Women: Europe Between the Two World Wars,* New York and Oxford: Berghahn, 1998, xvi + 591pp. West European chapters: Austria (Helmut Gruber), Belgium (Denise de Weerdt), Britain (Pamela Graves), Denmark (Hilda Romer Christensen), France (Helmut Gruber; Christine Bard and Jean-Louis Robert), Germany (Adelheid von Saldern; Atina Grossmann), Italy (Mary Gibson), The Netherlands (Ulla Jansz), Norway (Ida Blom), Spain (Mary Nash), Sweden (Renée Frangeur).

Tim Rees and Andrew Thorpe (eds), *International Communism and the Communist International, 1919–43,* Manchester and New York: Manchester University Press, 1998, x + 323pp. West European chapters: Britain (Andrew Thorpe; Yevgeny Sergeev), France (Guillaume Bourgeois), Germany (Aleksandr Vatlin), Greece (Artiem Ulunian), Italy (Aldo Agosti), The Netherlands (Gerrit Voerman), Portugal (Carlos Cunha), Spain (Tim Rees).

Ellen Furlough and Carl Strikwerda (eds), *Consumers Against Capitalism?,* Lanham, MD [etc.]: Rowman and Littlefield, 1999, 377pp. West European chapters: Austria (Gabriella Hauch), Belgium (Carl Strikwerda), Britain (Peter Gurney), Denmark (Niels Finn Christanssen), France (Ellen Furlough), Germany (Brett Fairbairn), Sweden (Peder Aléx).

Marcel van der Linden and Richard Price (eds), *The Rise and Development of Collective Labour Law,* Berne [etc.]: Peter Lang Academic Publishers, 2000, 458pp. West European chapters: Britain (Gerry R. Rubin), France (Norbert Olszak), Sweden (Susanne Fransson).

Gerd-Rainer Horn and Emmanuel Gerard (eds), *Left Catholicism 1943–1955: Catholics and Society in Western Europe at the Point of Liberation,* Leuven/Louvain: Leuven University Press, 2000, 320pp. Country chapters on Belgium (Jean-Louis Jadoulle), France (Jean-Claude Delbreil; Bruno Duriez; Yvon Tranvouez), Germany (Andreas Lienkamp), Italy (Antonio Parisella; Giorgio Vecchio).

A BRIEF GUIDE TO RELEVANT WEBSITES

Given that the World Wide Web is worldwide, many websites are not specifically dedicated to matters European. What are included here are sites that offer relevant materials for European Labour History, but many of these offer much more.

The richest internet source on labour history is without doubt the World Wide Web Virtual Library on Labour and Business History at http://www.iisg.nl/~w3vl/index.html. Most, if not all of the information presented below is on offer there, and is updated regularly, whereas this printed version was updated last in January 2002. Among other things, the WWW Virtual Library on Labour and Business History contains links to sites of numerous International Labour History Organisations, of relevant discussion lists, of Labour Unions and Political Organisations, thematic lists of sites (among other topics on Anarchism, Britain and Ireland, Culture, France, Germany, Individuals, Industry-Specific Information, Labour, Marxism, Russia and the Soviet Union, Spain and Portugal) and many other resources.

The WWW Virtual Library on Labour and Business History's very complete list of web sites of scholarly institutes (at http://www.iisg.nl/~w3vl/vl-inst.html) is organised by country and mentions whether the site gives general information, information on holdings, digitised and other publications, and the availability of online catalogues. The IALHI, the International Association of Labour History Institutions, unites most Labour History Institutions worldwide. Its members and links to their sites can be found at http://www.ialhi.org/imembers.html. Its Scandinavian members present themselves at http://www.ialhi.org/inordic.html

Archival indexes and library catalogues available on the web are listed at http://www.ialhi.org/icats.html. Among the larger libraries whose catalogues are accessible through the internet are:

- the Bibliothèque de Documentation internationale contemporaine (Nanterre) at http://www.u-paris10.fr/bdic/
- the Friedrich Ebert Stiftung (Bonn) of the Sozialistische Partei Deutschlands at http://library.fes.de/library/index_gr.html.
- the International Institute of Social History (Amsterdam) at http://www.iisg.nl/

Other sites with many resources and links relevant for European Labour History generally include 'Le Maitron, Site d'histoire sociale' at http://www.maitron.org/

Labour History Research tools are found at http://www.qbradley.freeserve.co.uk/links.html and as a part of the WWW Virtual Library on Labour and Business History at http://www.iisg.nl/~w3vl/vl-res.html. A number of bibliographies on aspects of labour history can be found at the 'Directory of Online Bibliographies for Historians' maintained by Stefan Blaschke at http://www.history-journals.de/hbg/hbg.html. A succinct bibliography on comparative labour history is available from http://www2.h-net.msu.edu/~labor/threads/thrclhb.html. 'Gender Issues in Contemporary Industrialization at the University of Warwick', an annotated bibliography by Diane Elson and Caroline Wright covering mainly the early 1970s to the mid-1990s, is available from http://www.warwick.ac.uk/fac/soc/complabstuds/caroline.htm.

Given the potential of the internet, sites which make available historical texts are surprisingly rare. The Modern History Sourcebook at http://www.fordham.edu/halsall/mod/modsbook.html contains links to numerous historical documents, including some texts relevant for European labour history. Links to sites with texts by Marx and Engels are provided by http://www.bbaw.de/vh/mega/linkliste.html. Sites that offer statistical data are listed at http://odwin.ucsd.edu/idata/.

Numerous historical journals, including journals specialising in labour history, can be consulted through the web. Some websites offer full articles, others abstracts or only tables of contents. There are 158 Labour and Business History journals at http://www.iisg.nl/~w3vl/vl-jour.html. For many of these journals the table of contents from 1997 on is available at http://www.ialhi.org/serials/. A survey of historical journals is to be found at http://www.history-journals.de (circa 2,500 journals, including information on downloadable articles). Seventy women history journals are listed at http://www.iisg.nl/~womhist/vlwhref.html#wsjours.

Relevant discussion lists for labour historians include H-Labor, part of the H-network of discussion lists maintained at Michigan State University. A list of the H-discussion list and information on subscription can be found at http://www2.h-net.msu.edu/lists/. Specific information on H-Labor is at http://www2.h-net.msu.edu/~labor/. Moderated by Seth Wigderson of the University of Maine at Augusta, in March 2001 it had 1,836 subscribers in thirty-six countries. Messages to be distributed over H-Labor should be sent to H-LABOR@H-NET.MSU.EDU. H-Labor is clearly a US-based list, but it carries many messages on European labour history too, and at times it is the site of lively exchanges about the state of labour history. Smaller, more focused on Europe, and less prone to engage in debate is LabNet, the discussion list of the European network of Labour Historians. LabNet had 553 subscribers in thirty-two countries in March 2001. (To subscribe, send a mail containing the message SUBSCRIBE LABNET to listserv@iisg.nl). LabNet is moderated by Aad Blok at the International Institute of Social History. Messages to be distributed over LabNet should be sent to Aad Blok at labmod@iisg.nl. IALHI offers a news service. For recent news, a news archive and subscription information consult http://www.ialhi.org/index.html.

Labour history exhibitions usually are strong on illustrations, documents, books and posters, all of which are easily reproduced on the web. Highlights from the collections of European IALHI members are exhibited at http://www.iisg.nl/exhibitions/ialhi/. Other examples include exhibitions on the 1848 revolution in Berlin (http://www.zlb.de/projekte/1848/), materials on Garibaldi (http://www.sc.edu/library/spcoll/hist/garib/garib.html), the Siege and Commune of Paris (http://www.library.nwu.edu/spec/siege/), Art for the people (http://www.iisg.nl/exhibitions/art/), William Morris (http://www.hrc.utexas.edu/exhibitions/morris/morris.html and http://www.lib.umich.edu/libhome/spec-coll/morris/), Soviet posters (http://www.brama.com/art/poster.html and http://www.iisg.nl/exhibitions/chairman/) and Soviet Archives (http://www.ibiblio.org/expo/soviet.exhibit/soviet.archive.html), Dutch Socialism (http://www.xs4all.nl/~rosmalen/index.html and http://www.iisg.nl/exhibitions/affiche/), The Spanish Civil War (http://orpheus.ucsd.edu/speccoll/posters/ and http://burn.ucsd.edu/scwtable.htm) and Paris in May 1968 (http://vicu.utoronto.ca/library/exhibitions/posters/ and http://burn.ucsd.edu/paristab.htm).

Good social history often is an interdisciplinary mix of input from history and other fields. The system of WWW Virtual Libraries offers a portal for information in many academic fields (an overview is available at http://vlib.org/Home.html). In the context of this book, other relevant WWW Virtual Libaries include those on the Social Sciences (http://www.vlib.org/SocialSciences.html), Sociology (http://socserv2.mcmaster.ca/w3virtsoclib), Women's History (http://www.iisg.nl/~womhist/vivalink.html), Women's Studies (http://libraries.mit.edu/humanities/WomensStudies/ wscd.html) and Regional Studies (http://www.vlib.org/ Regional.html). Portals for Religion Studies are 'Internet Resources in Religion and Theology' athttp://www.lib.duke.edu/divinity/ divlist.html, the 'Virtual Religion Index' at http://religion.rutgers.edu/ vri/index.html , the Religious Studies Page of 'Voice of The Shuttle' at http://vos.ucsb.edu/browse-netscape.asp?id=2730 and 'Finding God in Cyberspace' at http://www.fontbonne.edu/libserv/fgic/ contents.htm.

SELECTED AND ANNOTATED
BIBLIOGRAPHY, 1990–2000

This bibliography features a selection of titles of monographs and edited volumes in the broad field of class, gender, ethnicity, and religion in European labour history, which were annotated in the *International Review of Social History*, volumes 35–45 (1990–2000).

Alexander, Peter and Rick Halpern (eds), *Racializing Class, Classifying Race: Labour and Difference in Britain, the USA and Africa.* [St Antony's Series] Basingstoke: MacMillan Press; Oxford: St Anthony's College, 2000.
The ten essays in this volume, originating with a conference on labour and difference, held in Oxford in 1997, explore the interplay of race and class in the construction of working-class identities across three continents (Europe, North America and Africa). Included are, among others, a meditation on the international dimension of working-class mobilisation by David Montgomery, three essays on the functioning of racial difference in American settings (Yvette Huginnie, Venus Green and Colin Davis), an overview of the British historiography on race by Kenneth Lunn, and a concluding essay by Frederick Cooper, who inventories the different ways of understanding the relationship between race and class.

Amin, Shahid and Marcel van der Linden (eds), *'Peripheral' Labour? Studies in the History of Partial Proletarianization.* [International Review of Social History, Supplement 4] Cambridge: Cambridge University Press, 1997.
The seven essays in this fourth Supplement to the *International Review of Social History* all deal with what the editors have labelled as intermediary forms of labour relations, which can be located in the 'grey zones' between pure free wage labour, unfree labour and independent labour. The contributions by Gyan Prakash, Dilip Simeon, Madhavi Kale and Samita Sen present Indian examples of these intermediary forms of wage

labour. Erick D. Langer's study of nineteenth-century Bolivian mineworkers and Juan A. Giusti-Cordero's essay on early twentieth-century Puerto Rican canefield labour offer a Latin American perspective, whereas Alain Faure's contribution on nineteenth-century Parisian rag-pickers offers a European example of a partially proletarianised group.

Aminzade, Ronald, *Ballots and Barricades: Class Formation and Republican Politics in France, 1830–1871*. Princeton NJ: Princeton University Press, 1993.

Using a comparative case study design Dr Aminzade explores political activity among workers in three mid-nineteenth-century cities: Toulouse, Saint-Etienne and Rouen. The author reconstructs how the interaction between industrialisation, class relations and party development fostered revolutionary communes in some cities but not in others, thus providing an explanation of the failed municipal revolutions of 1871 and the triumph of liberal-democratic institutions.

Applewhite, Harriet B. and Darline G. Levy (eds), *Women and Politics in the Age of the Democratic Revolution*. Ann Arbor: The University of Michigan Press, 1990.

The nine essays collected in this volume explore the participation of women in eighteenth-century rebellions in the United States, Belgium, England, France and the Netherlands. Included are studies about, among other subjects, women's role in English food riots (John Bohstedt), in the French Revolution (Dominique Godineau, the editors), in revolutionary Brussels (Janet Polasky), in the American Revolution 1765–76 (Alfred F. Young) and in the Dutch Patriot and Batavian revolutions (Wayne Ph. te Brake, Rudolf M. Dekker and Lotte C. van de Pol).

Arnold, Georges, *Dans la ville, des témoins: Histoire de l'ACO en Ile-de-France*. Paris: Les Éditions de l'Atelier/Les Éditions Ouvrières, 1998.

Published in honour of its fiftieth anniversary in 2000, this is a short history of the *Action Catholique Ouvrière* (ACO), a Catholic trade union in the region of Ile-de-France. Based on interviews with many current and former activists, Mr Arnold sketches the rise of this Christian trade union according to some of the main labour events in Paris in this period, such as: the *La Défense* construction project; workers' struggles in the automobile industry and activism in the health care sector; and May 1968.

Auer, Frank von and Franz Segbers (eds), *Sozialer Protestantismus und Gewerkschaftsbewegung. Kaiserreich – Weimarer Republik – Bundesrepublik Deutschland*. Köln: Bund-Verlag, 1994.

This collection aims to redress the lack of attention that prevails, according to the editors, among historians with respect to the role of socially committed Protestants in the rise of the German labour movement. The fifteen contributions cover the period from the *Kaiserreich*, through the Weimar Republic, to the beginnings of the Federal Republic and focus, among others, on social theorists espousing a Protestant perspective, the development of Christian trade unions, their relation to the socialist labour movement, and their role in the struggle for co-determination during the Weimar era and under the Federal Republic.

Banks, Olive, *The Politics of British Feminism, 1918–1970*. Aldershot: Edward Elgar, 1993.
In this study, focusing on the political struggle of autonomous feminist groups, women in the labour movement and female MPs, Professor Banks aims to analyse what happened to the British women's movement between the victory of the suffrage movement after the First World War and the arrival of the modern women's movement in the 1960s. This period is generally seen as one of decline for feminism. Setting the development of the British women's movement in a broader political and economic context, the author concludes that one of the major reasons for the lack of success in these years was an overoptimism on the part of the feminists themselves about their own power and possibilities and an underestimation of the forces working against them.

Barry, David, *Women and Political Insurgency: France in the Mid-Nineteenth Century*. Basingstoke: Macmillan, in assoc. with University of Durham; New York: St. Martin's Press, Inc., 1996.
This book provides a survey of female insurgency in France from 1789 to 1871, focusing on Paris and the period between 1830 and 1851. Dr Barry concludes that although women's presence in traditional subsistence riots declined in this period, they remained deeply involved in riots where economic issues predominated. Exploring the links between contemporary feminism and insurgency, the author challenges the view that women retreated from popular movements during the nineteenth century and suggests that they developed their own means of public expression.

Beddoe, Deirdre, *Out of the Shadows: A History of Women in Twentieth-Century Wales*. Cardiff: University of Wales Press, 2000.
This is a comprehensive overview of the everyday experience of ordinary women in Wales during the twentieth century. Paying attention to both regional variations and differing linguistic and cultural traditions, the author examines key areas of women's lives: education, health, home life, leisure, politics and waged work. She also assesses the contributions of a number of hitherto neglected female pioneers in various social and political movements.

Belchem, John, *Class, Party and the Political System in Britain, 1867–1914*. [Historical Association Studies] Oxford: Basil Blackwell, 1990.
This is 'a stock-taking exercise of a personal kind', attempting 'to assess the significance of some of the most important recent historiography' of the English working class from 1750 to 1900. The period dealt with is divided into three parts (1750–1850, 1850–75, 1875–1900); for each part subjects like the economic context, living standards, housing, work, popular culture and working-class politics are dealt with. The treatment of

the different periods is uneven, the first part receiving much more attention than the latter two.

Belchem, John, *Industrialization and the Working Class: The English Experience, 1750–1900*. Aldershot: Scolar Press, 1990.
'Between the Second Reform Act and the First World War, the patterns and codes of political behaviour in Britain changed decisively. The nature of these changes, however is hotly debated. Historians are widely at odds in their interpretations of electoral sociology and party performance between 1867 and 1914. This short study is designed to introduce students to some of the more complex and controversial issues in the political history of the late-Victorian and Edwardian Britain and seeks to elucidate the impact of class and the role of party in local, constituency, Westminster and national politics.'

Belchem, John and Neville Kirk (eds), *Languages of Labour*. Aldershot: Ashgate, 1997.
The eight essays in this volume – the revised versions of the papers presented at the Spring 1996 conference of the British Society for the Study of Labour History (held in Manchester) – all deal with the broad theme of language and identity from pronounced 'realist' – as opposed to 'postmodernist' or 'anti-representational' – methodology and epistemology. Contributors included are Richard Price (on postmodernism as theory for historical research), Eileen Janes Yeo (on language and contestation), Karen Hunt, Susan Levine (on gender), the first editor and Melanie Tebbutt (on community and workplace) and Leon Fink and Roger Fagge (on labour-movement development, language and worker consciousness).

Berger, Stefan and David Broughton (eds), *The Force of Labour: The Western European Labour Movement and the Working Class in the Twentieth Century*. Oxford: Berg, 1995.
This textbook aims to provide a comprehensive overview and comparative analysis of European labour movements from 1900 to 1990. The authors examine the links between workers and organised labour in seven European countries – Britain (Chris Williams), France (Susan Milner), Germany (Stefan Berger), Italy (Tobias Abse), The Netherlands (Lex Heerma van Voss), Spain (Angel Smith), and Sweden (James Fulcher) – and focus on areas such as the role of the state, labour markets, and occupations and class. In a concluding chapter the first editor sketches the comparative perspective. An appendix with statistical data is included.

Berger, Stefan and Angel Smith (eds), *Nationalism, Labour and Ethnicity 1870–1939*. Manchester: Manchester University Press, 1999; distr. excl. in the USA by St. Martin's Press, New York.
The nine case studies and general introductory essay in this volume explore the interplay between identity, nation and labour in five European countries (Britain/Germany, Spain, France, Poland and Russia), and in the United States, Australia, South Africa and India in the period

1870–1939, the Age of Imperialism. The editors aim to offer through these case studies, based on a common set of questions, a comparative history of the position of labour and ethnicity within the nation during a crucial formative period of nation building and imperialism.

Berlanstein, Lenard R. (ed.), *Rethinking Labor History: Essays on Discourse and Class Analysis*. Urbana IL: University of Illinois Press, 1993.
Focusing on French labour history, this collection of nine essays discusses the advantages and disadvantages of the renovation of labour history from the 1980s onward by the rise of discourse analysis, which opposed revisionist Marxist class analysis. Advocates of both currents are represented. Contributors are: Ronald Aminzade, Leora Auslander, Lenard R. Berlanstein, Laura Lee Downs, Gay L. Gullickson, Michael Hanagan, Christopher H. Johnson, Donald Reid, and William H. Sewell, Jr.

Beynon, Huw and Terry Austrin, *Masters and Servants: Class and Patronage in the Making of a Labour Organisation, The Durham Miners and the English Political Tradition*. London: Rivers Oram Press, 1996.
This historical sociological study of the development of the labour movement in the Durham mining district focuses on the pivotal role of the Durham Miners' Association (DMA) in the process and on daily life and culture among the Durham miners. The authors analyse the influence of the specific, semi-feudal and paternalistic social relations in the area in the initial phase of the labour movement, and the role of the strongly religious and Liberal leadership of the DMA in the union's moderate political course.

Bielenberg, Andy (ed.), *The Irish Diaspora*. Harlow: Longman, 2000.
The seventeen essays in this collection, all originating from a conference on the Irish diaspora, held in Cork in the autumn of 1997, aim to provide an overview of the Irish diaspora in the major migration destinations in North America, Britain, and the British colonies. The contributors, including historians, demographers, economists, sociologists, and geographers, question myths associated with the religious character, identity, and relations between host community and Irish migrants, and re-evaluate the economic and social success and failure of Irish immigrants in different contexts, also addressing gender differences. In three concluding general contributions, the contemporary Irish migration patterns are dealt with.

Bolognese-Leuchtenmüller, Birgit and Michael Mitterauer (eds), *Frauen-Arbeitswelten. Zur historischen Genese gegenwärtiger Probleme*. [Beiträge zur historischen Sozialkunde, Beiheft 3] Wien: Verlag für Gesellschaftskritik, 1993.
The nine contributions to this collection are primarily intended to give an overview of the essential aspects in the development of the daily work routine among women in the context of structural long-term regional, economic and social conditions. The authors focus on the duality in the experiences of these women, who need to divide their attention between wage labour and housework. The contributions deal with the preindustrial and industrial period and cover rural and urban experiences. The

contributors are Erna Appelt, Birgit Bolognese-Leuchtenmüller, Josef Ehmer, Andrea Komlosy, Bärbel Kuhn, Juliane Mikoletzky, Michael Mitterauer, and Eva Tesar.

Boris, Eileen and Angélique Janssens (eds), *Complicating Categories: Gender, Class, Race and Ethnicity*. [International Review of Social History, Supplement 7] Cambridge: Cambridge University Press, 1999.

The seven essays in this 1999 Supplement to the *International Review of Social History* combine the categories of class, gender and/or ethnicity as complicating central concepts in the understanding of economic and social history. The essays reflect two groupings. The first three (Sandra E. Green, Ileen A. DeVault and Laura Dudley Jenkins) offer three approaches to complicating categories: intersectionality, seriality and the materiality of identity. The next four, by Michele Mitchell, Raelene Frances, Laura Levine Frader and Fatima El-Tayeb, address the conjuncture of racialised gender and sexuality in relation to colonisation and nationbuilding.

Budde, Gunilla-Friederike (ed.), *Frauen arbeiten. Weibliche Erwerbstätigkeit in Ost- und Westdeutschland nach 1945*. [Sammlung Vandenhoeck] Göttingen: Vandenhoeck & Ruprecht, 1997.

The eleven contributions to this volume explore and compare women's wage labour in East and West Germany from 1945 to 1989. Women's participation in wage labour has traditionally been viewed as a barometer of their emancipation. The contributors examine this relationship for both Germanies in various sectors of the economy and conclude that although a larger share of women in East Germany was involved in wage labour, the professional and social status of East German women was not necessarily better than that of their West German counterparts.

Candela Soto, Paloma, *Cigarreras madrileñas: trabajo y vida (1888–1927)*. Madrid: Editorial Tecnos, 1997.

This is a history of women working in Madrid's tobacco industry between 1888 and 1927. After reviewing the industry's history, the author discusses the organisation of work within the tobacco factory and the problems with the mechanisation of the labour process. Next, she deals with the position of the women workers as well as their working conditions. She also considers the living conditions of these women outside the factories, their social-demographic origins and their methods of organisation. Various statistical overviews conclude this book, which is a commercial edition of a thesis defended at Madrid's *Universidad Complutense* in 1996.

Cannadine, David, *Class in Britain*. New Haven CT: Yale University Press, 1998.

In this history of class in Britain from the eighteenth to twentieth century, Professor Cannadine aims to explain how past generations have perceived their society and their own place within it. Interpreting class as one of multiple identities, he analyses how class in Britain has been perceived in three different ways: as hierarchical, with multiple gradations ruled over by a traditional elite; as dichotomous ('us' versus 'them') and as a three-class model: 'upper', 'middle' and 'lower'. The author emphasises the use politicians have made of class in shaping social identities.

Carbonell i Esteller, Montserrat, *Sobreviure a Barcelona: Dones, pobresa i assistència al segle XVII*. [Referències, 20] Vic: Eumo Editorial, 1997.
Confronted in the late eighteenth century with the consequences of incipient industrialisation, the workers in Barcelona devised survival strategies, including reliance on poor relief. The author has used the vast but previously virtually unexplored archives of the poorhouse (the *Casa de Misericòrdia*) to reconstruct the women's lives as a cohesive element in the study and to explain the poverty among the urban masses. She illustrates another strategy by touching on the role of the Credit Bank.

Clark, Anna, *The Struggle for the Breeches: Gender and the Making of the British Working Class*. [Studies on the History of Society and Culture, 23] Berkeley CA: University of California Press, 1995.
Focusing on working people in Glasgow, Lancashire and London in the period 1780–1850, Professor Clark analyses in this study the formation of the working class from the gender perspective. At the end of the eighteenth century working people faced a persistent sexual crisis, according to the author. While artisans sought a solution for this crisis in misogyny and libertinism, male textile workers opted to cooperate with women at work and at home. Eventually, however, the adoption by the radicals of a rhetoric of domesticity solved the sexual crisis but narrowly defined the working class movement as masculine.

Clark, Linda L., *The Rise of Professional Women in France: Gender and Public Administration since 1830*. Cambridge: Cambridge University Press, 2000.
In this study of professional women in France in positions of administrative responsibility from 1830 onward, Professor Clark traces several generations of women working in public administration from 1830 onward, to analyse women's changing relationship to the public sphere. Examining public policy and politics, attitudes towards gender, women's work and education, as well as women's own perceptions and assessments of their positions, the author compares the situation of French women administrators with their counterparts in Great Britain and the United States.

Clements, Barbara Evans, *Bolshevik Women*. Cambridge: Cambridge University Press, 1997.
This study is a history of the women who joined the Soviet Communist Party before 1921. It examines their reasons for becoming revolutionaries, the work they did in the underground before 1917, their participation in the revolution and civil war and their service in establishing the Soviet Union. The author argues that women were important members of the Communist Party's lower echelons during its formative years and launched a remarkable effort to achieve emancipation from traditional society.

Coffin, Judith G., *The Politics of Women's Work: The Paris Garment Trades 1750–1915*. Princeton NJ: Princeton University Press, 1996.
This study combines a social history of women's work in the nineteenth-century Parisian garment industry with the intellectual history if the way women's work in this industry was represented in the economic and cultural policy debates of social scientists, reformers, labour unions, and politicians of the time. Covering the period from the unravelling of the guilds in the late eighteenth century to the first minimum wage bill in 1915, Professor Coffin examines the development in the industry, trade union politics, and working-class family incomes and household strategies, alongside the nineteenth-century development of social science and the views on women's work.

Copelman, Dina M., *London's women teachers. Gender, class and feminism 1870–1930*. London: Routledge, 1996.
In her study of London's women elementary-school teachers in the period 1870–1930 Dr Copelman argues that these women offer a model of gender and class identity that differs from the one constructed by historians of middle-class gender roles and middle-class feminism, known as the 'separate spheres' model. She explores the social and professional identities of these women teachers, who came mostly from 'labour aristocratic' and lower-middle-class families, and places their story in the context of the developing state education system, metropolitan life and the feminist political movement.

Corbin, J.R., *The Anarchist Passion: Class conflict in Southern Spain, 1810–1965*. [Studies in Spanish Anthropology, 3.] Avebury, Aldershot 1993.
This book is a social and anthropological study of the history of class conflict in southern Spain in the period between 1810 and 1965 and of the role played in that conflict by the anarchist movement between 1870 and 1939. Starting from an ethnographic perspective on the underlying social structure of the local communities in Andalusia, the author concludes that the 'base structure' on a local level remained stable during the whole period under observation and that the anarchists could not win full popular support because they wanted to change this structure.

Creighton, Margaret S. and Lisa Norling (eds), *Iron Men, Wooden Women: Gender and Seafaring in the Atlantic World, 1700–1920*. [Gender Relations in the American Experience] Baltimore MD: The Johns Hopkins University Press, 1996.
The present collection of ten essays examines the formulation of gender within seafaring communities, among sailors and by authors of sea fiction in the Anglo-American age of sailing and considers how these formulations have influenced or reflected norms created elsewhere. Topics include the careers of some female pirates (Marcus Rediker), 'transvestite heroines' who dressed as men to serve on the crews of sailing ships (Dianne Dugaw), the importance of the gender-race relationship for African American seamen (W. Jeffrey Bolster) and British merchant crews (Laura Tabili).

Crompton, Rosemary, *Class and Stratification: An Introduction to Current Debates*. Oxford: Polity Press, 1993.

This textbook offers a comprehensive review of the different theoretical and methodological approaches to the study of social class and stratification, developed after 1945, including quantitative approaches (Goldthorpe, Wright), as well as the investigation of class processes in history, politics and sociology. Issues dealt with in this volume are consumption, the growth of the middle classes, gender, citizenship and the 'underclass'. Dr Crompton argues that the examination of structural social inequality – for example class – remains a key topic in sociology, notwithstanding the modern trend to consider these categories as no longer relevant.

D'Cruze, Shani, *Crimes of outrage: Sex, Violence and Victorian Working Women*. [Women's History] London: UCL Press, 1998.

Based on judicial sources, in this study Dr D'Cruze examines sexual and physical violence against working-class women in Victorian Britain. Sketching how the neighbourhood, along with home and work, provided the spatial and social context of reported violence, the author then explores how the legal system filtered, defined and classified violence. She notes how in some cases the women's interests in being protected against violent crimes coincided with the courts' agenda to discipline the unruly behaviour of working men, but how more often the women's reputations and personal integrity were on trial more than those of their attackers.

Devine, Fiona, *Social Class in America and Britain*. Edinburgh: Edinburgh University Press, 1997.

This textbook aims to provide an accessible study of social class in the United States and Great Britain from a comparative perspective. Dr Devine covers the most recent controversies over the relationship between class and other social divisions, such as gender, race and ethnicity, over mobility and meritocracy, polarisation and social exclusion. She argues that both the United States and Britain may be characterised as class societies, with broadly similar class structures, class processes and class consciousness.

Diamond, M.J. (ed.), *Women and Revolution: Global Expressions*. Dordrecht: Kluwer Academic Publishers, 1998.

Partly originating from a commemoration of the bicentennial of the French Revolution, the nineteen contributions to this collection offer a broad range of work of women scholars from a variety of disciplines on the representations of women in movements of social transformation. Historical examples are taken from the Western world, Africa, India, Latin America and China. Included are, among many others, studies of women in the French Revolution and the Paris Commune; women in the Iranian Revolution; and the position of women in post-Mao China.

Downs, Laura Lee, *Manufacturing Inequality: Gender Division in the French and British Metalworking Industries, 1914–1939.* [The Wilder House Series in Politics, History, and Culture] Ithaca NY: Cornell University Press, 1995.

This study compares the process whereby employers in French and British metalworking industries introduced women into the hitherto all-male world of metal working from 1914 onward and then reorganised work procedures and managerial structures to accommodate the new workforce. Dr Downs analyses the transformation of sexual difference from a principle for excluding women into a basis for dividing labour within the newly structured production process, exploring issues such as wage discrimination and occupational segregation, the gendered redefinition of job skills and the implantation of scientific management techniques. She critiques both neoclassical and feminist explanations of gender discrimination in industry.

Eder, Klaus, *The New Politics of Class. Social Movements and Cultural Dynamics in Advanced Societies.* [Theory, Culture & Society] London: Sage Publications, 1993.

In this study Professor Eder aims to provide a cultural theory of class that incorporates the changing forms of collective action and the new social movements in contemporary societies. The author sees class as a social construction and states 'that the mobilisation of collective action is the basic mechanism that changes the boundaries between classes and shapes class relationships'. The model developed re-evaluates the role of the middle classes and links class to social theories of power and cultural capital.

Eijl, Corrie van, *Maandag tolereren we niets meer. Vrouwen, arbeid en vakbeweging 1945–1990.* Amsterdam: Stichting beheer IISG/Stichting FNV-Pers, 1997.

This study of the changing role of women in the trade union movement in the Netherlands in the period between 1945 and 1990 was published in honour of the thirtieth anniversary of the women's secretariat of the NVV/FNV, the general confederation of trade unions. Dr van Eijl examines the trade union's progression in the decades after 1970 from an organisation dedicated almost exclusively to protecting the interests of the male breadwinners to one that increasingly advocated a different distribution of labour between men and women.

Ferenschild, Sabine, *'Die Bestimmung des Weibes' und die Standeserziehung der Arbeiterinnen. Ein Beitrag zur Geschichte und Soziologie der katholischen Arbeiterinnenorganisationen im Rheinland (1867–1914).* [Arbeit und Menschenwürde] Bornheim: Ketteler-Verlag-GmbH, 1994.

This dissertation (Paderborn, 1993) deals with the organisation among women textile workers in the German Rhineland into Catholic unions of women workers in the period 1867–1914. Dr Ferenschild asserts that another important objective of these organisations involved educating women workers to conform to the bourgeois ideal of womanhood. She argues that this endeavour did not merely entail adaptation to bourgeois life, but that it also had origins in Catholic ethics.

Fielding, Steven, *Class and Ethnicity: Irish Catholics in England, 1880–1939*. [Themes in the Twentieth Century] Buckingham: Open University Press, 1993.

Focusing on the large and politically active Irish population of Manchester in the period 1880–1939, Dr Fielding here examines how an Irish and catholic identity survived in a long-settled community. He challenges the predominant view that class consciousness had largely transcended the remnants of a separate Irish Catholic ethnic identity by 1914.

Finn, Margot C., *After Chartism: Class and nation in English radical politics, 1848–1874*. [Past and Present Publications] Cambridge: Cambridge University Press, 1993.

This book charts the course of working- and middle-class radical politics in England from the continental revolutions of 1848 to the fall of Gladstone's Liberal government in 1874. According to Professor Finn the radical tradition, which was shared by middle- and working-class radicals, was problematised in the nineteenth century by middle-class radicals' acceptance of classical liberal economics. She traces this divide by contrasting the middle- and working-class responses to the continental revolutions in 1848–9, Polish and Italian nationalism in the 1860s and the Paris Commune in 1871, arguing that these events led to a diminution of middle-class radicals' commitment to liberal economics and helped in shaping the 'new liberalism' of the 1880s.

Fletcher, Ian Christopher, Laura E. Nym Mayhall, and Philippa Levine (eds), *Women's Suffrage in the British Empire: Citizenship, Nation, and Race*. [Routledge Research in Gender and History] London: Routledge, 2000.

Analysing suffrage movements in Palestine under British Mandate, in Southern Africa, in New Zealand and Australia, in India and Iran, in Canada and the United States, as well as in Great Britain, the fourteen essays in this collection explore the politics of women's suffrage from the age of empire to the eve of decolonisation. The emphasis in the essays is both on the transnational connections between suffrage campaigns around the British Empire, and complex interactions with other social movements in the metropolis and colonies. The general conclusion of the volume is that women's suffrage had engaged and reshaped important issues in modern politics, such as nation building and democratic citizenship.

Frader, Laura L. and Sonya O. Rose (eds), *Gender and Class in Modern Europe*. Ithaca NY: Cornell University Press, 1996.

This book explores the importance of gender among European working classes during the industrial, social and political transformations from 1800 through the 1930s. While the thirteen essays focus mainly on Britain and France, contributions on Germany, Ireland and the Soviet Union are also present. A broad variety of topics is covered, including the false notion of unitary and harmonious households; the gendered relationship between public and private domains in workers' lives; the gendered nature of state regulation and intervention; and the ways in which working-class claims to citizenship were simultaneously informed by notions of masculinity and femininity as well as by class.

Fraser, Kay M., *Same or Different: Gender Politics in the Workplace*. Aldershot: Ashgate, 1999.
    Basing herself on poststructuralist feminist theory, the author of this study explores the competing debates about women workers as they were constructed by organisations, institutions and individuals interested and involved in the employment of women in Great Britain during the 1960s. Looking at the way visions of government officials, industrial employers and trade union leaders on the issue of sameness and difference were translated into workplace and government policies, Dr Fraser aims to analyse how the notion of women workers as subordinate and inferior to man was, and according to the author still is, continually repeated and reinforced.

Frost, Diane (ed.), *Ethnic Labour and British Imperial Trade: A History of Ethnic Seafarers in the UK*. London: Frank Cass, 1995.
    This collection of seven essays examines the role of ethnic labour drawn from Britain's colonies in West Africa, the Middle East and Asia in British maritime history. Themes addressed include race and ethnicity, colonialism and migration, social class and the complex nature of racial hostility meted out by organised white labour. Contributors include Norma Myers, Dick Lawless, Neil Evans, David Byrne, Tony Lane and Marika Sherwood.

Frost, Diane, *Work and Community among West African Migrant Workers since the Nineteenth Century*. Liverpool: Liverpool University Press, 1999.
    The Kru, a group of West Africans who worked as ship's labourers and seafarers in the British colonial trade were among the earliest black people to settle in Britain in the nineteenth century. This book deals with the social history of this group both in West Africa and in Britain, and especially Liverpool, where they formed a black community long before the arrival of black British subjects after Second World War. Drawing on oral accounts of Kru themselves (both in Liverpool and return migrants in West Africa), Dr Frost focuses on the group's experiences, their perception of their own history, and their beliefs and values.

Furlong, Paul and David Curtis (eds), *The Church Faces the Modern World: Rerum Novarum and its Impact*. N.p. [Winteringham]: Earlsgate Press, 1994.
    The fourteen contributions to this collection – both in English and in French – are a selection of papers presented at a conference held at Hull in April 1991 to mark the centenary of the publication of the papal encyclical *Rerum Novarum*. The contributors analyse the development of Catholic social policy in the twentieth century and assess the influence of this encyclical. Two papers deal with the encyclical as such. The second section deals with the development of Catholic social policy in general, while the third section contains a consideration of the reception of the encyclical and the development of Catholic social organisation in several European and American countries.

Gans, Evelien, *De kleine verschillen die het leven uitmaken. Een historische studie naar joodse sociaal-democraten en socialistisch-zionisten in Nederland*. Amsterdam: Vassallucci, 1999.
This dissertation (University of Amsterdam, 1999) examines Dutch social-democratic Jews and their shifting identification with the socialist movement on the one hand and, under the influence of major political shifts and calamities, their personal passions and preoccupations with Judaism and Zionism on the other. Focusing on the period between the *Machtsübernahme* in Germany and 1949, Dr Gans examines these shifts in the identity of Jewish socialists and socialist Zionists by sketching biographical portraits of ten Dutch Jews who figured prominently in the social-democratic or Zionist movements and by portraying both the social-democratic and the Zionist or Jewish circles and organisations in which they were involved.

Garscha, Winfried R. and Stefan Weigang (eds), *Arbeiterbewegung – Kirche – Religion*. [ITH-Tagungsberichte, Band 27.] Wien: Europaverlag, 1991.
The thirteen case studies in this collection all deal with the relation between the labour movement on the one side and church and religion on the other. Among the subjects are: 'Religion and Working Class in India' (Uddalak Roy), 'Muslim Brotherhood and Workers (Egypt 1928–1952)' (Rifaat Said), 'The Catholic Church. Religion and Labour Movement as Exemplified by Poland' (Andrzej Chwalba *et al.*) and 'Social Catholicism and Labour Movement in Spain' (Antonio Elorza).

Gerber, Haim, *Islam, Guerrilla War, and Revolution: A Study in Comparative Social History*. Boulder CO: Lynne Rienner Publishers, 1988.
Based on case studies of the communist revolutions in Albania and South Yemen, the Algerian war of independence, and the communist revolution in Afghanistan in1978, the author examines in this book the relationship between Islam and communism, and, on a more general level, sets out to develop a theory of guerrilla war and political radicalism. He argues, among others, that a precondition for the radicalisation of a guerrilla movement is for it to take place in a society riven by class differences and conflicts.

Gluck, Sherna Berger and Daphne Patai (eds), *Women's Words. The Feminist Practice of Oral History*. New York: Routledge, 1991.
This is a collection of thirteen essays devoted to exploring the theoretical, methodological and practical problems that arise when women utilise oral history as a tool of feminist scholarship. Topics include: interview techniques and analyses (Kathryn Anderson and Dana C. Jack), interpretative conflict in oral narrative research (Katherine Borland), the practice of oral history among working-class women and men (Karen Olson and Linda Shopes) and scholarly collaboration and community outreach (Laurie Mercier and Mary Murphy).

Godineau, Dominique, *The Women of Paris and Their French Revolution*, trans. Katherine Streip. [Studies on the History of Society and Culture, vol. 26] Berkeley CA: University of California Press, 1998.

This is the English translation of *Citoyennes tricoteuses: Les femmes du peuple à Paris pendant la Révolution française* (Aix-en-Provence, 1988), a study of ordinary women's lives during the French Revolution. Professor Godineau uses sources, including police reports and demographic resources, to describe the private and public lives of these women who have remained anonymous in the accounts of the Revolution. Placing them within their political, social and gender-specific contexts, she aims to restore these women to their rightful historical place as instigators, activists, militants and decisive revolutionary individuals.

Goerner, Martin Georg, *Die Kirche als Problem der SED. Strukturen kommunistischer Herrschaftsausübung gegenüber der evangelischen Kirche 1945 bis 1958*. [Studien des Forschungsverbundes SED-Staat an der Freien Universität Berlin] Berlin: Akademie Verlag, 1997.

The Protestant churches in East Germany can be considered the only democratic societal organisation in the one-party system of the Communist SED. This dissertation (Potsdam, 1995) examines the changes in the SED policy regarding the churches, which continued to work with West-German churches in the 'Evangelische Kirche in Deutschland' (EKD). Dr Goerner finds that whereas in the period 1945–53 SED policy towards the churches was very incoherent, alternating between fierce oppression and tactical offers to cooperate, from the middle of 1953 onward a more strategic, long-term policy was devised at the instigation of the Soviet Union.

Goldman, Wendy Z., *Women, the State and Revolution. Soviet Family Policy and Social Life, 1917–1936*. [Soviet and East European Studies, 90] Cambridge: Cambridge University Press, 1993.

During the years following the October Revolution, conventional family and marriage structures came under a fierce attack aimed at eroding the traditional family and emancipating women socially and economically. Yet by 1936, this social experimentation had made way for increasingly conservative solutions intended to strengthen traditional family ties and women's reproductive role. This book examines this reversal in Bolshevist policies, focusing on the relationship between state, society and revolutionary ideology. Professor Goldman concludes that this regressive trend under Stalin ruined an important opportunity for socializing household labour and fostering greater equality between women and men.

Gomersall, Meg, *Working-class Girls in Nineteenth-century England: Life, Work and Schooling*. (Consultant Editor: Jo Campling) Basingstoke: Macmillan Press Ltd, New York: St. Martin's Press, Inc., 1997.

This study relates the education of working-class girls in nineteenth-century England to the changing social, economic and cultural context in various economically different regions. Dr Gomersall aims to combine a detailed examination of schooling with a review of the changes in the organisation of agricultural and industrial production and developments and tensions in responses to social change to chart the complex and multiple realities that informed the context of women's lives and education.

Gordon, Eleanor, *Women and the Labour Movement in Scotland, 1850–1914*. Oxford, Clarendon Press, 1991.
This is a study of working women in Scotland in the period 1850–1914. Dr Gordon discusses the patterns of their employment, their involvement in and relationship to trade unions and the forms of their workplace resistance and struggles, focusing particularly on women working in Dundee's jute industry. The book challenges assumptions about the organisational apathy of women workers and about the inevitable division between workplace and domestic ideologies.

Gould, Roger V., *Insurgent Identities: Class, Community, and Protest in Paris from 1848 to the Commune*. Chicago: The University of Chicago Press, 1995.
In this study of insurgency and social protest in Paris in the period between 1830 and the Commune in 1871, Professor Gould focuses on the collective identities that framed conflict during this period to advance the argument against seeing the Commune as a continuation of the class struggles of the 1848 Revolution. While class solidarity played a pivotal role in 1848, neighbourhood solidarity was, according to the author, the decisive organizing force in 1871. He demonstrates that the fundamental rearrangement in the patterns of urban social life, caused by Baron Haussmann's massive urban renovation projects between 1852 and 1868, gave rise to a neighbourhood insurgent movement.

Graves, Pamela M., *Labour Women: Women in British Working-Class Politics, 1918–1939*. Cambridge: Cambridge University Press, 1994.
Although thousands of working-class women joined the Labour Party and Co-operative Movement in the two decades after they achieved women's suffrage in 1918, they failed to win Labour over to a policy of sexual equality and woman-centred social reform. Using oral and questionnaire testimony, this study offers a group portrait of female and male grass-roots activists, contrasting the failure by labour women to win policy-making power in the national organisations with their achievements in community politics, poor law administration, and municipal government. Dr Graves argues that for most labour women, dedication to the class cause far outweighed their desire for power.

Gray, Marion W., *Productive Men, Reproductive Women: The Agrarian Household and the Emergence of Separate Spheres during the German Enlightenment*. New York: Berghahn Books, 2000.
Joining with the discussion on the origins of modern gender norms, Professor Gray argues in this study of the agrarian household in Germany during the Enlightenment that the modern ideal separate spheres originated in this era. According to the author, Enlightenment economist transformed the tradition gender paradigms, which prescribed active

interdependent economic roles for both men and women, by postulating a market exchange system directed exclusively by men. The emerging bourgeois value system subsequently affirmed the new civil society and the market place as exclusively male realms, defining women's options largely as marriage and motherhood.

Green, Nancy L., *Ready-to-Wear and Ready-to-Work: A Century of Industry and Immigrants in Paris and New York*. Durham: Duke University Press, 1997.

In this comparative study of the women's garment industry in New York and Paris from the end of the nineteenth to the end of the twentieth century, Professor Green covers a broad terrain of urban growth, the comparative economic development of an industry dictated by fashion, the differences between the cities with regards to markets, labour movements, labour legislation, the organisation and flexibility of the garment work, and the role of gender, ethnicity and class. She adopts a 'poststructuralist structuralist' approach that focuses on the similarities in the structure of the industry in both cities as well as on the semiology of differences.

Grever, Maria and Berteke Waaldijk, *Feministische Openbaarheid. De Nationale Tentoonstelling van Vrouwenarbeid in 1898*. Amsterdam: Stichting beheer IISG/IIAV, 1998.

In the summer of 1898 a national exhibition of women's labour was organised in The Hague, the Netherlands, in honour of Queen Wilhelmina's coronation. This richly-illustrated study describes the exhibition's structure and the aspects of women's labour that were featured. Dr Grever and Dr Waaldijk explore the backgrounds and motives of the organizing committee and assess the exhibition's impact on the gender relations discourse in the Netherlands at the turn of the century.

Grieco, Margaret, *Workers' dilemmas: Recruitment, reliability and repeated exchange: an analysis of urban social networks and labour circulation*. London: Routledge, 1996.

Focusing on the women and children seasonal workers who travelled annually from London's East End to work in the hop picking fields of Kent and Hampshire from the 1850s to the 1960s, this study explores the high level of management and occupational skills possessed by the urban poor in their construction of household survival strategies. The author stresses the key entrepreneurial role played by women in this labour market, the complexity of neighbourhood and household organisation it required and the importance of the financial support provided by this regular seasonal labour for household survival.

Groot, Gertjan de and Marlou Schrover (eds), *Women Workers and Technological Change in Europe in the Nineteenth and Twentieth Centuries*. London: Taylor & Francis, 1995.

Drawing on research from a number of European countries in the nineteenth and twentieth centuries, the nine contributions to this collection explore the origins of segregation between women's work and men's work by focusing on the relationship between technological change and the sexual division of labour. The contributions cover subjects including the Danish and Dutch textile industries (Marianne Rostgård, the first editor), the British civil service preceding the First World War (Meta Zimmeck), the British and Swedish pottery industries (Jacqueline Sarsby, Ulla Wikander), and the Dutch food industries (the second editor).

Gruber, Helmut and Pamela Graves, *Women and Socialism, Socialism and Women: Europe Between the Two World Wars*. New York: Berghahn Books, 1998.

This collection of fifteen essays compares the often complex relationship between feminism and the women's movement and socialism in eleven North and West European countries in the interwar years: Austria, Belgium, Britain, Denmark, France, Germany, Italy, the Netherlands, Norway, Spain and Sweden. A general introduction to the feminist expectations in 1914 is provided by Michelle Perrot. The collection deals with four main themes: social experiments; grass-roots initiatives; political fractures; and the social question and the development of the welfare states. Every theme is introduced separately, and general reflections on the issues of women and political power, and women and the social question, by Louise Tilly and Geoff Eley, conclude the volume.

Haan, Francisca de, *Gender and the Politics of Office Work, the Netherlands 1860–1940*. Amsterdam: Amsterdam University Press, 1998.

This is a comprehensive study of gender contestation over office work in the Netherlands between 1860 and 1940. According to Dr de Haan, reactions to women entering office work were exceedingly protracted and intense in the Netherlands, because the debate on female office workers extended to the foundations of Dutch society, in particular to the tradition of social compartmentalisation (by political ideology and religious denomination). The author argues that compartmentalisation can be seen as a successful patriarchal campaign against the feminist conception of society; the broad resistance to women's entry into the workforce is to be understood in this context.

Hagemann, Karen, *Frauenalltag und Männerpolitik. Alltagsleben und gesellschaftliches Handeln von Arbeiterfrauen in der Weimarer Republik*. Bonn: Verlag J.H.W. Dietz Nachf., 1990.

Among the women who took part in the struggle for the interests and rights of women in the Republic of Weimar were relatively many working-class women. The present voluminous monograph investigates the motives of predominantly social-democratic women, their working and living conditions and the social restrictions hampering their activities. Making use of extensive archival research and of interviews, the author presents a detailed picture of the daily lives, including housing, house work, birth control, wage labour, activities in the trade unions, consumer cooperatives, the SPD and the women's movement, mainly concentrating on the city of Hamburg.

Hannagan, Michael P., *Nascent Proletarians: Class Formation in Post-Revolutionary France*. [Studies in Social Discontinuity] Oxford: Basil Blackwell, 1989.

In this sequel to his *The Logic of Solidarity* (1980) Dr Hannagan explores the relationship between industrialisation, the growth of consciousness and the origins of popular politics in the area around Saint-Etienne (the 'Stephanois'), employing a broad conception of class formation. The author shows that 'a well-rounded portrait of class formation requires an understanding of migration, fertility behaviour, and household employment patterns as well as political ideology and the logic of class coalitions'.

Harrison, Barbara, *Not Only the 'Dangerous Trades': Women's Work and Health in Britain, 1880–1914*. [Feminist Perspectives on the Past and Present] London: Taylor & Francis, 1996.

This book examines the relationship of women's work to their health in Britain in the period 1880–1914, including health problems not only in industrial employment but also in other forms of paid work, such as domestic service, office work, nursing and teaching. Issues such as maternity and infant welfare are also discussed, as well as factory legislation and regulation that focused on the protection of women. Professor Harrison argues that, ultimately, factory legislation failed as a preventive health strategy, but that regulation and the encompassing discourse were successful in preserving male power and privileges by ensuring women's material disadvantage and social and political subordination.

Hart, Vivien, *Bound by Our Constitution: Women, Workers, and the Minimum Wage*. [Princeton Studies in American Politics: Historical, International, and Comparative Perspectives] Princeton NJ: Princeton University Press, 1994.

Comparing the course of minimum wage policies in Britain and the United States in the twentieth century, Dr Hart examines in this study the reciprocal influence between the question of the legal basis for the minimum wage and the debate on women, work and the role of the state. The most important difference between the two countries is that in Britain the minimum wage never became the constitutional issue it was in the United States. She argues that, contrary to general belief, the American constitutional system has had the advantage in the long run.

Hauch, Gabriella (ed.), *Geschlecht – Klasse – Ethnizität. 28. Internationale Tagung der Historikerinnen und Historiker der Arbeiterinnen- und Arbeiterbewegung*. [ITH-Tagungsbericht, Band 29.] Wien: Europaverlag, 1993.

This volume is a selection from papers presented at the 28th International Conference of Labour Historians (ITH), held at Linz (Austria) in 1992. The annual Conference's theme for that year was gender in relation to class and ethnicity. In her preface, the editor notes that this conference signified an historic departure from male domination for the ITH. All but two of the twenty-one contributions are by women and deal with, *inter alia*, gender and family (Dorothy Thompson, Tamara K. Hareven), the use of oral history in women's history (Shena Berger Gluck, Regina

Becker-Schmidt, Irene Bandhauer-Schöffmann), and women and the GULAG (Irina Sherbakova, Meinhard Stark).

Hausen, Karin (ed.), *Geschlechterhierarchie und Arbeitsteilung. Zur Geschichte ungleicher Erwerbschancen von Männern und Frauen.* [Sammlung Vandenhoeck] Göttingen: Vandenhoeck & Ruprecht, 1993.
This collection addresses the gender-based distribution of labour that results from a historically dictated hierarchy of the sexes. The nine contributions here explore the development and the consequences of this gender-specific distribution of labour over different periods and economic brackets in Germany. Contributions deal with, *inter alia*, gender-specific labour distribution and evaluation in the early modern era (Heide Wunder), gender-related labour allocation in the context of mechanisation in the textile industry during the nineteenth century (Karin Zachmann), as well as the reinstatement of the gender hierarchy following the First World War (Susanne Rouette) and gender divisions in the field of social work in the 1920s (Christine Eifert).

Henderson, John and Richard Wall (eds), *Poor Women and Children in the European Past.* London: Routledge, 1994.
Extending from the Middle Ages to the early twentieth century, and covering Denmark, England, France, Iceland, Italy, Ireland and Spain, the fifteen contributions to this volume offer a comparative survey of the impact of poverty on the lives of women and children. In their introduction, the editors consider the distinctive nature of women's poverty over the life cycle, as well as the relation between family and demographic systems and the level of poverty. The contributors test the applicability of the concept of the poverty life cycle in the various periods and countries.

Henkes, Barbara, *Heimat in Holland. Deutsche Dienstmädchen 1920–1950.* (trans. Maria Csollány, with a Foreword by Gerhard Hirschfeld) Straelen: Straelener Manuskripte, 1998. 319 pp.
Between 1920 and 1933 tens of thousands of young German women migrated to the Netherlands to enter domestic service. This study, the German translation of a Dutch dissertation (University of Amsterdam, 1995), explores the women's motives for migrating, their experiences, and the Dutch reactions to these migrant workers, whose presence remains firmly established in Dutch collective memory. Based on archival sources and on many interviews with those concerned, Dr Henkes shows how after 1933 both economic and political pressures led most of the migrants to return to Germany.

Hennesy, Rosemary and Chrys Ingraham (eds), *Materialist Feminism: A Reader in Class, Difference, and Women's Lives.* New York: Routledge, 1997.
This reader comprises thirty-three essays on Marxist feminism, most of which were published previously between 1969 and 1996. The collection is divided into three parts: the essays in the first part offer possible uses for historical materialism in explaining and changing women's oppression

and exploitation under capitalism; the second part focuses on Marxist feminists' critique of the concept of identity politics; and in the third part, which features five previously unpublished essays, more recent social changes (e.g. reproductive engineering and ecofeminism) are discussed from a historical materialist viewpoint.

Hettling, Manfred, Claudia Huerkamp, Paul Nolte and Hans-Walter Schmuhl (eds), *Was ist Gesellschaftsgeschichte? Positionen, Themen, Analysen*. München: Verlag C.H. Beck, 1991.

The present *Festschrift* on the occasion of Professor Hans-Ulrich Wehler's sixtieth birthday contains over thirty short essays about a wide range of sociohistorical subjects, varying from 'Ordo and *dignitas* as social categories in the Roman Republic' (Rolf Rillinger), via 'Max Weber and the race problem' (the fourth editor) to the East European revolutions of 1989–91 (Jürgen Kocka).

Hilden, Patricia Penn, *Women, Work, and Politics. Belgium, 1830–1914*. Oxford: Clarendon Press, 1993.

In this study of the working women of Belgium from the country's independence in 1830 until the First World War, Professor Hilden argues that the success of Belgium's industrial revolution was uniquely dependent on female labour. Women in Belgium were active in almost every industrial sector, unrestricted by the labour legislation that controlled female wage labour in other countries. According to the author, this unique deviation from the historical pattern elsewhere also had a clear influence on the emerging politics of the Belgian working class, with women participating in male-led organisations, as well as organising their own movements.

Hofmeester, Karin, *Van talmoed tot statuut. Joodse arbeiders en arbeidersbewegingen in Amsterdam, Londen en Parijs, 1880–1914*. [IISG-Studies + Essays; 15] Amsterdam: Stichting beheer IISG, 1990.

At the end of the nineteenth century Amsterdam was the only city in western Europe with a numerous autochthonous Jewish proletariat, which was to a large extent employed in the diamond industry. Together with their non-Jewish colleagues these workers established a successful mixed trade union. In London and Paris at the same time the opposite development took place: the Jewish immigrants from eastern Europe, who took up a marginal position in the clothing industry, established separate Jewish (sections of) unions and political organisations. The present monograph tries to explain these differences.

Hopkin, Deian R. and Gregory S. Kealey (eds), *Class, Community and the Labour Movements: Wales and Canada, 1850–1930*, with an introduction by David Montgomery. N.p. [St. John's Nfld.]: Llafur/CCLH, 1989.

The twelve papers collected in this volume were first presented at a conference of Canadian and Welsh labour historians (Gregynog Hall, 1987). Most contributions are concerned with the period 1890–1930. Among the subjects treated are a comparison of the labour movement in a Canadian and a US-American manufacturing and transportation town (Robert Babcock), women's work in Wales (Dot Jones), women's activities in the Canadian labour revolt of 1919 (Linda Kealey), and the Great Unrest in Wales, 1910–1913 (Deian R. Hopkin).

Hudson, Pat and W.R. Lee (eds), *Women's Work and the Family Economy in Historical Perspective*. Manchester Manchester University Press, 1990.
This collection of eleven essays explores the extent to which market and non-market work by women affected the internal and external relations of the family and the household. Besides an extensive historiographical commentary on recent work in the field by the editors, contributions have been included about, among other things, women and proto-industrialisation in Württemberg, 1590–1760 (Sheilagh C. Ogilvie), family structure, family income and women's work in nineteenth-century France (Anne Meyering), changes in women's work and family responsibilities in Norway since the 1860s (Ida Blom), Russian women in urban employment 1880–1917 (Jane McDermid) and the hidden economy of dockland families in Liverpool during the 1930s (Pat Ayers).

Hüchtker, Dietlind, *'Elende Mütter' und 'liederliche Weibspersonen'. Geschlechterverhältnisse und Armenpolitik in Berlin (1770–1850)*. [Theorie und Geschichte der bürgerlichen Gesellschaft, Band 16] Münster: Westfälisches Dampfboot, 1999.
This dissertation (Technical University, Berlin, 1996) relates the changes in the policy towards paupers and poverty in Berlin in the period 1770–1850 to the evolving gender relations and progressive institutionalisation and disciplinary control. Dr Hüchtker explores the everyday experience of beggars and paupers, considers the changes in the concepts of poverty, pauperism, unemployment and the spatial and social rearrangements with respect to pauperism and prostitution that occurred during in this period and focuses on the emergence of concepts of immorality and debauchery in relation to poor women.

Hunt, Karen, *Equivocal feminists: The Social Democratic Federation and the Woman Question 1884–1911*. Cambridge: Cambridge University Press, 1996.
A detailed examination of the relationship between socialism and feminism within the Social Democratic Federation (SDF), Britain's first Marxist party, is contained in the present revised doctoral thesis (Manchester, 1988). Dr Hunt reassesses the history of the SDF by exploring SDF ideas and practice on issues such as marriage and 'free love', women and work and suffrage. She also considers the party's attitudes toward women as potential socialists, its understanding of women's politicisation and the role women assumed within the party.

Hunt, Margaret R., *The Middling Sort: Commerce, Gender, and the Family in England, 1680–1780*. Berkeley CA, University of California Press, 1996.
This study of the 'middling sort', the swelling ranks of shopkeepers, tradesmen, merchants, financiers, professionals and white-collar workers

in late seventeenth and eighteenth-century urban England, highlights the role and place of the family in the middling society. Professor Hunt finds that commercial and social needs largely coincided in entrepreneurial families and, investigating the intertwinement of gender with class and family hierarchy, that more women ran businesses than is commonly thought. According to the author, the growing middling class was largely responsible for the significant expansion in trade and commerce that preceded the take-off to industrialisation.

Hyman, Paula E., *The Jews of Modern France*. [Jewish Communities in the Modern World, vol. 1] Berkeley CA: University of California Press, 1998.
This study gives a chronological overview of the complex relationship between France and its Jews from the years just before the French Revolution to the present day. Professor Hyman focuses, among others, on the opportunities for integration and acculturation, which began when French Jews were offered citizenship during the Revolution, on the secular political anti-Semitism during the Dreyfus Affair and the Holocaust, and on the way French Jews have asserted the compatibility of their French identity with various versions of Jewish particularity, including Zionism.

Jacoby, Robin Miller, *The British and American Women's Trade Union Leagues, 1890–1925: A Case Study of Feminism and Class*. [Scholarship in Women's History: Rediscovered and New, 7] Brooklyn: Carlson Publishing Inc., 1994.
From the end of the nineteenth century in Britain and the United States, Women's Trade Union Leagues existed as autonomous, but nevertheless related, reform organisations, composed of both upper-class and working-class women concerned with the problems of women in the industrial labour force. This study compares the Leagues in both countries between 1890 and 1925 by focusing on the relationship between the intrinsic issues of feminism and class within these organisations. In the concluding chapter, Dr Jacoby examines The International Federation of Working Women (1919–25). The author submits that the fate of this international organisation was a conclusive indication of the successes and failures of the British and American Leagues.

Joannou, Maroula and June Purvis (eds), *The Women's Suffrage Movement: New Feminist Perspectives*. Manchester: Manchester University Press, 1998.
The editors of this collection of fourteen new essays present new trends in feminist historiography of the women's suffrage movement in Britain. Attention is paid to hitherto neglected groups that participated in the campaign: the Women's Franchise League, the Women's Freedom League, the Women's Tax Resistance League and the United Suffragists. The other topics include the poetry, fiction and drama that emerged from the women's struggle for the vote, a reappraisal of the rank-and-file activist Mary Leigh and the suffragist movement outside London.

Jordan, Ellen, *The Women's Movement and Women's Employment in Nineteenth Century Britain.* [Routledge Research in Gender and History, vol. 1] London: Routledge, 1999.

This study examines the expansion of middle-class women's work in nineteenth-century Britain, the reasons for this expansion and the influence of the early women's movement on this process. After 1850 young women entered previously all-male areas such as medicine, pharmacy, librarianship, the civil service, clerical work and hairdressing. The author aims to show how the women's movement, by redefining femininity and promotion of academic education of girls, targeted employers to show the advantages of employing young women, and persuaded young women that working outside the home would not endanger their femininity.

Kalb, Don, *Expanding Class: Power and Everyday Politics in Industrial Communities, The Netherlands, 1850–1950.* [Comparative and International Working-Class History] Durham: Duke University Press, 1998.

This study studies two cases: the shoemaking industry and the electrical industry of the Philips Corporation in the Catholic Dutch province of North Brabant from the middle of the nineteenth to the middle of the twentieth century. With these two case studies Professor Kalb aims to reveal a dynamic relationship between capitalist industrialisation, locality and cultural class identities. The author introduces the concept of 'flexible familism', whereby family daughters were employed to ensure the discipline and loyalty of the working-class community, thus facilitating cheap and able labour.

Kassel, Brigitte, *Frauen in einer Männerwelt. Frauenerwerbsarbeit in der Metallindustrie und ihre Interessenvertretung durch den Deutschen Metallarbeiter-Verband (1891–1933).* [Schriftenreihe der Otto Brenner Stiftung, Band 66] Köln: Bund-Verlag, 1997.

This dissertation (Technical University, Berlin, 1995) examines gender relations and the rise of female wage labour in the German metal industry between 1891 and 1933 and the role of the trade union, the *Deutsche Metallarbeiter-Verband* (DMV) in devising the social-political structure of the gender relations and the hierarchic place of women working in the industry. Dr Kassel concludes, among others, that the attitude of the DMV towards female wage labour was conducive to the establishment of a gender hierarchy, in which women became subordinate both on the job market and in the household.

Kent, Susan Kingsley, *Gender and power in Britain, 1640–1990.* London: Routledge, 1999.

This textbook survey aims to offer a synthesising history of the interaction of gender and power in political, social, cultural, and economic life in Britain from the middle of the seventeenth through the twentieth century. Structured in chronological order, the book examines a wide range of issues and topics, including: the Civil War; industrialisation; Victorian morality; the role of empire in the development of British institutions and identities; twentieth-century suffrage; the World Wars; second-wave feminism; how power relationships were established within the various gender systems that were developed over the centuries; and class, racial and ethnic considerations.

Kerchner, Brigitte, *Beruf und Geschlecht. Frauenberufsverbände in Deutschland 1848–1908*. [Kritische Studien zur Geschichtswissenschaft, Band 97] Göttingen: Vandenhoeck & Ruprecht, 1992.

This Ph.D. thesis (Münster, 1990) deals with the goals and strategies of women's organisations in Germany in the period 1848–1908. The author aims to explore with what kind of expectations working women got organised, what means they used to pursue their goals and to what extent they found a typically feminine method. Although the first forms of an emancipated promotion of their own interests are apparent, this certainly cannot be said of every women's organisation in the period.

Kessler, Mario (ed.), *Arbeiterbewegung und Antisemitismus. Entwicklungslinien im 20. Jahrhundert*. [Podium Progressiv, 25] Bonn: Pahl-Rugenstein-Verlag Nachf., 1993.

The thirteen contributions to this collection all originate from a workshop on the labour movement and anti-Semitism, held in Berlin in December 1992. The main focus is on the relation between communism and anti-Semitism. Contributions included deal with, *inter alia*, the attitude of the SPD towards eastern-European Jews in 1919/1920 (Lothar Elsner), Léon Blum on the Jewish question and anti-Semitism (Johannes Glasneck), the unsolved Jewish question in the Soviet Union (1917–53) (Mario Keßler), the German Democratic Republic, the Holocaust and anti-Zionism (Angelika Timm) and conflicts within the West German Left on Israel (Martin W. Kloke).

Kessler, Mario, *Zionismus und internationale Arbeiterbewegung 1897 bis 1933*. Berlin: Akademie Verlag, 1994.

In this study of the relationship between Zionism and the international workers' movement in the period 1897–1933, Dr Kessler investigates the view of Zionism among major international socialist organisations. Focusing on the Second International, the Comintern and the Socialist and Labour Internationals, the author examines several themes, including the solutions drafted by the international labour movement for the Jewish question, its reactions to Zionist ideas and initiatives and the attempts by leftist zionist movements to join the various Internationals.

Kirk, Neville, *Change, Continuity and Class: Labour in British Society 1850–1920*. [New Frontiers in History] Manchester: Manchester University Press, 1998; distrib. excl. in the USA by St. Martin's Press, New York.

This book aims to critique old and new approaches and debates within British social and labour history from the mid-Victorian period to the immediate post-First World War years. Assuming a general malaise in British labour history, which, in contrast to social history, has failed to engage with new trends and forces, Dr Kirk argues that British labour history can regenerate itself by means of a synthesis and further development of the best elements in both traditional and new approaches. A selection of documents reflecting the dominant concerns and themes in the book is appended.

Klausmann, Christina, *Politik und Kultur der Frauenbewegung im Kaiserreich. Das Beispiel Frankfurt am Main.* [Geschichte und Geschlechter, Band 19] Frankfurt am Main: Campus Verlag, 1997.
This dissertation examines the rise of the women's movement in Frankfurt am Main between 1871 and 1914. Dr Klausmann offers a comparative analysis of the bourgeois and proletarian sections of the women's movement from the perspective of the sociology of social movements and examines the distinctive and common elements in their movement's culture and their programmatic and organisational development. In a separate chapter, the author provides a collective biography of the participants in both sections of the Frankfurter women's movement.

Klein, Gotthard, *Der Volksverein für das katholische Deutschland 1890–1933. Geschichte, Bedeutung, Untergang.* [Veröffentlichungen der Kommission für Zeitgeschichte, Reihe B: Forschungen, Band 75] Paderborn: Ferdinand Schöningh, 1996.
In the first decade of the twentieth century one of the most important and influential Catholic organisations in Germany was the *Volksverein für das katholische Deutschland.* This dissertation (Eichstätt, 1995) reconstructs the origins, successful development and subsequent demise of this social association in the Weimar Republic, which was founded by laymen in 1890 and comprised over 800,000 members (concentrated in the Rhineland-Westphalia industrial region) in its heyday. According to Dr Klein, its intensive training and schooling activities, based on a Catholic social doctrine, contributed considerably to the social integration of Catholics in imperial Germany.

Klein, Marian van der, *Kranig en dwars. De Vrouwenbond NVV/FNV 1948–1998.* Amsterdam: Stichting beheer IISG, 1998.
This book offers an overview of the history of the Vrouwenbond FNV (the largest women's trade union in the Netherlands) in honour of its fiftieth anniversary. Mrs van der Klein sketches how the Vrouwenbond evolved from an organisation supporting the 'real' trade union into an independent operation that protected the interests of women doing both paid and unpaid labour and established a link between traditional women's organisations and new, autonomous feminist initiatives in the 1970s.

Knoblich, Susanne, *"Mit Frauenbewegung hat das nichts zu tun". Gewerkschafterinnen in Niedersachsen 1945 bis 1960.* [Veröffentlichungen des Instituts für Sozialgeschichte e.V. Braunschweig, Bonn] Bonn: Verlag J.H.W. Dietz Nachfolger, 1999.
On the basis of the example of the regional branch of postwar German trade union, the Deutsche Gewerkschaftsbund (DGB), in Niedersachsen,

and the local branch in Braunschweig, Dr Knoblich examines what demands, especially for women female trade union members, were formulated in the 1950s, how they sought to realise and advertise these goals within the male dominated DGB. The author concludes that when the women's interest conflicted with the trade union's general interest, the female trade unionists willingly conform to the general interests.

Kocka, Jürgen, _Arbeitsverhältnisse und Arbeiterexistenzen. Grundlagen der Klassenbildung im 19. Jahrhundert._ [Geschichte der Arbeiter und der Arbeiterbewegung in Deutschland seit dem Ende des 18. Jahrhunderts, Band 2] Bonn: Verlag J.H.W. Dietz Nachf., 1990.

These are the first two volumes of a planned four-volume publication on the history of the working class and the labour movement in Germany, 1800–75, by Professor Kocka. This again is part of a project continuing up to 1933, to which Gerhard A. Ritter, Klaus Tenfelde and Heinrich August Winkler contribute. The present volumes deal with the economic and social circumstances respectively, as well as the experiences and the social consciousness of the lower classes about 1800, and the changing social conditions of various professional groups in the period up to 1875 (servants, agricultural labourers, home workers and proto-industry, journeymen and masters, navvies and wage workers in mining and factories.

Kulczycki, John J., _The Foreign Worker and the German Labor Movement: Xenophobia and Solidarity in the Coal Fields of the Ruhr, 1871–1914._ Oxford: Berg, 1994.

Through this extensive examination of the major strikes and developments within the labour movement in the Ruhr between 1871 and 1914, Dr Kulczycki questions the generally accepted view that regards the Polish migrant workers in this region – because of their rural origins and traditional Catholic beliefs – as obstacles to the labour movement and resistant to working-class consciousness. Focusing on the mass strikes of 1899, 1905 and 1912, and on the 'Polish Revolt' of 1899, he counters that Polish militancy generally surpassed that of native miners.

Kulczycki, John J., _The Polish Coal Miners' Union and the German Labor Movement in the Ruhr, 1902–1934: National and Social Solidarity._ Oxford: Berg, 1997.

In this sequence to his _The Foreign Worker and the German Labor Movement. Xenophobia and Solidarity in the Coal Fields of the Ruhr, 1871–1914_, Professor Kulczycki gives in this study a comprehensive account of the history of the _Zjednoczenie Zawodowe Polskie_ (ZZP), the Polish Trade Union in the Ruhr Region, from its founding in 1902 to its final demise in 1934. The history of the ZZP must be divided, according to the author, into two clearly different periods: the period from 1902 to 1914, in which the ZZP formed an integral part of the labour movement in the Ruhr; and the period after the First World War, when the involvement in the labour movement decreased, and the Polish nationalist course prevailed.

Laslett, John H.M., *Colliers Across the Sea: A Comparative Study of Class Formation in Scotland and the American Midwest, 1830–1924.* [The Working Class in American History] Urbana IL: University of Illinois Press, 2000. Between 1865 and 1868 several hundred mine workers from the Clyde Valley in the south-west of Scotland migrated to the recently opened coalfields in Northern Illinois. In this comparative study, Professor Laslett charts the similarities and differences in the development of these two coal-mining communities in the period between 1830 and 1924. Challenging the exceptionalist paradigm of American labour history, the author analyses the American and Scottish divergent approaches to collectivist solutions, and traces the heightened militancy and rise of industrial unionism on both sides of the Atlantic. He argues that, with the exception of electoral politics, the process of class formation in Scotland and Northern Illinois was surprisingly similar.

Lawrence, Elizabeth, *Gender and Trade Unions.* [Gender & Society: Feminist Perspectives on the Past and Present] London: Taylor & Francis, 1994. This book, which is based on a study of male and female shop stewards in a local branch of the National and Local Government Officers Association (NALGO) in England, conducted between 1987 and 1990, explores the impact of work and gender roles on union activism and aims to identify factors that support or impede women's representation in trade unions. Dr Lawrence concludes that to increase women's representation within trade unions, unions should pay more attention to the operation of union facility agreements and to affirmative action in employment.

Levine, Rhonda F. (ed.), *Social Class and Stratification: Classic Statements and Theoretical Debates.* Lanham: Rowman & Littlefield Publishers, Inc., 1998. This reader brings together sixteen classical and more recent essays on social class and stratification. The essays are divided into four groups: the first covering classical perspectives on social class, including Marx's and Engels's Communist Manifesto and Max Weber's 'Class, Status, Party'; the second focusing on American stratification theory; the third on Neo-Marxian and Neo-Weberian perspectives; and the fourth on gender and racial stratification, ranging from Friedrich Engels, 'The Patriarchal Family', via Gunnar Myrdal, 'Facets of the Negro Problem', to Patricia Hill Collins, 'Toward a New Vision: Race, Class and Gender as Categories of Analysis and Connection'.

Liedtke, Rainer and Stephan Wendehorst (eds), *The Emancipation of Catholics, Jews and Protestants. Minorities and the Nation State in Nineteenth-Century Europe.* Manchester: Manchester University Press, 1999. The ten essays in this collection compare and contrast the emancipation of Catholics, Jews and Protestants in four core European nation states, Britain, France, Germany and Italy, during the nineteenth century. Sketching the changing attitudes of nineteenth-century states and societies towards nondominant religious groups, and addressing the fragmented nature of the emancipation experience within the minorities, the collection aims to present the struggle for political, civic and social equality in an integrated framework. The editors suggest that the treatment of religiously defined minorities was symptomatic of changing notions of citizenship and national identity, as well as of shifting balances in relation between the public and religious spheres.

Linden, Marcel van der and Jan Lucassen (eds), *Racism and the Labour Market: Historical Studies*. (in collaboration with Dik van Arkel, Els Deslé, Fred Goedbloed and others) [International and Comparative Social History, Band 1] Bern: Peter Lang, 1995.

The twenty-three contributions in this collection, based on a conference organised by the International Institute of Social History in September 1991, deal with three types of historical situations. The first are former slave economies, which had turned into free labour markets after the abolition of slavery. The second are situations where white settlers subjugated peripheral societies, thereby creating a new labour market. The main issue in these situations is whether and how they brought about racial segmentation. The third are situations where a labour market, segmented by class but not along racial lines, is confronted with immigration. Here, the research focuses on determining the conditions for integrating or segregating immigrants. The contributions address countries on all continents in the period after 1830.

Linden, Marcel van der and Jürgen Rojahn (eds), *The Formation of Labour Movements 1870–1914. An International Perspective*. [Contributions to the History of Labour and Society, 2] Leiden: E.J. Brill, 1990.

The twenty-eight articles presented in this collection mark the first stage of an international research project set up by the Internationaal Instituut voor Sociale Geschiedenis in Amsterdam. Using a general questionnaire, each article gives a survey of the development of the working class and the labour movement in one country during the period 1870–1914, in order to simplify comparative research as a second step. Dealt with are all West European countries, the Czech lands, Hungary, Romania, Bulgaria, Serbia, Greece, Russia, Poland, the USA, Australia, New Zealand, South Africa, Argentina and Japan. A substantial bibliography has been appended. Contributors include Franco Andreucci, Victoria E. Bonnell, Santiago Castillo, Keith Hitchins, Hans Ulrich Jost, David Kirby, Jiří Košalka, Kazuo Nimura, Birger Simonson and Klaus Tenfelde.

Lischke, Ute, *Lily Braun: 1865–1916. German Writer, Feminist, Socialist*. [Studies in German Literature, Linguistics, and Culture] Rochester: Camden House, 2000.

This is a biographical study of Lily Braun (1865–1916), a leading German feminist of the late nineteenth and early twentieth centuries, and a successful writer of both novels and feminist political tracts. Active both in groups as the *Verein Frauenwohl*, and in the Social Democratic Party, she did her best on issues such as maternity insurance and better education and housing for women. Professor Lischke sketches how she came into increasing conflict with other leading socialist women, who were suspicious of Braun's aristocratic origins, and how she retreated from politics to pursuit a literary career. By 1914, Braun was espousing extreme nationalistic and racial hygiene ideas, and had repudiated many of her earlier feminist stances.

Lockman, Zachary, *Comrades and Enemies: Arab and Jewish Workers in Palestine, 1906–1948*. Berkeley CA: University of California Press, 1996.
This book explores the interactions among Arab and Jewish workers, trade unions, labour movements, and labour-oriented political parties in Palestine during the British mandate period, 1906–48. Focusing on the Arab and Jewish workers who operated the Palestine railway system during the mandate period, the author pays particular attention to the thought and practice of the left wing of the Zionist movement and the complex interaction between Palestine's Arab working class and labour Zionism.

Long, Jane, *Conversations in Cold Rooms: Women, Work and Poverty in Nineteenth-Century Northumberland*. [Studies in History New Series] Woodbridge: The Royal Historical Society/The Boydell Press, 1999.
This book explores the relations between gender, poverty and women's work in the context of nineteenth-century Northumberland. Dr Long examines urban and rural conditions for women, poor relief debates and practices, philanthropic activity, working-class cultures, 'protective' intervention in women's employment. She also looks at cultural codes around women and womanhood, and the way in which representations of women's bodies, the contemporary discourse of domestic life, respectability and Victorian 'progress' contributed to the meanings of poverty in nineteenth-century Northumberland, arguing that poverty was far more gendered than often is acknowledged.

McDermid, Jane and Anna Hillyar, *Women and Work in Russia 1880–1930: A Study in Continuity through Change*. [Women and Men in History] London: Longman, 1998.
This study aims to give a comprehensive picture of the variety of female work in Russia and of working women themselves from 1881 to 1930. Throughout this period of political and economic upheaval, Russia remained a patriarchal society dominated by a peasant economy. Yet the stereotype of women as passive, subordinate beasts of burden during the immense changes in this period, needs, according to the authors, to be differentiated: working women of all social classes were manoeuvring within, and not simply submitting to, a patriarchal system, and seeming continuity in women's work should not obscure change.

McKibbin, Ross, *The Ideologies of Class. Social Relations in Britain 1880–1950*. Oxford: Clarendon Press, 1990.
To a certain extent the nine essays in this collection – eight of which have been published before – are a sequel to Dr McKibbin's book *The Evolution of the Labour Party* (1974). The themes of the contributions are connected and are more or less closely related to the social character of the British

working class from the 1880s to the early 1950s. Among the subjects dealt with are 'Why was there no Marxism in Great Britain?', 'The Franchise Factor in the Rise of the Labour Party', 'Working-Class Gambling in Britain, 1880–1939', 'The "Social Psychology" of Unemployment in Inter-War Britain' and 'Class and Conventional Wisdom: The Conservative Party and the "Public" in Inter-War Britain'.

McLeod, Hugh, *Religion and Irreligion in Victorian England: How Secular was the Working Class?* [Headstart History Papers] Bangor: Headstart History, 1993.

In this small booklet, intended for students and the general reader, Dr McLeod examines the historiography of the Victorian working class and religion. Based on the existing literature, the author concludes that approximately one-third of the working class had a strongly religious ethos, one-third an ethos indifferent or hostile to religion, while one-third is to be situated between these extremes and can be described as 'one hundred per cent Christians, but no church-goers'.

McMillan, James F., *France and Women 1789–1914: Gender, Society and Politics.* London: Routledge, 2000.

In this study, Professor McMillan considers the role played by women in French politics, culture and society throughout the nineteenth century. Portraying French women both as individuals and as members of different social classes and regional and cultural communities, the author explores the redefinition of the role and sphere of women as a result of the French Revolution, the resulting dichotomy between a male, public domain and female, private domain in the first half of the nineteenth century, the subsequent emergence of a discourse on womanhood in the third quarter of the nineteenth century, and the crisis in French gender relations in the period 1880–1914.

Marshall, Gordon, *Repositioning Class: Social Inequality in Industrial Societies.* London: Sage Publications, 1997.

Professor Marshall, an expert in modern class analysis who published *Social Class in Modern Britain* in 1988 and coedited *Against the Odds?* (1997), has gathered in this volume ten essays (written and previously published over the past twelve years) that are intended as an illustration of his methodological principles. The issues dealt with include the debate about the unit of class composition, the question of meritocracy, the relationship between class and gender, cross-national similarities and differences in mobility regimes, and proletarianisation, distributional struggles, collective identities and the nature of the so-called underclass in advanced societies.

Marshall, Gordon, Adam Swift and Stephen Roberts, *Against the Odds? Social Class and Social Justice in Industrial Societies.* Oxford: Clarendon Press, 1997.

Drawing on political theory and sociological analysis, the authors of this study explore the implications of social class for social justice by studying patterns of social mobility in contemporary Britain. Using statistical data sets from large-scale social surveys, Drs Marshall, Swift and Roberts focus on the role of education in generating equal opportunities for social mobility. They conclude that, even when educational attainment remains constant, social origins continue to exert considerable influence on class destinations.

Medick, Hans and Anne-Charlott Trepp (eds), *Geschlechtergeschichte und Allgemeine Geschichte. Herausforderungen und Perspektiven.* (With contributions from Karin Hausen, Lynn Hunt, Thomas Kühne and others) [Göttinger Gespräche zur Geschichtswissenschaft, Band 5] Göttingen: Wallstein Verlag, 1998.
The five essays in this collection, based on a colloquium held in Göttingen in July 1996, discuss the challenges that gender history offers for general history and the chances and opportunities for incorporating the gender perspective in general historiography. Contributors are Karin Hausen (on the historical relevance of gender history), Lynn Hunt (on the deconstruction of categories), Gianna Pomata (on combining the specific and the general in gender history), Helmut Puff (on the relevance of the history of homosexuality for gender history) and Thomas Kühne (on political history as gender history).

Mengus, Raymond (ed.), *Cent ans de catholicisme social en Alsace: De l'encyclique Rerum Novarum (1891) à la fin du XXe siècle.* Strasbourg: Presses Universitaires de Strasbourg, 1991.
In November 1990, a colloquium was held at the University of Strasbourg to celebrate the centennial of the papal encyclical *Rerum Novarum* (1891). The ten contributions in this volume, which were presented at this colloquium, deal with the reception of this encyclical among Alsatian Catholics, social democrats and employers, as well as with its influence on the emergence of a Catholic social movement in the Alsace from the appearance of *Rerum Novarum* to the present. In his concluding contribution, Raymond Mengus explores the present-day significance of Catholic social movements.

Miles, Robert, *Racism after 'Race Relations'.* London: Routledge, 1993.
This book examines the scope of the concept of racism in the light of the problematic status of the idea of 'race' and the histories of migration and racism. Dr Miles opposes the idea that racism is always linked to colonialism and focuses on the formation of nations in Europe in relation to migration and a number of 'interior racisms' that resulted from it. The author concludes with an analysis of the current relationships between, migration, nationalism and racism in the European Community today.

Miliband, Ralph, *Divided Societies: Class Struggle in Contemporary Capitalism.* Oxford: Clarendon Press, 1989.
The present book, resulting from the Marshall Lectures, which the author gave at the University of Cambridge, attempts to 'theorise' socioeconomic and political developments in advanced capitalist countries. From a Marxist point of view, Professor Miliband analyses the class structure, labour movements, 'new' social movements and the class struggle 'from above' and strongly pleads the cause of socialist democracy.

Misgeld, Klaus and Klas Amark (eds), *Arbetsliv och arbetarrörelse modern historisk forskning i Sverige*. Stockholm: Arbetarrörelsens arkiv och bibliotek, 1991.

The six contributions to this small volume deal with several aspects of Swedish labour historiography such as working-class daily life (Lars Edgren and Lars Olsson), trade unions and labour markets (the second editor), the Social Democratic Party (Lars Bjorlin), women and the labour movement (Gunnel Karlsson), workers' educational institutions (Marion Leffler), and a survey of labour history institutions and periodicals (the first editor). An extensive list of relevant publications has been appended.

Müller, Dirk H., *Arbeiter – Katholizismus – Staat. Der Volksverein für das katholische Deutschland und die katholischen Arbeiterorganisationen in der Weimarer Republik*. [Reihe Politik- und Gesellschaftsgeschichte, Band 43] Bonn: Verlag J.H.W. Dietz Nachfolger, 1996.

Focusing on two Catholic working-class laymen's organisations (the *Volksverein für das katholische Deutschland* and the *Reichsverband katholische Arbeitervereine*), this study, part of a series comparing the history of social-democratic and Catholic organisations in the Weimar Republic, explores the relationship between the working class, Catholicism and the German state from the 1890s to the end of the Weimar Republic and the signing of the *Reichskonkordat* in 1934.

Murray, Mary, *The Law of the Father? Patriarchy in the Transition from Feudalism to Capitalism*. London: Routledge, 1995.

This sociological study examines the relationship between patriarchy and class during the transition from feudalism to capitalism. Focusing on Anglo-Saxon feudal and capitalist societies, she views class and patriarchy as particular expressions of the fundamental social relation of property that they constitute together. At the heart of the transition from feudalism to capitalism was, according to Dr Murray, a fundamental shift in property relations which were patriarchally structured.

Myers, Norma, *Reconstructing the Black Past: Blacks in Britain c. 1780–1830*. [Studies in Slave and Post-Slave Societies and Cultures] London: Frank Cass, 1996.

Whereas most studies of the black population in Britain in the eighteenth and nineteenth centuries have focused on intellectuals, this study concentrates on the working class, which accounted for the vast majority of black people in Britain in this period. Dr Myers examines, on the basis of little-used sources, the sex ratios, age structure, family patterns and occupations of black men and women to give a more complete historical impression of Britain's black community.

Nash, Mary, *Defying Male Civilization: Women in the Spanish Civil War*. [Women and Modern Revolution Series] Denver CO: Arden Press, Inc., 1995.

This is a study of the social and political mobilisation of women in Republican Spain during the Spanish War. Professor Nash addresses both

the contributions made by women on the home front and the accom-
plishments of female republican leaders and women who fought on the
war fronts. Based on, among others, women activists from the Spanish
Civil War, the author explores the effects of women's involvement in the
anti-fascist struggle for the gender relation. A Spanish translation
appeared in 1999: *Rojas. Las mujeres republicanas en la Guerra Civil* (trans.
Irene Cifuentes) [Pensamiento] Madrid: Taurus, 1999), which has been
adapted for Spanish readers and contains substantial revisions with respect
to the original English edition.

Nienhaus, Ursula, *Vater Staat und seine Gehilfinnen. Die Politik mit der
Frauenarbeit bei der deutschen Post (1864–1945)*. [Reihe 'Geschichte und
Geschlechter', Band 11] Frankfurt am Main: Campus Verlag, 1995.
In this study of women workers for the German postal services, an
abridged edition of this scholar's dissertation (Hannover, 1993), Dr
Nienhaus examines employment opportunities for women, as well as the
social policy that covered women working for the state from the beginning of the modern postal services in the 1860s until 1945. Comparing
the German developments to other European countries and the United
States, the author concludes that the German state maintained a gender-
specific policy with respect to its employees throughout the period. On
the one hand, single women received increasing employment opportunities as cheap labour. On the other hand, the social policy catered to male
breadwinners.

Offen, Karen, *European Feminisms 1700–1950: A Political History*. Stanford
CA: Stanford University Press, 2000.
This broad-ranging study aims to provide a comprehensive, comparative
account of feminist developments in European societies from 1700 to
1950, focusing especially on France, but also offering comparative material on developments in German-speaking and other countries, and on the
development of international feminist organisations. By rereading European history from a feminist perspective, Dr Offen also aims to address
issues under discussion by contemporary feminist theorists: about, among
others, the Enlightenment, reason and nature, public vs. private, and
equality vs. difference. She concludes that gender is not merely a useful
category of analysis, but lies at the heart of human thought and politics.

O'Leary, Paul, *Immigration and Integration: The Irish in Wales, 1798–1922*.
[Studies in Welsh History, vol. 16] Cardiff: University of Wales Press, 2000.
Dr O'Leary examines in this study the Irish emigration to Wales in the
nineteenth and first decades of the twentieth centuries, and sketches the
experience of Irish immigrants in Wales. Although initially the Irish immigrants met with the same violent hostility as in other parts of Britain, by
the late nineteenth century the integration appeared to be relatively trou-
ble-free. The author considers key aspects of immigrant life, such the role
of the Irish in the labour force; criminality and drink; the establishment
of community organisation, among which friendly societies and political

organisations; the mobilisation of support for the Irish nationalist organisation; and Irish participation in the Welsh labour movement.

Omnès, Catherine, *Ouvrières parisiennes. Marchés du travail et trajectoires professionnelles au 20e siècle*. Paris: Éditions de l'École des Hautes Études en Sciences Sociales, 1997.

This study, pertaining to both women's history and labour history, describes women's work in the Paris area from the early twentieth century onward. Using a wealth of quantitative and qualitative sources, Dr Omnès reconstructs the labour market's professional, sectoral and geographic segmentation; the changes on the labour market; and the personal history of wage-earning women.

Pakulski, Jan and Malcolm Waters, *The Death of Class*. London: Sage Publications, 1996.

In this book, Professors Pakulski and Waters set out to show that the concept of class, as used in the so-called 'weak' class theory, is no longer a viable description of social systems of inequality and occupational structure because it no longer provides an adequate account of modern society. They argue that class is a purely historical phenomenon, applying to societies divided into exploitation-based class communities, and that postmodernisation, globalisation, increasing unemployment and the collapse of state socialism have exposed the limitations of class analysis.

Pasture, Patrick, *Christian Trade Unionism in Europe Since 1968: Tensions Between Identity and Practice*. Aldershot: Avebury, 1994.

This study surveys the development of Christian trade unionism in Western, Central and Eastern Europe (excluding the former Soviet Union) since 1968, examining national membership, developments within the international Christian trade union movement, and international trade action. The author concludes that, despite vast national variations and differences, the general trend is univocal: Christian trade unionism has tended to merge with the free trade union movement as a result of the progressive secularisation and diminishing political power of Christian Democracy.

Pasture, Patrick, *Histoire du syndicalisme chrétien international: La difficile recherche d'une troisième voie.* (trans. from Dutch by Serge Govaert) [Chemins de la mémoire] Paris: Éditions L'Harmattan, 1999.

In this study of International Christian trade unionism from its origins in Europe at the end of the nineteenth century to the 1970s, Dr Pasture sees as a general characteristic of the international Christian trade-union movement the continuous search for an independent third way. A third way between laissez-faire liberalism and socialism in the first phase, between socialism and fascism in the interwar years, and between the capitalist West and communist East during the Cold War. The author concludes his comprehensive chronological account of the developments with the transformation in more recent decades of International Christian trade unionism into a solidarity movement with Third World countries.

Pazos, Antón M. (ed.), *Un siglo de catolicismo social en Europa 1891–1991*. [Colección Historia de la Iglesia, 22.] Pamplona: EUNSA, S.A., 1993.
  In 1991 a colloquium on 100 years of social Catholicism in Europe was held in the Spanish town of Pamplona to commemorate the centennial of the papal encyclical *Rerum Novarum* (1891). The editors of the present work emphasise the movement's European character. The volume comprises five contributions about countries with a strong Catholic presence: Spain, France, Italy, Belgium and Germany. The authors discuss the characteristics of social Catholicism in each country and describe its political and social influence. They also consider recent research on this subject. A critical bibliography accompanies each chapter.

Peled, Yoav, *Class and Ethnicity in the Pale: The Political Economy of Jewish Workers' Nationalism in Late Imperial Russia*. Basingstoke and London: MacMillan, 1989.
  In this study of the ideological development of the Jewish labour movement in late imperial Russia, organised in the Bund, Dr Peled aims to explore the emergence of a particular type of ethno-class consciousness among Jewish workers in Russia, which was reflected in the increasingly nationalist ideology adopted by the Bund. With this examination the author also aims to test the analytic usefulness of the concept of 'reactive nationalism' and shed some new light on the debate between the Bund and its main political rivals: the Russian social democrats and the socialist Zionist.

Piguet, Marie-France, *Classe: Histoire du mot et genèse du concept des Physiocrates aux Historiens de la Restauration*. Lyon: Presses universitaires de Lyon, 1996.
  Using a sociolinguistic approach and discourse analysis, Dr Piguet examines in this book how and when in France the word 'class' took over as the central indicator of social division from 'order'. She claims that this transition can be traced in the second half of the eighteenth century, starting with the writing of the Physiocrats (Quesnay and his followers) and completed in the writings of the historians of the Restoration period.

Planert, Ute, *Antifeminismus im Kaiserreich. Diskurs, soziale Formation und politische Mentalität*. [Kritische Studien zur Geschichtswissenschaft, Band 124] Göttingen: Vandenhoeck & Ruprecht, 1998.
  The central theme in this revised and abridged dissertation (Tübingen, 1996) is the origin and growth of institutionalised opposition to the feminist demands for emancipation in Imperial Germany since the 1890s. Dr Planert aims to show that in response to the emerging women's movement, with its political and social demands for more influence, a widespread anti-feminist network arose that was closely connected to anti-semitic, nationalist and anti-parliamentary movements.

Poelstra, Jannie, *Luiden van een andere beweging. Huishoudelijke arbeid in Nederland 1840–1920*. Amsterdam: Het Spinhuis, 1996.
  This dissertation (University of Amsterdam, 1996) analyses changing views in the Netherlands between 1840 and the 1920s on domestic ser-

vants and the 'servants' issue' with respect to social concerns and women's emancipation. Dr Poelstra explores the discourse in which servants were labelled as 'others' in social terms and the implications of this status. She examines living and working conditions among domestic servants, trends in the labour market for these workers and their social and legal rights.

Posadskaya, Anastasia (eds), *Women in Russia: A New Era in Russian Feminism*. (trans. Kate Clark, originated by Ruth Steele) London: Verso, 1994.
In 1989, the Moscow Centre for Gender Studies was founded as a result of the growing desire among a group of female researchers to deal with the women's issue in the USSR. This collection presents translations of twelve recent articles by Russian feminist authors, all employed at or closely affiliated with the Centre. Subjects range from the myth of women's equality in the socialist society, through women's rights under *perestroika* and in post-Soviet Russia, the emergence of an independent women's movement in Russia, women and the labour market, to the history of feminism in Russia.

Purvis, June and Sandra Stanley Holton (eds), *Votes for Women*. [Women's and Gender History] London: Routledge, 2000.
The twelve contributions in this volume aim to provide an innovative re-examination of the British women's suffrage movement, from its origins in the nineteenth century to the post-First World War period. The opening chapter by Sandra Stanley Holton deals with the historiography of the movement. Other contributions include, among others, reassessments of the roles of leading figures, such as Lily Maxwell (Jane Rendall), Mrs Henry Fawcett (Janet Howarth), Emmeline Pankhurst (June Purvis), and Constance Lytton (Marie Mulvey-Roberts), and essays on the Women's Social and Political Union (June Purvis), the Women's Freedom League (Hilary Frances), and the suffrage movement in the regions (June Hannam).

Reed, Mick and Roger Wells (eds), *Class, Conflict and Protest in the English Countryside, 1700–1880*, London, Savage MD: Frank Cass, 1990.
In 1979 Dr Roger A.E. Wells published an article about 'The Development of the English Rural Proletariat and Social Protest, 1700–1850'in *The Journal of Peasants Studies*. This was followed by a debate in which Andrew Charlesworth, J.E. Archer, Dennis Mills, Brian Short and Mick Reed took part. In addition to introductory and concluding dissertations, the present volume contains reprints of the various contributions to the discussion, as well as an extensive new essay by Dr Wells.

Richards, Andrew J., *Miners on Strike: Class Solidarity and Division in Britain*. Oxford: Berg, 1996.
This book offers an explanation for the differences between the outcomes of the British miners' strikes in 1972 and 1974 – which resulted in a total victory for the miners and reinforcement of the National Union of Mineworkers' (NUM) position – and the dramatic strikes in 1985, which ended in bitter defeat for the NUM. Professor Richards goes against main-

stream interpretation by arguing that these differing outcomes illustrate the complexity rather than the disappearance of collective identity and class consciousness among miners and maintains that remarkably high levels of solidarity were achieved in 1985, despite the inherently divisive issue.

Roberts, Elizabeth, *Women and Families. An Oral History, 1940–1970*. [Family, Sexuality and Social Relations in Past Times] Oxford: Blackwell, 1995.
This volume is based on in-depth interviews conducted in three towns in northern England. This study shows that the period 1940–70 is marked by a dramatic increase in the number of women doing paid work, along with the growth of the welfare state and the privatisation of the family. According to the author, these developments were accompanied by a diminishing sense of community and neighbourliness and by a loss of confidence in previously accepted standards and values.

Roberts, Michael and Simone Clarke (eds), *Women and Gender in Early Modern Wales*. Cardiff: University of Wales Press, 2000.
The eleven contributions to this volume examine the material, social and cultural experiences of women in Wales from the late middle ages to the eve of the Industrial Revolution, and explore how those experiences were defined alongside or against those of men. Issues addressed in the essays include female contributions to the poetic tradition, attitudes towards witchcraft and female abduction, the role of women in the emerging Nonconformist movements, the changing political and social responsibilities following the Acts of Union, and an exploration of women's experiences as presented in such varied sources as records from the law courts and the work of the embroiderer.

Rogard, Vincent, *Les catholiques et la question sociale Morlaix 1840–1914: L'avènement des militants*. (preface by Jean-Marie Mayeur) [Histoire] Rennes: Presses Universitaire de Rennes, 1997.
In this revised edition of a dissertation (Sorbonne, 1991) Dr Rogard examines the emergence of the Catholic social movement in and around the Morlaix, a town in the western part of Brittany, between 1840 and 1914. After dealing with the Catholic charity efforts, directed primarily at alleviating poverty, he subsequently explores the emerging Catholic youth movement at the end of the nineteenth century and its rivalry with the socialist movement to incorporate the growing workers' movement.

Rose, Sonya O., *Limited Livelihoods: Gender and Class in Nineteenth-Century England*. London: Routledge, 1992.
By analysing a range of industries, Professor Rose reviews the influence of gender distinctions and gender relations on the development of capitalism in nineteenth-century England. Integrating analytical tools from feminist theory, cultural studies and sociology with detailed archival research, the author argues that gender was a central organizing principle of industrial transformation and working-class responses to industrialisation in England in this period.

Rouette, Susanne, *Sozialpolitik als Geschlechterpolitik. Die Regulierung der Frauenarbeit nach dem Ersten Weltkrieg*. [Reihe Geschichte und Geschlechter, Band 6] Frankfurt am Main: Campus Verlag, 1993.
   In this revised doctoral thesis (Berlin, 1991) Dr Rouette examines to what extent the social and labour-market policies in the Weimar Republic between 1918 and 1923 can be seen as gender policies, directed at restoring the prewar gender hierarchy and forcing women back into their traditional role as mothers and housewives. She does so on the basis of a regional case study of Greater Berlin. She concludes that after the Weimar Revolution of 1918/19 the discrimination of women in the labour market was legalised in the newly developed social-security policy and in the labour-market policy.

Rowbotham, Sheila, *Women in Movement: Feminism and Social Action*. [Revolutionary Thought/Radical Movements] New York: Routledge, 1992.
   This textbook aims to give a historical introduction to a range of women's movements from the late eighteenth century to the present, tracing the origins of feminism in relation to political thought and activities, and describing other economic, social and political movements in which women participated in Europe, North America and the Third World. Themes dealt with include equality, women's differences from men, personal and political individualism, collectivity, the scope of rights and the definition of needs.

Savage, Mike and Andrew Miles, *The Remaking of the British Working Class, 1840–1940*. [Historical Connections] London: Routledge, 1994.
   The historical significance and validity of the concept of class, and therefore also the historical study of the working class, have been subjects of extensive discussions over the past decade. This short textbook is designed to introduce these debates. The authors argue that ample grounds exist for a sophisticated, adapted approach to class analysis. They substantiate their argument by reviewing the complex (but nonetheless distinctive) process of 'working-class formation' that took place in British society between 1840 and 1940.

Schmitt, Sabine, *Der Arbeiterinnenschutz im deutschen Kaiserreich. Zur Konstruktion der schutzbedürftigen Arbeiterin*. [Ergebnisse der Frauenforschung, Band 37] Stuttgart: Verlag J.B. Metzler, 1995.
   In this revised edition of a dissertation (Technical University, Berlin, 1994), Dr Schmitt uses methods of discourse analysis to study the origins of the forms of legal protection designed specifically for women workers in Germany in the period 1890–1914. The author views the development and implementation of these measures as a construction process that embedded the need for extra protection as a specific characteristic of women's labour in public awareness, reinforced gender segregation and hierarchisation in the industrial workplace and increased the perception that women workers were exceptions.

Schneider, Bernhard, *Katholiken auf die Barrikaden? Europäische Revolutionen und deutsche katholische Presse, 1815–1848*. [Veröffentlichungen der Kommission für Zeitgeschichte, Reihe B: Forschungen, Band 84] Paderborn: Ferdinand Schöningh, 1998.

Following an inventory of the emerging German Catholic press in the early nineteenth century, this *Habilitationsschrift* (Freiburg im Breisgau, 1996/97) examines the reaction of the various Catholic mainstreams, in their respective press media, to the revolutionary events and changes in Europe between 1815 and 1848, and the interpretations by the Catholic commentators and opinion leaders, from these various mainstreams, of the events, and the ways they used them to serve their own religious-political and theological purposes.

Scholz, Rüdiger, *Kritik der Sozialgeschichtsschreibung. Zur Diskussion gegenwärtiger Konzepte*. (With contributions from Hans Peter Herrmann, Georg G. Iggers, Rüdiger Scholz, Immanuel Wallerstein) [Argument-Sonderband AS 166] Hamburg: Argument-Verlag, 1991.

This book focuses on the Marxist interpretation of social history. The contributions deal with the analysis of the transition from feudalism to capitalism in more recent East- and West-German reference books (the editor), 'The West, Capitalism and the Modern World System' (Immanuel Wallerstein), the theoretical basis of Hans-Ulrich Wehler's *Deutsche Gesellschaftsgeschichte* (the editor), historiography in the former GDR (Georg G. Iggers) and the relation between (German) literary and social history (Hans Peter Herrmann).

Scott, Gillian, *Feminism and the politics of working women; The Women's Co-operative Guild, 1880s to the Second World War*. [Women's History] London: UCL Press, 1998.

This study investigates the development of the British Women's Co-operative Guild from the 1880s to Second World War. Predominantly composed of working-class housewives, the organisation managed, according to the author, to balance in its policies class and gender issues with an awareness of the cultural, ideological and sexual dimensions of the oppression of working women. Dr Scott aims to assess the political significance of the movement during the decades of its greatest influence and to examine the causes and circumstances of its demise.

Sellier, Ulrich, *Die Arbeiterschutzgesetzgebung im 19. Jahrhundert. Das Ringen zwischen christlich-sozialer Ursprungsidee, politischen Widerständen und kaiserlicher Gesetzgebung*. [Rechts- und Staatswissenschaftliche Veröffentlichungen der Görres-Gesellschaft; Neue Folge, Band 82] Paderborn: Ferdinand Schöningh, 1998.

This dissertation (Trier, 1995) examines the emergence of the German labour protection legislation from the 1860s into the 1890s, emphasizing the role of Catholic social ideology and Catholic politicians. Dr Sellier devotes separate chapters to the proposals and parliamentary strategies of

German social democracy and the papal encyclical, *Rerum Novarum*, and its influence on German social policy.

Shiach, Morag, *Discourse on Popular Culture, Class, Gender and History in Cultural Analysis: 1730 to the Present*. Stanford CA: Stanford University Press, 1989.

This book (originally a Cambridge doctoral thesis) focuses not on 'popular culture' as such, but on 'continuities in the ways in which popular culture has been described and evaluated' from about 1730 to the present. Several sets of responses to popular cultural forms are examined 'in order to identify the relation between theorisation of the 'dominant' and of the 'popular'.

Simonton, Deborah, *A History of European Women's Work: 1700 to the Present*. London: Routledge, 1998.

This study aims to offer a comprehensive and detailed description of the multitude of various productive activities undertaken by women in Europe over the last three centuries, contrasting countries such as Britain, France and Germany. Dr Simonton subdivides her overview chronologically, dealing with a number of recurrent key themes in each of the three centuries, including, among others: household and the social construction of domesticity; skill as a gendered category; the invisibility of women's work; the gendering of the workplace; the difference between men's and women's relationship to machinery; and the gendering of technology.

Smith, Harold L. (ed.), *British Feminism in the Twentieth Century*. Aldershot: Edward Elgar, 1990.

'This book contains [ten] chapters written especially for it on major developments in [British] feminist thought and action since 1900.' Included are more or less biographical studies about Emmeline Pankhurst, Vera Brittain and Eleanore Rathbone and more structural contributions about, *inter alia*, 'Gender Reconstruction after the First World War' (Susan Kingsley Kent), 'The Women of the British Labour Party and Feminism, 1930–1950' (Martin Pugh) and 'British Feminism from the 1960s to the 1980s' (Elizabeth Meehan).

Sklar, Kathryn Kish, Anja Schüler, and Susan Strasser (eds), *Social Justice Feminists in the United States and Germany. A Dialogue in Documents, 1885–1933*. Ithaca NY: Cornell University Press, 1998.

Women reformers between 1885 and 1933, in various organisations in the United States and Germany, engaged in a dialogue covering a wide array of social injustices caused by the rise of industrial capitalism, such as child labour and the exploitation of women in the workplace. This book presents and interprets documents from that exchange, which show how these interactions reflected the political cultures of the two nations. The documents shed light on the influence of German factory legislation on debates in the United States, the differing contexts of the suffrage movements and the shifts in the feminist movements of both countries after the First World War.

Sperling, Valerie, *Organizing Women in Contemporary Russia. Engendering Transition*. Cambridge: Cambridge University Press, 1999.

In this study, Professor Sperling gives a comprehensive analysis of the contemporary women's movement in Russia and of the social, political, economic, historical and international context that surrounds it. She pays particular attention to the key challenges facing social movements in postcommunist Russia, with its virtual absence of civil society and constant flux in political institutions. The author also discusses the problems women's organisations face in the context of societal attitudes towards feminism in Russia. Her study is based on participant observation, primary source materials, and interviews conducted in Moscow and the provincial cities of Cheboksary and Ivanovo. Included are tables and appendices with comprehensive information on women's organisations, including age, education and occupation of members.

Steinberg, Mark D., *Moral Communities: The Culture of Class Relations in the Russian Printing Industry 1867–1907*. [Studies on the History of Society and Culture] Berkeley CA: University of California Press, 1992.

The evolution of the Russian printing industry from a state-run handicraft to a technologically developed capitalist industry changed the conduct and structure of class relations and added meaning to the values, norms and perceptions that guided these relations. To explore these developments, this study focuses on the exercise of authority and the varieties of resistance and rebellion. Professor Steinberg aims to show that while workers and employers shared ideas of community and morality, they differed in their methods of interpretation and application. These shared ideas resulted in a persistent element of ambiguity in the evolving class struggle.

Stewart, Mary Lynn, *Women, Work, and the French State: Labour Protection and Social Patriarchy, 1879–1919*. Kingston, Montreal and London: McGill-Queen's University Press, 1989.

During the 1880s and 1890s the protection of women and girls in the workplace was advocated by numerous reformers of virtually every hue. In this thorough book Dr Stewart traces the implementation of the restrictive legislation enacted in response. She argues that these laws, though initiated to protect women and girls, were actually a method of exploiting woemn's dual role of short-time wage worker and unpaid housewife and mother.

Stone, Marilyn and Carmen Benito-Vessels (eds), *Women at Work in Spain: From the Middle Ages to Early Modern Times*. New York: Peter Lang, 1998.

Based on extensive archival research, the seven essays in this volume aim to document the contribution of women to economic and cultural change on the Iberian Peninsula from the Middle Ages to the early modern period by their 'public' work (i.e. production of goods and rendering of services in return for which compensation). The contributions included cover the role of peasant and aristocratic women in the rural economy, the work of women in monasteries and women in the printing industry.

Szreter, Simon, *Fertility, Class and Gender in Britain, 1860–1940*. [Cambridge Studies in Population, Economy and Society in Past Time, 27] Cambridge: Cambridge University Press, 1996.

Based on a new analysis of the 1911 British fertility census, this study aims to offer a new interpretation of the history of falling fertilities in the period 1860–1940. Integrating a social science and demographic perspective with gender, labour and intellectual history, Dr Szreter argues that the orthodox view of a national, unitary class-differential fertility decline is based on statistical inadequacy. He finds many diverse fertility regimes, differentiated by distinctively gendered labour markets and changing family roles. The author proposes a new general approach to the study of fertility change, as well as a new conception of the relationship between class, community and fertility change, and a new evaluation of the positive role of feminism.

Tabili, Laura, *'We Ask for British Justice': Workers and Radical Difference in Late Imperial Britain*. [The Wilder House Series in Politics, History, and Culture] Ithaca NY: Cornell University Press, 1994.

Focusing on the labour market in merchant shipping in Britain during the Interbellum, this study aims to trace the sources of racial conflict to the structure of this market. Reconstructing the social meaning of race in late imperial Britain, Professor Tabili shows the combined struggle by unions, workers, and British and colonial governments to define who was black and what this designation meant in relation to the prerogatives of British identity. She concludes that racial confrontation resulted more from the decision of influential institutional actors than from the racist impulses of ordinary people.

Terrar, Edward F., *Social, Economic, and Religious Beliefs Among Maryland Catholic People During the Period of the English War 1639–1660*. San Francisco: Catholic Scholars Press, 1996.

In this study Dr Terrar explores the particular beliefs of Catholic labourers who came to Maryland at the turn of the seventeenth century and were at odds with the traditional English Catholic gentry, in opposition to their crown, parliament, clergy and papacy. The author aims to provide a complete economic, intellectual, legal and social history of the Maryland Catholics during the English Civil War and to compare the situation to related developments in Europe, Latin America and Africa, analysing the labourers' ideology, their position with regard to the official Catholic ideology of the time and their relation to the liberation theology and the Reformation.

Thom, Deborah, *Nice Girls and Rude Girls: Women Workers in World War I*. London: I.B. Tauris Publishers, 1998.

In this study of the myths and realities of women workers' experience in Great Britain in the First World War, Dr Thom examines the effect of 'dilution and substitution' in compensating for the loss of industrial workers, the role of 'patriotic fervour', the industrial roles of women, wages, the function of trade unions, the impact on health and family life, and demobilisation in 1918–19. She concludes that the circumstances of war work were so circumscribed that any change in the position of women as workers was not enduring and was not regarded as affecting women's nature as workers or as citizens.

Thompson, Dorothy, *Outsiders: Class, Gender and Nation*. London: Verso, 1993.
This volume brings together six essays plus an autobiographic introduction, written by Dr Thompson over the course of twenty-five years. The main theme of the collection is a consideration of nineteenth-century English radicalism, including three previously published, well-known essays on Chartism: 'The Early Chartist' (1971), 'Women and Nineteenth-Century Radical Politics' (1976), and 'Ireland and the Irish in English Radicalism' (1983).

Webster, Wendy, *Imagining Home: Gender, 'Race' and National Identity, 1945–64*. [Women's History] London: UCL Press, 1998.
Questioning the popular view that the 1950s were a nadir for women, this study examines the ideas and images of 'home' during a period of national decline in Great Britain and loss of imperial power. Basing herself on sources such as oral narratives and autobiographical writings of women, Dr Webster analyses the ways in which women negotiated, appropriated or opposed the different roles assigned to them within discourses of race, class, health and nation, and explores the multiple meanings of 'home' for women. The experience of migrant women is highlighted.

Weinstock, Nathan, *Couleur espérance. La mémoire ouvrière juive, Textes autobiographiques, prés. et trad. du yiddish par Nathan Weinstock*, Genève: Les éditions Metropolis, 2000.
In this book, Dr Weinstock, who has published widely on the Jewish labour movement in pre-revolutionary Russia and the *Bund*, has brought together and translated from Yiddish (extracts from) autobiographies of four *Bund* activists: Leon Bernstein, Laybetshke Berman, Sholem Levine, and "A Litwak". Dr Weinstock has selected four autobiographies from the rank-and-file of the Bund, rather than its leadership. In his general introduction, and in the presentations of the texts, he sketches the historical background of the Jewish working-class milieu and the *Bund* in turn-of-the-century Russia.

White, Carol and Sian Rhiannon Williams (eds), *Struggle or Starve: Women's Lives in the South Wales Valleys between the Two World Wars* Dinas Powys: Honno, 1998.
Combining fragments of recollections by previously unpublished writers with extracts from published autobiographies, the fifty-five short essays in this collection aim to convey the lives of working-class women in the south Wales valleys in the interwar period. The texts are arranged thematically on topics including childhood, school, work, strikes and poverty,

and women and politics. The introduction aims to situate the individual experiences within a wider social and political context of a period of mass unemployment and labour unrest.

Wightman, Clare, *More than Munitions: Women, Work and the Engineering Industries, 1900–1950.* [Women and Men in History] London: Longman, 1999.

Taking women's employment in the engineering industries in Britain between 1900 and 1950 as her focus, Dr Wightman analyses in this study the complexity of women's working lives and the role of gender in explaining the experiences of women and men at work. Women, according to the author, figured prominently as workers, not only in munitions and weapons production during the world wars but also in the newly emerging manufacturing industries that played a key role in producing mass consumer goods. Looking at women's relations with employers and trade unions, she examines the changes in the concepts of 'women's work' and 'women's pay'.

Wilkinson, Alan, *Christian Socialism: Scott Holland to Tony Blair, The 1998 Scott Holland Lectures.* London: SCM Press, 1998.

With the rise of Tony Blair, who derives his political beliefs from his Christian faith, the Christian socialist tradition is resurrecting within the Labour Party. In this book, Dr Wilkinson sketches the nineteenth-century background to the Christian socialism of F.D. Maurice, the contributions to the Christian socialist ideas by Henry Scott Holland and Charles Gore, the influence of Christian socialism on R.H. Tawney and William Temple, the relation with Roman Catholic social teaching and the more radical, dissenting current within British Christian socialism, represented by Alan Ecclestone, Donald Soper and Kenneth Leech. A survey of British Christian socialist politicians concludes this book.

Willson, Perry R, *The Clockwork Factory: Women and Work in Fascist Italy.* Oxford: Clarendon, 1993.

Focusing on the Magneti Marelli company, a light engineering firm near Milan during the fascist period, this study addresses gender divisions and the experience of women in the workforce, as well as the introduction of scientific management. Contrary to fascist ideology, half the workforce was and remained female. The author aims to show the impact of the combination of modern, Taylorist labour management and fascist paternalist ideology on the work experience of women in this fascist model firm.

Winslow, Barbara, *Sylvia Pankhurst: Sexual politics and political activism,* foreword by Sheila Rowbotham. [Women's History] London: UCL Press, 1996.

Focusing on her life as a committed political activist, Professor Winslow examines in this study Sylvia Pankhurst's political involvement in the suffrage, working-class and socialist movements. Though best known for her role in the suffrage movement, she did, according to the author, far more than that: she applied both socialist and feminist theory in practice by building a working women's suffrage and community organisation, which fought for full social, political and economic emancipation of women.

Wood, Andy, *The Politics of Social Conflict: The Peak Country, 1520–1770*. [Cambridge Studies in Early Modern British History] Cambridge: Cambridge University Press, 1999.

This study is a detailed reconstruction of economic and social change, as well as change in cultural meanings of diverse phenomena, such as custom, gender, locality, skill, literacy, orality and magic, in the region of the Peak Country in Derbyshire from around 1520 to 1770. According to Dr Wood, this local history of social conflict offers important insights into the early modern social and gender identities, civil war allegiances, the appeal of radical ideas and the making of the English working class. The author challenges the idea that early modern England was a hierarchical, 'pre-class' society.

Walsh, Margaret (ed.), *Working Out Gender: Perspectives from Labour History*. [Studies in Labour History] Aldershot: Ashgate, 1999.

The twelve essays in this collection, all originating from the Spring 1998 Conference of the British Society for the Study of Labour, aim to illustrate a variety of ways of making gender more central to labour history. Spanning the eighteenth through the twentieth centuries, the contributions cover both Great Britain and the United States and explore the different ways that primarily European historians have interpreted gender as a valuable lens for refocusing on issues connected with work, workers, the working classes and their politics.

Wright, Erik Olin, with Uwe Becker, Johanna Brenner, Michael Burawoy, *The Debate on Classes*. London and New York: Verso, 1989.

In 1985 Erik. O. Wright's *Classes* appeared, which gave rise to much debate among Marxist sociologists. A number of the contributions to the discussion in *Politics and Society, Berkeley Journal of Sociology, Capital and Class, Critical Sociology* and *Sociology* have been collected in this volume. Professor Wright opens the book with an essay, also published before, in which he expounds his theory, and concludes it with an extensive reply to his critics, entitled 'Rethinking, Once Again, the Concept of Class Structure'.

Yeo, Eileen Janes, *The Contest for Social Science: Relations and Representations of Gender and Class*. London: Rivers Oram Press, 1996.

Covering the long period from 1789 through the twentieth century, Professor Yeo explores in this study the development of social science in Britain as a contest for class and gender power. Starting with the period of revolutions between 1789 and 1850, she examines how scientific philanthropy, socialist 'social science' and the middle-class urban statistical movement competed to create an activist science of social improvement, how in the second half of the nineteenth century confrontation subsided, and in the twentieth century with the ongoing professionalisation the dominance of universities and the state in the production of knowledge increased.

Yeo, Eileen Janes (ed.), *Radical Femininity: Women's Self-Representation in the Public Sphere*. Manchester: Manchester University Press, 1998; distrib. excl. in the USA by St. Martin's Press, New York.

The eight essays in this volume explore how, between 1790 and 1914, women in Britain attempted to represent themselves in the public sphere and to establish empowering identities. The contributions address class, ethnicity and motherhood in the works of the Quaker educationalist writer Hannah Kilham (Alison Twells), the political rhetoric of Chartist women (Michelle de Larrabeiti), the image of married working women in the Industrial Women's Movement (Gerry Holloway) and representations of working-class femininity in the Women's Co-operative Guild (Gillian Scott).

Young, Glennys, *Power and the Sacred in Revolutionary Russia: Religious Activists in the Village*. University Park: The Pennsylvania State University Press, 1997.

This study examines the relationship among Orthodox clergy, laity and Communist party cadres during the establishment of Soviet power in the Russian countryside in the period of New Economic Policy (NEP), 1921–8, when an intensive anti-religious campaign, led by organisations such as the League of the Godless, was launched by the Bolshevist party. Professor Young concludes that rural Orthodox clergy and laity organised themselves in opposition to the Bolshevist campaign and revived factional politics within the village soviets to defend their religious interests, thus forcing the Bolsheviks to adapt their strategies.

NOTES ON CONTRIBUTORS

John Belchem is Professor of History and Head of the School of History at the University of Liverpool. He recently published *Popular Radicalism in Nineteenth-Century Britain* (Basingstoke, 1996), *Merseypride: Essays in Liverpool Exceptionalism* (Liverpool, 2000) and co-edited *Languages of Labour* (Aldershot, 1997).
email: J.C.Belchem@liverpool.ac.uk

Lex Heerma van Voss is Research Fellow at the International Institute of Social History (Amsterdam) and Professor of Economic and Social History at the University of Utrecht. He recently co-edited *Dock Workers: International Explorations in Comparative Labour History, 1790–1970* (Aldershot, 2000).
email: lhv@iisg.nl

Alice Kessler-Harris is Professor of History at Rutgers University. She is the author of *Out to Work: A History of Wage-Earning Women in the United States* (Oxford, 1983) and recently co-edited *Protecting Women: Labor Legislation in Europe, the United States, and Australia, 1880–1920* (Urbana and Chicago, 1995) and *U.S. History as Women's History: New Feminist Essays* (Chapel Hill, 1995).
email: akh@rci.rutgers.edu

Jürgen Kocka is President of the Wissenschaftszentrum Berlin für Sozialforschung and Professor of the History of the Industrial World at the Free University Berlin. He recently published *Industrial Culture and Bourgeois Society: Business, Labor and Bureaucracy in Modern*

Germany, 1800–1918 (New York, 1999) and co-edited *Bourgeois Society in Nineteenth-Century Europe* (Oxford, 1993).
email: kockafu@zedat.fu-berlin.de

Marcel van der Linden is head of the Research Department at the International Institute of Social History (Amsterdam) and Professor in the History of Social Movements at Amsterdam University. He recently edited *The International Confederation of Free Trade Unions* (Berne, 2000) and co-edited *The Rise and Development of Collective Labour Law* (Berne, 2000).
email: mvl@iisg.nl

Janaki Nair is a fellow of the Centre for the Study of Culture and Society, Bangalore, India. She recently published *Women and Law in Colonial India* (New Delhi, 1996) and *Miners and Millhands: Work, Culture and Politics in Princely Mysore* (New Delhi, 1998) and co-edited *A Question of Silence: The Sexual Economics of Modern India* (New Delhi, 1998).
email: ssmids@ren.nic.in (Janaki Nair)

Patrick Pasture is Professor of History at the Catholic University of Leuven. He recently published *Christian Trade Unionism in Europe since 1968: Tensions between Identity and Practice* (Aldershot, 1994) and *Histoire du syndicalisme chrétien international. La difficile recherche d'une troisième voie* (Paris, 1999) and co-edited *Working Class Internationalism and the Appeal of National Identity: Historical Dilemmas and Current Debates on Western Europe* (Oxford/ New York, 1998).
email: Patrick.Pasture@arts.kuleuven.ac.be

Mike Savage is Professor of Sociology at the University of Manchester. He recently co-edited *Social Change and the Middle Classes* (London, 1995) and co-authored *Careers and Organisations: Recent Developments in Banking, Local Authorities and Nursing* (Houndmills, 1997).
email: m.savage@man.ac.uk

Eileen Yeo is Professor of Social and Cultural History at the University of Strathclyde in Glasgow. She recently published *The Contest for Social Science: Relations and Representations of Gender and Class* (London, 1996) and edited *Radical Femininity: Women's Self-Representation in the Public Sphere* (Manchester, 1998).
email: eileen.yeo@strath.ac.uk

INDEX

Lightning Source UK Ltd.
Milton Keynes UK
UKHW020645280120
357701UK00005B/331